Assessing Spanish–English Bilingual Preschoolers

Assessing Spanish–English Bilingual Preschoolers

A Guide to Best Approaches and Measures

by

Sandra Barrueco, Ph.D.
The Catholic University of America
Washington, D.C.

Michael López, Ph.D.
National Center for Latino Child & Family Research
Laytonsville, MD

Christine Ong, Ph.D.
University of California, Los Angeles
Los Angeles, CA

and

Patricia Lozano, M.A.
Early Childhood Education Expert
Sherman Oaks, CA

·P·A·U·L·H·
BROOKES
PUBLISHING CO.®

Baltimore • London • Sydney

Paul H. Brookes Publishing Co.
Post Office Box 10624
Baltimore, Maryland 21285-0624
USA

www.brookespublishing.com

Typeset by Spearhead Global, Inc., Bear, Delaware.
Manufactured in the United States of America by
Sheridan Books, Chelsea, Michigan.

Library of Congress Cataloging-in-Publication Data

Assessing Spanish-English bilingual preschoolers : a guide to best approaches and measures / by
Sandra Barrueco ... [et al.].
     p.   cm.
   Includes bibliographical references and index.
   ISBN-13: 978-1-59857-219-3 (pbk.)
   ISBN-10: 1-59857-219-9 (pbk.)
   1. Education, Bilingual—United States—Evaluation.   2. English language—Study and teaching
(Preschool)—Spanish speakers.   3. Preschool tests—United States.   I. Barrueco, Sandra.
   LC3723.A88 2011
   370.117'5—dc23

                                                                                              2011048105

British Library Cataloguing in Publication data are available from the British Library.

2016   2015   2014   2013   2012

10   9   8   7   6   5   4   3   2   1

Contents

About the Authors

Sandra Barrueco, Ph.D., Assistant Professor of Psychology and Fellow, Institute for Policy Research & Catholic Studies, Department of Psychology, The Catholic University of America, Washington, D.C.

Dr. Barrueco is Assistant Professor of Psychology and Fellow of the Institute for Policy Research & Catholic Studies at The Catholic University of America. Dr. Barrueco specializes in the prevention and early intervention of developmental difficulties, particularly among language-minority, immigrant, and migrant children. Much of her grant-funded research has focused on early bilingual, socioemotional, and acculturative processes within the Latino community.

Dr. Barrueco specializes in the assessment, prevention, and early intervention of developmental difficulties, particularly among language-minority, immigrant, and migrant children. Dr. Barrueco began her career as a preschool teacher assistant and is now a licensed clinical psychologist in Maryland and Washington, D.C. She obtained her doctorate at the University of Denver in child clinical psychology with an emphasis in cognitive neuroscience and completed an internship at Children's National Medical Center in clinical child and pediatric psychology. Dr. Barrueco subsequently focused on the early childhood identification and prevention of developmental and mental health difficulties as a postdoctoral fellow in the Department of Neuropsychology at Kennedy Krieger Institute. She also completed a research postdoctoral fellowship in the Department of Mental Health at the Johns Hopkins Bloomberg School of Public Health, where she designed and conducted prevention and intervention science investigations. Most recently, she participated in a faculty fellowship in the National Center for Research on Early Childhood Education at the University of Virginia.

Throughout her training and career, Dr. Barrueco has been dedicated to learning and utilizing advanced statistics to advance scientific knowledge and practice with young immigrant children and families. This approach is rooted in a community-based participatory research framework involving strong collaborations with families and the local and national programs that serve them. This is reflected in her involvement in local and national studies with Head Start, Early Head Start, and Migrant and Seasonal Head Start as well as her appointments as Board Vice Chair of the DC Bilingual Public Charter School and on the Advisory Committee of the American Psychological Association Presidential Task Force on Immigration.

Michael López, Ph.D., Executive Director, National Center for Latino Child & Family Research, Laytonsville, MD

Dr. Michael López is Executive Director of the National Center for Latino Child & Family Research, which is dedicated to research on issues relevant to practices and policies affecting the lives of Latino children and families. Previously,

Dr. López directed the Child Outcomes Research and Evaluation team in the Administration for Children and Families, where he managed a number of large-scale national, Head Start research studies, including the Head Start Family and Child Experiences Survey; the Head Start Transition Evaluation; and the National Head Start Impact Study, a nationally representative, randomized study examining the impact of Head Start on children's school readiness. Dr. López's current work is focused on applied policy research and programmatic activities on such topics as early childhood care and education; language and literacy development; bilingual education; early childhood prevention and intervention programs; and young children's mental health, with an emphasis on at-risk, low-income, and/or culturally and linguistically diverse populations.

Christine Ong, Ph.D., Senior Researcher, University of California Los Angeles, National Center for Research on Evaluation, Standards, and Student Testing, Los Angeles, CA

Christine Ong recently joined the University of California, Los Angeles's National Center for Research on Evaluation, Standards, and Student Testing as a Senior Researcher. Previously, Dr. Ong was a visiting researcher at the National Center for Children in Poverty at Columbia University, participating in studies that examined state-level professional development initiatives linked to quality improvement rating systems as well as innovative early childhood mental health policies. Dr. Ong also served as a Senior Research Analyst at First 5 LA—a child-advocacy organization dedicated to improving the lives of young children and their families in Los Angeles County. She was involved in several First 5 LA projects related to early learning and assessment, including the Los Angeles Universal Preschool Child Outcomes Studies and the evaluation of the Healthy Kids Initiative. While completing a doctorate in Psychological Studies in Education at UCLA, she was involved in numerous projects related to early language and literacy development at the National Center for Research on Evaluation, Standards, and Student Testing. Dr. Ong also was a Research Fellow at UCLA Seeds University Elementary School and the UCLA Center for Healthier Children, Families and Communities.

Patricia Lozano, M.A., Early Childhood Education Expert, Sherman Oaks, CA

Patricia Lozano is an Early Childhood Education expert with more than 10 years of experience in the field. She has worked extensively in conducting research and program evaluations of early care, education, and family programs with organizations such as First 5 Los Angeles, University of California, Los Angeles (UCLA), and many others. Ms. Lozano is actively involved in the selection and adaptation of child assessments measures for English Language Learners across various research studies and observes various early childhood education programs using measures like the Early Childhood Environment Rating Scale and the Classroom Assessment Scoring System™ (CLASS™). In addition to her research experience, Ms. Lozano also evaluates children with special needs and works with parents in selecting the best therapies for their children.

Preface

This text—the only known book that analyzes actual early childhood bilingual measures, rather than generally discussing bilingual assessment approaches—provides a culturally and linguistically grounded examination of assessment measures available for use with the growing population of bilingual preschoolers. Thirty-seven measures of childhood development available in English and Spanish are examined and compared across translation, linguistic, cultural, and psychometric characteristics.

This book assists psychologists, educators, and speech-language pathologists in their practice and research activities, as well as propel the respective fields forward in considering the critical cultural and psychometric facets of bilingual assessment. It provides clinicians, teachers, program staff, policy makers, and researchers with the facts to choose measures that are culturally, linguistically, and psychometrically appropriate.

From an initial list of 150 currently available measures, the final 37 measures were selected if they met an established set of criteria (e.g., could be administered by a range of professionals, had been standardized or extensively used in last decade). Each measure subsequently underwent an extensive set of analyses by the authors, including examination of technical manuals, web site materials, and published articles and critiques. In the final step, feedback from each measure's authors and publishers was solicited and any clarifying information incorporated.

The book provides a thorough analysis of measures in English and Spanish across multiple facets, from the most basic considerations (e.g., administration length) to the most advanced (e.g., the extent to which the Spanish and English versions are similar or dissimilar in their validity for use with young children). It also includes critiques and comparative analyses. The strengths and weaknesses of the English and Spanish versions of each respective measure are independently described and compared to each other (e.g., discussions on how the version of a measure in one language may have stronger or weaker reliability than the other version). Furthermore, each version and measure is rated along various linguistic, cultural, and psychometric dimensions. It also provides a graphic overview of where the early childhood field currently stands in the development of solid measures in both English and Spanish for use with preschool-age children.

Acknowledgments

Our colleagues, families, and friends provided unwavering support during the book's development. For example, the authors appreciate the encouragement provided by Dr. Katie Fallin, Dr. Armando Jimenez, and Evelyn Martinez from First 5 LA, as well as Dr. Tom Schultz who is now Project Director for Early Childhood Initiatives at the Council of Chief State School Officers. Further, Sandra and Michael thank their wonderful children, Jessica, Koji, and Sofía, for their love, patience, and encouragement during the many hours dedicated to this book.

We acknowledge the following individuals from the research team at The Catholic University of America for their contributions: Corine Bell, Stephanie Lockwood, Joanna Melon, Anusha Natarajan, and Saleem Hue Penny. Further, various aspects of the activities that led to this book were supported by The Catholic University of America, the U.S. Department of Education, First 5 LA, The Pew Charitable Trusts' Task Force on Early Childhood Accountability, The Foundation for Child Development, and the Joyce Foundation. In addition, we thank the many authors and publishers who provided feedback on their measure's review prior to publication.

Finally, the authors acknowledge the publishing house of Brookes. Collaborating with Astrid Pohl Zuckerman and her team has been an exceptional experience. Their grounded understanding of early childhood development and assessment facilitated the execution of this book. We also appreciate the solid copyediting contributions by Yvette Chin and her colleagues.

Bilingual Assessment During Early Childhood

I

1

Assessing Young Children within and Across Two Languages

There has been an explosion in the availability of assessment measures for use with linguistically and culturally diverse preschoolers. Such development is related in part to the striking demographic changes in the United States. The cultural and linguistic diversity of young children is growing, and providers of early education can expect to see continuing increases over time (Reyes & Moll, 2005; U.S. Census Bureau, 2009). Specifically, the U.S. education system has witnessed a dramatic increase in the number of children who speak a language other than English in the home, both *English language learners* and *dual language learners*.[1]

SETTING THE STAGE: DEFINITION, PREVALENCE, AND DEMOGRAPHIC CHANGES

Although the education system has long included such young learners, only recently have they made up such a large percentage of the nation's school-age population. Differences in official classifications of English language learners and

---

[1]Multiple terms with somewhat different definitional criteria are used to refer to children from diverse linguistic backgrounds. Children whose home language is not English, who primarily speak a language other than English in the home, and who may experience difficulties achieving in classrooms where the language of instruction is English are often referred to as *limited English proficient* or *English language learners*. In contrast, the terms *dual language children* or *dual language learners* are typically used to refer to a broader group of children who come from homes where a language other than English is spoken. The latter terms acknowledge that many of these children not only may be learning a second language but also may still be acquiring their first language (Administration for Children and Families, 2008; Paradis, Genesee, & Crago, 2011). For the purposes of this book, we use *dual language children* or *dual language preschoolers* to refer more broadly to this group of preschool-age children unless otherwise specified. Similarly, the primary focus is on measures for Spanish-speaking *dual language children*, although many of the issues and recommendations are relevant to measures for *dual language children* from other home language backgrounds.

3

dual language children make tracking their exact numbers difficult, but many researchers have noted that the population of linguistically diverse children is growing at a much more rapid rate than the overall student population. Between 1995 and 2005, the population of English language learners increased at about 7 times the rate of the total school population (National Clearinghouse for English Language Acquisition [NCELA], 2006). English language learners make up about 10% of the nation's overall school-age population (NCELA, 2009), and the broader group of dual language children represents 20% of the school-age population (Capps, Fix, Ost, Reardon-Anderson, & Passel, 2004). These estimates are even higher when one looks at the proportion of children served by preschool programs targeting low-income populations, such as Head Start. In 2006, 27% of children in Head Start were from homes where a language other than English was spoken most frequently to the child, and 43% came from homes where a language other than English was spoken (Administration for Children and Families, 2006, 2009). Thus, it is clear that early childhood education providers and educators at every level of the education system must be prepared for a continuing increase in the proportion of linguistically diverse children among the school-age population.

In addition to the general increase in the population of young dual language children, the geographical distribution of this group has been changing. Historically speaking, dual language children have been clustered in several states, including California, Texas, Florida, New York, Illinois, and Arizona (NCELA, 2006). García, Kleifgen, and Falchi (2008) noted that between the academic years of 1994–1995 to 2004–2005, the greatest increases have occurred in states that have not typically served a large dual language population, including South Carolina, Kentucky, Indiana, North Carolina, and Tennessee. These states, as well as others that previously have not seen large numbers of dual language children in the school system, will need to be prepared to serve the needs of this unique population as it continues to grow and change.

Though there is great diversity within the population of children who speak a language other than English at home, the vast majority of dual language children in the United States come from homes where Spanish is spoken. Goldenberg (2008) noted that although more than 400 different home languages are spoken by dual language children, 80% of dual language children speak Spanish. The next largest group of dual language children is children who speak Asian languages; this mixed-language group makes up approximately 8% of the dual language population. Not only are the majority of today's dual language children Spanish speakers, but also they represent a large portion of one of the fastest growing population subgroups in the country (U.S. Census Bureau, 2009). In 2003, Latino infants made up approximately 25% of all live births in the United States, and approximately 75% of these infants were exposed to Spanish in the home (López, Barrueco, & Miles, 2006). By the year 2050, Latino children, many from homes where Spanish is spoken, are projected to make up between 25% and 39% of the population of children younger than 5 years of age (U.S. Census Bureau, 2008). Thus, there is reason to expect Spanish–English dual language learning to be relevant to the U.S. school system for some time to come. To date, most research into dual language learning has concerned Spanish–English dual language children. As this research continues to expand and inform education policy, it will be important to focus on other language-minority groups as well.

VARIABILITY IN BILINGUAL LANGUAGE DEVELOPMENT

With the increasing linguistic diversity represented in early childhood education programs, one must be aware of what is known about the complexities of early bilingual language development and the heterogeneity that exists within the broader population of dual language children. There is considerable variability in the timing, rate, and sequence of young children's language development among both monolingual and bilingual language learners. Children may acquire a second language *simultaneously* or *sequentially* in relationship to the development of their home language (McLaughlin, 1984). The rate of both first and second language acquisition is influenced by a range of factors both within the child (e.g., intrinsic motivation and personality) and external to the child (e.g., age of first exposure to a second language, as well as the quantity and quality of exposure to a second language), including experiences that occur within the home and/or other care settings (Birdsong, 2006; Pan, Rowe, Singer, & Snow, 2005; Tabors, 1997). However, much of this variation in the language development of young dual language children is related to the type and range of language and literacy experiences within the home as well as parental demographic characteristics (Garcia & Jensen, 2009). Barrueco, López, and Miles (2007) described the variability in home language environments for a nationally representative sample of Latino infants. They found, for example, that 19% of the children lived in homes where only Spanish was spoken; 35% were exposed primarily to Spanish, with some English; 22% were exposed primarily to English, with some Spanish; and 21% were in only English-speaking homes. Clearly, such differences in the amount of exposure to the home and second languages will shape the early linguistic development of these young children.

In the process of acquiring a second language, there is often variability across time with respect to one language being more dominant than the other. During such periods of *language imbalance,* dual language children may not perform as well as monolingual speakers of either language. For example, many young dual language children may demonstrate greater proficiency on measures of receptive vocabulary versus expressive vocabulary, as the latter requires a more advanced set of language-related skills and abilities (Tabors & Snow, 1994). This is a common and temporary characteristic of emergent bilingualism (Paradis, Genessee, & Crago, 2011) rather than an indicator of a language delay. As young dual language children continue to become more proficient in their second language, their expressive abilities may reflect the use of *telegraphic* or *formulaic speech* (using commonly heard words and phrases), *code-switching* (switching languages for portions of a sentence), and *language mixing* (inserting single items from one language into another), all of which are also normal elements of dual language acquisition (McLaughlin, Blanchard, & Osanai, 1995; Tabors, 1997; Tabors & Snow, 1994). Thus, it is important for all early childhood professionals, when assessing dual language children's abilities and functioning, to take into consideration these critical factors associated with variability in the timing and rate of developing different language skills and abilities.

The demographic data presented previously emphasize the dramatic increase in the number and percentage of culturally and linguistically diverse children across the country, both nationally and even more so within certain states and localities. These demographic changes, in combination with variability in the timing and sequencing of bilingual language development, have implications not only for the nature and timing of instructional practices within classrooms but also for the types of dual language assessment strategies utilized. It is important to understand and to take into consideration some of the key dimensions associated with the variability in dual language children's language and literacy development at any given point in time as well as the dynamic nature of their linguistic development over time. Similarly, early childhood professionals and providers must be familiar with the common characteristics and sequencing of bilingual language development in order to provide high-quality learning environments that appropriately differentiate and individualize instructional practices according to the children's prior learning experiences and current linguistic proficiency levels. The demographic data highlight the fact that *within* the population of dual language children and families there is considerable variability across a number of important factors that predict important differences in children's rate and level of development. Thus, in addition to having implications for individualized instructional strategies, assessment approaches utilized across different contexts and for different purposes must be responsive to within-group heterogeneity, the dynamic nature of bilingual language development, as well as critical differences between monolingual and dual language children.

APPROPRIATE AND VALID ASSESSMENT OF YOUNG DUAL LANGUAGE LEARNERS

Given the increasing diversity of the population of young children along with the considerable variability in children's bilingual language development, there has been a related increase in the development and availability of assessment measures for use with linguistically diverse preschoolers. However, this increase in the availability of assessment measures has not been attributable solely to population changes, as it also has been fueled by several additional factors.

Growth in the Use of Assessments in the Field

First, many state and local agencies across the United States have increased investments in early care and education activities (Barnett, Epstein, Friedman, Sansanelli, & Hustedt, 2009). For example, Florida, Georgia, Illinois, Iowa, New York, Oklahoma, and West Virginia have committed to providing expanded access to universal prekindergarten programs. Thus, greater proportions of eligible young children, including culturally and linguistically diverse children, attend early childhood programs than ever before (e.g., Barnett & Yarosz, 2007).

Second, as more early childhood programs are implemented and/or expanded, a greater emphasis has been placed on the development of accountability systems to examine programs' success in improving children's school readiness outcomes (Kallemeyn & DeStefano, 2009). This is consistent with the broad paradigm shifts at the federal, state, and local levels in education and other fields toward increased accountability of all publicly funded education programs (Espinosa & López, 2007; National Association for the Education of Young Children [NAEYC], 2009; Padilla & Borsato, 2008; U.S. Department of Education, 2002).

The net result is a greater utilization of assessments to examine children's abilities and growth over time. This includes both using content-focused measures to track children's everyday learning and to guide instructional practices in the classroom and using standardized, developmentally focused measures to examine the rate of children's improvement in comparison to typical growth at the same age. Given this increased use of assessments, it is critical that the strategies and measures used be appropriate for use within different contexts, by different professionals, and for different accountability purposes. Multiple professional guidelines exist to provide recommendations regarding the appropriate use of assessments and to minimize the potential iatrogenic consequences of the use of assessments for different purposes (e.g., American Educational Research Association, American Psychological Association, & National Council on Measurement in Education [AERA/APA/NCME], 2010; Division for Early Childhood, 2007; Meisels, 2007; NAEYC & National Association of Early Childhood Specialists in State Departments of Education [NAECS/SDE], 2003; Snow & Van Hemel, 2008). For example, the *Principles and Recommendations for Early Childhood Assessments*, developed by the National Education Goals Panel (Shepard, Kagan, & Wurtz, 1998), identified four broad purposes for early childhood assessments:

1. To promote the learning and development of individual children
2. To identify children with special needs and health conditions for intervention purposes
3. To monitor trends in programs and evaluate program effectiveness
4. To obtain benchmark data for accountability purposes at the local, state, and national levels

To date, each of the four purposes for assessment has often required its own instruments, procedures, and technical standards and has carried its own potential for cultural, linguistic, and method bias. For example, individual child-level assessment strategies utilized by teachers for daily instructional purposes are typically less formal and more frequently implemented than assessment strategies used for broader program accountability or evaluation purposes. The latter often involve larger groups of children and historically have relied more on standardized, **norm-referenced** assessment measures.

Although there may be some overlap or similarities across the different types of assessments and their targeted purposes (e.g., the importance of measures having documented psychometric properties that are appropriate for their intended use, the use of assessment data for individual children versus groups of children), it is nevertheless critical to understand the unique considerations, strengths, limitations, and recommendations of assessing dual language children within each of the stated purpose areas. Such an understanding of the complexity of these issues is essential to providing the necessary guidance regarding the selection of the most appropriate measures. The following section provides an overview of some of the important differences in the assessment terminology and approaches used for different purposes by different sectors of the early childhood professional community.

The Use of Assessments for Tracking and Affecting Individual Improvement

At the intervention or instruction level, early childhood professionals (including those in education, psychology, and speech-language pathology) have often viewed assessments as a process or set of activities to guide practices and monitor the development of children on an ongoing basis. The assessments used to guide practices typically consist of less formal, nonstandardized approaches that may include the use of observational notes, checklists, rating scales, work samples, and portfolios. These types of ongoing assessment approaches can provide valuable information regarding a child's performance that then allows professionals to individualize their practices to best address each child's unique needs. Some researchers have argued that the use of such a comprehensive assessment system that is closely tied to improvement is an essential aspect of a quality program that should directly affect children's early achievement (Hills, 1992; Meisels, Atkins-Burnett, Xue, Nicholson, Bickel, & Son, 2002).

Regarding culturally and linguistically diverse children, the NAEYC (2005) position statement *Screening and Assessment of Young English-Language Learners* provided more specific guidance, recommending that for the purpose of promoting learning,

> Assessment of young English-language learners should be used to (a) guide curriculum planning, teaching strategies, and the provision of learning opportunities in all areas;… (b) monitor development and learning in all domains—including children's content knowledge, skills, and capabilities; (c) determine language proficiency and ongoing language development in both the child's home language and English, as appropriate; and (d) identify children with developmental disabilities or delays, emotional impairments, physical disabilities, and other conditions that indicate the need for special services. (p. 6)

Despite the rather broad level of support that has emerged from various position statements and recommendations regarding the use of authentic assessments, there are continued debates within the field with respect to the strengths and weaknesses of such approaches in comparison with other assessment approaches. Some professionals within the early childhood field, especially early childhood education providers, have cautioned against an overreliance on the use of decontextualized, standardized, norm-referenced measures when assessing young children, particularly children from culturally and linguistically diverse backgrounds (Duarte & Gutierrez, 2004; Santos, 2004; Trister-Dodge, Herman, Charles, & Maiorca, 2004). For the specific purpose of guiding practice for individual and groups of children, many of these professionals recommend using primarily alternative or authentic assessment approaches that include ongoing assessments that take into account the child's background characteristics and prior experiences while also respecting the child's primary language and home culture. These types of informal, instructionally embedded assessment approaches have frequently been praised for their ecological validity and authentic nature (Meisels, 1998; Wortham, 2001).

One important consideration is the potential for assessor variance or rater effects that may occur with the use of some "authentic" assessment measures (Bennett, Gottesman, Rock, & Cerullo, 1993; Hoyt, 2000; Myford & Wolfe, 2003). *Rater effects* refers to a systematic source of variability in ratings or assessment scores that is attributable to the person conducting the assessment and not to the child's actual performance or behavior. Some of the extraneous factors that influence ratings beyond the child's actual ability, particularly by teachers on subjective measures, include child factors (e.g., language ability, personality, behavior) and teacher factors (e.g., their interpretation of individual items and scoring criteria, beliefs), among others (Bennett et al., 1993; Llosa, 2008; Myford & Wolfe, 2003). Estimates suggest that as much as 37%–50% of the variation in teacher assessment scores or observer ratings may be attributable to rater bias and/or measurement error, as opposed to the child's actual performance or the behavior that the assessment was intended to measure (Cote & Buckley, 1987; Hoyt & Kerns, 1999). This is why the guidelines of the National Research Council regarding the use of assessments in early childhood recommend including at least some standardized assessments for assessing individual children, so that important decision making regarding children's placement is not potentially biased by factors more attributable to the assessor than the child's actual abilities (Snow & Van Hemel, 2008). Such factors may include explicit or implicit biases on the part of the assessor about the child. Thus, various professional guidelines regarding the selection and use of assessments clearly stipulate the importance of documented psychometric integrity of assessments (**reliability** and **validity**), especially those used for the purposes of high-stakes assessment (AERA/APA/NCME, 2010; NAEYC & NAECS/SDE, 2003; Snow & Van Hemel, 2008). The higher the stakes of the assessment, the more important it is to have the most reliable and valid information guiding critical decision making for children's educational placements, services, and experiences.

The Use of Assessments for Identifying Special Needs

In addition to helping guide practice, a related but distinct purpose for screening and assessing children is to identify potential disabilities or other special needs. Relatively brief developmental screening tools are typically administered quickly to a large number of children as an initial step in the broader assessment process. If the results of the developmental screening indicate a potential problem, individual children can then be referred to a multidisciplinary team for more in-depth assessment.

For those children identified through an initial screening approach, the NAEYC and NAECS/SDE position statement on early childhood curriculum, assessment, and program evaluation recommended the use of a multimodal assessment process that "emphasizes repeated, systematic observation, documentation, and other forms of criterion- or performance-oriented assessment using broad, varied, and complementary methods" (2003, p. 11). This recommendation does not argue for the exclusive use of more informal, **criterion-referenced** or portfolio assessments versus standardized, norm-referenced assessments or vice versa. In contrast, this recommendation, along with similar recommendations from the Division for Early Childhood (2007) of the Council for Exceptional Children and AERA/APA/NCME (2010), argued for the use of multiple sources of relevant and complementary information, including information gathered in natural settings and using a family-centered approach. Given the considerable variability in the rate and timing of young children's growth and development and in the strengths and weaknesses of different assessment approaches, the use of such a multimodal approach allows for the convergence of information, which is more likely to increase the accuracy of the assessment of potential disabilities or other special needs (Campbell, 2002; McLean, 2004).

An underlying dilemma for clinicians is how to distinguish between *language differences* and *language disorders*. This is especially difficult when interpreting assessment information for children who are acquiring English as a second language, because many of the characteristics of second language acquisition can easily be mistaken for disordered language. For example, many children who are nonnative English speakers may have low verbal language assessment scores but average nonverbal scores. This is a common finding for monolingual students with reading disabilities (Barrera, 1995; Brown, 2004; Gunderson & Siegel, 2001). Similarly, a dual language child can be more proficient in basic oral language skills (e.g., simple conversational language, receptive oral language) than in other areas (e.g., expressive language, more advanced vocabulary, literacy skills). However, the fact that a dual language child may demonstrate proficiency in a few more narrow linguistic skills does not necessarily mean that the child is equally proficient in other areas of language or literacy development. Thus, if not properly used, the assessment results for English language proficiency and home language ability can be misleading and can underestimate the child's true language competency.

The NAEYC position statement on assessing young linguistically diverse children recommends that English language learners be "regularly screened using linguistically and culturally appropriate screening tools" (2009, p. 6). This screening is conducted to determine whether there is a possible problem with any aspects of the child's development that will require more in-depth assessment, including a possible problem with the child's first and second language development. The NAEYC position statement further recommends that screenings occur in the child's home language as well as in English and that the screeners accept the use of code-switching, as necessary. Furthermore, some researchers have recommended screening procedures that also include ongoing developmental surveillance and parent reports in conjunction with direct child assessments (Alberts, Davis, & Prentice, 1995; Hanson & Lynch, 1995).

In assessing dual language children for eligibility for special services, many of the previously noted recommended assessment practices apply: using multiple measures, using a multidisciplinary team, including information gathered in natural settings, and using a family-centered approach (Bondurant-Utz, 1994; McLean, 2004). In addition, each dual language child's language proficiency and language dominance must be assessed, which is a complex task with all dual language children and especially challenging for young children. Clearly, in assessing young children's learning, care must be taken to distinguish true developmental difficulties from cultural and linguistic differences, including typical developmental variations in the rate and timing of language development of young dual language children.

As discussed more thoroughly in Chapter 2, clinicians must carefully consider the cultural, linguistic, and psychometric features of measures they are selecting. Although there have been vast improvements in the development of measures for use with dual language children, many standardized, norm-referenced assessments were designed and normed on monolingual speakers of English and therefore have some limitations in their use with young English language learners (APA, 1990; Cole & Mills, 1997; Klee & Carson, 2000; MacSwan, Rolstad, & Glass, 2002). Dual language children may perform poorly on such assessments because 1) they are truly delayed or 2) they are being assessed with a weak or even inappropriate measure. Furthermore, the context of the testing situation as well as the specific aspect of language being assessed can influence the child's language use (Paradis, Genesee, & Crago, 2011).

In sum, the use of assessments to identify potential disabilities and/or other special needs requires great care and attention, especially when one is assessing culturally and linguistically diverse children. A comprehensive approach that utilizes multiple assessment methods and combines information gathered from teachers, families, and careful observation with information obtained from more informal assessments and psychometrically sound direct assessments will best guide appropriate decision making about the functioning of, and recommendations for, young dual language children.

The Use of Assessments for Program Accountability

Program accountability refers to the various approaches used by stakeholders to examine the extent to which programs are accomplishing their intended goals. Within the context of early childhood educational programs, program accountability efforts typically place a primary emphasis on assessing the quality of teacher's instructional activities, as well as the key outcomes reflecting children's developmental and academic progress. As described by Espinosa & López (2007), "assessment efforts often are focused on examining one or more of the following descriptive, structural, process, or outcome areas of the program:

- Group-level descriptions of the characteristics of children and families in states or local communities, at one point in time or longitudinally over several points in time;
- The structural quality of early education or other care programs or settings;
- The quality of classroom processes, including the quality of instructional practices;
- Group-level descriptions of children's developmental and academic progress, and rates and levels of accomplishments; and
- The assessment or cost–benefit analysis of the investment of public resources for early childhood programs and services" (26).

It is important to make the distinction between the previously discussed focus of assessment for individual purposes and the broader program-level focus of assessment for program accountability purposes. Although assessments used to track the progress of individual children (or a small group of children) and those used for broader program accountability purposes may share some similarities, very few existing assessment procedures and measures work equally well for both purposes. The primary goal of program accountability assessments typically is not to guide decision making about specific children but rather to examine how well programs are achieving their intended goals. Thus, program accountability efforts have tended to focus more on the structural and dynamic aspects of the instructional or intervention context as well as a group-level description of children's developmental progress. Early childhood professionals who focus on program accountability have historically relied on standardized, norm-referenced assessments to examine the progress made by groups of children (as opposed to individual children) at the program, state, or even national level. The use of standardized assessment measures in this context allows for a comparison of the performance of a given group of children to that of children at the national or another aggregate level.

Although there have been various recommendations to date regarding the optimal characteristics of effective program accountability assessment approaches, few have adequately addressed the unique issues associated with assessing dual language children (e.g., Baker, Linn, Herman, & Koretz, 2002; Goff, 2000; Meisels, 2005; NAEYC & NAECS/SDE, 2003; Walberg, 2002). For example, efforts to examine group-level descriptive data on the characteristics of dual language children and families must be cognizant of the considerable variability that exists within the dual language population on key dimensions related to bilingual language exposure, experiences, and development both within the classroom as well as within the child's home and neighborhood. In addition, different definitions and approaches are used across communities to determine status as a dual language or English language learner. The criteria used to establish children's status as a dual language or English language learner may be formally defined by a school district in a given community or state or may be more informally determined by program staff based on a wide range of possible criteria and informants. Most approaches use a definition that includes the primary language spoken in the home and some information about the child's degree of English proficiency. Thus, efforts to collect descriptive data on the characteristics of groups of dual language children and families should clearly articulate the specific definitions, informants, and procedures used to determine the status as a dual language or English language learner of children and their families.

Assessment for program accountability should also reflect the program's goals for children's growth and development. For dual language children, an important long-term consideration is progress toward both English acquisition (a goal of most preschool programs) and ongoing development in the home language. Although this may not be an explicit goal of the program, these processes are important underlying aspects of a child's overall development and predict future academic functioning in English across most academic domains (Garcia, 2005; Oller & Eilers, 2002).

The assessment measures used for broader program or classroom accountability purposes ideally are correlated with more in-depth assessments used for other purposes and therefore can serve as proxy measures of children's outcomes. For example, a dual language child's performance on English and Spanish receptive vocabulary measures that contain limited sets of English and Spanish vocabulary words likely will not capture the full range of the child's English and Spanish language and literacy skills and abilities at a given point in time. However, if used in combination with similar data from other children within the same classroom or program, and examined over time, such assessments may yield important information about the average or aggregated growth in and development of the children's general English and Spanish receptive vocabulary, especially if a particular emphasis was placed on improving the activities targeting the oral language development of children in the particular program. Similarly, differences in children's performance across languages can be compared with the type and proportion of instruction or intervention provided in each language to provide further input and guidance on the match between activities and children's progress.

Regardless of the different ways in which aggregated assessment data can be used for program accountability purposes, a good program accountability indicator assessment measure not only should be correlated with other more in-depth assessment measures but also should be reasonably predictive of other related aspects of children's growth and development over time. Thus, if a more narrow measure of dual language children's receptive vocabulary is correlated with more in-depth assessments of language skills and abilities and is also predictive of later reading achievement, then it could be a very useful and efficient program-level indicator assessment, but only within a more comprehensive and integrated program accountability system. As may be expected, it is essential for such measures to have adequate documented psychometric properties (e.g., reliability, validity) consistent with recommendations regarding the selection and use of assessments, especially those related to the use of data for important accountability purposes, such as program evaluation and funding (AERA/APA/NCME, 2010; NAEYC & NAECS/SDE, 2003).

The Use of Assessments for Research and Evaluation

At this juncture, it is important to describe the similarities and differences among program accountability, evaluation, and basic and applied research. As described previously, program accountability initiatives have emerged as important mechanisms for policy makers, public officials, and other key decision makers and stakeholders to evaluate the degree to which programs are accomplishing their intended goals and therefore justify the expenditure of public funds. Thus, the primary audience is typically found within the broader public.

In comparison, *program evaluation* consists of the "systematic application of social science research procedures for assessing the conceptualization, design, implementation, and utility of social intervention programs" (Rossi & Freeman, 1983, p. 5). Program evaluations focus on examining the mechanisms by which program development and implementation influence, or do not influence, outcomes. Therefore, they examine the multiple questions inherent to continued program improvement in the next stage of development: Why? How? When? Where? With whom? Much has been written on the nature and essential aspects of good program evaluation (e.g., Rossi & Freeman, 1983; Scriven, 1991; Shadish, Cook, & Leviton, 1991; Unrau, Gabor, & Grinnell, 2001). Although program evaluation may be initiated by policy makers or other public decision makers and stakeholders for specific accountability purposes, it often is conducted within the context of the broader academic research community without necessarily the direct link to funding or other similar decision-making processes that program accountability has.

In addition, there are distinctions to be made between program evaluation and basic developmental research. Whereas program evaluation strives to determine how a particular program or intervention has accomplished the intended goals and how effective it has been with the population served, more basic developmental research tends to focus on both typical and atypical developmental processes as they naturally occur both within and outside the program (Scriven, 1991). Thus, general developmental research aims to increase understanding of the processes by which children grow and learn. It is critical to developing knowledge of indicators of positive growth and at-risk development as well as identifying potential new methods for intervening in the lives of children and families. Given the relatively limited body of research on the complexities of typical language and literacy development in young dual language children and bilingual curricular models, much more basic research needs to be conducted.

Although program accountability, evaluation, and research may be initiated for slightly different purposes and by different stakeholders, they share various characteristics. For example, the issues, concerns, and recommendations discussed previously for program accountability also apply to dual language assessment measures and approaches used in program evaluation and research. Specifically, the NAEYC and NAECS/SDE (2003) position statement on early childhood curriculum, assessment, and program evaluation presented a common set of recommendations or indicators of effectiveness that apply equally well to all three efforts:

- Evaluation is used for continuous improvement.
- Goals become guides for evaluation.
- Comprehensive goals are used.
- Evaluations use valid designs.
- Multiple sources of data are available.
- Sampling is used when assessing individual children as part of large-scale program evaluation.
- Safeguards are in place if standardized tests are used as part of evaluations.
- Children's gains over time are emphasized.
- Well-trained individuals conduct evaluations.
- Evaluation results are publicly shared.

Most of these recommendations emphasize the importance of carefully selecting procedures and methods in an intentional, ethical, and appropriate manner—important features of all accountability, evaluation, and research practices. Similarly, the previously mentioned guidelines regarding the importance of selecting and using assessments that have adequately documented psychometric properties (reliability and validity) are particularly applicable to the use of assessments for research and evaluation purposes (AERA/APA/NCME, 2010; NAEYC & NAECS/SDE, 2003; Snow & Van Hemel, 2008). In addition, accountability, evaluation, and research efforts share a focus on the importance of selecting measures developed adequately and systematically with the intended population and a strong emphasis on carefully aligning evaluation design and assessment strategies with a program's content standards, curriculum, and actual classroom instructional practices. However, as is discussed in subsequent chapters, there are many different challenges related to the technical limitations of many of the available dual language assessment measures.

RATIONALE FOR A FOCUS ON STANDARDIZED ASSESSMENTS WITH DUAL LANGUAGE LEARNERS

There is little doubt that the use of different types of assessment measures and measurement approaches plays a powerful and important role across various clinical, educational, and policy settings. The dramatic increase in the availability of early childhood programs along with the related increased emphasis on the accountability of program investments has further fueled the use of assessments within various contexts and for different purposes. This growth in demand has been accompanied by a related increase in the development and availability of assessment measures, both general measures as well as those for use with the rapidly growing population of linguistically diverse children. Standardized, norm-referenced assessments often play an important role within an overall assessment approach.

Despite this increase in the availability of measures and the various professional standards and recommendations providing guidance on the appropriate use of assessments, there remains a relative lack of resources describing and reviewing specific measures and measurement approaches, particularly standardized assessments, for use with young dual language children. Without appropriate resources and specific guidance on the selection and use of specific measures, early childhood professionals assessing dual language children may use assessments inappropriately, resulting in serious consequences. Common errors that may occur include, but are not limited to, the following:

- Informal translation of an existing measure without a careful examination of the psychometric properties or measure equivalence of the translated version compared with the original English version
- Selection of a non-English version of an assessment based solely on the psychometric properties of the English version and not those of the translated or adapted version
- Collection of inadequate information from parents and providers on the amount and timing of a child's prior language exposure and the child's current proficiency levels in both the native language as well as English, essential information to help guide the appropriate selection of specific measures and measurement approaches
- Use of family members during the administration of a standardized assessment in ways that do not adhere to the publisher's administration procedures
- Use of a measure's published normative data that does not match a particular child's or group of children's background characteristics
- Misdiagnosis of a child's abilities as a language disorder or disability rather than a typical lag in performance due to typical differences in the developmental trajectories of dual language children
- Making program funding decisions based on the overall progress of a group of children as measured against a single standard rather than relative growth data for certain subgroups that more accurately reflect differences in the children's initial abilities at the beginning of the program year
- Analysis and reporting of classroom- or program-level assessment data without regard for disaggregated data presented for important subgroups of children, such as linguistically diverse children

Thus, the focus of this book is to provide a valuable resource that offers specific guidance to early childhood professionals on the selection and use of different standardized measures when assessing young, dual language children. The goal of this careful review of the psychometric properties of measures available in both English and Spanish is to maximize the appropriate use of available measures and to minimize any unintended, negative consequences for bilingual children.

2

Selecting Appropriate Dual Language Approaches and Measures

Assessments in both Spanish and English are being increasingly included as part of efforts to improve knowledge, services, programs, and policies for the growing population of Spanish–English dual language children in the United States. However, along with the increased use of Spanish and English assessment measures, there is a concomitant need for improved guidance to the field in both the selection and appropriate use of such measures. In particular, the language(s) to be used while assessing language skills is a primary question. It is discussed first here, followed by a description of the psychometric, linguistic, and cultural features of assessment that also necessitate careful consideration.

SELECTING THE ASSESSMENT APPROACH

The selection of the most appropriate measures and measurement approaches when assessing young dual language children should be guided by a number of factors. It is critical to carefully collect information from parents and other caregivers regarding the child's prior and current language exposure and abilities. This information can then be used in combination with information on characteristics and technical properties of different measures and measurement approaches to best address the specific developmental, diagnostic, or research questions of interest.

Language Assessment and the Language of Assessment

Given the variability that exists within the linguistically diverse population, there are multiple strategies for approaching the measurement of language skills among young DLLs, whether one is using direct child assessments or parent reports. The following sections discuss 1) common strategies used to determine a child's primary or dominant language, 2) approaches for choosing the best language in which to assess dual language children, and 3) advantages and disadvantages of assessing bilingual children in different languages or combinations of languages.

Determining a Child's Primary Language(s)

One key consideration for direct assessments of bilingual children is determining the child's primary or dominant language(s). The subsequent decision then focuses on the language or languages in which to conduct the assessment: the child's primary language (i.e., the language that the child uses most often and/or most accurately) or a combination of languages. Because each of these approaches yields different information, the choice should be guided in part by the intended purposes of the assessment results. Therefore, the accurate initial determination of a child's primary or dominant language(s) informs assessment choices and interpretation of the resulting data.

Sources of Information on a Child's Primary or Dominant Language(s)

When deciding how best to determine a child's primary or dominant language, early childhood professionals must take into account the relative reliability of the available reporters. Many approaches used to determine a young dual language child's primary language proficiency status involve collecting parent reports about prior home language exposure, the language(s) spoken most often in the home, and the child's current level of proficiency in both English and the home language (Espinosa & López, 2007; Gutiérrez-Clellen, Restrepo, & Simon-Cereijido, 2006). For the youngest children, reports on primary language would likely be made by parents, teachers, or other care providers. Yet depending on how long a child has been in a given out-of-home care setting, and the formality of both intake, screening, and assessment procedures and teacher–parent interactions, a care provider or teacher may not be able to confidently report on the primary or dominant home language of the child. Unless the care provider has specifically attempted to gather information from parents about the child's home language experiences and his or her current use of and proficiency in each language with all household members, it may be difficult for the care provider to accurately determine the child's primary language, language dominance, and/or relative proficiencies across different languages.

Sensitivity of Measures

Given the variability in the timing and rate of acquiring different language skills and abilities, care must be taken when assessing a child's relative language proficiencies at any given point in time. The onset and rate of language acquisition depend on factors within both the child and the child's home and other learning environments (Anderson, 2004; Pan et al., 2005). The child's personality, aptitude for languages, interest, and motivation interact with the quantity and quality of language inputs and opportunities for use to influence the rate of language acquisition and eventual fluency levels (Romaine, 1994). Multiple skills are involved in language use, and a child's profile of dual language skills could be complex or even contradictory. Depending on his or her age, the amount of prior English exposure and the particular stage of English language acquisition, and the stage of home language acquisition, a child may perform differently on different types of assessments.

For example, many young dual language children demonstrate greater proficiency on measures of receptive vocabulary than measures of expressive vocabulary, as the latter requires a more advanced set of language-related skills and abilities (Tabors & Snow, 1994). Therefore, the fact that a child may demonstrate proficiency in a few narrow linguistic skills (e.g., items on a language screener that assess receptive language skills) does not necessarily mean that the child is equally proficient in other areas of language.

Thus, efforts to determine an individual dual language child's primary or dominant language(s) should clearly articulate the specific definitions and factors used in the assessment process, such as the type of informants used, information on exposure to both primary and secondary languages, and related information collection procedures that will be used. The process chosen to determine a child's primary or dominant language(s) would then shape subsequent decisions about selecting the corresponding direct child assessments.

Different Approaches to Choosing the Language(s) of Assessment

More complex than determining the child's primary language(s) is choosing assessment processes that will gather meaningful information in one or both languages. Many of the different assessment approaches used with dual language children acknowledge the complexities of bilingual language and literacy development and try to overcome the limitations of many of the assessment tools discussed here. Different assessment approaches range from a sole focus on the use of English assessment measures or the total exclusion of non–English-speaking dual language children in research and accountability assessment, to relatively sophisticated efforts that take into account an array of developmental skills and abilities both within and across languages (Espinosa & López, 2007). The following sections review three methods of using information on a child's primary or dominant language to guide related decisions pertaining to the assessment of dual language children. Each method yields different information, which is often used for different purposes. The methods are as follows:

- Preliminary screening for primary language(s), followed by administration of assessments in a single language
- Separate administration of measures in each language
- **Conceptual scoring** of measures administered in a combination of two languages

The selection of a particular assessment approach should be guided in large part by the specific developmental, diagnostic, and research questions at hand and the types of data that will be needed to answer those questions.

Formal Prescreening of Language Proficiency   The most commonly used language proficiency prescreening approach, a *monolingual language prescreening,* is more applicable for research and accountability assessment purposes than for instructional planning or diagnostic purposes. Several major evaluation studies have screened for minimal proficiency in English prior to administering each wave of English-language assessments. The Early Childhood Longitudinal Study–Kindergarten (ECLS-K; National Center for Education Statistics, 2000) is one example of dual language assessment conducted primarily in a single language.

In this study, children from non–English-speaking homes were initially screened using the English version of the Oral Language Development Scale (OLDS), which was developed using several subtests of the *preLAS 2000* (Duncan & De Avila, 1998). The non–English-speaking children who scored above an empirically derived threshold score on the OLDS indicating a minimal level of English oral proficiency were subsequently assessed using English direct assessments of reading, general knowledge, and mathematics. However, those Spanish-speaking children who scored below the cutoff on the OLDS completed only a limited set of assessments in Spanish (i.e., only the translated mathematics and psychomotor direct assessments).

This type of monolingual prescreening procedure helped ensure that assessment results better reflected the children's abilities in the content areas rather than their proficiency in English (or lack of English proficiency). In other words, children were directly assessed on the broader array of assessments only when they demonstrated a certain minimum level of English proficiency. Furthermore, this approach kept children with little to no English from having to complete frustrating assessments that they likely were not able to understand. However, it is important to note the differential impact that this screening process had on the composition of the final sample, especially the sample of children from Spanish-speaking backgrounds. Overall, 15% of the total ECLS-K sample screened with the OLDS; 62% of those screened were children whose home language was Spanish (9% of the total sample). About half of the children who were screened were not administered the full direct child assessment battery because their English skills were below the threshold (National Center for Education Statistics, 2000). However, those screened out were primarily Spanish speakers (58% of the children screened out; 4% of the total sample). These screened-out children represented almost a 48% reduction in the number of Spanish-speaking children who participated in the full battery. Excluding this number of children significantly undermined the knowledge gained regarding the early childhood development targeted by the ECLS-K. Again, such a strategy would not be appropriate for assessments of dual language children for instructional planning or diagnostic purposes. Nor would such an approach be appropriate for use in research or accountability efforts when such efforts are expected to contain anything more than a minimal percentage of Spanish-dominant children, who would be likely to be screened out by such an approach.

A somewhat similar prescreening approach involves separate *bilingual language prescreening* conducted in both English and Spanish. In this approach, a child first completes brief language screening measures in both languages to determine his or her minimal proficiency in both languages and/or the more dominant language. Then the child completes the rest of the assessment battery in the more dominant language. Results obtained using this method more accurately reflect a child's peak skills in his or her more dominant language than likely would have occurred if the decision about the language of assessment had been guided by more informal information on the child's language abilities. One strength of this approach for use in research or accountability efforts is that a greater percentage of children then participate in the assessment process either in Spanish or in English.

However, there are some important limitations to both the monolingual and bilingual language prescreening approaches. Assessing children in one language only makes it difficult to understand both their separate and comparative linguistic proficiencies in each separate language. Key understanding of separate (English and Spanish) bilingual developmental trajectories and outcomes is lost. Bilingual screening would be most meaningful if it occurred periodically, because children may switch dominant languages over time (McLaughlin et al., 1995).

Dual Language Administration of Assessments   Another dual language assessment strategy overcomes some of the inherent limitations of the monolingual or bilingual language prescreening approaches by conducting assessments in both English and the child's home language (Espinosa & López, 2007; Hammer, Lawrence, & Miccio, 2007; Páez & Rinaldi, 2006). This dual administration approach allows for the simultaneous examination of children's performance in both their home language and English at any given point in time as well as the examination of developmental variations at different ages and over time.

The dual language assessment approach has many obvious advantages over the previously described approaches, mainly with respect to matching the language(s) of assessment with one or more language(s) in which the child is actually proficient. In other words, children would be assessed separately in each language in which they are at least minimally proficient. However, there also are some limitations. When young dual language children enter more formal care and education settings, they not only face the challenges of rapidly learning a new language (typically English) but also may experience changes in their rate of acquisition of their home language (Genesee et al., 2004; Hammer, Lawrence, & Miccio, 2007). If data are gathered at only one point in time, the results from a dual language administration approach need to be interpreted with extra care for children during this transitional period, as their performance on either measure may be substantially lower than that of either their predominantly English-speaking peers or their dual language peers who are not undergoing such a transition. Furthermore, current research provides little clear guidance on how to either statistically analyze or interpret the separate information obtained on children's English language versus home language developmental trajectories. In addition, a dual administration approach can also involve extensive additional testing time, cost, and practice effects.

Conceptual Scoring Approaches   An emerging strategy in the field of multilingual measure development is the use of measures that have standardized conceptual scoring of items, wherein a child's correct responses are accepted regardless of the language in which he or she provides them. Some advocate that this approach measures children's overall knowledge, skills, and abilities irrespective of the language in which their responses are provided (Pearson, Fernandez, & Oller, 1993). For measurement tools developed intentionally for such use, individual items are typically developed (written, tested, refined, and standardized) simultaneously in both English and Spanish. Extensive care needs to be taken to ensure that each item in each language is answered correctly by the same percentage of children of the same age. These matching questions are then used during the actual administration; usually the tester is allowed to provide prompts in both English and Spanish. In addition to recording the child's response for each item, the assessor also indicates the language of the response. Measures that are specifically developed for this purpose also tend to have appropriate normative samples to compare with the child's score. One example is the Expressive One-Word Picture Vocabulary Test–Spanish-Bilingual Edition (EOWPVT-SBE; Brownell,

2001). The EOWPVT-SBE was standardized with a sample of 1,050 children who generally matched the demographic characteristics of the U.S. Hispanic population. The normative sample included an oversampling of individuals from the Western region whose dialect was Mexican-Spanish, whereas Hispanics from other geographic and dialectical regions were somewhat underrepresented. Thus, scores derived from the EOWPVT-SBE can be compared with normative scores for Spanish-speaking bilingual children in the United States.

The resulting standardized score from such conceptually scored measures could be considered to reflect a child's combined or total knowledge within the given **domain** assessed irrespective of his or her primary language or languages. This approach thereby overcomes one of the main limitations of the dual language or prescreening approaches described previously: the possible loss of information about a child's overall abilities due to assessment in only one language or separately by language. The method may be particularly appropriate within the context of research or accountability data collection efforts that include a substantially high proportion of bilingual children and/or studies designed to assess bilingual children over time, as the relative balance of the children's respective language abilities is also likely to change (e.g., Hammer et al., 2008; Páez, Tabors, & Lopez, 2007).

Although the standardized conceptual scoring approach has many advantages (e.g., it is less burdensome, it is more cost effective, and it captures an overall or combined perspective of a child's language or literacy functioning), there are some important limitations. For example, on receptive language assessments, the child is only required to provide a correct response in one language or the other, which does not accurately assess the child's full range of receptive language abilities in each separate language. Furthermore, if the purpose is to assess the development of children's separate language abilities both at any given point in time as well as longitudinally, the use of such an approach would not be warranted. In sum, the decision to utilize such an approach needs to be guided by the specific question of interest that the assessment is intended to address. Another major limitation is the scarcity of measures that have been developed and standardized to reliably and validly gather conceptual scores across languages.

SELECTING APPROPRIATE MEASURES

As discussed previously, the most critical tasks for clinicians, educators, program staff, policy makers, and researchers are being clear about the intended purpose of the assessment being undertaken and then identifying the desired assessment approach that is aligned with this primary assessment purpose. The next step is to review and to choose from among the available options a specific measure or set of measures whose use is appropriate for both the intended purpose and the targeted assessment approach. This section provides an overview of some of the more critical factors that professionals should use to guide their review and selection of the most culturally, linguistically, and psychometrically appropriate measures for use with DLLs.

Unfortunately, measures often may be chosen out of convenience, out of familiarity, or because they appear adequate in English. However, the existence of a basic translation of an English measure in Spanish in itself is neither adequate nor sufficient to ensure that it is appropriate for use with dual language children (e.g., Peña, 2007). Furthermore, a Spanish measure may be published and readily available to the field, but, as evidenced in this review, that is no guarantee that it has solid psychometric properties or that the necessary array of cultural and linguistic measurement approaches were utilized when the measure was developed, translated, or adapted. Thus, careful examination and comparison of available measures across translation, linguistic, cultural, and psychometric characteristics are always needed. This includes an examination of both the Spanish and English versions of measures, because it is not uncommon to administer measures to dual language children in one or both languages over time as the children develop bilingually. This book was thus developed to aid professionals in their measure selection decision making through a careful, exhaustive, and detailed analysis of measures available for use with young Spanish-speaking dual language children. It is intended to assist educators and psychologists in their practice and research activities as well as to propel their respective fields forward in considering the critical cultural, linguistic, and psychometric facets of bilingual assessment.

PSYCHOMETRIC, LINGUISTIC, AND CULTURAL PROPERTIES OF ASSESSMENTS

Two primary considerations in selecting measures for use with dual language children are their basic psychometric properties and their cultural and linguistic appropriateness. The central importance of these features is reflected in their inclusion in professional standards across the psychological, educational, and evaluation fields (American Educational Research Association, American Psychological Association, & National Council on Measurement in Education, 1999, 2010; American Psychological Association, 1990, 1999, 2002; National Association for the Education of Young Children, 2009; National Association for the Education of Young Children & National Association of Early Childhood Specialists in State Departments of Education, 2003). Professionals are thus obligated to select and use psychometrically, linguistically, and culturally appropriate measures in research and practice. An essential first step in this process is to understand the meaning of these terms and the methods used to assess the adequacy of measures across these dimensions. The goal of this book is to provide a conceptual overview of these issues and to lay the framework for the approach utilized in reviewing the measures presented here. These concepts, as well as others, are also described in the glossary and in other available resources.[1]

Basic Psychometric Features of Measures

When a measure's *psychometric properties* are discussed or described, attention is usually focused on one or more aspects of its *reliability* and *validity*. *Reliability* refers to how precise or trustworthy a test score is in capturing the skills, attitudes,

---

[1]Readers interested in learning more about these topics are referred to the growing body of literature in this area, including Atkins-Burnet (2007); Basterra, Trumbull, and Solano-Flores (2010); Bravo (2003); Dana (2005); Educational Testing Service (2009); Geisinger (1994); Hambleton, Merenda, and Spielberger (2005); Kazdin (2003); Kopriva (2008); Leong and Austin (2006); Snow and Van Hemel (2008); Stubbe Kester and Peña (2002); Suzuki and Ponterotto (2008); and Tabors (2008) as well as the 2011 issue of *Child Development Perspectives*, focused on cross-cultural measurement (Eisenberg, 2011).

| 2.1 | Basic Psychometric Features of Measures—Reliability |

Test–retest reliability: The stability of an individual's score on a given measure over time. Specifically, individuals complete the same measure (or an equivalent form of the measure) on two separate occasions under as close to the same conditions as possible in a certain time interval (e.g., 2 weeks). Their scores on these two occasions are then correlated. Test–retest reliability **correlations** are considered acceptable if greater than .80.

Alternate-form reliability: The comparability of two forms of the same measure that share the same purpose but include different questions or items. Test takers complete both forms, and their scores are then correlated. Alternate-form reliability correlations are considered acceptable if greater than .80. Most measures do not have alternate forms.

Internal consistency: The degree to which scores on items within a given **scale** or test correlate with one another or measure the same **construct**. One can assess the internal consistency of a measure using various indicators, including *split-half reliability* (i.e., correlating an individual's score on half of the items with his or her score on the other half) and Cronbach's alpha (i.e., using coefficient alphas to see how well items "hang together" statistically). Correlations are considered acceptable if greater than .80.

Interrater or *interscorer agreement:* The level of agreement across two or more independent scorers that demonstrates that the assessment, rather than the assessor, is measuring the ability consistently. Interrater agreement is generally reported using Pearson's *r*. Correlations of test scores $\geq$ .80 are considered acceptable.

or abilities it is purported to measure. The reliability of a measure is examined across multiple dimensions, such as **test–retest reliability**, **internal consistency**, **interrater** or **interscorer agreement**, and **alternate-form reliability** (see Box 2.1). In turn, *validity* reflects the degree to which all accumulated evidence supports the interpretation and use of test scores for a particular purpose. Validity can also be examined at multiple levels, including **face validity**, **content validity**, **construct validity**, and **criterion validity** (see Box 2.2).

Additional Cultural and Linguistic Features of Measures Used with Dual Language Learners

Beyond the basic psychometric properties of measures, additional considerations pertain to the unique cultural and linguistic features of measures developed for use with dual language children. The fact that a measure has been translated from English to Spanish neither ensures that the psychometric properties automatically carry over from the English version to the Spanish version nor ensures that the cultural and linguistic characteristics are appropriate for use with any given Spanish-speaking population. Rather, it is necessary to use intensive qualitative and quantitative approaches to determine the adequacy of the measures' items, content, and functioning both within and across languages. These approaches can include reviews of curricula and developmental assessments from Latin American countries; input from panels of content experts; translation/back-translation

2.2	Basic Psychometric Features of Measures—Validity

Face validity: The extent to which a given assessment appears at first glance to measure the phenomenon it is designed to measure. Face validity is often examined by internal and external expert review.

Content validity: The extent to which a measure reflects the range of content present in the domain that it is designed to measure. For example, a measure that is reported to comprehensively examine children's language development should contain both receptive and expressive questions rather than questions in only one of those areas. Generally speaking, content validity is assessed without using statistics. Activities used to assess content validity can include expert panel review and analyses of textbooks, curricula, and dictionaries.

Construct validity: A broad concept that refers to the extent to which a given assessment measures the domain of interest. Multiple terms are utilized when discussing construct validity:

1. **Internal construct validity** is examined when a measure is composed of subscales. For example, separate receptive language and expressive language subscale scores, rather than only a total language score, should be empirically supported. Factor analysis is a common type of statistical analysis.

2. **External construct validity** assesses the extent to which the complete measure taps a domain. For example, a test created to assess language and literacy development should be able to distinguish between younger and older children and between children with and without disabilities in this area. In addition, this test should correlate with other measures designed to assess the same domain (i.e., have *convergent validity*) but not with measures designed to assess other areas of development, such as motor skills (i.e., have *divergent/discriminant validity*).

Criterion validity: The extent to which an assessment correlates with expected outcomes as evidenced by correlations with other measures. Two of the most common types of criterion validity are the following:

1. **Concurrent validity:** The degree to which an assessment correlates with performance on another measure at the same point in time.

2. **Predictive validity:** The degree to which an assessment can be used to predict future behavior or future performance on another measure.

methodologies to ensure accurate interpretations across English and Spanish; **standardization** of measures with an appropriate Spanish-speaking normative sample (or samples); and advanced statistical procedures such as **differential item functioning, item response theory** analyses, or **Rasch item modeling,** which help to identify potential biases in any particular question. Multiple resources are available that inform professionals in the field about these and other related procedures for use in appropriately developing measures across different languages and cultures (see the list of references in Footnote 1).

The measures review in this book utilizes many of the terms and guidelines summarized by Bravo (2003) as a foundation for examining the cultural and linguistic characteristics of dual language measures. The first set of important cultural and linguistic features includes aspects related to the process of developing and standardizing measures in another language (see Box 2.3).

2.3   Cultural and Linguistic Features of Measures

Content equivalence of items and measure: Refers to whether the domains and questions are relevant to the cultural group or population. In other words, are the domains and items appropriate for the population? For example, questions regarding children's influence in making family decisions may be less relevant in cultures that have more traditional or hierarchical family structures. Geographical differences must also be considered (e.g., asking individuals from tropical climates about winter weather may not be meaningful). Test developers may conduct interviews or focus groups or convene a panel of experts representing different cultural groups to review items for potential biases and cultural relevance.

Semantic equivalence: The degree to which versions of a measure possess the same meaning across languages or even across distinct dialects within a given language. For example, in the United States there are many different dialects of Spanish, with Mexican dialects being the most prevalent, followed by Caribbean (e.g., Puerto Rican, Dominican, Cuban) and Central American dialects. Essential questions in this area are the following: If a measure was translated, how was it done, what were the background characteristics of the individual or individuals who did the translation work, and does the resulting translation maintain the same meaning as the original English version? If discordance was identified in particular items, how was it fixed? One way to assess the semantic equivalence of a translated measure is to translate it back into its original language and compare the result with the initial measure (i.e., translation/back translation). Dialectical variations that exist within languages are also increasingly being considered in measure development and translation and are generally examined using a mix of qualitative and quantitative procedures.

Structural consistency across versions: The extent to which the structure (e.g., length, item/response format) of the items on the original and adapted/translated version(s) of a measure are uniform and comparable to one another. In other words, how similar are the items, length, and format of the measure across the languages? This *may* be important if **raw scores** across both English and Spanish measures are being utilized to compare children's development. Measures for which items are simultaneously developed in both English and Spanish are more likely to have corresponding morphological and syntactical structure in both languages.

Standardization: The sample and procedures utilized to develop the measure. Within the bilingual assessment field, particular attention is paid to the representation of Spanish-speaking children. Was the measure standardized across various Latin American countries with monolingual Spanish-speaking children? Or with bilingual children throughout the United States? Or with Spanish-dominant children in one area of the United States? Additional important characteristics of the **standardization sample** include the socioeconomic and education levels of the parents of the children included in the sample. Different normative populations may be preferred depending on the purpose of the assessment and the subsequent population of interest being assessed. Thus, there is no one correct sample to include in standardization. However, it is important to be knowledgeable about the standardization sample, as this assists in both measure selection and the accurate interpretation of results.

Comparison of the Psychometric Properties of Measures in English and Another Language

The second set of important cultural and linguistic features is related to the extent to which the psychometric properties of a translated or adapted measure are comparable to those of the English version of the measure (see Box 2.4).

SUMMARY

Early childhood professionals working with dual language children need to consider each of the following features when selecting measures:

- What language approach is needed?
- What content area is the measure intended to measure?
- Who can administer it and for what purpose?
- How much training and time are needed?
- How were young dual language children included when developing the measure?
- What is the demographic composition of the normative samples across ethnicity, socioeconomic status, language, region, and so forth? How well does the norming sample match the population of interest?
- How strong are its psychometric properties (across the different types of reliability and validity)? How do these compare or differ across the English and Spanish versions?
- How strong are its cultural and linguistic measurement properties for use with Spanish-speaking children?

Early childhood professionals are beginning to understand the *need* to consider the full range of cultural, linguistic, and psychometric properties of measures prior to selecting them for use in assessment or research. However, the *actual application and utilization* of such procedures are either not fully understood or are thwarted

---

2.4   Technical Equivalence Across Measures

Technical equivalence in reliability: The extent to which an adapted or translated version of a given assessment has similar reliability psychometrics as the original assessment. In essence, technical equivalence in reliability indicates how similar the data are across, for example, Spanish and English versions in terms of test–retest reliability, internal consistency, and interrater agreement. Statistical coefficients are usually examined visually, though they can be examined statistically.

Technical equivalence in validity: The extent to which an adapted or translated version of a given assessment has similar validity results as the original assessment. Technical equivalence in validity indicates how similar the validity of, for example, Spanish and English versions is, particularly as it examines how culturally relevant the domains tested are, what their meanings are, and how they relate to other child development measures or outcomes. This process entails a review of both qualitative and quantitative data.

by lack of time, effort, money, or technical resources. Thus, the latter part of this book is dedicated to filling this gap by providing a thorough description of measures available in both English and Spanish. For example, information and analysis are provided on everything from the most basic considerations of a measure (e.g., administration length, cost, required training) to the most advanced technical aspects (e.g., the extent to which the Spanish and English versions are similar or dissimilar in their reliability and validity for use with young children). In addition, the strengths and weaknesses of the English and Spanish versions of each measure are independently described and compared to each other. Furthermore, each version and measure is rated along various linguistic, cultural, and psychometric dimensions. Appendix B provides readers with a quick visual representation of how individual measures compare to one another. It also provides a graphic overview of where the early childhood field stands in the development of psychometrically sound measures in both English and Spanish for use with preschool-age children.

3

Techniques for Administering Assessments to Dual Language Preschoolers

In addition to overall language and measure selection considerations, the actual techniques utilized to administer assessments to dual language preschoolers require specialized knowledge and experience. First, examiners assessing young children, *regardless of whether they are monolingual English speakers, monolingual Spanish speakers, or have dual language proficiencies,* need to have good interpersonal skills and adequate knowledge about early childhood development. Second, examiners assessing young dual language children must be grounded in understanding and addressing cultural, linguistic, and pragmatic influences on the assessment process. Each of these is described in turn here.

ASSESSING YOUNG CHILDREN

Approaches related to interpersonal techniques, measure knowledge and skills, and physical setting are specifically addressed in this section. For more about these topics and other general approaches to assessing young children, please see Bracken (2004) and Sattler (2008).

Interpersonal Techniques

Young children respond well to examiners who are both warm and structured. Such examiners are generally positive and upbeat with young children yet are attuned to cues from the children and can quickly adapt their tone and address any potential concerns or stress. Examiners also should become adept at using both verbal and nonverbal approaches to facilitate engagement, such as smiles and high-fives to provide encouragement. Such reinforcement should not be contingent on correct responses; rather, it is provided to support and acknowledge the child's efforts. Although positive reinforcers that are social in nature work very well, young children also respond well to concrete reinforcers, such as stickers, incorporated between subtests or measures. Finally, examiners must balance time spent playing or in general discussion with children with the actual administration of the standardized assessment. Indeed, extended play can fatigue the linguistic and attentional resources of children, which may limit their performance and scores on the assessment. On a positive note, many children enjoy the tasks that have been developed for assessments at their developmental level and will follow the examiner's structure and lead to engage in the measure. If at any point the child becomes disinterested or discouraged, reinforcement and emotional support should be provided along with frequent breaks as may be necessary. Often, young children will respond quite positively. Otherwise, one should consider discontinuing the assessment either until another day or altogether.

Measure Knowledge and Skills

It is critical that those examining young children have a thorough knowledge of, and facility with, the specific measure being administered, including all of its items, **basal** and **ceiling** rules, and scoring. The attention spans of young children are relatively short, and children can be easily distracted or fatigued if examiners are not adequately prepared and spend an extended amount of time looking at their manuals, rereading items, or even reading stiffly from the manuals. Thus, the measures should be memorized to the greatest extent possible in order to provide the child with the most fluid and optimal assessment. With experience and full knowledge of a measure (including knowledge of the order and presentation of items), the examiner can more easily engage young children as items are presented following standardized procedures. This experience also enhances the examiner's ability to quickly shift to appropriate developmental levels across and within different domains.

Physical Setting

Finally, the environment of the administration setting also requires forethought and preparation. Examiners should use a room or an area of a room that is visually pleasing and welcoming to a child but that has relatively few distractions within the child's immediate reach or view. Furthermore, the placement of a child-size table and chairs close to a wall or near a corner can safeguard against chair tipping and can contribute to focused attention and behavioral self-regulation during the session. Including a focal point of interest, such as an appealing photo or a small fish tank, can facilitate quickly placing the young child at ease and can provide ample opportunity for spontaneous language sampling and greater engagement on the part of the child in the assessment activities. Finally, it can also be helpful to have a large plastic container or drawer with toys to use during breaks and observations.

DUAL LANGUAGE ASSESSMENT WITH YOUNG CHILDREN

Professionals must also develop a deep understanding of dual language development and variation in order to fully engage, and appropriately assess, young children who have proficiencies across two languages.

Understanding the Variability in Children's Dual Language Development

Early dual language development in the United States can become uneven as one language is developed (e.g., English) while the other plateaus or weakens (e.g., Spanish). Unfortunately, such trajectories can be more commonly observed than full dual language development in the United States. Importantly, uneven dual language development reflects sociocultural influences on language development in the United States (where English is dominant and a status language) more so than young children's cognitive capabilities for learning two or more languages. (See Hammer, Miccio, & Rodríguez, 2004, for more about the socialization process in dual language development and Paradis, Genesee, & Crago, 2011, for more about typical and atypical dual language development.)

As children switch dominance from one language to another, they may enter a nonverbal (or silent) period in which they may be reticent to express themselves in either language (e.g., Tabors, 2008). More empirical examination of the incidence of this period, its length, and other related characteristics is needed. An examiner assessing a child undergoing a dominance switch must reflect on the intended purpose(s) of testing for that child as well as its advantages and disadvantages. Being in such a transitional period of dual language development does not negate the utility of expressive language testing in either language. Indeed, this utility can be heightened, as a deeper understanding of a child's expressive skills may be utilized to refine interventions and/or instructional activities with the child. Most important, it is critical that the child feel comfortable with the examiner and be interested in the tasks; otherwise, any nonresponses may reflect reticence rather than linguistic limitations.

Ordering of Tasks

When administering a measure, the examiner should administer the subtests and items in the order prescribed by the publisher to be consistent with the standardization of the test, unless there is a compelling reason to do otherwise. If more than one measure is being administered across a range of domains, then it is recommended that motor or nonverbal tasks be presented prior to assessing verbal abilities. Young children, and particularly children who are just learning a second language, enjoy the physicality of these tasks and will become even more conversational over time. When engaging in dual language assessment, it is advisable to administer receptive measures prior to expressive ones. Young dual language children generally feel more confident demonstrating their receptive linguistic *understanding* in either language (which often entails pointing or demonstration) and will then more easily progress to *expressing* themselves verbally.

Dual Language Assessment

When using the dual language assessment approach, which entails measuring children's abilities separately within each language, at least two separate testing sessions may be necessary. It is preferable to assess across two different days or, if this is not possible, to give a substantial break in between each assessment session. At the beginning of the first session, the examiner should describe to the child the dual language approach that is being used. For example, the examiner could say, "I hear that you speaking [or are learning] two languages. Wow, me too! Let's practice with each other, first by speaking [language] and then by speaking [language]. Of course, if either of us gets stuck, it is okay to switch back to the other language."

Testing in the Dominant Language

It is typically beneficial to spend some time conversing with the child in his or her dominant language before beginning the assessment. If the dominant language is one other than English and the child is enrolled in an early education program, it is possible that he or she has just spent part, if not all, of the day actively hearing and processing his or her second language (English). Thus, it is advisable to reacclimate the child to speaking in his or her dominant language prior to assessing.

Testing in the Nondominant Language

Children (and adults alike) may be more hesitant or have difficulty responding in their nondominant language (e.g., Tabors, 2008). Thus, the tone and quality of the examiner's interpersonal engagement with the young child are central to making him or her feel at ease. Demonstrating excitement about "trying out" the nondominant language is beneficial, as is providing social or tangible reinforcements. Many children are proud to demonstrate what they have learned, and they may perform better than examiners initially expect when provided with support and opportunities. As when assessing in the dominant language, the examiner should spend time speaking with the child in the nondominant language prior to beginning administration. If the child responds in his or her dominant language when development in the nondominant language is being assessed, the decision to score the response as correct, score it as incorrect, or prompt again in the nondominant language depends on how each specific measure was developed and its intent (e.g., conceptual scoring across languages or separate assessment of each language).

Code-Switching

Dual language children frequently use two languages within a sentence, utterance, or conversation, a phenomenon referred to as *code-switching* or *code-mixing* (e.g., Miccio, Hammer, & Rodriguez, 2009; Nicoladis & Genesee, 1997). Some measures have been intentionally designed to allow for the use of code-switching in order to assess overall or combined development across languages through conceptual scoring (e.g., the Expressive One-Word Picture Vocabulary Test–Spanish-Bilingual Edition), whereas others have been developed to account for code-switching in the responses (e.g., the Preschool Language Scale–Fifth Edition). If the examiner is assessing in a specific language with a measure that does not incorporate other-language responses in order to provide an estimate of skills within a particular language, then he or she should continue to model the assessment language in conversation and maintain rapport. Code-switching should not be actively rejected by the examiner.

Dialect

Although there are vast similarities in vocabulary and grammar across Spanish-speaking countries, some dialectical variation exists that should be accounted for in assessment. For example, *car* may be *coche, auto,* or *automóvil* depending on the country. Anglicisms are also present for some Spanish-speaking communities, such as the use of *carro* for *car*. Differences in linguistic features such as prosody and articulation also exist. For example, those from the Caribbean are more likely to drop final phonemes (e.g., saying *pa'* instead of *para* [for]), among other phonological variations (e.g., Goldstein, 2007). In addition, verb finite errors may be less indicative of language impairments among some Latino groups in the United States (such as Caribbeans in the northeast) but may serve as a distinct indicator of language impairments among others (such as Mexican Americans in the southwest; Gutiérrez-Clellen, Simon-Cereijido, & Wagner, 2008).

Some measures have been standardized with distinct Spanish dialects, whereas others have been developed with items used across multiple dialects. Thus, appropriate dialectical variations for various Spanish-speaking populations have already been examined and incorporated into the creation and standardization of the measure. Other test developers have not explicitly done this. In such cases, the examiner needs to reflect on the items used in the measure and consider whether any may not be appropriate for a particular child's regional and dialectical background. Substitutions may be considered; however, care must be taken to avoid inadvertently changing the difficulty level of the question (e.g., making it harder or easier) or even the purpose of the question (e.g., from a semantic question to a lexical one) given that such changes likely may negatively affect the psychometrics and therefore the validity of the results.

Qualifications of the Examiner and the Use of an Interpreter

Finally, it is preferable that the examiner be completely fluent in the language(s) being assessed in order to validly examine the child's competency in this area. Semilingualism on the part of the examiner could potentially influence the child's performance or engagement and thus ultimately his or her results. Thus, bilingual examiners should be fully aware of the extent of their respective language proficiencies and their potential impact on their ability to administer dual language assessments.

Because of the general dearth of bilingual examiners, interpreters can be utilized if no other suitable options are available. Indeed, it is preferable to use an interpreter than to not fully assess a child's abilities. Three key elements contribute to a successful collaboration with an interpreter. First, the interpreter should be a professional interpreter, to the extent possible, rather than a family member or an older sibling of the child. Second, the interpreter needs to be trained in conducting assessments, both general assessment approaches (including the rationale for and methods of maintaining standardized procedures) and the dual language assessment approaches described previously. Third, the examiner and the interpreter need to establish a strong working relationship. This includes describing how and when communication will occur between them as well as with the child and family. Power dynamics and potential triangulated conversations can be averted by anticipating these potential scenarios (e.g., Miller, Martell, Pazdirek, Caruth, & Lopez, 2005). For example, the examiner must be aware that there can be a strong pull to speak or look to the interpreter and not directly to the family or child. However, the focus should be on direct communication between the examiner and child/family, with the interpreter providing assistance with the translation (e.g., Langdon, 2002).

4

Guide to the Measure Reviews and State of the Field

A systematic approach was utilized to identify, select, and critically review measures that directly assess preschool-age children's language and literacy development in both English and Spanish.[1]

STEP 1: INITIAL IDENTIFICATION OF POTENTIAL MEASURES

The first step in the selection process consisted of identifying measures related to 1) early childhood, 2) language, 3) literacy, and/or 4) dual language children. Multiple sources were used to identify potential dual language measures. Exhaustive reviews of the *Mental Measurements Yearbook*, publisher web sites, academic articles, and technical reports (including those by Albarran-Rivero, 1999; Berry, Bridges, & Zaslow, 2004; Del Vecchio & Guerrero, 1995; Midwest Equity Assistance Center, 1999) were conducted. At the conclusion of Step 1, nearly 150 potential measures were identified.

STEP 2: IDENTIFICATION OF A SHORT LIST OF MEASURES FOR REVIEW

Descriptions of each measure were subsequently obtained and reviewed in order to identify measures fitting all three of the following selection criteria:

a. A target age range that included 3- to 5-year-olds

b. Ample coverage of language and/or literacy domain

---

[1]Because preschool dual language assessments are often centered on young children's language and literacy development, and because the vast majority of the non-English measures are available only in Spanish, this book focuses on English and Spanish measures of early language and literacy development.

c. Translation/adaptation available, or indication by publisher of utility with dual language populations

This step dramatically reduced the total pool of candidate measures to a much shorter list of 36 dual language measures to review.

STEP 3: SELECTION OF FINAL MEASURES

The last step in the selection process consisted of identifying the final measures for review. The 19 measures selected (see Table 4.1) possessed all of the following characteristics:

a. They were available in English and Spanish for similar age groups.
b. They included a direct child assessment component.[2]
c. They were useful with the general population rather than just children with potential disorders.

Table 4.1. Measures reviewed in English and Spanish

Battelle Developmental Inventory–Second Edition (BDI-2)

Bilingual Vocabulary Assessment Measure (BVAM)

Boehm Test of Basic Concepts–Third Edition Preschool

BRIGANCE Preschool Screen–II

Clinical Evaluation of Language Fundamentals–Preschool®–Second Edition (CELF® Preschool-2)

Compton Speech and Language Screening Evaluation of Children

Developmental Indicators for the Assessment of Learning–Fourth Edition (DIAL-4)

Early Literacy Skills Assessment (ELSA)

Early Screening Inventory•Revised (ESI•R) 2008 Edition/*Inventario para la Detección Temprana•Revisado* (IDT•R) 2008

Expressive One-Word Picture Vocabulary Test–Fourth Edition (EOWPVT-4): English/Expressive One-Word Picture Vocabulary Test–Spanish-Bilingual Edition (EOWPVT-SBE)

FirstSTEp: Screening Test for Evaluating Preschoolers: English/*PrimerPASO* Screening Test for Evaluating Preschoolers: Spanish

Get Ready to Read! Screening Tool (GRTR)

Merrill-Palmer–Revised Scales of Development (M-P-R)

Peabody Picture Vocabulary Test–Fourth Edition (PPVT-4): English/*Test de Vocabulario en Imágenes Peabody* (TVIP)

preLAS 2000: English/*preLAS* 2000 *Español*

Preschool Language Scale–Fifth Edition (PLS-5): English/Preschool Language Scale–Fourth Edition (PLS-4): Spanish

Receptive One-Word Picture Vocabulary Test–Fourth Edition (ROWPVT-4): English/Receptive One-Word Picture Vocabulary Test–Spanish-Bilingual Edition (ROWPVT-SBE)

Woodcock-Muñoz Language Survey–Revised, Normative Update (WMLS-R NU)[a]

Young Children's Achievement Test (YCAT): English/*Prueba de Habilidades Académicas Iniciales* (PHAI)

[a]Because of the focus here on language and literacy skills, the WMLS-R NU was reviewed rather than the broader Woodcock-Johnson III batteries (WJ-III) and *Batería III Woodcock-Muñoz* (*Batería III*). As appropriate, information about the WJ-III is provided here. For more details about the WJ-III, see the reviews by Berry, Bridges, and Zaslow (2004), Cizek (2003), and Sandoval (2003). For more details about the *Batería III*, see the reviews by Doll and LeClair (2007), Olivarez and Boroda (2007), and Otero (2006).

---

[2]This book focuses on examining and comparing one type of assessment approach (i.e., direct child assessment) used across various disciplines and for multiple purposes. Observational measures, along with parent and teacher reports, also play important roles in assessing young children's language and literacy development and need to be examined for their own psychometric, cultural, and linguistic properties.

d. They had been standardized or used extensively in studies published since 1995.

e. They could be administered by teachers, examiners, and/or researchers.

STEP 4: INTERNAL AND EXTERNAL EVALUATION OF MEASURES

Once selected, each measure underwent extensive internal and external analysis. The review process began with a careful examination of published and unpublished manuals as well as information provided on publisher web sites. In addition, published critiques or studies about the measures were identified via *Mental Measurements Yearbook,* the Education Resources Information Center, PsycINFO, and Google Scholar. After the initial review draft for each measure was created, we cross-checked it on multiple occasions among ourselves. A final important step was the predistribution of the reviews to both the publishers and the authors of all measures. This provided an ability to solicit clarifying or unpublished information, which was subsequently incorporated into the reviews. In addition, it provided an opportunity to establish an open, collaborative endeavor to continue to improve the state of assessment for dual language children.

OVERVIEW OF CONTENTS IN EACH REVIEW

The detailed reviews of each measure address the following items:

a. Overview
   1. Manual citation
   2. Publisher contact information
   3. Cost
   4. Type of measure (e.g., norm, criterion, mixed)
   5. Intended age range
   6. Description of the measure
   7. Key constructs/domains assessed in the measure
   8. Available languages and formats
   9. Primary strengths of the measure
   10. Primary weaknesses of the measure
b. Administration
   1. Time needed
   2. Procedure
   3. Administration and interpretation
   4. Scoring method
   5. Adaptations or instructions for use with individuals with disabilities
c. Functional Considerations
   1. Measure development (for Spanish versions of measures, this includes content equivalence of items and measure, semantic equivalence of translations, structural consistency across English and Spanish versions)
   2. Standardization sample

3. Norming

4. Reliability (test–retest reliability, internal consistency, interrater agreement, other [e.g., equivalent forms])

5. Validity (face and content, internal construct, external construct, criterion validities)

6. Comparison of psychometric properties between English and Spanish versions (at the end of the reviews of the Spanish versions)

d. Relevant Studies Using the Measure

e. Additional References

Note that this book provides a detailed analysis of the psychometric properties of some of the most frequently used direct assessments of preschoolers' language and literacy development in Spanish and English available to assist clinicians, teachers, researchers, and policy makers in their work with dual language preschoolers. We have worked to check the accuracy of these reviews against information available from publishers and published in the literature. However, additional information may be available from other sources. When selecting measures to use, readers are strongly encouraged to read and consider all documentation available. In addition, readers are reminded that measures are continually updated and that they should check to see whether new editions or updates of measures of interest have been released. Updates usually reflect improvements in one or more of the areas examined in these reviews.

DESCRIPTION OF THE STATE OF THE FIELD OF DUAL LANGUAGE ASSESSMENT BASED ON THE REVIEWS

As evidenced across the individual measure reviews and particularly by the table in Appendix B, the available measures for assessing young preschool children *in English* are now overwhelmingly adequate in their reliability and validity. The field had been faced with a dearth of well-developed, well-examined, and appropriate measures that reliably and validly provided an understanding of early development among English-speaking children. Yet the availability and quality of state-of-the-art assessment measures for use with young children has improved rapidly since then. The field, including the publishers and authors, is to be commended for this growth born from focused attention to this area.

The reviews also show that although a measure may have been carefully developed and examined in English, its Spanish version may not have received the same attention in terms of its development and adaptation in Spanish. In some cases the basic psychometric properties of Spanish versions are weak, with inadequate documentation and/or feeble support for the cultural or linguistic relevance of constructs, items, or approaches across language versions. Thus, an important lesson is not to make *any* assumptions about a non-English measure based solely on the characteristics and psychometric properties of the respective English version.

Moreover, the available pool of Spanish-language versions of early childhood linguistic assessments is a mixed bag for clinicians, researchers, and educators. Some Spanish versions of measures are quite poor (and even weak in English in a very few cases), whereas other Spanish measures have been born from an exhaustive, iterative, and detailed development and examination process using qualitative and quantitative approaches. On a positive note, it is becoming increasingly likely that more Spanish-language measures will undergo such extensive development over time. Thus, attention to and discussion about adequate dual language measure development must continue its momentum.

Thus, although great strides have been made, additional work is necessary to refine direct child assessments for use with diverse groups of children and for different purposes. There is no perfect assessment tool for all scenarios; yet careful consideration of the psychometric, cultural, and linguistic properties described here will assist professionals in optimizing their choices of measures to use with the growing population of young dual language children.

A

Alphabetical List of All Measures Originally Considered

As detailed in Chapter 4, the assessment field was systematically examined to identify measures for review that met all of the following criteria:

a. They were available in English and Spanish for similar age groups.
b. They included a direct child assessment component.[1]
c. They were useful with the general population rather than just children with potential disorders.
d. They had been standardized or used extensively in studies published since 1995.
e. They could be administered by teachers, examiners, and/or researchers.

A total of 19 measures identified met these characteristics, whereas the following 114 measures did not at the time of the review:

1. ABC Inventory to Determine Kindergarten and School Readiness
2. *Aprenda*
3. Assessment, Evaluation, and Programming System, for Infants and Children (AEPS), Second Edition
4. Assessment of Literacy and Language
5. Austin Spanish Articulation
6. Australian Developmental Screening Checklist

---

[1]This book focuses on examining and comparing one type of assessment approach (i.e., direct child assessment) used across various disciplines and for multiple purposes. Observational measures, along with parent and teacher reports, also play important roles in assessing young children's language and literacy development and need to be examined for their own psychometric, cultural, and linguistic properties.

7. Bankson Language Test–Second Edition (BLT-2)
8. Bankson-Bernthal Test of Phonology (BBTOP)
9. Basic English Skills Test (BEST)
10. Basic Inventory of Natural Language (BINL)
11. Basic School Skills Inventory–Third Edition (BSSI-3)
12. Ber-Sil Spanish Test
13. Bilingual Syntax Measure (BSM)
14. Bilingual Verbal Ability Test (BVAT)
15. British Ability Scales (BAS)–Second Edition
16. The Carolina Curriculum for Infants and Toddlers with Special Needs (CCITSN)
17. The Carolina Curriculum for Preschoolers with Special Needs (CCPSN)
18. Cattell Infant Intelligence Scale
19. Central Institute for the Deaf Preschool Performance Scale (CID-PPS)
20. Child Development Inventory
21. Children's Progress Academic Assessment (CPAA)
22. Chinese Proficiency Test (CPT)
23. Clinical Evaluation of Language Fundamentals®–Preschool (CELF®-Preschool)
24. Cognitive Abilities Scale–Second Edition (CAS-2)
25. Combined English Language Skills Assessment in a Reading Context (CELSA)
26. Communication and Symbolic Behavior Scales (CSBS)
27. Communication and Symbolic Behavior Scales Developmental Profile (CSBS DP), First Normed Edition
28. Comprehensive Adult Student Assessment Systems (CASAS)
29. Comprehensive Assessment of Spoken Language (CASL)
30. Comprehensive Receptive and Expressive Vocabulary Test–Second Edition (CREVT-2)
31. Concepts of Print and Writing
32. Crane Oral Dominance Test (COD): Spanish/English
33. Detroit Tests of Learning Aptitude–Primary: Third Edition (DTLA-P:3)
34. Developing Skills Checklist (DSC)
35. Developmental Assessment of Young Children (DAYC)
36. Developmental Observation Checklist System (DOCS)
37. Developmental Profile–II
38. Developmental Readiness Scale–Revised (DRS-R)
39. Diagnostic English Language Tests (DELTA)
40. Diagnostic Evaluation of Articulation and Phonology (DEAP)
41. Diagnostic Evaluation of Language Variation (DELV–Criterion Referenced)
42. Diagnostic Evaluation of Language Variation—Screening Test (DELV–Screening Test)
43. Differential Ability Scales (DAS)
44. *Dos Amigos* Verbal Language Scales

45. Dynamic Indicators of Basic Early Literacy Skills–Sixth Edition (DIBELS)
46. Early Childhood Observation System (ECHOS)
47. Early Childhood System: Developing Skills Checklist Score Sheet
48. Early Reading Diagnostic Assessment–Second Edition (ERDA-II)
49. Early Screening Profiles
50. Early Years Early Screen
51. English as a Second Language Oral Assessment (ESLOA)
52. Evaluation of Basic Skills (EBS)
53. Expressive Vocabulary Test (EVT)
54. Fluharty Preschool Speech and Language Screening Test–Second Edition (Fluharty-2)
55. Galileo System
56. Gesell Child Developmental Age Scale (GCDAS)
57. Gesell Developmental Schedules
58. Gesell Preschool Test[2]
59. Gray Oral Reading Tests–Fourth Edition (GORT-4)
60. Henderson-Moriarty ESL Placement (HELP)
61. Hodson Assessment of Phonological Patterns (HAPP-3)
62. Humanics National Child Assessment
63. Hundred Pictures Naming Test (HPNT)
64. Infant Reading Tests
65. Joliet 3-Minute Preschool Speech and Language Screen
66. Kaufman Developmental Scale (KDS)
67. Kaufman Survey of Early Academic and Language Skills (K-SEALS)
68. Khan-Lewis Phonological Analysis–Second Edition (KLPA-2)
69. Language Arts Objective Sequence
70. Language Assessment Battery (LAB)–English
71. Language Proficiency Test Series (LPTS)
72. Lexington Developmental Scales
73. Lindamood Auditory Conceptualization Test–Third Edition (LAC-3)
74. Listening Comprehension Test-2 (LCT-2)
75. Listening Skills Test (LIST)
76. MacArthur-Bates Communicative Development Inventories (CDI)–Second Edition
77. Maculaitas Assessment Program
78. McCarthy Scales of Children's Abilities (MSCA)
79. *Medida Espanola de Articulacion* (*La Meda*)
80. Metropolitan Performance Assessment (MPA)
81. Michigan English Language Institute College English Test (MELICET)
82. Miller Assessment for Preschoolers (MAP)

[2]The upcoming Gesell Early Screener and Gesell Developmental Observation–R measures will be available in Spanish.

83.   Mini-Battery of Achievement (MBA)
84.   Mullen Scales of Early Learning
85.   Multicultural Vocabulary Test (MVT)
86.   Norris Educational Achievement Test (NEAT)
87.   Oral and Written Language Scales (OWLS)
88.   Oral Language Evaluation–Second Edition
89.   Phelps Kindergarten Readiness Scale (PKRS)
90.   Pre-Kindergarten Screen (PKS)
91.   Pre-Reading Inventory of Phonological Awareness (PIPA)
92.   Pre-School Screening Instrument (PSSI)
93.   Preschool Development Inventory (PDI)
94.   Preschool Evaluation Scale (PES)
95.   Quick Informal Assessment–Second Edition (QIA-2)
96.   Rapid Automatized Naming and Rapid Alternating Stimulus Tests (RAN/ RAS)
97.   Ready to Learn
98.   Reynell Developmental Language Scales (RDLS)
99.   Secondary Level English Proficiency Test (SLEP)
100. Slosson Oral Reading Test (SORT)
101. Smit-Hand Articulation and Phonology Evaluation (SHAPE)
102. Spanish/English Reading Comprehension Test–Revised
103. STAR Early Literacy
104. Test for Auditory Comprehension of Language–Third Edition (TACL-3)
105. Test of Academic Achievement Skills–Revised (TAAS-R)
106. Test of Auditory-Perceptual Skills–Revised (TAPS-R)
107. Test of Early Language Development–Third Edition (TELD-3)
108. Test of Early Reading Ability–Third Edition (TERA-3)
109. Test of Early Written Language–Second Edition (TEWL-2)
110. Test of English Proficiency Level (TEPL)
111. Test of Kindergarten/First Grade Readiness Skills (TKFGRS)
112. Test of Language Development–Primary: Third Edition (TOLD-P:3)
113. Test of Preschool Early Literacy (TOPEL)
114. Test of Spoken English (TSE)

B

Measures at a Glance

A Visual Representation of the Relative Strengths and Weaknesses of the Measures Reviewed

In this appendix, the strengths and weaknesses of the English and Spanish versions of each measure are visually represented in two tables. Table B1 presents an analysis of the basic psychometric properties of the measures for each language, which are important foundations for measures. Table B2 presents an analysis of the cultural and linguistic equivalence of each measure across the languages, which is a critical feature for measures used with dual language learner children.

The following is the key to the tables:

○ Indicates not enough information provided *or* the psychometric data is weak

◑ Indicates only partial information provided *or* the psychometric data is low to moderate

● Indicates comprehensive information provided *and* the psychometric data is moderate to high

Please note that a measure may receive a dot when key information is missing from the manual or otherwise unknown. Other data within an area may be quite strong. For example, many measures received a partial dot for Technical Equivalence in Validity. Although they may have solid equivalence in terms of face and content validity, they may have presented only limited studies on criterion validity.

The following tables provide an overview of the measures. Readers should review the detailed descriptions in Section II for information on each measure's adequacy for the intended use. Furthermore, definitions of measurement terminology can be found in the glossary.

TABLE **B.1.** Degree of reliability and validity among English and Spanish forms of measures

Measure	Reliability			Validity			
	Test–retest reliability	Internal consistency	Interrater agreement	Face and content	Internal construct	External construct	Criterion
Battelle Developmental Inventory–Second Edition (BDI-2): English	●	●	●	●	●	●	●
Battelle Developmental Inventory–Second Edition (BDI-2): Spanish	○	○	○	◐	○	○	○
Bilingual Vocabulary Assessment Measure (BVAM)	○	○	○	○	○	○	○
Boehm Test of Basic Concepts–Third Edition Preschool: English	●	●	○	●	N/A	●	◐
Boehm Test of Basic Concepts–Third Edition Preschool: Spanish	●	●	○	●	N/A	●	○
BRIGANCE Preschool Screen–II: English	●	●	○	●	●	●	◐
BRIGRANCE Preschool Screen–II: Spanish	○	○	○	○	○	○	○
Clinical Evaluation of Language Fundamentals®–Preschool–Second Edition: English (CELF® Preschool-2: English)	●	●	●	●	●	●	●
Clinical Evaluation of Language Fundamentals®–Preschool–Second Edition: Spanish (CELF® Preschool-2: Spanish)	●	●	●	●	◐	●	●
Compton Speech and Language Screening Evaluation of Children: English	○	○	○	◐	○	○	○
Compton Speech and Language Screening Evaluation of Children: Spanish	○	○	○	◐	○	○	○
Developmental Indicators for the Assessment of Learning–Fourth Edition (DIAL-4): English	◐	●	●	●	●	●	●
Developmental Indicators for the Assessment of Learning–Fourth Edition (DIAL-4): Spanish	●	●	●	●	●	●	●

Measure	1	2	3	4	5	6	7
Early Literacy Skills Assessment (ELSA): English	○	●	○	●	●	◑	◑
Early Literacy Skills Assessment (ELSA): Spanish	○	◑	○	●	●	◑	○
Early Screening Inventory–Revised (ESI–R) 2008 Edition	●	●	●	●	N/A	●	●
Inventario para la Detección Temprano–Revisado (IDT–R) 2008	◑	●	○	●	N/A	◑	◑
Expressive One-Word Picture Vocabulary Test–Fourth Edition (EOWPVT-4): English	◑	●	○	●	N/A	●	◑
Expressive One-Word Picture Vocabulary Test–Spanish-Bilingual Edition (EOWPVT-SBE)	●	●	○	●	N/A	●	◑
FirstSTEp: Screening Test for Evaluating Preschoolers: English	●	●	◑	●	●	●	●
PrimerPASO Screening Test for Evaluating Preschoolers: Spanish	○	●	○	●	○	○	○
Get Ready to Read! Screening Tool (GRTR): English	○	◑	○	●	●	●	●
Get Ready to Read! Screening Tool (GRTR): Spanish	○	◑	○	●	●	●	●
Merrill–Palmer–Revised Scales of Development (M-P-R): English	●	●	◑	●	●	●	●
Merrill–Palmer–Revised Scales of Development (M-P-R): Spanish	○	○	◑	●	○	○	○
Peabody Picture Vocabulary Test–Fourth Edition (PPVT-4): English	●	●	○	●	N/A	●	●

(continued)

47

Table B.1. *(continued)*

Measure	Reliability			Validity			
	Test–retest reliability	Internal consistency	Interrater agreement	Face and content	Internal construct	External construct	Criterion
Test de Vocabulario en Imágenes Peabody (TVIP)	○	◐	○	○	N/A	◐	◐
preLAS 2000: English	●	●	●	●	◐	◐	○
preLAS 2000: *Español*	○	◐	●	●	◐	○	○
Preschool Language Scale–Fifth Edition (PLS-5): English	●	●	●	●	◐	●	●
Preschool Language Scale–Fourth Edition (PLS-4): Spanish	●	●	●	●	◐	●	◐
Receptive One-Word Picture Vocabulary Test–Fourth Edition (ROW-PVT-4): English	◐	●	◐	●	N/A	●	◐
Receptive One-Word Picture Vocabulary Test–Spanish-Bilingual Edition (ROWPVT-SBE)	●	●	○	●	N/A	●	◐
Woodcock-Muñoz Language Survey–Revised, Normative Update (WMLS-R NU): English	●	●	○	●	●	●	○
Woodcock-Muñoz Language Survey–Revised, Normative Update (WMLS-R NU): Spanish	○	●	○	●	●	◐	◐
Young Children's Achievement Test (YCAT): English	●	●	●	●	◐	●	●
Prueba de Habilidades Académicas Iniciales (PHAI)	◐	●	●	●	◐	◐	◐

Key: N/A, not applicable.

48

TABLE **B.2.** Degree of cultural, linguistic, and psychometric equivalence between English and Spanish forms of measures

Measure	Content equivalence of items and measure	Semantic equivalence of translations	Structural consistency across English and Spanish	Technical equivalence in reliability	Technical equivalence in validity
Battelle Developmental Inventory–Second Edition (BDI-2)	●	●	●	○	○
Bilingual Vocabulary Assessment Measure (BVAM)	○	◐	●	○	○
Boehm Test of Basic Concepts–Third Edition Preschool	●	●	●	●	◐
BRIGANCE Preschool Screen–II	○	○	◐	○	○
Clinical Evaluation of Language Fundamentals®–Preschool–Second Edition (CELF® Preschool-2)	●	●	◐	●	◐
Compton Preschoolers Screening Evaluation	◐	◐	●	○	○
Developmental Indicators for the Assessment of Learning–Fourth Edition (DIAL-4)	●	●	●	●	◐
Early Literacy Skills Assessment (ELSA)	●	◐	◐	◐	●
Early Screening Inventory•Revised (ESI•R) 2008 Edition/ *Inventario para la Detección Temprano•Revisado (IDT•R)* 2008	●	●	●	●	○
Expressive One-Word Picture Vocabulary Test–Fourth Edition (EOWPVT-4): English/ Expressive One-Word Picture Vocabulary Test–Spanish-Bilingual Edition (EOWPVT-SBE)	●	●	◐	●	◐
FirstSTEp: Screening Test for Evaluating Pre-schoolers: English/*PrimerPASO* Screening Test for Evaluating Preschoolers: Spanish	●	●	●	◐	◐
Get Ready to Read! Screening Tool (GRTR)	●	●	●	●	●

(continued)

Table B.2. *(continued)*

Measure	Content equivalence of items and measure	Semantic equivalence of translations	Structural consistency across English and Spanish	Technical equivalence in reliability	Technical equivalence in validity
Merrill-Palmer–Revised Scales of Development (M-P-R)	◐	●	◐	○	○
Peabody Picture Vocabulary Test–Fourth Edition (PPVT-4): English/*Test de Vocabulario en Imágenes Peabody* (TVIP)	○	●	○	◐	○
preLAS 2000: English/*preLAS* 2000 *Español*	●	◐	●	◐	◐
Preschool Language Scale–Fifth Edition (PLS-5): English/Preschool Language Scale–Fourth Edition (PLS-4): Spanish	●	●	●	●	◐
Receptive One-Word Picture Vocabulary Test–Fourth Edition (ROWPVT-4): English/Receptive One-Word Picture Vocabulary Test–Spanish-Bilingual Edition (ROWPVT-SBE)	●	●	◐	●	◐
Woodcock-Muñoz Language Survey–Revised, Normative Update (WMLS-R NU)	●	●	●	◐	●
Young Children's Achievement Test (YCAT): English/*Prueba de Habilidades Académicas Iniciales* (PHAI)	●	●	●	●	●

50

II

Individual
Review of Measures

Battelle Developmental Inventory– Second Edition (BDI-2): English

Manual

Newborg, J. (2005). *Battelle Developmental Inventory, 2nd Edition*. Rolling Meadows, IL: Riverside.

Publisher

Riverside Publishing Company
3800 Golf Road, Suite 100
Rolling Meadows, IL 60008
http://www.riverpub.com

Cost

Complete kit (with manipulatives): $629 ($1,075). Complete kit with software (with manipulatives): $826 ($1,335). BDI-2 Screener Kit (with manipulatives and manual): $202 ($340). Items are also sold separately.

Type of Measure

Direct child assessment, parent interview, and observation

Intended Age Range

Birth to 7;11 years

Key Constructs/Domains

The full BDI-2 assesses five domains:

- Adaptive (ADP)
- Personal-Social (P-S)
- Communication (COM)
- Motor (MOT)
- Cognitive (COG)

Description of Measure

According to the manual, the BDI-2 serves four specific purposes:

- Assessing the typically developing child
- Assessing and identifying a child with a disability or developmental delay
- Planning and providing instruction and intervention
- Evaluating programs serving children

Newborg pointed out that the goal of any evaluation using the English and/or Spanish BDI-2 is "to obtain a comprehensive picture of the child's developmental strengths and opportunities for learning" (2005, p. 5).

Available Languages and Formats

A Spanish version of the measure is available.

Examiners can use the shorter screening version of the BDI-2, which consists of 100 items that are "the best predictors of a child's level of development" (Newborg, 2005, p. 62). The purpose of the screening is to identify children who may have a developmental disability or who are at risk. An additional difference between the BDI-2 Screening Test and the full measure is that basal and ceiling levels are established for the broader domains instead of the subdomains for the screening measure.

Strengths

The English version of the BDI-2 has undergone extensive reliability and validity investigations in English.

The BDI-2 incorporates multiple types of information as part of the assessment. Namely, data are collected regarding a child's development via direct assessment; via interviews with parents, caregivers, or teachers; as well as via observations.

Weaknesses

The scoring procedures entail multiple steps, potentially making them difficult to learn and execute correctly. However, an electronic scoring system is available to assist with scoring.

Examiners may need extended contact with children in order to engage in the observations. This may make the measure difficult to use in some settings.

ADMINISTRATION

Procedure

The BDI-2 assesses five domains and 13 subdomains of child development. The BDI-2 incorporates multiple forms of information as part of the assessment. Namely, data are collected regarding a child's development via direct assessment, observations, and interviews with teachers, parents, or caregivers. The manual provides guidelines for the use of multiple approaches. The ADP and P-S domains are assessed through parent or caregiver interviews, whereas the MOT, COM, and COG domains are assessed primarily through direct child assessment. For many items in all five domains, the manual indicates that naturalistic observations may be used to "evaluate skills that a child would probably not display during a test session" (Newborg, 2005, p. 29). A small number of fine motor items, for example, may require multiple observations. Given the role of observation in the measure, the manual recommends that observers have extended contact with children during the observation period. Finally, observations related to children's behavior during the testing session are also recorded.

Time Needed

Entire Measure

Approximately 60–90 minutes, depending upon age:

- Birth to 2 years: 60 minutes
- 3 years to 5 years: 90 minutes
- 5 years to 7 years: 60 minutes

The manual indicates that testing may occur over several days but must be completed within a 2-week period.

Screening Test

Approximately 10–30 minutes, depending upon age:
- Birth to 3 years:
  10–15 minutes
- 3 years to 5 years:
  20–30 minutes
- 5 years to 7 years:
  10–15 minutes

Adaptive (ADP)

- Self-care (e.g., toileting, eating)
- Personal responsibility (e.g., ability to carry out tasks, initiate play)

Personal-Social (P-S)

- Adult interaction (e.g., helps adult with simple tasks)
- Peer interaction (e.g., shares toys, plays cooperatively)
- Self-concept and social role (e.g., ability to express emotions, aware of gender differences)

Communication (COM)

- Receptive (e.g., responds to who/what questions, identifies initial sounds in words)
- Expressive (e.g., produces vowel sounds, articulates familiar words)

Motor (MOT)

- Gross motor (e.g., throws ball, walks up/down stairs)
- Fine motor (e.g., picks up small objects, cuts paper with scissors)
- Perceptual motor (e.g., stacks cubes, copies letters)

Cognitive (COG)

- Attention and memory (e.g., follows auditory, visual stimuli)
- Reasoning and academic skills (e.g., identifies names, matches colors)
- Perception and concepts (e.g., compares objects by size, color, etc.)

Administration and Interpretation

According to Newborg, the BDI-2 is "primarily designed for use by infant interventionists; preschool, kindergarten, and primary school teachers; and special educators. Speech pathologists, school psychologists, adaptive physical education specialists, clinical diagnosticians, and health care professionals will also find the BDI-2 effective in measuring the functional abilities in young children" (2005, p. 1).

Because there are multiple uses for the BDI-2, individuals' training may vary. In general, administrators should have "college-level training in measurement and statistical concepts," familiarity with child development, as well as "a thorough understanding of the purposes of the instrument, the characteristics of the child to be assessed relative to the normative sample used in the standardization, the administration procedures, and scoring" (p. 10). Such training is especially important given the detail needed to score the BDI-2.

A checklist to use before, during, and after the test is included for administrators to ensure the best possible testing and scoring conditions. A familiar adult (i.e., parent, teacher) may be present when a young child is being directly assessed.

Scoring Method

The BDI-2 (Paper) Record Form contains three sections: 1) a scoring summary; 2) a Test Session Behavioral Observations Form; and 3) subdomain item response areas, where scores are assigned and the procedural method is documented for each item (e.g., structured, interview, observation). A student workbook is also utilized by older children to complete some motor and cognitive items.

After administering the subdomains, examiners using the paper record form calculate children's raw score totals to derive age equivalents and a developmental quotient from tables provided within the manual. Normal curve equivalents, z and T scores, and percentile rankings for developmental quotient scores are also provided. Examiners can also create profile graphs for children's scores across domains and subdomains in order to visually see their performance.

BDI-2 Data Manager software and Palm-powered personal digital assistants are available for purchase. If used, the personal digital assistant takes the place of the paper forms, allowing for potentially more efficient and accurate scoring of children's performance.

Adaptations or Instructions for Use with Individuals with Disabilities

Suggestions for possible accommodations are provided for children with motor, vision, hearing, or speech impairments as well as emotional disturbances or multiple disabilities.

FUNCTIONAL CONSIDERATIONS

Measure Development

The BDI was initially designed for use in an evaluation of a federally funded network of early childhood programs in the early 1970s. It was created in a multistep fashion. First, more than 4,000 items from various other measures were reviewed. Second, the domains and behaviors covered across these measures were identified and evaluated on how critical they were to children's development. Third, these behaviors were organized into the domains and subdomains of the BDI. Finally, the selected items were pilot-tested on 152 children living in Ohio.

In developing the BDI-2, the developers conducted an extensive literature review on the original BDI and on issues surrounding service mandates for young children and early childhood literature. Sets of newly written items were field-tested with groups of 10–20 children. Modifications were made based on children's performance on these items and comments made by administrators conducting the field tests.

More than 150 new items were added to the measure for the tryout edition of the BDI-2. Data from more than 850 tryout cases were collected from children living in the Atlantic/Mid-Atlantic region and analyzed. In addition, more than 45 examiners were surveyed about their experience using the measure. Potential item bias was investigated statistically and through examiner accounts. The manual outlines the criteria used to select items for the standardized edition of the BDI-2 (e.g., high subdomain internal consistency; evidence of content, criterion, and construct validities). A total of 492 items were included in the standardized edition (with approximately 40 of these items dropped prior to its formal publication).

Standardization Sample

Data from 2,500 children were collected. The stratified standardization sample was selected to correspond to 2000 Census data on a range of variables, including age, sex, race/ethnicity, geographic region, and socioeconomic status. A total of 310 examiners from diverse locations within Census regions (Northeast, Midwest, South, West) were selected to engage in the standardization process with examiner teams located in major metropolitan cities such as New York and Los Angeles. Detailed charts in the manual demonstrate that the standardization sample matches U.S. Census data within a percentage point across variables of sex, race/ethnicity, education level, and region.

Children in the standardization sample were administered the BDI-2 in English. "The examiner was responsible for ensuring that the child had an adequate command of English" (Newborg, 2005, p. 99).

Norming

Norm referenced

Reliability

Test–Retest Reliability

Among young children, a sample of children (*n* = 252) organized into two age groupings (2- and 4-year-old children) were tested twice over an interval of 2–25 days (median = 8 days). The ethnic/racial composition of the sample was 63% white, 18% Hispanic, 15% African American, and 4% Asian American. Pearson correlations for subdomains and domains were generally in the medium range for both age groups (i.e., > .80) except for the subdomains of Attention and Memory, which had test–retest coefficients ranging from .74 to .77. Athanasiou (2007) suggested that the data indicate weaker stability coefficients with the COM and COG domains, though they appear adequate.

Internal Consistency

Split-half reliability correlations for the BDI-2 (corrected using the Spearman-Brown formula) are presented for all 13 subdomain scales and across 16 age groupings. Reliability coefficients across age groupings are generally good (i.e., > .80). The reliability coefficients for BDI-2 Total Score and Total Screening Score are high (.99 and .91, respectively). Athanasiou (2007) noted concerns about the ADP and MOT domains for children older than 6 years of age. The

average standard error of measurement (SEM) for domain scores ranges, from 3.04
(P-S domain) to 4.81 (ADP domain). The SEM for the BDI-2 Total Score is relatively stronger in
comparison (1.81), as may be expected.

Interrater Agreement

Some BDI-2 items found in the Fine Motor and Perceptual Motor sections require examiners
to assign scores for children's written responses (e.g., copy a line, circle, and triangle).
Approximately 40 protocols with scores of 0, 1, or 2 were gathered (for a total of 120
protocols) to examine interrater agreement across 17 items. Two trained administrators then
rescored these protocols. Pearson correlations were high (i.e., greater than .90), indicating
that the BDI-2 can be reliably scored.

Other Forms of Reliability (e.g., Equivalent Forms)

Analyses were also conducted to examine the reliability of information ascertained from
different sources (i.e., child assessment, parent/caregiver interview, and observation). Data
from items utilized in the tryout phases were examined. "Only 4% of the item-method
pairs involving only 7% of the items were flagged for further inspection by test developers"
(Newborg, 2005, p. 115). Developers concluded that there were no systematic bias and
relatively few problematic items, suggesting the equivalence of information gathered from
the three different data collection methods.

Validity

Face and Content

The measure's face and content validity appear solid. Experts assisted in developing the
BDI-2 by reviewing items and ensuring coverage of different domains and subdomains. In
developing the BDI-2, developers conducted an extensive literature review on the first edition
of the BDI, as well as current service mandates for young children. In addition, items were
analyzed using examiner feedback and classical and item response theory methods for both
tryout and standardization tasks. Overall, this measure appears to assess what it purports to.

Internal Construct

Both exploratory and confirmatory factor analyses were conducted for the BDI. Overall, there
is strong support for the presence of the five domains on the BDI-2: ADP, P-S, COM, MOT,
and COG.

External Construct

The manual includes growth curve plots that illustrate the progression of mean scores across
age groups as evidence of the measure's construct validity. These curves demonstrate positive
growth trends across domains, with steeper increases for children younger than age 3.

A study was also conducted to investigate whether distinctive score profiles emerged for
various special groups in relation to those of children who were typically developing. Namely,
the BDI-2 was administered to children with identified special needs (e.g., autism, motor
delay). The results showed, for example, that 44 children with autism matched with children
from the standardization sample had significantly lower scores across BDI-2 domains (i.e.,
effect sizes ranged from 2.11 to 2.87).

The classification accuracy (i.e., sensitivity, specificity) of BDI-2 Domain and Total scores as well
as for the BDI-2 Screening Test for identifying children in need of further testing is presented
in the manual. Sensitivity values across different special needs areas ranged from .75 (Motor
Delay Group) to .93 (Cognitive Delay Group). Specificity values across different special needs

areas ranged from .75 (Speech/Language Delay Group) to .91 (Autistic Delay Group). In other words, the BDI-2 has moderate to high classification accuracy. Similar levels of specificity and sensitivity are found for the BDI-2 Screening Test.

Support for its convergent and discriminant validity is also indicated by some of the correlational studies described in "Criterion."

Criterion

As described in the manual, children's performance on the BDI-2 was compared with several measures. These included the older form of the BDI and the Bayley Scales of Infant Development–Second Edition, Comprehensive Test of Phonological Processing, Denver Developmental Screening Test, Preschool Language Scale–Fourth Edition (PLS-IV), Vineland Social Emotional Early Childhood Scales, Wechsler Preschool and Primary Scale of Intelligence–Third Edition, and Woodcock-Johnson III Tests of Achievement (WJ-III).

Overall, the results are supportive of the BDI-2's criterion validity and, as appropriate, its convergent and discriminant validities. For example, correlations between expressive scales for the BDI-2 and the PLS-IV are .73. In addition, the BDI-2 Reasoning and Academic Skills domain and the WJ-III Pre-Academic Skills composite score are correlated at .64. As may be expected, correlations with other WJ-III subtests vary depending on their nature.

RELEVANT STUDIES USING THE MEASURE

A brief literature review using PsycINFO and Google Scholar did not yield any published studies whose abstracts specified use of the BDI-2. The BDI-2 has been used in dissertations. Numerous studies, however, have utilized previous versions of the BDI.

ADDITIONAL REFERENCES

Athanasiou, M. (2007). Test review of the Battelle Developmental Inventory, 2nd edition. In K.F. Geisinger, R.A. Spies, J. F. Carlson, & B. S. Plake (Eds.), *The seventeenth mental measurements yearbook.* Retrieved from the Buros Institute's *Test Reviews Online* web site: http://www.unl.edu/buros

Barton, L.R., & Spiker, D. (2007). Test review of the Battelle Developmental Inventory, 2nd edition. In K.F. Geisinger, R.A. Spies, J. F. Carlson, & B.S. Plake (Eds.), *The seventeenth mental measurements yearbook.* Retrieved from the Buros Institute's *Test Reviews Online* web site: http://www.unl.edu/buros

Bliss, S.L. (2007). Test reviews: Battelle Developmental Inventory–Second Edition. *Journal of Psychoeducational Assessment, 25,* 409–415.

Information pertaining specifically to the Spanish version of the measure is in bold and italics. The remainder is equivalent information provided in the English review.

Manual

Newborg, J. (2005). *Battelle Developmental Inventory, 2nd Edition, Spanish, User's Guide*. Itasca, IL: Riverside Publishing.

Publisher

Riverside Publishing Company
3800 Golf Road, Suite 100
Rolling Meadows, IL 60008
http://www.riverpub.com

Type of Measure

Direct child assessment, parent interview, and observation

Intended Age Range

Birth to 7;11 years

Key Constructs/Domains

The full BDI-2 assesses five domains:
- Adaptive (ADP)
- Personal-Social (P-S)
- Communication (COM)
- Motor (MOT)
- Cognitive (COG)

Cost

A Spanish kit that includes the User's Guide, scoring booklets, CD, and other items in Spanish is available for $300 (items also sold separately). However, additional materials are also needed from the English BDI-2 Complete Kit. There is not a separate manual for the Spanish version. The short User's Guide is available for download from the publisher's web site.

Description of Measure

According to the manual, the BDI-2 serves four specific purposes:
- Assessing the typically developing child
- Assessing and identifying a child with a disability or developmental delay
- Planning and providing instruction and intervention
- Evaluating programs serving children

Newborg pointed out that the goal of any evaluation using the English and/or Spanish BDI-2 is "to obtain a comprehensive picture of the child's developmental strengths and opportunities for learning" (2005, p. 5).

Available Languages and Formats

An English version of the measure is available.

Examiners can use the shorter screening version of the BDI-2, which consists of 100 items that are "the best predictors of a child's level of development" (Newborg, 2005, p. 62). The purpose of the screening is to identify children who may have a developmental disability or who are at risk. An additional difference between the BDI-2 Screening Test and the full measure is that basal and ceiling levels are established for the broader domains instead of the subdomains for the screening measure.

Strengths

The BDI-2 incorporates multiple forms of information as part of the assessment. Namely, data are collected regarding a child's development via direct assessment; via interviews with parents, caregivers, or teachers; as well as via observations.

The English version of the BDI-2 was developed with input from the Spanish translation team in order to create a version that could work as well with Spanish-speaking children.

Weaknesses

No standardization of the Spanish version has been conducted. A short User's Guide that outlines major modifications to materials, scoring, and so forth, is available online.

The manual provides few details regarding how the translation and content reviews were conducted.

The scoring procedures entail multiple steps, potentially making them difficult to learn and execute correctly. However, an electronic scoring system is available to assist with scoring.

Although also a strength, examiners may need extended contact with children in order to engage in the observations. This may make the measure difficult to use in some settings.

ADMINISTRATION

Procedure

The BDI-2 assesses five domains and 13 subdomains of child development. Specific domains may be administered in any order and by different individuals if necessary, though this is not preferable. The BDI-2 incorporates multiple forms of information as part of the assessment. Namely, data are collected regarding a child's development via direct assessment, observations and interviews with teachers, parents, or caregivers. The manual provides guidelines for the use of multiple approaches. The ADP and P-S domains are assessed through parent or caregiver interviews, whereas the MOT, COM, and COG domains involve direct child assessment. For the latter three domains, the manual indicates that naturalistic observations may be used to "evaluate skills that a child would probably not display during a test session" (Newborg, 2005, p. 29). A small number of fine motor items, for example, may require multiple observations. Given the role of observation in the measure, the manual recommends that observers have extended contact with children during the observation period. Finally, observations related to children's behavior during the testing session are also recorded.

Time Needed

Entire Measure

Approximately 60–90 minutes, depending upon age:

- Birth to 2 years: 60 minutes
- 3 years to 5 years: 90 minutes
- 5 years to 7 years: 60 minutes

The manual indicates that testing may occur over several days but must be completed within a 2-week period.

Screening Test

Approximately 10–30 minutes, depending upon age:

- Birth to 3 years: 10–15 minutes
- 3 years to 5 years: 20–30 minutes
- 5 years to 7 years: 10–15 minutes

Adaptive (ADP)

- Self-care (e.g., toileting, eating)
- Personal responsibility (e.g., ability to carry out tasks, initiate play)

Personal-Social (P-S)

- Adult interaction (e.g., helps adult with simple tasks)
- Peer interaction (e.g., shares toys, plays cooperatively)
- Self-concept and social role (e.g., ability to express emotions, aware of gender differences)

Communication (COM)

- Receptive (e.g., responds to who/what questions, identifies initial sounds in words)
- Expressive (e.g., produces vowel sounds, articulates familiar words)

Motor (MOT)

- Gross motor (e.g., throws ball, walks up/down stairs)
- Fine motor (e.g., picks up small objects, cuts paper with scissors)
- Perceptual motor (e.g., stacks cubes, copies letters)

Cognitive (COG)

- Attention and memory (e.g., follows auditory, visual stimuli)
- Reasoning and academic skills (e.g., identifies names, matches colors)
- Perception and concepts (e.g., compares objects by size, color, etc.)

Administration and Interpretation

Administering the Spanish version is "nearly identical" to administering the English version (Newborg, 2005, p. 4). The User's Guide recommends that a bilingual examiner experienced in administering both English and Spanish assessments serve as an examiner. Another option is to utilize an assessment team (e.g., a Spanish speaker conducts the assessment with assistance from or under the supervision of an English-speaking assessor).

Depending upon the child and his or her family's proficiency in English, a child may be assessed in English while his or her parents respond to the interview portions of the assessment in Spanish (or vice versa). "Using this model, followed by the readministration in Spanish of any structured items the child missed in English, offers an opportunity to determine the child's maximum developmental level across both languages" (Newborg, 2005, p. 5).

According to Newborg, the BDI-2 is "primarily designed for use by infant interventionists; preschool, kindergarten, and primary school teachers; special educators. Speech pathologists, school psychologists, adaptive physical education specialists, clinical diagnosticians, and health care professionals will also find the BDI-2 effective" (2005, p. 1).

Because there are multiple uses for the BDI-2, individuals' training may vary. In general, administrators should have college-level training in measurement and statistical concepts and child development as well as "a thorough understanding of the purposes of the instrument, the characteristics of the child to be assessed relative to the normative sample used in standardization, the administration procedures, and scoring" (p. 10). Such training is especially important given the detail needed to score the BDI-2.

A checklist to use before, during, and after the test is included for administrators to ensure the best possible testing and scoring conditions. A familiar adult (i.e., parent, teacher) may be present when a young child is being directly assessed.

Scoring Method

Item scoring procedures are identical for the Spanish and English versions of the BDI-2. Age equivalents are not available for the Spanish version, and examiners may use the English tables to estimate these results. However, according to Newborg, "There is no reason to believe that there would be any significant differences between scores for Hispanic/Latino and non-Hispanic/Latino children" (2005, p. 5). Nonetheless, examiners wishing to calculate scaled scores and standard scores for Spanish results should do so "only experimentally" using English norms. In light of this, the COM domain is the area of most concern, as *"several of the items were modified to align the behavioral milestone with appropriate content for the two languages" (p. 5).*

Newborg stated that administrators can retest children on items for which they received a score of 0 or 1 in the alternative language. Using this test–retest procedure may provide a more accurate picture of the child's total development.

The BDI-2 (Paper) Record Form contains three sections: 1) a scoring summary; 2) a Test Session Behavioral Observations Form; and 3) subdomain item response areas, where scores are assigned and the procedural method is documented for each item (e.g., structured, interview, observation). A student workbook is also utilized by older children to complete items.

After administering the subdomains, examiners using the paper record form calculate children's raw score totals to derive age equivalents and a developmental quotient from tables provided within the manual. Specifically, examiners sum standard scores across subdomains. Normal curve equivalents, z and T scores, and percentile rankings for developmental quotient scores are also provided. Examiners can also create profile graphs for children's scores across domains and subdomains in order to visually see their performance.

BDI-2 Scoring Pro software and Palm-powered personal digital assistants are available for purchase. If used, the personal digital assistant takes the place of paper forms, allowing for potentially more efficient and accurate scoring of children's performance.

Adaptations or Instructions for Use with Individuals with Disabilities

Suggestions for possible accommodations are provided for children with motor, vision, hearing, or speech impairments as well as emotional disturbances or multiple disabilities.

FUNCTIONAL CONSIDERATIONS

Measure Development

According to the User's Guide, "Because most of the developmental milestones assessed by the BDI-2 are neither language nor culture specific, it was possible to develop an instrument that largely paralleled the English version" (Newborg, 2005, p. 1). According to Newborg's estimates, the majority of BDI-2 items and materials are translations from English to Spanish. Namely, instructions, questions, and visual stimuli with text for children and parents/caregivers were translated into Spanish. In addition, "Only 20 of the 450 BDI-2 items required any significant modification" (p. 2). Most of these items were part of the COM domain.

Content Equivalence of Items and Measure

The English version of the BDI-2 was developed with input from the Spanish translation team in order to create a version that could work as well with Spanish-speaking children.

Semantic Equivalence of Translations

Translation occurred in stages using "three groups of mostly independent translators from numerous Spanish-speaking countries" (Newborg, 2005, p. 4). According to the User's Guide, the goal was to reach a "consensus translation" at each stage that is appropriate for children and families from various Spanish-speaking cultures living in the United States. During the first stage, tryout items from the English version were examined in order to identify potential challenges to developing a Spanish version (e.g., grammar, cultural biases). Next, while the English version of the BDI-2 was undergoing standardization, "items were reviewed and translated as needed by a different team of native Spanish speakers" (p. 4). Prior to publication, there was a "final review of the translation for universality of the test and faithfulness to the context and content of items" (p. 4). There is no specific description of what procedures were used to ensure such faithfulness (e.g., back translation, item-level analyses).

Structural Consistency Across the English and Spanish Versions

The Spanish version is very similar to the BDI-2 English version in terms of its structure (i.e., items, length, and format). Only 20 out of 450 items were substantially modified during the translation process (Newborg, 2005). In fact, some Spanish items are administered solely as placeholders to allow for an equal number of items in the Spanish and English assessments. For example, children given the English version are asked about irregular plural nouns (e.g., goose, geese). Although Spanish does not have such irregularities, conceptually similar, albeit easier, items are found in the Spanish version. Although this approach contributes to the measure's structural consistency, it may negatively influence other aspects of measurement equivalence (such as the validity of the normed scores with Spanish speakers) given that these changes have not yet been empirically examined.

Standardization Sample

The Spanish version has not yet been standardized. As described by Barton, "No normative information or reliability/validity information is provided for the Spanish-translation version. This lack of information yields uncertainty about the measurement properties and effectiveness of the BDI-2 for [this] group" (2007).

Norming

Norm referenced

Reliability

Test–Retest Reliability

The reliability of the Spanish form has not yet been examined.

Internal Consistency

The reliability of the Spanish form has not yet been examined.

Interrater Agreement

The reliability of the Spanish form has not yet been examined.

Other Forms of Reliability (e.g., Equivalent Forms)

The reliability of the Spanish form has not yet been examined.

Validity

Face and Content

Spanish reviewers were engaged in three phases of the measure's development, including during the development of the English BDI-2. Although this contributes to the face validity of the Spanish BDI-2, its content validity is weakened by the limited discussion in the manual of how potential Spanish items were identified and which specific translation method was used and absence of psychometric item-level analyses for the Spanish version.

Internal Construct

The statistical validity of the Spanish form has not yet been examined.

External Construct

The statistical validity of the Spanish form has not yet been examined.

Criterion

The statistical validity of the Spanish form has not yet been examined.

Comparison of Psychometric Properties Between English and Spanish Versions

Technical Equivalence in Reliability

Not available because the Spanish version has not yet been standardized.

Technical Equivalence in Validity

Not available because the Spanish version has not yet been standardized.

RELEVANT RECENT STUDIES USING THE MEASURE

A brief literature review using PsycINFO and Google Scholar did not yield any published studies whose abstracts specified use of the BDI-2. The measure may have been utilized in studies that were not found in these searches.

ADDITIONAL REFERENCES

Barton, L.R. (2007). Test review of the Battelle Developmental Inventory, 2nd edition. In K.F. Geisinger, R.A. Spies, J.F. Carlson, & B.S. Plake (Eds.), *The seventeenth mental measurements yearbook*. Retrieved from the Buros Institute's *Test Reviews Online* web site: http://www.unl.edu/buros

Bilingual Vocabulary Assessment Measure (BVAM)

This measure does not have independent English and Spanish versions but is intended to be presented bilingually at one sitting. Thus, it has one review.

Manual

Mattes, L.J. (1995). *Bilingual Vocabulary Assessment Measure*. Oceanside, CA: Academic Communication Associates.

Publisher

Academic Communication Associates
P.O. Box 586249
Oceanside, CA 92058-6249
http://www.acadcom.com

Cost

$52

Description of Measure

"The instrument was developed primarily for use with children between 4 and 8 years of age who have been referred for testing because of problems using basic vocabulary in the classroom setting" (Mattes, 1995, p. 1). This 48-item measure is a basic screening tool that can be utilized by paraprofessionals and administered in multiple languages.

Available Languages and Formats

English, Spanish, French, Italian, and Vietnamese versions have been created.

Strengths

It is a short, easy-to-use measure that can be used by paraprofessionals as an initial screening tool.

Weaknesses

There are no explicit instructions for administering the instrument (e.g., particular prompts). The BVAM has not been standardized for norm or criterion scoring in any language.

Type of Measure
Direct child assessment

Intended Age Range
The manual indicates that the measure can be used for children between 4 and 8 years old, although the web site advertises use with children as young as 3.

Key Constructs/Domains
Expressive vocabulary

ADMINISTRATION

Procedure

The child sits directly across from the examiner and is asked to name each of the 48 items drawn in the toolkit in each of his or her languages. There are four black-and-white drawings per page. No set prompt (e.g., "Tell me what this is") is provided.

The examiner records the child's responses on a score sheet (one column for each language with room for the child's response and whether the item is correct or incorrect). No information about basal or ceiling levels is provided, nor are there

Time Needed
No time estimate is provided. Given the number of items, one could estimate that the measure requires 10–15 minutes to complete.

explicit instructions for administering the measure in multiple languages (e.g., first English, then Spanish).

Administration and Interpretation

There is no discussion in the manual about training requirements, although it appears that paraprofessionals can administer this measure with little training.

Scoring Method

A 1-page score sheet is used. The examiner hand-scores the child's responses as either correct (+) or incorrect (–). The total number of correct responses is then calculated and recorded at the bottom of the sheet. Minimal information is provided regarding how to interpret the scores, but it is stated that the frequent production of errors in both languages merits further examination for potential language disorders (Mattes, 1995).

Adaptations or Instructions for Use with Individuals with Disabilities

This information is not provided.

FUNCTIONAL CONSIDERATIONS

Measure Development

Information is not provided on the measure's initial development in English or any other language.

Content Equivalence of Items and Measure

No information is provided in the manual.

Semantic Equivalence of Translations

Although answers are provided in different languages, there is no discussion in the manual about the translation procedures utilized. The items do not appear to have been analyzed statistically. Mattes (1995) suggested that native speakers review the answer key and make any necessary modifications. In our review of the items, we noted two translation issues:

- The measure has only one option in Spanish for the word *sock* (*calcetín*). Another Spanish word for *sock* (*media*) could be added, as it is frequently used by Spanish speakers.
- The translation for the word *house* is incorrect (it gives *cama* instead of *casa*).

Structural Consistency Across the English and Spanish Versions

The format, items, and length are the same across languages.

Standardization Sample

The BVAM has not been standardized in any language.

Norming

Criterion referenced, although there is not any information regarding how to interpret scores.

Reliability

Test–Retest Reliability

Reliability is not reported in the manual.

Internal Consistency

Reliability is not reported in the manual.

Interrater Agreement

Reliability is not reported in the manual.

Other Forms of Reliability (e.g., Equivalent Forms)

Reliability is not reported in the manual.

Validity

Face and Content

Although the BVAM looks like an interesting vocabulary measure, the absence of information about the sources of information for the measure, reviewers, or analyses limits the ability to examine its face and content validity.

Internal Construct

Statistical validity is not reported in the manual.

External Construct

Statistical validity is not reported in the manual.

Criterion

Statistical validity is not reported in the manual.

Comparison of Psychometric Properties Between English and Spanish Versions

Technical Equivalence in Reliability

Not available because the measure has not yet been standardized.

Technical Equivalence in Validity

Not available because the measure has not yet been standardized.

RELEVANT STUDIES USING THE MEASURE

A brief literature search using PsycINFO and Google Scholar did not yield any mentions of the BVAM in study abstracts. However, it is possible that this measure has been utilized in studies.

ADDITIONAL REFERENCES

None

Boehm Test of Basic Concepts–Third Edition
Preschool: English

Manual

Boehm, A.E. (2001). *Boehm Test of Basic Concepts–3rd Edition Preschool.* San Antonio, TX: The Psychological Corporation.

Publisher

The Psychological Corporation
19500 Bulverde Road
San Antonio, TX 78259
http://www.PsychCorp.com

Cost

Complete kit: $186. Items sold separately.

Type of Measure

Direct child assessment

Intended Age Range

3 years to 5;11 years

Key Constructs/Domains

The measure assesses receptive language and cognitive abilities by testing "basic relational concepts" (Boehm, 2001, p. 2) such as size and direction.

Description of Measure

"The *Boehm Test of Basic Concepts, Third Edition–Preschool* (Boehm-3 Preschool) was designed to assess young children's understanding of the basic relational concepts important for language and cognitive development, as well as for later success in school" (Boehm, 2001, p. 1). Later in the manual, it states that it can be "used as part of a battery of tests to determine what, if any, special services may be needed for a given child" (p. 69).

Available Languages and Formats

Spanish, Finnish, and French versions are also available.

Strengths

The Boehm-3 Preschool has been well standardized, and its psychometrics are generally solid.

Test developers paid close attention to content validity when developing the measure.

Detailed item-level information (e.g., difficulty by age bands) is provided.

Weaknesses

Only one study is available to examine the criterion validity of the Boehm-3 Preschool.

There are potential ceiling issues for older children. That is, it may be difficult to obtain a solid understanding of the development of older children because there are relatively fewer items for that age range.

The mix of easy and difficult items within the test protocol may make it more challenging for examiners to attain an adequate basal level for children and/or deflate the confidence of some children.

ADMINISTRATION

Procedure

The administrator presents the child with a series of picture cues from an easel-back book with directions in English and Spanish visible to the administrator. Directions are read in the child's home language,

---

Time Needed

15–20 minutes

---

and the child is first asked to complete a few practice items. For each item, the child is asked to point to the part of the picture that best depicts the meaning of the concept words. The administrator is told to emphasize the italicized concept word in the directions for each item.

The Boehm-3 Preschool covers 26 relational concepts. As described by Graham (2005), these include, among others, the following:

- Size (e.g., *tallest*)
- Direction (e.g., *in front*)
- Position in space (e.g., *nearest*)
- Time (e.g., *before*)
- Quantity (e.g., *some, but not many*)
- Classification (e.g., *all*)
- General (e.g., *another*)

Each concept is tested in two contexts, with easier items interspersed with more difficult items and organized into three item sets. There are two starting points for the test according to age (3 and 4–5), with some overlap of items.

Administration and Interpretation

"The Boehm-3 Preschool was designed for use by knowledgeable professionals who have experience in test administration and interpretation, including speech language pathologists, special educators, teachers, educational diagnosticians and school psychologists" (Boehm, 2001, p. 8).

According to Boehm (2001), one can use the Boehm-3 Preschool with children outside the age range of the standardization sample (3;0–5;11 years) to determine their level of understanding of these basic concepts. Specifically, one can report a raw score as criterion-referenced information. According to the publisher, one can administer the Boehm-3 Preschool to children bilingually (in Spanish and English), although what language to begin with is not specified. This may provide the examiner with a sense of how well the child is doing across the two languages.

Scoring Method

Record forms include a miniature reproduction of each picture cue with the correct response circled. In addition to basic scoring, code letters can be used by the administrator to denote qualitative information related to children's responses (e.g., did not respond, provided antonym or opposite response) for an optional error analysis as detailed by Boehm (2001). Namely, the administrator can examine children's errors for systematic patterns that may provide a more detailed portrait of their understanding of basic concepts. The error analysis may include informally interviewing the children about their strategy for answering particular items. Boehm also provided suggestions for "mini-teaching" or intervention activities to help children in their learning of basic concepts.

Results can be reported as a raw score, percent correct, performance range (i.e., 1 = child knows basic concepts, 2 = child knows most basic concepts, 3 = child lacks understanding of basic concepts), and percentile. The record form includes space for noting each of these test results as well as comments and the reason for testing.

Adaptations or Instructions for Use with Individuals with Disabilities

Boehm (2001) provided possible modifications or adaptations for use with children with disabilities (e.g., fewer test items per sitting, the use of concrete objects versus pictures). Boehm cautioned, however, that performance ranges and percentiles cannot be reported if such modifications or adaptations are used.

FUNCTIONAL CONSIDERATIONS

Measure Development

The Boehm-3 Preschool is a revision of the Boehm–Preschool (Boehm, 1986) and a downward extension of the Boehm Test of Basic Concepts (Boehm, 1971, 1986). According to the manual, the test was developed after a review of the literature related to basic concept acquisition.

According to Boehm (2001), the items presented in the Boehm-3 Preschool were selected to represent basic concepts that young children are most likely to encounter during their early school years. In order to understand the relative frequency of particular concepts in preschool and kindergarten activities, curricular materials were consulted. Boehm–Preschool users (e.g., speech-language pathologists, special educators) were also surveyed. The ease of creating pictures to illustrate these concepts was also a factor in developing the test items. An expert panel was convened for a review of items for gender, ethnic, class, cultural, and regional bias.

The tryout edition contained 88 items (52 of which were revisions of Boehm–Preschool items). More than 300 children participated in tryout testing. The tryout sample was designed to be nationally representative. Test items for standardization were selected based on a statistical analysis of tryout items (i.e., item-level difficulty). Similar analyses were conducted in order to develop norms. Three items (*away, ahead, after*) were discarded prior to publication because *away* and *ahead* were more difficult in Spanish and *after* was difficult for children in both languages.

The percentage of children answering an item correctly is presented in tables in the manual for both the English and Spanish editions according to 6-month age intervals. Generally speaking, children administered the English version get more items correct, especially at older age levels.

There are potential ceiling issues for older children, as described by Graham (2005). Nearly 50% of children ages 5;6–5;11 years missed three or fewer items (such scores are not necessarily surprising, however, as kindergartners are expected to master many of these concepts). Thus, missing a question alters an older child's percentile rank. For example, a 5;6-year-old child with a raw score of 48 out of 52 would be placed in the 54th percentile, whereas a child of the same age with a raw score of 47 out of 52 would be placed in the 40th percentile (Graham, 2005). Thus, Boehm (2001) stressed that percentiles must be interpreted with caution.

Standardization Sample

A sample of 660 children ages 3;0–5;11 years (110 children in each 6-month band) was tested beginning in 1999 to develop national norms for the English version of the Boehm-3 Preschool. The sample, stratified according to age, gender, race/ethnicity, parent education level, and geographic region, was designed to replicate 1998 U.S. Census data. Approximately 11% of the children had identified disabilities or special needs but were able to complete the test without adaptations or modifications. Parent education levels tended to be higher than the national average (i.e., more than 50% of parents had had at least some college). No information is available regarding the children's English language proficiency.

Norming

Norm referenced (criterion scores are also available).

Reliability

Test–Retest Reliability

The test was administered to 98 children ages 4;0–5;11 years. Pearson correlation coefficients ranged from .90 to .94 (the time between tests ranged from 2 to 21 days, with an average interval of 1 week), indicating high test–retest reliability. No information is available for test–retest reliability for 3-year-olds.

Internal Consistency

Cronbach's coefficient alphas ranged from .85 to .92 across all six age bands (3;0–5;11 years), indicating medium to high internal consistency. The corresponding standard error of measurement ranged from 1.98 to 2.88 across all age bands.

Interrater Agreement

Information is not provided in the manual.

Other Forms of Reliability (e.g., Equivalent Forms)

Not applicable

Validity

Face and Content

The face and content validities of the measure are strong. According to Boehm (2001), preschool and kindergarten curricula were reviewed for their frequency of basic relational concepts. In addition, word lists were consulted for the Boehm-3 Preschool (see the manual for more detailed information), as was the content of preschool teacher speech samples.

Experts also provided feedback regarding potential biases in the assessment (i.e., gender, ethnic, culture, class bias). Stimuli were modified in order to lessen potential bias based on expert opinion, including enhancing the illustrations to denote greater diversity.

Internal Construct

Not applicable as the Boehm focuses on one domain—relational concepts.

External Construct

A study was conducted to investigate the extent to which the Boehm-3 Preschool differentiated between children ages 3;0–5;11 years ($n = 290$) with and without diagnosed receptive language disorders. The expected significant differences between the two groups were found.

Support for the measure's convergent and discriminant validity is also indicated by one correlational study described in "Criterion."

Criterion

A total of 62 children (33 children ages 3;0–3;11 years and 29 ages 5;0–5;11 years) were administered the Boehm-3 Preschool and the Bracken Basic Concept Scale–Revised. The tests were counterbalanced; the average interval between tests was 2–21 days, with an average of 1 week. The correlation between these two tests was moderate to high ($r = .80$ for 3-year-olds and $r = .73$ for 5-year-olds). This suggests that Boehm-3 Preschool scores relate well to another similar measure. This provides preliminary indication of the measure's criterion validity. However, more studies are needed.

RELEVANT STUDIES USING THE MEASURE

A brief literature search using PsycINFO and Google Scholar yielded the following studies that described using the Boehm-3 Preschool. The measure has also been used in dissertation studies, and it is also possible that it has been utilized in additional studies.

Li, Atkins, and Stanton (2006) examined the impact of computer use (i.e., 15–20 minutes of developmentally appropriate computer software activity daily) on school readiness and psychomotor skills for children attending Head Start programs in West Virginia (*n* = 122). Li and colleagues found significant differences between the intervention and control groups on the Boehm-3 Preschool even after controlling for baseline differences between the groups. In a related study, Fish et al. (2008) found that computer use in the home related to Boehm-3 Preschool scores in a Head Start sample in Michigan. Finally, the Boehm-3 has been utilized in Istanbul to study preschools and orphanages (Balat, 2006).

ADDITIONAL REFERENCES

Balat, G.U. (2006). Temel kavram bilgilerinin okul öncesi eğitim alma ve kurumda kalma durumlarına göre karşılaştırılması [A comparison of the effects of experiencing preschool education and living in an orphanage on basic concepts acquisition]. *Kuram ve Uygulamada Egitim Bilimleri, 6,* 939–945.

Boehm, A.E. (1971). *Boehm Test of Basic Concepts.* New York: Psychological Corporation.

Boehm, A.E. (1986). *Boehm Test of Basic Concepts–Preschool Edition.* San Antonio, TX: Psychological Corporation.

Fish, A.M., Li, X., McCarrick, K., Butler, S.T., Stanton, B., Brumitt, G.A.,…Partridge, T. (2008). Early childhood computer experience and cognitive development among urban low-income preschoolers. *Journal of Educational Computing Research, 38*(1), 97–113.

Graham, T. (2005). Test review of the Boehm Test of Basic Concepts—3rd Edition Preschool. In R.A. Spies & B.S. Plake (Eds.), *The sixteenth mental measurements yearbook.* Retrieved from the Buros Institute's *Test Reviews Online* web site: http://www.unl.edu/buros

Kutsick Malcom, K. (2005). Test review of the Boehm Test of Basic Concepts—3rd Edition Preschool. In R.A. Spies & B.S. Plake (Eds.), *The sixteenth mental measurements yearbook.* Retrieved from the Buros Institute's *Test Reviews Online* web site: http://www.unl.edu/buros

Li, X., Atkins, M., & Stanton, B. (2006). Effects of home and school computer use on school readiness and cognitive development among Head Start children: A randomized controlled pilot trial. *Merrill-Palmer Quarterly, 52,* 239–263.

Boehm Test of Basic Concepts–
Third Edition Preschool: Spanish

Information pertaining specifically to the Spanish version of the measure is in bold and italics. The remainder is equivalent information provided in the English review.

Manual

Boehm, A.E. (2001). *Boehm Test of Basic Concepts—3rd Edition Preschool Spanish Edition.* San Antonio, TX: The Psychological Corporation.

Publisher

The Psychological Corporation
19500 Bulverde Road
San Antonio, TX 78259
http://www.PsychCorp.com

Cost

Complete kit: $186. Items sold separately.

Description of Measure

"The *Boehm Test of Basic Concepts, Third Edition–Preschool* (Boehm-3 Preschool) was designed to assess young children's understanding of the basic relational concepts important for language and cognitive development, as well as for later success in school" (Boehm, 2001, p. 1). Later in the manual, it states that it can be "used as part of a battery of tests to determine what, if any, special services may be needed for a given child" (p. 69).

Available Languages and Formats

English, Finnish, and French versions are also available.

Strengths

Multiple checks and balances were used to create the Spanish version (e.g., translation, independent review, expert panel review).

The Spanish edition was concurrently standardized with the English version.

Various types of reliability coefficients were examined with the Spanish version.

Detailed item-level information (e.g., difficulty by age bands) is provided in both English and Spanish.

Weaknesses

Limited validity evidence is available for the Spanish edition.

More detailed information about the Spanish standardization sample (e.g., Latino descent, English/Spanish language proficiency) would be helpful.

There are potential ceiling issues for older children. That is, it may be difficult to obtain a solid understanding of the development of older children because there are relatively fewer items for that age range.

The mix of easy and difficult items within the test protocol may make it more challenging for examiners to attain an adequate basal level for children and/or the deflate confidence of some children.

Type of Measure
Direct child assessment

Intended Age Range
3 years to 5;11 years

Key Constructs/Domains
The measure assesses receptive language and cognitive abilities by testing "basic relational concepts" (Boehm, 2001, p. 2) such as size and direction.

ADMINISTRATION

Procedure

The administrator presents the child with a series of
picture cues from an easel-back book with directions
in English and Spanish visible to the administrator.
Directions are read in the child's home language,

Time Needed
15–20 minutes

and the child is first asked to complete a few practice items. For each item, the child is
asked to point to the part of the picture that best depicts the meaning of the concept words.
The administrator is told to emphasize the italicized concept word in the directions for each
item.

The Boehm-3 Preschool covers 26 relational concepts. As described by Graham (2005), these
include, among others, the following:

- Size (e.g., *tallest*)
- Direction (e.g., *in front*)
- Position in space (e.g., *nearest*)
- Time (e.g., *before*)
- Quantity (e.g., *some, but not many*)
- Classification (e.g., *all*)
- General (e.g., *another*)

Each concept is tested in two contexts, with easier items interspersed with more difficult
items and organized into three item sets. There are two starting points for the test according
to age (3 and 4–5), with some overlap of items.

Administration and Interpretation

"The Boehm-3 Preschool was designed for use by knowledgeable professionals who have
experience in test administration and interpretation, including speech language pathologists,
special educators, teachers, educational diagnosticians and school psychologists" (Boehm,
2001, p. 8).

According to Boehm (2001), one can use the Boehm-3 Preschool with children outside
the age range of the standardization sample (3;0–5;11 years) to determine their level of
understanding of these basic concepts. Specifically, one can report a raw score as criterion-
referenced information.

*According to the publisher, one can administer the Boehm-3 Preschool to children
bilingually (in Spanish and English), although what language to begin with is not
specified. It is not discussed whether the examiner should go back and forth between
the languages during the test or administer the language versions sequentially.
Overall, use of the two language forms can provide the examiner with a sense of
how well the child is doing across the two languages. However, if the examiner goes
back and forth in English and Spanish, deciding which normed data to use will be
difficult because of the performance differences in the English and Spanish samples
during standardization.*

Scoring Method

Record forms include a miniature reproduction of each picture cue with the correct response
circled. In addition to basic scoring, code letters can be used by the administrator to denote
qualitative information related to children's responses (e.g., did not respond, provided
antonym or opposite response) for an optional error analysis as detailed by Boehm (2001).
Namely, the administrator can examine children's errors for systematic patterns that may

provide a more detailed portrait of their understanding of basic concepts. The error analysis may include informally interviewing the children about their strategy for answering particular items. Boehm also provided suggestions for "mini-teaching" or intervention activities to help children in their learning of basic concepts.

Results can be reported as a raw score, percent correct, performance range (i.e., 1 = child knows basic concepts, 2 = child knows most basic concepts, 3 = child lacks understanding of basic concepts), and percentile. The record form includes space for noting each of these test results as well as comments and the reason for testing.

For example, the manual provides detailed information regarding children's performance on English and Spanish items. The percentage of children answering an item correctly is presented in tables in the manual for both the English and Spanish editions according to 6-month age intervals as well as the type and difficulty of each item. Overall, English-speaking children are more likely to get items correct than their Spanish counterparts. There are several potential and reasonable explanations for these discrepancies (e.g., differences in parent education levels, relative frequency of use of words in Spanish).

Thus, the percentile rankings vary between the English and Spanish standardization samples, as has been found for other measures. An example used in the English review showed that a 5;6-year-old Spanish-speaking child with a raw score of 48 out of 52 would be placed at the 85th percentile, whereas his or her English-speaking counterpart would be placed at the 54th percentile. This may be due in part to the sociodemographic factors of the families in the respective standardization samples. For example, parent education levels for the Spanish standardization sample were substantially lower (nearly 15% of parents in the Spanish sample had some college compared with more than 50% of parents in the English sample). This discrepancy could also relate to the varying difficulty of concepts across the languages (e.g., a concept may be less frequently used in Spanish than in English). Thus, it was likely rarer for a Spanish-speaking 5;6-year-old child in the standardization sample to obtain 48 correct. Therefore, this raw score in Spanish falls at the 85th percentile. Given these considerations, comparison of percentiles across the English and Spanish versions should be undertaken with caution. Similarly, performance range designations must be considered in light of decreasing variability in scores as children grow older.

Adaptations or Instructions for Use with Individuals with Disabilities

Boehm (2001) provided possible modifications or adaptations for use with children with disabilities (e.g., fewer test items per sitting, the use of concrete objects versus pictures). Boehm cautioned, however, that performance ranges and percentiles cannot be reported if such modifications or adaptations are used.

FUNCTIONAL CONSIDERATIONS

Measure Development

The Boehm-3 Preschool is a revision of the Boehm–Preschool (Boehm, 1986) and downward extension of the Boehm Test of Basic Concepts (Boehm, 1971, 1986). According to Boehm (2001), basic concepts covered within the assessment were selected to represent concepts that young children are most likely to encounter during their early school years. In order to understand the relative frequency of particular concepts in preschool and kindergarten activities, curricular materials were consulted. Boehm–Preschool users (e.g., speech-language pathologists, special educators) were also surveyed. The ease of creating pictures to illustrate these concepts was also a factor in developing the test items.

The tryout edition was first created in English and tested with a sample of more than 300 English-speaking children. Test items for the English standardization were selected based on a statistical analysis of tryout items (i.e., item-level difficulty). The Spanish translation was created from the English tryout version as well. A professional Spanish translator knowledgeable about various dialects was hired to translate these tryout items. When difficulties arose in translating English items into Spanish (e.g., lack of an equivalent term in Spanish), experts in Spanish grammar and semantics were called upon to make modifications and recommendations. Independent reviewers with expertise in the Spanish language and in multicultural issues were then asked to evaluate items for their equivalency. Reviewers also assessed the appropriateness of items in relation to different Spanish dialects and the familiarity of situations as depicted in illustrations for Spanish speakers. Furthermore, an expert panel was convened for a review of items for gender, ethnic, class, cultural, and regional bias. Panel recommendations led to changes in items (e.g., using more familiar vocabulary) and illustrations (including different body types) in order to be more inclusive.

Subsequently, both the English and Spanish language measures were standardized with their respective samples, though the Spanish sample was half the size of the English sample. The results were then examined and three items (away, ahead, after) were discarded prior to publication (i.e., away and ahead were more difficult in Spanish, and after was difficult for children in both languages).

Content Equivalence of Items and Measure

Although the Spanish version of the Boehm-3 Preschool was standardized in conjunction with the English version, the initial content was developed by examining the English research literature and curricula and surveying users of the prior English version of the Boehm-3 Preschool. Many different approaches were then used to provide input on the Spanish version, and item-level analyses were subsequently conducted.

Semantic Equivalence of Translations

The utilization of a translator, multiple reviews, and an expert panel contributed to this measure's semantic equivalence.

Structural Consistency Across the English and Spanish Versions

The structure, number of items, and stimuli are the same for the English and Spanish versions.

Standardization Sample

A sample of 300 children ages 3;0–5;11 years (50 children in each 6-month band) was tested beginning in 1999 to develop national norms for the Spanish edition of the Boehm-3 Preschool. All examiners completed a Spanish proficiency check prior to participating in the study. Similar to the English edition, approximately 11% of the children in the sample had identified disabilities or special needs.

Although the children came from across the United States, the majority resided in either the West (40%) or South (52%). Information regarding the children's relative English and Spanish language proficiency and ethnic background is not provided. More than 50% of Latino parents had completed up to 11 years of education. In contrast, parent education levels for the English edition tended to be higher than the national average (i.e., more than 50% of parents had had at least some college). In other words, the two standardization samples are not demographically similar in terms of parent education levels, making it a little difficult to compare performance across the tests. This is typical for many measures. However, Graham wondered whether "a larger population of Spanish-speaking children needed to be included in the standardization given the potential significant diversity in language background of the Spanish-speaking children (e.g., what is their home language environment, exposure to English)" (2005).

Norming

Norm referenced (criterion scores are also available).

Reliability

Test–Retest Reliability

The Spanish measure was administered to 125 children ages 3;0–5;11 years. Pearson correlation coefficients were generally within the medium range (.76–.88). The time between tests ranged from 2 to 21 days, with an average interval of 1 week. These coefficients are lower than those of the English version but included children at the younger age bands. (Test–retest reliability is reported for children ages 4;0–5;11 years only for the English version.)

Internal Consistency

Cronbach's coefficient alphas were relatively medium to high and ranged from .80 to .91 across the six age bands.

Interrater Agreement

Information is not provided in the manual.

Other Forms of Reliability (e.g., Equivalent Forms)

Not applicable

Validity

Face and Content

As described in "Measure Development," the initial content was developed by examining the English research literature and curricula and surveying users of the prior version of the English Boehm-3 Preschool. Though the corresponding Spanish literature was not also examined, many different approaches were used to provide input on the translated Spanish version. Item-level analyses were also conducted.

Internal Construct

Not applicable as the Boehm focuses on one domain—relational concepts.

External Construct

A study was conducted to investigate the extent to which the Boehm-3 Preschool Spanish edition differentiated between children aged 3;0–5;11 years (n = 120, roughly 80 of whom were male) with and without diagnosed receptive language disorders. The expected significant differences between the two groups were found.

Data on convergent and discriminant validity with other measures are not presented in the manual.

Criterion

No information specific to the Spanish version is provided.

Comparison of Psychometric Properties Between English and Spanish Versions

Technical Equivalence in Reliability

The reliability results for both language versions are generally strong. Test–retest reliability and internal consistency are a bit higher for the English version. The interrater reliability of both versions has not yet been examined.

Technical Equivalence in Validity

Both editions were able to differentiate between children with and without diagnosed receptive language disorders. However, there have been fewer validity studies conducted on the Spanish edition.

RELEVANT STUDIES USING THE MEASURE

A brief literature search using PsycINFO and Google Scholar did not yield any published studies whose abstracts specified use of the Boehm-3 Preschool: Spanish. However, it is possible that this measure has been utilized in studies.

ADDITIONAL REFERENCES

Boehm, A.E. (1971). *Boehm Test of Basic Concepts.* New York, NY: Psychological Corporation.

Boehm, A.E. (1986). *Boehm Test of Basic Concepts–Preschool Edition.* San Antonio, TX: Psychological Corporation.

Graham, T. (2005). Test review of the Boehm Test of Basic Concepts—3rd Edition Preschool. In R.A. Spies & B.S. Plake (Eds.), *The sixteenth mental measurements yearbook*. Retrieved from the Buros Institute's *Test Reviews Online* web site: http://www.unl.edu/buros

Kutsick Malcom, K. (2005). Test review of the Boehm Test of Basic Concepts—3rd Edition Preschool. In R.A. Spies & B.S. Plake (Eds.), *The sixteenth mental measurements yearbook*. Retrieved from the Buros Institute's *Test Reviews Online* web site: http://www.unl.edu/buros

BRIGRANCE Preschool Screen–II: English

Manual

Glascoe, F.P. (2005). *Technical Report for the BRIGRANCE Screen.* North Billerica, MA: Curriculum Associates.

Publisher

Curriculum Associates, Inc.
P.O. Box 2001
North Billerica, MA 01862
http://www.curriculumassociates.com

Cost

2011 price data: $259. Items sold separately.

Description of Measure

"The *BRIGRANCE Screens* identify quickly and accurately those who may have developmental problems such as language impairments, learning disabilities, or cognitive delays....Unlike many other measures, the BRIGRANCE Screens also identify children who may have academic talent or intellectual giftedness" (Glascoe, 2005, p. 1). Glascoe also noted that because the items are criterion referenced and the overall measure is norm referenced, the BRIGRANCE allows teachers to create instructional goals and allows for comparisons of children's performance with that of other children across the country. The BRIGRANCE Screens can also be used to track children's progress over time.

Available Languages and Formats

A Spanish version is available. In addition, screening measures for various age groups have been created, including the Infant & Toddler Screen, the Early Preschool Screen–II, and the K&1 Screen–II.

Strengths

The manual indicates that because items are criterion referenced, the measure can be used to monitor progress over time.

The manual describes well how to differentiate children who score low on the measure because of developmental delay rather than psychosocial risk factors. Adjusted cutoff scores are presented.

Weaknesses

The manual presents data on interrater reliability and criterion validity that are inferred from the Screen's longer counterpart, the BRIGRANCE Diagnostic Inventory of Early Development (IED). Additional studies of these coefficients are needed.

Type of Measure

Direct child assessment and parent questionnaire

Intended Age Range

3;0 years to 4;11 years

Key Constructs/Domains

- Motor
- Communication
- Academic/preacademic skills
- Self-help (questionnaire)
- Socioemotional (questionnaire)

ADMINISTRATION

Procedure

Children are presented with either manipulatives or picture plates. The children are asked to either follow simple directions or identify (either verbally or

Time Needed

15 minutes

nonverbally) which item represents the stimulus word. The following domains are assessed on the Preschool Screen–II:

- Motor (e.g., visual motor, fine motor, and graphomotor skills; gross motor skills)
- Communication (e.g., receptive language, expressive vocabulary, articulation, verbal fluency, syntax)
- Academic/Preacademic (e.g., quantitative concepts, personal information, prereading/reading skills)

Additional questionnaires that are unstandardized are also available for use with the BRIGRANCE Screen. These include a Screening Observations Form, a Teacher's Rating Form, a Parent's Rating Form, and a Registration and Background Information Form. A form entitled Supplemental Assessments includes items to administer to higher-performing children.

Administration and Interpretation

This measure was designed for use by teachers, paraprofessionals, special educators, psychologists, physicians, occupational and physical therapists, child care and early childhood teachers, and speech-language pathologists. Experience or a background in child development is needed. Finally, knowledge of test administration and score interpretation is essential, and the examiner should be thoroughly familiar with the instrument.

Scoring Method

The BRIGRANCE Screen provides age-based standard scores, percentiles, quotients, age equivalents, percentages of delay, deviation scores, and growth indicators. The subscale raw scores are obtained by recording the number of correct responses for each assessment and multiplying this by the point value assigned. The total score is calculated by adding the weighted values of each subscale (a total maximum score of 100 can be achieved at each level). A child's score can then be compared to cutoff scores to identify concerns about the child's development. Raw scores can be converted using charts in the manual or specialized scoring software.

The manual reports that examiners should consider making adjustments to cutoff scores when administering to children with "four or more psychosocial risk factors (such as limited parental education and income, single-parent household, more than three children in the home, frequent household moves or other disruptive events, parental mental health problems including depression, anxiety, and substance abuse, ethnic/racial minority, and an authoritarian parenting style)" (Glascoe, 2005, p. 29). This is done in order to help discriminate "at-risk children who are likely to make adequate gains by attending prevention programs from at-risk children with undetected disabilities" (p. 29). These modifications are described in Chapter 5 of the manual.

Adaptations or Instructions for Use with Individuals with Disabilities

The manual includes a discussion on adapting the BRIGRANCE Screen for use with children with exceptionalities. Extensive adaptations are described for specific populations, including children with motor, hearing, vision, speech, and emotional/behavioral impairments. Also described are testing approaches for use with children with autism, traumatic brain injury, and giftedness.

FUNCTIONAL CONSIDERATIONS

Measure Development

The BRIGRANCE Screens were developed as a screening counterpart to the longer IED. The present IED-II is a criterion- and norm-referenced measure of developmental skills for use with children between birth and 7 years of age.[1] Tryout items for the Preschool Screen–II were selected if 90% of teachers, diagnosticians, and curriculum supervisors indicated through a survey that the items corresponded to curriculum. The measure was subsequently pilot-tested throughout the United States.

Standardization Sample

The BRIGRANCE Screens were originally standardized in 1979 and revised in 1995. The present set of screens was standardized in 2005 with a representative sample of the population stratified by parent education level, geographic region, and race. The sample consisted of 1,366 children ages birth (infant) to 6+ years (first grade; 50% male, 50% female). Powell (2007) noted that this corresponds to the use of 95 three-year-olds and 86 four-year-olds to norm the Preschool Screen–II, which he suggested is not an adequate sample. Unfortunately, this is similar to the procedures used for numerous other preschool measures in the field. In addition, Spanish-speaking children were included in the original standardization: "Children whose primary language was Spanish were tested in that language using standardized Spanish directions while their parents were interviewed with Spanish versions of the demographics questionnaire and other measures" (Glascoe, 2005, p. 97). The number of Spanish-speaking children included in the standardization sample is not given in the manual.

Norming

According to the manual, the items are criterion referenced, and the measure is norm referenced.

Reliability

Test–Retest Reliability

Unlike that of the screens for the other age groups, the test–retest reliability of the preschool screens has yet to be directly assessed. However, an analysis of about 12 identical items from the longer IED-II indicated high test–retest reliability (.91 for 3-year-olds and .89 for 4-year-olds).

Internal Consistency

High reliability coefficients were obtained using Guttman lambda scalability coefficients for total BRIGRANCE Screen scores (Emmons & Alfonso, 2005). Correlations were .99 for the 3- and 4-year-olds, with standard errors of measurement (SEMs) between 1.26 and 1.29.

The internal consistency was also examined for the rating forms. Among the preschoolers, coefficients ranged from .89 to .93 (SEMS = 0.74–1.30). Correlations for the socioemotional scales were .84–.90, with SEMs between .76 and .79.

Interrater Agreement

Interrater agreement for the Preschool Screen–II has not yet been directly assessed. The manual presents correlations that are averaged estimated coefficients for children ages 2 and older across the IED-II and the measure's elementary school version (the Comprehensive Inventory of Basic Skills–Revised, CIBS-R). These ranged from .88 to .96 for the direct assessment portions and from .80 to .93 for the rating forms. However, the broad age range included in these averages, along with the approach of combining across measures, limits the interpretation of these coefficients.

---

[1]The Preschool Screen–II is reviewed here rather than the IED-II as the latter is not yet available in Spanish.

Other Forms of Reliability (e.g., Equivalent Forms)

Not applicable

Validity

Face and Content

The BRIGRANCE Screens appear to assess the domains indicated and were developed with input from educators and researchers. For example, a sample of readiness skills included in the BRIGRANCE was developed based on the developmental and readiness literature and collaboration with educators who assisted with item selection.

Internal Construct

Varimax factor analysis was used to examine the factor structure by age group. Three factors are clearly present (Language, Motor, and Academic/Preacademic). Together, they explain about 74% of the variance in performance, which is strong. As may be expected based on child development, more items loaded on the Language factor among 3-year-olds, whereas more items loaded on the Academic/Preacademic factor among 4-year-olds.

External Construct

As may be expected, older children scored higher than younger children. In addition, children with developmental problems scored significantly lower (1 *SD*) across the full family of BRIGRANCE Screens than children who had been in the average range on the CIBS-R or IED-II. Furthermore, children who scored above average on these measures also scored higher (1 *SD*) than other children on the BRIGRANCE Screen–II. Among 3- and 4-year-olds, the Academic/ Preacademic Domain correlated most strongly with disability categorization (in the range of .89–.91). Among gifted/talented children, the Communication domain was correlated highly among 3-year-olds (.97) and the Academic/Preacademic Domain was correlated with giftedness at .82.

In terms of sensitivity and specificity, the BRIGRANCE Preschool Screen–II was analyzed for its ability to identify children who score below the 20th percentile on the IED-II (and thus who may have developmental difficulties). Specificity ranged from .72 to .80, and sensitivity ranged from .73 to .76. Its specificity and sensitivity were high for identifying children who had scored in the top 10th percentile on the IED-II (0.86–1.00). Given the strong relationship between the Screen and the IED-II, these coefficients may need to be reexamined with groups of children with formal diagnoses of disabilities.

Support for its convergent and discriminant validity is also indicated by some the correlational studies described in "Criterion."

Criterion

The manual presents correlations between the Preschool Screen–II and the IED-II. These ranged from .87 to .93 for the domain scores on direct assessment portions and from .46 to .86 for the rating forms. Given the strong relationship between the Screen and the IED-II, the criterion validity of the Preschool Screen–II is in need of further examination.

RELEVANT STUDIES USING THE MEASURE

A brief literature search using PsycINFO and Google Scholar did not yield abstracts that indicated the use of the present version of the BRIGRANCE Screen–II, though the older version has been utilized in studies. Given that the measure is relatively new, publications are likely to be forthcoming.

ADDITIONAL REFERENCES

Emmons, M.R., & Alfonso, V.C. (2005). A critical review of the technical characteristics of preschool screening batteries. *Psychoeducational Assessment, 23,* 111–127.

Powell, S. (2007). Test review of the BRIGRANCE Preschool Screen–II. In K.F. Geisinger, R.A. Spies, J. F. Carlson, & B.S. Plake (Eds.), *The seventeenth mental measurements yearbook*. Retrieved from the Buros Institute's *Test Reviews Online* web site: http://www.unl.edu/buros

Vacca, J.J. (2007). Test review of the BRIGRANCE Preschool Screen–II. In K.F. Geisinger, R.A. Spies, J.F. Carlson, & B.S. Plake (Eds.), *The seventeenth mental measurements yearbook*. Retrieved from the Buros Institute's *Test Reviews Online* web site: http://www.unl.edu/buros

BRIGRANCE Preschool Screen–II: Spanish

Information pertaining specifically to the Spanish version of the measure is in bold and italics. The remainder is equivalent information provided in the English review.

Manual

Glascoe, F.P. (2005). *Technical Report for the BRIGANCE Screen.* North Billerica, MA: Curriculum Associates.

Publisher

Curriculum Associates, Inc.
P.O. Box 2001
North Billerica, MA 01862
http://www.curriculumassociates.com

Type of Measure

Direct child assessment and parent questionnaire

Intended Age Range

3;0 years to 4;11 years

Key Constructs/Domains

- Motor
- Communication
- Academic/preacademic skills
- Self-help (questionnaire)
- Socioemotional (questionnaire)

Cost

2011 price data: $259. The booklet of Spanish directions costs $25. Items sold separately.

Description of Measure

"The *BRIGANCE Screens* identify quickly and accurately those who may have developmental problems such as language impairments, learning disabilities, or cognitive delays....Unlike many other measures, the BRIGANCE Screens also identify children who may have academic talent or intellectual giftedness" (Glascoe, 2005, p. 1). Glascoe also noted that because the items are criterion referenced and the overall measure is norm referenced, the BRIGANCE allows teachers to create instructional goals and allows for comparisons of children's performance with that of other children across the country. The BRIGANCE Screen can also be used to track children's progress over time.

Available Languages and Formats

An English version is available. In addition, screening measures for various age groups have been created, including the Infant & Toddler Screen, the Early Preschool Screen–II, and the K&1 Screen–II.

Strengths

The manual indicates that because items are criterion referenced, the measure can be used to monitor progress over time.

The manual describes well how to differentiate children who score low on the measure because of developmental delay rather than psychosocial risk factors. Adjusted cutoff scores are presented. *However, the utility of the cutoff scores with Spanish-speaking children is unknown.*

Weaknesses

The translation and development of the Spanish version are not described in the manual.

The BRIGANCE Screens have not been standardized in Spanish. The standardization sample for the English BRIGANCE Preschool Screen–II included Spanish speakers, but the sample size is unknown.

ADMINISTRATION

Procedure

Children are presented with either manipulatives or picture plates. The children are asked to either follow simple directions or identify (either verbally or nonverbally) which item represents the stimulus word. The following domains are assessed on the Preschool Screen–II:

Time Needed
15 minutes

- Motor (e.g., visual motor, fine motor, and graphomotor skills; gross motor skills)
- Communication (e.g., receptive language, expressive vocabulary, articulation, verbal fluency, syntax)
- Academic/Preacademic (e.g., quantitative concepts, personal information, prereading/ reading skills)

Additional questionnaires that are unstandardized are also available for use with the BRIGRANCE Screen. These include a Screening Observations Form, a Teacher's Rating Form, a Parent's Rating Form, and a Registration and Background Information Form. A form entitled Supplemental Assessments includes items to administer to higher-performing children.

Spanish Direction Booklets can be purchased separately and include translations of assessor scripting and reproducible Spanish Data Sheets. It is unknown which of the additional forms are available in Spanish, though it appears that the Registration and Background Information Form is available in Spanish.

Administration and Interpretation

This measure was designed for use by teachers, paraprofessionals, special educators, psychologists, physicians, occupational and physical therapists, child care and early childhood teachers, and speech-language pathologists. Experience or a background in child development is needed. Furthermore, knowledge of test administration and score interpretation is essential, and the examiner should be thoroughly familiar with the instrument. *Finally, proficiency in Spanish is needed to administer the Spanish version of the BRIGRANCE Screen.*

Scoring Method

The standardization charts created for the English version are used for the Spanish version. The BRIGRANCE Screens provide age-based standard scores, percentiles, quotients, age equivalents, percentages of delay, deviation scores, and growth indicators. The subscale raw scores are obtained by recording the number of correct responses for each assessment and multiplying this by the point value assigned. The total score is calculated by adding the weighted values of each subscale (a total maximum score of 100 can be achieved at each level). A child's score can then be compared to cutoff scores to identify concerns about the child's development. Raw scores can be converted using charts in the manual or specialized scoring software.

The manual reports that examiners consider making adjustments to cutoff scores when administering to children with "four or more psychosocial risk factors (such as limited parental education and income, single-parent household, more than three children in the home, frequent household moves or other disruptive events, parental mental health problems including depression, anxiety, and substance abuse, ethnic/racial minority, and an authoritarian parenting style)" (Glascoe, 2005, p. 29). This is done in order to help discriminate "at-risk children who are likely to make adequate gains by attending prevention programs from at-risk children with undetected disabilities" (p. 29). These modifications are described in Chapter 5 of the manual.

Adaptations or Instructions for Use with Individuals with Disabilities

The manual includes a discussion on adapting the BRIGANCE Screen for use with children with exceptionalities. Extensive adaptations are described for specific populations, including children with motor, hearing, vision, speech, and emotional/behavioral impairments. Also described are testing approaches for use with children with autism, traumatic brain injury, and giftedness.

FUNCTIONAL CONSIDERATIONS

Measure Development

The translation and development of the Spanish version are not described in the manual.

In terms of the English version, the BRIGANCE Screen was developed as a screening counterpart to the longer BRIGANCE Diagnostic Inventory of Early Development (IED). The present IED-II is a criterion- and norm-referenced measure of developmental skills for use with children between birth and 7 years of age.[1] Tryout items for the Preschool Screen–II were selected if 90% of teachers, diagnosticians, and curriculum supervisors indicated through a survey that the items corresponded to curriculum. The measure was subsequently pilot-tested throughout the United States.

Content Equivalence of Items and Measure

It appears that the content of the Spanish version is the same as the English version, potentially indicating that when creating the Spanish version, test developers did not consider Spanish language development or instructional criteria.

Semantic Equivalence of Translations

This information is not provided in the manual.

Structural Consistency Across the English and Spanish Versions

Given that the Spanish version appears to be a straight translation of the English version, the two versions are structurally consistent.

Standardization Sample

A separate standardization of the Spanish version does not appear to have been conducted. Instead, Spanish-speaking children were involved in the original standardization of the BRIGANCE Screen: "Children whose primary language was Spanish were tested in that language using standardized Spanish directions while their parents were interviewed with Spanish versions of the demographics questionnaire and other measures" (Glascoe, 2005, p. 97). The number of Spanish-speaking children included in the standardization sample is not given in the manual.

The BRIGANCE Screens were originally standardized in 1979 and revised in 1995. The present set of screens was standardized in 2005 with a representative sample of the population stratified by parent education level, geographic region, and race. The sample consisted of 1,366 children ages birth (infant) to 6+ years (first grade; 50% male; 50% female). Powell (2007) noted that this corresponds to the use of 95 three-year-olds and 86 four-year-olds to norm the Preschool Screen–II, which he suggested is not an adequate sample. Unfortunately, this is similar to the procedures used for numerous other preschool measures in the field. *Furthermore, it is unknown how many of these children were*

---

[1]The Preschool Screen–II is reviewed here rather than the IED-II as the latter is not yet available in Spanish.

Spanish speakers.

Norming

According to the manual, the items are criterion referenced and the measure is norm referenced.

Reliability

Test–Retest Reliability

Spanish-speaking children do not appear to have participated in the test–retest substudy.

Internal Consistency

This information is not provided in the manual for the Spanish version. Spanish data appear to be mixed with English data, and the number of Spanish speakers in the sample is unknown.

Interrater Agreement

Spanish-speaking children do not appear to have participated in this substudy.

Other Forms of Reliability (e.g., Equivalent Forms)

Not applicable

Validity

Face and Content

The content appears to be taken from the English version. The degree to which expert consultants were used or Spanish research literature was reviewed is unknown.

Internal Construct

This information is not provided in the manual for the Spanish version. The Spanish data appear to be mixed with English data, and the number of Spanish speakers in the sample is unknown.

External Construct

This information is not provided in the manual for the Spanish version. The Spanish data appear to be mixed with English data, and the number of Spanish speakers included in the standardization sample is unknown.

Criterion

The BRIGRANCE's criterion validity in Spanish may need to be separately examined given that some of the comparison measures are available in Spanish and themselves have varying psychometric properties in Spanish.

Comparison of Psychometric Properties Between English and Spanish Versions

Technical Equivalence in Reliability

The similarity of the reliability statistics for the English and Spanish versions could not be compared as Spanish data are not presented separately in the manual.

Technical Equivalence in Validity

The similarity of the validity statistics for the English and Spanish versions could not be compared as Spanish data are not presented separately in the manual.

RELEVANT STUDIES USING THE MEASURE

A brief literature search using PsycINFO and Google Scholar did not result in any study abstracts that specified using the BRIGRANCE Screen–Spanish. However, it is possible that this measure has been utilized in studies.

ADDITIONAL REFERENCES

Powell, S. (2007). Test review of the BRIGRANCE Preschool Screen–II. In K.F. Geisinger, R.A. Spies, J.F. Carlson, & B.S. Plake (Eds.), *The seventeenth mental measurements yearbook*. Retrieved from the Buros Institute's *Test Reviews Online* web site: http://www.unl.edu/buros

Clinical Evaluation of Language Fundamentals®–Preschool–Second Edition: English (CELF® Preschool-2: English)

Manual

Wiig, E.H., Secord, W.A., & Semel, E. (2004). *Clinical Evaluation of Language Fundamentals®, Preschool–2nd Edition.* San Antonio, TX: NCS Pearson.

Publisher

Pearson, Inc.
19500 Bulverde Road
San Antonio, TX 78259-3701
http://www.pearsonassessments.com

Cost

$366

Description of Measure

The CELF® Preschool-2 "is a practical and efficient clinical tool for identifying, diagnosing, and performing follow-up of language deficits in children 3–6 years" (Wiig, Secord, & Semel, 2004, p. 1).

Available Languages and Formats

The CELF® Preschool-2 is available in Spanish. It is a downward extension of the Clinical Evaluation of Language Fundamentals®–Fourth Edition (CELF®-4), which can be used with individuals between 5 and 21 years of age.

Strengths

The measure can be used to provide both quick and more detailed examinations of young children's language ability.

The steps undertaken in the measure's development and standardization were thorough and well documented.

The reliability and validity of the measure across multiple dimensions are solid, including for children of diverse backgrounds.

An appendix provides for the understanding and utilization of dialectical patterns in administration and scoring.

Weaknesses

Results from the reliability and validity studies indicate that the version for older children (CELF®-4) rather than the CELF® Preschool-2 should be used with 6-year-olds.

The criterion validity of the CELF® Preschool-2 could benefit from further investigation.

Type of Measure

Direct child assessment, parent/teacher report

Intended Age Range

3;0 years to 6;11 years

Key Constructs/Domains

- Receptive and expressive language
- Language content and structure
- Phonological, preliteracy, and pragmatic development

"Clinical Evaluation of Language Fundamentals" and "CELF" are trademarks, in the US and/or other countries, of Pearson Education, Inc. or its affiliate(s).

ADMINISTRATION

Procedure

The CELF® Preschool-2 is composed of

- Seven subtests that provide scaled scores and are norm referenced *(Sentence Structure, Word Structure, Expressive Vocabulary, Concepts & Following Directions, Recalling Sentences, Word Classes, Basic Concepts—Ages 3–4)*

- Two supplemental subtests that provide criterion scores or percentile ranges and are norm referenced *(Recalling Sentences in Context, Phonological Awareness—Ages 4–6,* as well as *Basic Concepts—Ages 5–6)*

- Two checklists that provide criterion scores and are norm referenced *(Pre-Literacy Rating Scale, Descriptive Pragmatics Profile)*

> **Time Needed**
>
> 15–20 minutes to administer the three subtests comprising the Core Language Score (Sentence Structure, Word Structure, Expressive Vocabulary)

The following standardized composite scores are available:

- Core Language Score (CLS)
- Receptive Language Index
- Expressive Language Index
- Language Content Index
- Language Structure Index

In the English version, the indexes are created from three subtests each. The Receptive Language Index and Language Content Index include the Basic Concepts—Ages 3–4 subtest for children ages 3–4 but substitute the Word Classes subtest for children ages 5–6.

The CELF® Preschool-2 can be administered in its entirety or in parts to examine language development at four levels:

- Overall language ability/presence of language disorder (entails administration of three subtests in the CLS)

- Description of child's language abilities/nature of disorder (entails administration of norm-referenced subtests)

- Evaluation of early classroom and literacy fundamentals (entails administration of supplementary norm-referenced measures)

- Evaluation of language and communication in context (entails administration of Descriptive Pragmatics Profile).

Administration and Interpretation

The CELF® Preschool-2 "can be used by speech-language pathologists, school psychologists, special educators, and diagnosticians who have been trained and are experienced in administration and interpretation of standardized tests" (Wiig et al., 2004, p. 1). One should also have "experience or training in testing children whose ages, linguistic, and cultural backgrounds, and clinical history are similar to those of the children [one is] testing" (p. 7).

A behavior checklist appears on the record form to track physical activity, attention levels, and other behaviors.

Case studies are provided in the manual and on the publisher's web site as examples of interpretation.

Scoring Method

Scoring considerations related to cultural diversity and dialectical variations are discussed in the manual. An appendix describes English dialectal patterns across various areas and communities, including Appalachia, the South, the African American community, and the Latino community.

The CELF® Preschool-2 is hand-scored. Generally speaking, the raw score is the number of items answered correctly by the child on each subtest. Some subtests use a 3-point scale that provides partial credit for answers that are not fully correct. After the initial scoring is complete, raw scores for the seven norm-referenced subscales are converted into scaled scores and then compiled into the CLS and Index scores. Scaled and standard scores, percentile ranks, confidence intervals, and age equivalents are available.

The degree to which children are experiencing discrepancies between their receptive and expressive language abilities and between the content and structure of their language can be analyzed both statistically and clinically.

Though full norms are not available, the CELF® Preschool-2 provides criterion (cutoff) scores for additional subtests and rating scales. These are used to determine whether children's development of basic concepts, phonological awareness, preliteracy skills, pragmatics, or sentence recollection is delayed.

Item analysis tables are available for each subtest to enable the researcher to qualitatively examine the error patterns in children's responses. Suggestions for extension testing and intervention/follow-up are provided in the manual.

Adaptations or Instructions for Use with Individuals with Disabilities

The manual provides examples of modifications to the CELF® Preschool-2 that support the use of norm-referenced scores as well as more extensive modifications that preclude the use of such scores. In the latter case, raw scores can be interpreted to describe children's performance.

FUNCTIONAL CONSIDERATIONS

Measure Development

The CELF® Preschool was first developed in 1992. Its counterpart, the CELF®, which is on its fourth edition, is used with individuals between 5 and 21 years of age. The CELF® Preschool-2 was released in 2004 with attention to its diagnostic power, psychometrics, utility, and appeal and with an aim to deepening the assessment of pragmatics, semantics, and morphosyntax. One of the principal changes was the development of the CLS, which is a composite score of the three subtests that can most accurately diagnose language disorders. This enables the examiner to obtain a quicker overall assessment than with the prior version, the CELF® Preschool. Another adaptation was the development of Language Content Index and Language Structure Index scores, which are available along with Receptive Language Index and Expressive Language Index scores. Furthermore, an assessment process was developed to guide the clinician "in administering only those measures relevant to the specific objectives for an evaluation" (Wiig et al., 2004, p. 94).

The revision effort also entailed developing and piloting the following subtests and scales: 1) Word Classes subtest (ability to understand and explain words that are categorical or related by a semantic class feature), 2) Phonological Awareness subtest, 3) Recalling Sentences subtest (ability to recall and reproduce sentence structures without a story context), 4) Pre-Literacy Rating Scale (checklist of early reading skills), and 5) Descriptive Pragmatics Profile (checklist of reported observations of communication in context). In addition, new items were developed at the lower and higher levels of the prior version subtests, and other items were adapted in some of the original subtests. For example, a new story was developed for the Recalling Sentences in Context subtest.

(continued)

A comprehensive approach was utilized in developing the CELF® Preschool-2. Input came from a literature review, feedback from CELF® Preschool users, and a panel of experts in language disorders and early speech and language development. Items were reviewed for their appropriateness for assessing children across ethnic, gender, regional, and socioeconomic factors.

A pilot study, a national tryout study, and nationwide standardization were also undertaken. The pilot sample was comprised of 40 typically developing children and 18 children with language disorders. All children spoke English as their primary home language, but the sample included a substantial proportion (64%) of Latino children. The pilot research led to further refinements. For example, 3-year-olds were no longer administered the Phonological Awareness subtest and expressive part of the Word Classes subtest because of their difficulty level.

A total of 487 children without diagnosed language disorders and 230 children diagnosed with language disorders participated in the national tryout study. The children in the tryout study sample spoke English as their primary home language, and approximately 31% and 12% of children with and without language disorders were of Latino heritage, respectively. Among other endeavors, the tryout study entailed scoring studies, a bias and content review, and statistical analyses. Items were eliminated based on fairness, clinical utility, difficulty, and ease of scoring. The item order was also examined. At this point, the remainder of the Word Classes subtest was completely eliminated at the 3-year-old level.

Standardization Sample

In 2003, 800 children were part in the standardization sample, and about 350 children were involved in related reliability and validity studies. A total of 100 children in all eight 6-month age groups were included. The sample was stratified by age, sex, race/ethnicity, geographic region, and primary caregiver's education level. The sample's distribution across these characteristics closely matched the distribution in the 2000 Census. Children were excluded if they could not speak, necessitated modifications, or had been diagnosed with a behavior or emotional disorder.

English was the primary language of all participants, though they could be bilingual. A total of 10% of children lived in multilingual homes (79% Spanish, 10% Asian languages, 11% other languages). Also, 12% of the sample spoke with "regional and cultural patterns that represent variations from Mainstream American English" (Wiig et al., 2004, p. 107). Moreover, 13% of the sample received services, with about 9% receiving both speech and language therapies. Finally, 4% were participating in Head Start, 27% in other early education services, 21% in kindergarten, and 19% in first grade.

The scoring studies used during the standardization process led to scoring rule adjustments for various subtests. Furthermore, all examiners scored responses that reflected dialectical variations. Each record form in the standardization sample was then scored by two trained scorers.

Final adjustments were also subsequently made to the CELF® Preschool-2. For example, item orders were adjusted and items were deleted based on item difficulty, differential item functioning, and scoring ease and reliability. Furthermore, discontinue rules, standard scores, age equivalents, and percentile ranges were developed based on empirical examination. Criterion scores were developed at 1 *SD* below the standardization sample on the following subtests and checklists: Basic Concepts—Ages 5–6, Phonological Awareness, Pre-Literacy Rating Scale, and Descriptive Pragmatics Profile. The Phonological Awareness subtest also has a criterion at the 40th percentile based on the University of Oregon Assessment Committee guidelines. For the Descriptive Pragmatics Profile, a criterion score was determined by examining sensitivity and specificity levels between the standardization sample and the samples of children with a language or autism spectrum disorder who had participated in the validity studies.

Norming

Norm referenced and criterion referenced

Reliability

Test–Retest Reliability

A total of 120 children were administered the CELF® Preschool-2 twice between 2 and 24 days apart (M = 9.3 days, SD = 4.9). Demographics were well balanced, and analyses were conducted by age group and on the sample as a whole. Overall, the corrected correlations were in the strong range for the CLS and Index scores across the full sample (.91–.94). The coefficients were somewhat lower for the 6-year-olds, suggesting possible ceiling effects. Thus, the CELF®-4, rather than the CELF® Preschool-2, may be preferable for use with children in this age range. Among the subtests and across the age groups, the Sentence Structure subtest exhibited the lowest coefficients and generally moderate temporal stability (.75–.81).

Internal Consistency

Internal consistency was examined by two methods (Cronbach's coefficient alpha and split-half reliability), among age groups (3;0–6;11 years), and among various populations (standardization sample and clinical samples).

Overall, the CLS yielded a Cronbach's alpha of .90, with Index scores in the .91–.92 range. Thus, strong internal consistency is indicated. When individual age subgroups were considered, the CLS alpha was much lower (.76) for the oldest children in the sample (6;6–6;11 years). Overall, the Sentence Structure and Basic Concepts subtests were among the weaker subtests (.77–.78). Others (i.e., Eigenbrood, 2007; Schwarting, 2007) have noted the lower reliability of a couple of the subtests, which is similar to variations seen on other measures. Thus, the diagnostic value of these subtests is lower than that of other subtests.

Similar findings were evidenced using the split-half method. Here, the coefficients for the CLS and Index scores were solid in the .92–.94 range. The general pattern across subtests and ages is similar to that for Cronbach's alpha.

Using the split-half coefficients, the corresponding standard errors of measurement were as follows for the whole sample: 4.24 (CLS) and 3.75–4.37 (Index scores).

Internal consistency was also examined in a sample of 233 children with hearing difficulties and with language and autism spectrum disorders. The reliability coefficients (.88–.97) suggest that the "CELF® Preschool-2 is equally reliable for measuring the language skills of children from the general population or children with clinical diagnoses" (Wiig et al., 2004, p. 120).

Interrater Agreement

All protocols in the standardization sample were scored by two raters. Interrater agreement on the following subtests, which require more subjective judgment, was high: Word Structure (.97), Expressive Vocabulary (.97), and the expressive part of Word Classes (.95).

Other Forms of Reliability (e.g., Equivalent Forms)

Not applicable

Validity

Face and Content

The comprehensive literature review, item reviews, examiner feedback, and utilization of an expert panel contribute to the face and content validity of the CELF® Preschool-2.

Internal Construct

Confirmatory factor analyses at two age ranges were conducted to examine the fit of the structure of the CELF® Preschool-2 indexes and items. A two-level model was supported, with overall language ability reflecting the high correlation of language skills assessed across all subtests and indexes. In addition, the manual states that "children with language disorders tend to exhibit global dysfunction on language measures and therefore would be expected to demonstrate relatively high correlation among the subtests" (Wiig et al., 2004, p. 129). This is also evidenced in the standardization sample, with a .76 correction between the Receptive Language Index and the Expressive Language Index and a .82 correlation between the Language Content Index and the Language Structure Index.

Unlike other measures, the indexes are not mutually exclusive, and the subtests may be pulled together in different combinations. For example, the Sentence Structure subtest loads onto the Language Structure Index and the Receptive Language Index. The overall fit of such an approach is generally supported by the factor analyses.

External Construct

To examine the ability of the CELF® Preschool-2 to distinguish between children with and without an identified language disorder, researchers matched 157 children with a language disorder with children from the standardization sample based on age, parent education level, and race/ethnicity. Significant mean effect sizes were demonstrated such that those with a language disorder scored lower on all components of the CELF® Preschool-2. In addition, the sensitivity of correctly identifying a child with a language disorder with the CLS criterion placed at 85 was .85 and the specificity was .82. The manual also presents the predictive powers relative to base rates seen in referral settings. The values suggest that the CELF® Preschool-2 should not be used in isolation for diagnostic purposes (Schwarting, 2007).

Similar studies were also conducted with children with an autism spectrum disorder ($n = 38$) and who were hard of hearing ($n = 33$). Significant mean effect sizes were demonstrated.

Support for the measure's convergent and discriminant validity is also indicated by some of the correlational studies described in "Criterion."

Criterion

The manual presents correlational studies between the CELF® Preschool-2, the original CELF® Preschool, the CELF®-4, and the Preschool Language Scale–Fourth Edition (PLS-4). The correlation between the CELF® Preschool and the CELF® Preschool-2 fell in the moderate to high range in a study of 96 children. Overall, the correlation between the CLS and the CELF® Preschool Total Language score was .86, which is strong.

A total of 102 children ages 5 and 6 were assessed with both the CELF®-4 and CELF® Preschool-2. The overall correlation between the CLSs was .69, which is lower than one might expect. Some indexes were as high as expected, such as the Language Content Index at .84. Lower ceilings on the CELF® Preschool-2 could have contributed to more restriction for the oldest children and for lower mean scores as well. That is, there were fewer difficult items for the oldest children on the CELF® Preschool-2 compared to the CELF®-4. Thus, examiners assessing older, higher functioning 6-year-olds may be advised to utilize the CELF®-4.

In another comparison, 81 children were administered the CELF® Preschool-2 and the PLS-4. A moderate relationship was evidenced between the two measures, with a correlation of .73 between the CLS and the PLS-4 Total Language Score. Thus, similar results will likely be evidenced on the two measures.

Eigenbrood (2007) noted that providing only one comparison between the CELF® Preschool-2 to one other external measure in the manual provides readers with minimal information on criterion validity.

RELEVANT STUDIES USING THE MEASURE

A brief literature search using PsycINFO, the Education Resources Information Center, and Google Scholar yielded a variety of studies describing the use of the CELF® Preschool-2.

For example, Riou, Ghosh, Francoeur, and Shevell (2009) reported the relationship of language, cognitive, and other skills among children diagnosed with a global developmental delay. Also, Gaines and Missiuna (2007) reported on a longitudinal study examining a pattern by which children first diagnosed with speech-language impairments later evidenced motor difficulties that affected academic learning. Furthermore, Glennen (2009) presented patterns of language impairments experienced by young children adopted from overseas.

Additional studies using the CELF® Preschool-2 have been published. In addition, older versions of the measure have been used in many studies.

ADDITIONAL REFERENCES

Eigenbrood, R. (2007). Test review of the Clinical Evaluation of Language Fundamentals® Preschool–Second Edition. In K.F. Geisinger, R.A. Spies, J.F. Carlson, & B.S. Plake (Eds.), *The seventeenth mental measurements yearbook*. Retrieved from the Buros Institute's *Test Reviews Online* web site: http://www.unl.edu/buros

Gaines, R., & Missiuna, C. (2007). Early identification: Are speech/language-impaired toddlers at increased risk for developmental coordination disorder? *Child: Care, Health and Development, 33,* 325–332.

Glennen, S. (2009). Speech and language guidelines for children adopted from abroad at older ages. *Topics in Language Disorders, 29,* 50–64.

Riou, E., Ghosh, S., Francoeur, E., & Shevell, M. (2009). Global developmental delay and its relationship to cognitive skills. *Developmental Medicine & Child Neurology, 51,* 600–606.

Schwarting, G. (2007). Test review of the Clinical Evaluation of Language Fundamentals® Preschool–Second Edition. In K.F. Geisinger, R.A. Spies, J.F. Carlson, & B.S. Plake (Eds.), *The seventeenth mental measurements yearbook*. Retrieved from the Buros Institute's *Test Reviews Online* web site: http://www.unl.edu/buros

Clinical Evaluation of Language Fundamentals®–Preschool–Second Edition: Spanish (CELF® Preschool-2: Spanish)

Information pertaining specifically to the Spanish version of the measure is in bold and italics. The remainder is equivalent information provided in the English review.

Manual

Wiig, E.H., Secord, W.A., & Semel, E. (2009). *Clinical Evaluation of Language Fundamentals®, Preschool–2 Spanish Edition.* San Antonio, TX: NCS Pearson.

Publisher

Pearson, Inc.
19500 Bulverde Road
San Antonio, TX 78259-3701
http://www.pearsonassessments.com

Cost

$385

Type of Measure

Direct child assessment, parent/teacher report

Intended Age Range

3;0 years to 6;11 years

Key Constructs/Domains

- Receptive and expressive language
- Language content and structure
- Phonological, preliteracy, and pragmatic development

Description of Measure

The manual describes the CELF® Preschool-2 Spanish as "an individually administered clinical tool for the identification, diagnosis, and follow-up evaluation of language and communication disorders in Spanish-speaking children" (Wiig, Secord, & Semel, 2009, p. 1). It is a parallel but not directly translated version of the CELF® Preschool-2 English. Given that there are some different items and scales, as well as a different norming sample, the resulting scores on the CELF® Preschool-2 Spanish are not comparable to scores from the CELF® Preschool-2 English version.

Available Languages and Formats

The CELF® Preschool-2 is available in English. It is a downward extension of the Clinical Evaluation of Language Fundamentals®–Fourth Edition (CELF®-4) Spanish, which can be used with individuals between 5 and 21 years of age.

Strengths

The measure can be used to provide both quick and more detailed examinations of young children's language ability.

The steps undertaken in applicability, development, and standardization for Spanish-speaking populations were thorough and well documented.

The reliability and validity of the Spanish version is generally solid across multiple dimensions.

The manual provides a detailed description of assessment approaches for use with monolingual and bilingual Spanish-speaking children.

Dialectical variations were carefully considered and incorporated into the measure.

Improvements in the CELF® Preschool-2 were evidenced between the time of the English version (2004) and the Spanish version (2009). For example, growth scores are now available.

Weaknesses

The criterion validity of the CELF® Preschool-2 Spanish could benefit from further investigation.

Use of the CELF® Preschool-2 with 3-year-olds likely needs further development. Only two subtests compose the Receptive Language Index and Language Content Index since Concepts & Following Directions subtest was dropped. The alphas on these scales for this age group are thus lower (.84–.88), though still somewhat acceptable. The Concepts & Following Directions subtest did not benefit from revision (particularly at the lower range) prior to the standardization study because it was not included in the pilot study.

Structural differences suggested by factor analyses may need further examination with a larger sample of Spanish-speaking children. In addition, the external construct validity remains to be examined for 3-year-olds, and the description of the use of the present model for 4-year-olds is unclear.

ADMINISTRATION

Procedure

The CELF® Preschool-2 Spanish is composed of

- Seven subtests that provide scaled scores *and growth scores,* and are norm referenced (*Sentence Structure, Word Structure, Expressive Vocabulary, Concepts & Following Directions, Recalling Sentences, Word Classes, Basic Concepts—Ages 3–4*)

- Two supplemental subtests that provide criterion scores and are norm referenced (Phonological Awareness—Ages 4–6 as well as Basic Concepts—Ages 5–6)

Time Needed

Core Language Score (for children ages 3;0 to 4;11 years: Basic Concepts, Work Structure, and Recalling Sentences; for children ages 5;0 to 6;11 years: Word Structure, Recalling Sentences, and Concepts & Following Directions): 15–20 minutes

- Two checklists that provide criterion scores and are norm referenced (Pre-Literacy Rating Scale, Descriptive Pragmatics Profile)

- *A Language Sample Checklist used to describe the quality of language in Spanish and/or another language during an unstructured interaction.*

Note that Recalling Sentences in Context (a supplemental norm-referenced subtest in the English version) is not part of the Spanish version of the CELF® Preschool-2 as it was not found to differentiate among Spanish-speaking children with and without a language disorder.

The following standardized composite scores are available:

- Core Language Score (CLS)
- Receptive Language Index
- Expressive Language Index
- Language Content Index
- Language Structure Index

In the English version, the indexes are created from three subtests each. The Receptive Language Index and Language Content Index include the Basic Concepts—Ages 3–4 subtest for children ages 3–4 but substitute the Word Classes subtest for children ages 5–6. *In the Spanish version, these indexes have three variations: for 3-year-olds, for 4-year-olds, and for children ages 5–6. Among the tests for the 3-year-olds, only two subtests*

(continued)

compose the indexes since the Concepts & Following Directions subtest was dropped. The difference between the indexes for Spanish-speaking 4-year-olds and children ages 5–6 is similar to that for the English version.

The CELF® Preschool-2 Spanish can be administered in its entirety or in parts to examine language development at four levels:

- Overall language ability/presence of language disorder (entails administration of three subtests in the CLS®, *which differ from the three in the English version*)
- Description of child's language abilities/nature of disorder (entails administration of norm-referenced subtests)
- Evaluation of early classroom and literacy fundamentals (entails administration of supplementary norm-referenced measures)
- Evaluation of language and communication in context (entails administration of the Descriptive Pragmatics Profile)

Administration and Interpretation

"The test can be administered by Spanish-speaking speech-language pathologists, school psychologists, special educators, and diagnosticians who have been trained and are experienced in administration and interpretation of standardized tests. An examiner must be a fluent Spanish speaker with near-native proficiency to administer the test and transcribe the child's responses. If the examiner does not have near-native proficiency in Spanish, the test can be administered in collaboration with a trained and qualified interpreter" (Wiig et al., 2009, p. 2). The manual provides a detailed 9-page description of the methods for successfully using an interpreter. Furthermore, a description of assessment considerations for use with Latino children is provided for the examiner, including how to interpret the performance of a child learning a second language.

Furthermore, interpersonal verbal and nonverbal communication patterns among Latinos are described in the manual to assist in the interpretation of the Pragmatics checklist. For example, physical proximity and contact customs are presented.

A Language Environment Checklist is provided on the Spanish record form to describe the use of languages at home and at school and the children's mastery of the two languages. A behavior checklist appears on the record form to track physical activity, attention levels, and other behaviors.

Cases studies are provided in the manual as examples of interpretation. *Unlike the English version, additional cases are not available on the publisher's web site.*

An English translation of the test stimuli and administration directions are also provided in the manual.

Scoring Method

Scoring considerations related to dialectical variations in Spanish are discussed: "Before the child is tested, review the information you have about the child and determine if you need to substitute alternate vocabulary for specific test stimuli, depending on the type/dialect of Spanish the child speaks. If you are not familiar with Caribbean or Central or South American variants of Spanish, you may want to have the primary caregiver or older sibling review the test and determine if all the words used are familiar to the child. Words that may need to be substituted for a stimulus word should ideally be identified before testing begins" (Wiig et al., 2009, p. 28). Alternative words are listed on the record form, and an expanded scoring guide is provided in the appendix.

In addition, the manual describes the scoring of articulation variations in Spanish, as well as the use of code-switching and Anglicisms. The research basis for such decisions is also presented.

The CELF® Preschool-2 Spanish is hand-scored. Generally speaking, the raw score is the number of items answered correctly by the child on each subtest. Some subtests use a 3-point scale that provides partial credit for answers that are not fully correct. After the initial scoring is complete, raw scores for the seven norm-referenced subscales are converted into scaled scores and then compiled into the CLS and Index scores. Scaled and standard scores, *growth scores,* percentile ranks, confidence intervals, and age equivalents are available.

The degree to which children are experiencing discrepancies between their receptive and expressive language abilities and between the content and structure of their language can be analyzed both statistically and clinically.

Though full norms are not available, the CELF® Preschool-2 Spanish provides criterion (cutoff) scores for additional subtests and rating scales. These are used to determine whether children's development of basic concepts, phonological awareness, preliteracy skills, or pragmatics is delayed.

Item analysis tables are available for each subtest to enable the researcher to qualitatively examine the error patterns in children's responses. Suggestions for extension testing and intervention/follow-up are provided in the manual.

Adaptations or Instructions for Use with Individuals with Disabilities

The manual provides examples of modifications to the CELF® Preschool-2 Spanish that support the use of norm-referenced scores as well as more extensive modifications that preclude the use of such scores. In the latter case, raw scores can be interpreted to describe children's performance.

FUNCTIONAL CONSIDERATIONS

Measure Development

The English version of the CELF® Preschool was first developed in 1992. Its counterpart, the CELF®, is on its fourth edition in English and in Spanish and is used with individuals between 5 and 21 years of age. The CELF® Preschool-2 was released in English in 2004 with attention to its diagnostic power, psychometrics, utility, and appeal and with an aim to deepening the assessment of pragmatics, semantics, and morphosyntax. *More about the development of the English version can be found in the review for the CELF® Preschool-2 English.*

The Spanish version of the CELF® Preschool-2 was published in 2009. The principal goal in its development is described as follows: "To develop a comprehensive and flexible Spanish assessment process parallel to that of CELF® Preschool-2, subtests and tasks were developed to match the formats of the English edition as closely as possible, while incorporating skills specific to Spanish vocabulary, morphology, and syntax" (Wiig et al., 2009, p. 131). Specifically, consideration was paid to research and trends in preschool development and assessment, Spanish language and bilingual development and variation, psychometrics, overlap with the CELF-4® Spanish, the appropriate floor for Spanish-speaking 3-year-olds with less advanced language skills, the differential performance of typically developing Spanish-speaking children and children with a language disorder, and the appropriate item-level difficulty sequence for Spanish-speaking children.

As with the English version, a comprehensive approach was utilized in developing the CELF® Preschool-2 Spanish. Input stemmed from a literature review on Spanish and bilingual development, feedback from CELF® Preschool-2 and CELF®-4 Spanish users, and a panel of experts in this area. Items were reviewed for their cultural and content relevance; clinical utility; and appropriateness for assessing children across ethnic, gender, regional, and socioeconomic factors.

A pilot study and nationwide standardization were also undertaken. (A national tryout study was utilized with the English version but not the Spanish one.) The pilot sample comprised 89 typically developing children from the United States and Puerto Rico. "All children lived in a Spanish-speaking home and spoke Spanish fluently enough to take CELF® Preschool-2 Spanish in a standard manner" (Wiig et al., 2009, p. 142). About 63% of the sample was of Mexican heritage, whereas about 17% was from Puerto Rico and 10% from Central America. A clinical pilot study was also conducted with 47 Spanish-speaking children with a language disorder. Similar demographics are presented for this sample.

Six of the norm-referenced subtests and one of the criterion-referenced subtests (Phonological Awareness) were examined in the pilot study. The exclusion of the Concepts & Following Directions subtest from the pilot study is not discussed. Its absence from the pilot study may have precluded it from being further refined before the standardization study. The subsequent standardization study found that the Concepts & Following Directions subtest had a floor effect, and thus it was dropped from the protocol for 3-year-olds. Thus, the Receptive Language Index and Language Content Index comprise only two subtests rather than three.

The pilot studies led to the development of scoring protocols (including examination and incorporation of regional/cultural variances) and adjustments to the measure based on statistical analyses. For example, 3-year-olds were no longer administered the Phonological Awareness and Word Classes subtests because of their difficulty levels. Furthermore, additional items were added to the Word Structure subtest to increase its ceiling. Instructions for required trial and optional trial items were also added.

Content Equivalence of Items and Measure

The CELF® Preschool-2 Spanish is not a straight translation of the English version. Careful attention was paid to appropriately selecting Spanish items. In addition, the application of the various content areas assessed on the subtests and indexes for the Spanish language is discussed from theoretical and empirical perspectives.

Semantic Equivalence of Translations

Children's responses in Spanish overall and in relation to dialectical variations were empirically examined and incorporated into the measure. Expert panelists also provided input, and feedback from participants in the pilot study was incorporated. Although the manual indicates that the test stimuli are typical of vocabulary used by Spanish-speaking children in the southwestern and western parts of the United States (who are more likely to speak with a Mexican dialect), the standardization sample included children from Puerto Rico. Further, the test development team included two language experts from Puerto Rico. The use of alternative vocabulary related to dialectical differences is acceptable.

Structural Consistency Across the English and Spanish Versions

Overall, the English and Spanish versions are structurally similar. They have the same indexes, and the same subtests compose the Expressive Language Index and the Language Structure Index. However, the composition of other indexes (including the CLS) varies across the language versions and across age groups. In addition, the measures vary in the number of items and discontinuation rules "based on the performance of children in their respective normative sample" (Wiig et al., 2009, p. 133).

Standardization Sample

In 2007–2008, 464 children participated in the standardization sample and about 236 children were involved in related reliability and validity studies. A total of 60 children from each of the eight 6-month age groups were included in the standardization sample, except for the 3;0–3;5 years sample, which was composed of 44 children. The youngest group was initially composed of 60 children. However, the longer standardization set was taxing to 16 children, and their protocols could not be utilized. The manual describes consulting with psychometric experts and deciding to base the norms of the youngest children on the available protocols.

Standardization occurred in the United States and Puerto Rico. The sample was stratified by age, sex, race/ethnicity, geographic region, and primary caregiver's education level. *The sample's distribution across these characteristics closely matched the distribution of the Hispanic young child population based on the U.S. Census.* Children were excluded if they could not use Spanish to communicate, necessitated modifications, or had been diagnosed with a behavioral or emotional disorder.

Spanish was the primary language of all participants, though they could be bilingual. A total of 24% of children lived in homes where English was also spoken. The parents' countries of origin were distributed as follows: Mexico (61%), Puerto Rico (18%), Central/South America (17%), Cuba (2%), the Dominican Republic (2%), and other (1%). In addition, 26% of the sample was receiving second language services (English as a second language learners, children with limited English proficiency, English language learners), and 23% were in bilingual education. About 7% of the sample received speech-language therapy. Moreover, 7% were participating in Head Start, 21% in other early education services, 15% in kindergarten, and 18% in first grade. In addition, the manual provides a description of the sample by home language use, child's English and Spanish fluency, Spanish dialect, recency of immigration, education level, and gender, among other factors.

The scoring studies engaged in during the standardization process led to scoring rule adjustments for various subtests. *Furthermore, all examiners scored responses that reflected correct variations in Spanish. For example, a child could say "para mimis" for "going to sleep."* Each record form in the standardization sample was then scored by two trained scorers.

Final adjustments were also subsequently made to the CELF® Preschool-2 Spanish. For example, item orders were adjusted and items were deleted based on item difficulty, differential item functioning, ease of scoring, and reliability. Furthermore, discontinue rules, standard scores, *growth scores,* age equivalents, and percentile ranges were developed based on empirical examination.

For the Spanish version, the criterion scores for all of the supplementary subtests and checklists were developed as they had been developed for the English Descriptive Pragmatics Profile. That is, the criterion scores were determined by examining sensitivity and specificity levels between the standardization sample and the samples of children with a language disorder participating in the validity studies. On the English version, criterion scores for Basic Concepts—Ages 5–6, Phonological Awareness, the Pre-Literacy Rating Scale, and the Descriptive Pragmatics Profile had been established by examining standard deviations. As with the English version, the Spanish Phonological Awareness subtest also has an available criterion at the 40th percentile based on the University of Oregon Assessment Committee guidelines.

The manual indicates that raw scores and norms of the English and Spanish versions are not directly comparable due to the demographic differences between the two samples.

Norming

Norm referenced and criterion referenced

Reliability

Test–Retest Reliability

A total of 66 children were administered the CELF® Preschool-2 Spanish twice between 2 and 29 days apart (M = 9.3 days, SD = 4.9). Demographics were well balanced, and analyses were conducted on the sample and by 2-year age spans (3;0–4;11 years and 5;0–6;11 years). Overall, the corrected correlations were in the strong range for the CLS and Index scores across the full sample (.88–.93). The coefficients were somewhat lower for the 5- to 6-year-old range (.81–.91). This may reflect possible ceiling effects for the 6-year-olds, as was evidenced in the English version. Thus, the CELF®-4 rather than the CELF® Preschool-2 may be preferable for use with children in this age range. Among the subtests and across the age groups, the Concepts & Following Directions subtest exhibited the lowest coefficients and generally moderate temporal stability (.69–.71).

The Spanish manual also presents an examination of the decision consistency between test and retest administrations for the criterion-referenced measures. Overall, decision consistency fell in the 97% to 100% range for the Basic Concepts subtest, the Phonological Awareness subtest, and the Pre-Literacy Rating Scale. The Pragmatics score was .94 for all age groups except for the 4-year-olds, which was .81. Because this was calculated on only about 15 children at this age level, it would be beneficial for future studies to reexamine consistency for 4-year-olds.

Internal Consistency

Internal consistency was examined by two methods (Cronbach's coefficient alpha and split-half reliability), among age groups (3;0–6;11 years), and among various populations (standardization sample and clinical samples).

Overall, the CLS yielded a Cronbach's alpha of .93, with Index scores in the .87–.93 range. As may be expected, lower values were evidenced for 3-year-olds on the indexes composed of only two subtests (Receptive Language Index and Language Content Index). Thus, strong internal consistency is indicated. Overall, the Basic Concepts (.76) and the Word Classes–Expressive (.75) subtests were among the weaker subtests. A ceiling effect appears to be present for the Word Classes subtest, with an alpha of .91 for the young 4-year-olds and .74 for the older 6-year-olds. Older children also have lower alphas on the Sentence Structure subtest (.63–.78). Thus, the diagnostic value of these subtests is lower than that of other subtests.

Similar findings were evidenced using the split-half method. The coefficients for the CLS and Index scores were solidly in the .89–.93 range. The general pattern across subtests and ages is similar to that presented for Cronbach's alpha.

Using the split-half coefficients, the corresponding standard errors of measurement were as follows for the whole sample: 3.90 (CLS) and 4.00–5.00 (Index scores).

Internal consistency was also examined in a sample of 90 children with language disorders. The reliability alpha coefficients at the subtest level (.83–.97) suggest that the "CELF® Preschool-2 Spanish has reliable scores for measuring the language skills of children with a diagnosis of language disorder, as well as children from the general population" (Wiig et al., 2009, p. 172).

Interrater Agreement

All protocols in the standardization sample were scored by two raters. Interrater agreement on the following subtests, which require more subjective judgment, was high: Word Structure (.97), Expressive Vocabulary (.98), Recalling Sentences (.95), and the expressive part of Word Classes (.93).

Other Forms of Reliability (e.g., Equivalent Forms)

Not applicable

Validity

Face and Content

The comprehensive literature review, item reviews, examiner feedback, and utilization of an expert panel contribute to the face and content validity of the CELF® Preschool-2 Spanish.

Internal Construct

Confirmatory factor analyses for 4- to 6-year-olds were conducted to examine the fit of the structure of the CELF® Preschool-2 Spanish's indexes and items. Three-year-olds were likely excluded because of their small sample size. Although the tables and figures present the data as for children ages 4–6, the structure presented was only consistent with that used for the 5- to 6-year-olds. For example, the standardized solutions for the Receptive Language Index are provided for three subtests (Concepts & Following Directions, Sentence Structure, Word Classes–Receptive). However, 4-year-olds are administered Basic Concepts—Ages 3–4 instead of Word Classes.

Unlike the English version, a two-level full model was not the best fit to the data. (In the English model, overall language ability reflected the high correlation of language skills assessed across all subtests and indexes, and there was support for the four concurrent indexes.) Rather, two separate models were supported in which the children's performance could be examined from a receptive/expressive perspective or a content/structure perspective. This is not surprising because it is generally unusual for subtests to load on more than one index. For example, the Sentence Structure subtest can be examined from its contribution to both the Language Structure Index and the Receptive Language Index. The factor analysis suggests considering results from receptive/expressive and content/structure perspectives rather than thinking of them as four separate indexes. There is also not separate confirmation of the CLS, though again this is likely because of the multiple loadings of subtests to the CLS and indexes and perhaps the relatively small sample size for such multilevel analyses (standardization sample = 464).

External Construct

The raw score means were examined to verify that they generally increased with age. In addition, performance on the CELF® Preschool-2 Spanish was examined by children's language comprehension and expressiveness across the two languages (i.e., child understands/speaks Spanish only, child understands/speaks Spanish and a little English, child understands/speaks both Spanish and English). The mean scores did not differ significantly, though variance did relate to language proficiency. As such, separate normative data were not needed by language group.

To examine the ability of the CELF® Preschool-2 to distinguish between children with and without an identified language disorder, researchers matched 90 children with a language disorder with children from the standardization sample based on age, parent education level, and race/ethnicity. Children lived in the United States, Puerto Rico, and Mexico. Significant mean effect sizes were demonstrated such that those with a language disorder scored lower on all components of the CELF® Preschool-2 Spanish. In addition, the sensitivity of correctly identifying a child with a language disorder with the CLS criterion placed at 85 was .86 and the specificity was .89. The manual also presents the predictive powers relative to base rates seen in referral settings. The values suggest that the CELF® Preschool-2 Spanish should not be used in isolation for diagnostic purposes (as is generally the case for measures; Schwarting, 2007), though its diagnostic power is stronger than that of the English version.

Support for the measure's convergent and discriminant validity is also indicated by some of the correlational studies described in the Criterion section.

Criterion

The manual presents correlational studies between the English version of the CELF® Preschool-2, the CELF®-4 Spanish, and the Preschool Language Scale–Fourth Edition (PLS-4) Spanish. Five bilingual children (ages 4 and 6) were administered the Spanish and English versions of the CELF® Preschool-2. Their scores and response patterns were examined qualitatively. Similar patterns in performance were evidenced; for example, some children scored poorly on both language versions, whereas other children performed well on both. Children with underlying morphology or syntax problems evidenced these problems on both exams. The largest discrepancy was in vocabulary knowledge in English and in Spanish, as may be expected in cases of bilingualism.

Moreover, 30 children ages 5 and 6 were assessed with the Spanish versions of both the CELF®-4 and the CELF® Preschool-2. The overall correlation between the CLSs was solid at .87. Some indexes were not as highly correlated as expected, such as the Expressive Language Index at .65. The manual suggests that the test differences reflect performance response reactions to the stimuli presented to the 5- to 6-year-olds. For example, animal drawings may be more appealing for this age group than the inanimate objects in the CELF®-4 Spanish.

In another comparison, 36 children were administered the CELF® Preschool-2 Spanish and the PLS-4 Spanish. A moderate correlation was evidenced between the two, with the correlation of .66 between the CLS and the PLS-4 Spanish Total Language Score. Thus, relatively similar results will likely be evidenced on the two measures, though they are not completely interchangeable.

Comparison of Psychometric Properties Between English and Spanish Versions

Technical Equivalence in Reliability

Overall, the reliability results of the English and Spanish versions are quite similar.

Technical Equivalence in Validity

The validity of the English and Spanish versions is generally equivalent. Both versions have good support in external construct and criterion validities. Structural differences suggested by factor analyses may need further examination with a larger sample of Spanish children. In addition, the external construct validity remains to be examined for 3-year-olds, and the description of the use of the present model for 4-year-olds is unclear.

RELEVANT STUDIES USING THE MEASURE

A brief literature search using PsycINFO, the Education Resources Information Center, and Google Scholar did not yield any published studies that mentioned using the CELF® Preschool-2 Spanish.

ADDITIONAL REFERENCES

None

Compton Speech and Language Screening Evaluation of Children: English

Manual

Compton, A.J. (1999). *Compton Speech and Language Screening Evaluation of Children.* San Francisco, CA: Carousel House.

Publisher

Carousel House
212C Arguello Boulevard
San Francisco, CA 94118
http://www.carouselhouse.com

Cost

Complete kit: $63

Description of Measure

"This screening evaluation is designed to provide a quick estimate of the speech and language development of preschool, kindergarten, and first-grade children (ages 3–6 years). It is intended to be used as a means of selecting out those children with potential speech and language handicaps, thereby alerting the tester and parents that a more extensive evaluation is warranted" (Compton, 1999, p. 1).

Available Languages and Formats

A Spanish adaptation is available.

Strengths

The measure examines multiple components of speech and language.

The nature of the tasks (i.e., the use of objects) is likely appealing to young children.

The assessment takes less than 10 minutes to administer (Compton, 1999).

Weaknesses

There is very little information regarding how scoring guidelines were developed, although more than 500 children were involved in tryouts of the measure.

Limited information related to reliability and validity is presented in the manual.

ADMINISTRATION

Procedure

Compton explains that the assessment is "object oriented" in that activities center on a small number of toy objects (1999, p. 1). The examiner begins by opening the measure's carrying case (i.e., a lunchbox) full of toys and inviting the child to come

Type of Measure

Direct child assessment

Intended Age Range

3 years to 6 years

Key Constructs/Domains

- Expressive/receptive language (e.g., articulation, vocabulary, fluency and voice)
- Cognitive skills (e.g., auditory-visual memory span)

Time Needed

6–10 minutes (a hearing screening can be added, resulting in an additional 5–8 minutes)

This measure is also referred to as the Pre-Schoolers Screening Evaluation.

see them. These objects are then used in a series of tasks. Specifically, the administrator covers items across nine broad sections:

- *Articulation and language.* The child is asked to name the objects *presented to him or her.* "To conserve time in testing for articulation, the objects have been chosen so that initial, intervocalic, and final consonants can be checked at the same time with each item" (Compton, 1999, p. 2).

- *Color recognition.* The child names the colors of different blocks.

- *Shape recognition.* The child is asked to point to blocks of various shapes.

- *Auditory-visual memory span.* The examiner places certain objects (selected according to the child's age) within the test carrying case, showing and saying each item first. The child is then asked to recall which items were placed in the case.

- *Language.*[1] The child completes various tasks, including

  - Creating plural forms for objects

  - Contrasting opposites

  - Completing ideas using progressive or past tense forms of verbs

  - Using appropriate prepositions

  - Following multiple commands

  - Using possessive pronouns

- *Spontaneous language sample.* The child is asked to describe one of the pictures for the examiner (who has his or her eyes closed). The examiner then guesses which picture the child has described. The examiner is asked to make a mental note of the average number of words per utterance as well as the intelligibility of the utterance. This task can be omitted, according to the manual, if the administrator has already obtained a sufficient sample of the child's conversational speech.

- *Fluency and voice.* The administrator should note any concerns about the child's fluency or voice quality based on his or her observations during the assessment thus far.

- *Oral mechanisms.* The administrator should note any concerns about the child's oral mechanisms (i.e., structural or functional problems such as poor tongue mobility that may interfere with speech) based on his or her observations during the assessment thus far.

Administration and Interpretation

"No special preparation is required for administration other than familiarity with the test materials and several practice trials to become acquainted with procedures for giving the evaluation" (Compton, 1999, p. 1). Nonetheless, given the focus on speech and language, individuals with training in this area (e.g., speech-language pathologists) are especially well suited to administer the Compton Speech and Language Screening Evaluation of Children.

Scoring Method

Administrators utilize a record sheet to document children's responses. For the Articulation and Vocabulary sections of the measure, administrators with training in speech-language pathology are encouraged to record the sound substitutions or distortions made by children. The total number of correct and incorrect responses is then tallied.

Guidelines are provided for characterizing children as 1) passing, 2) in need of rescreening, or 3) in need of a speech evaluation. These guidelines "are based upon several years of extensive research on normal and abnormal linguistic development, information available from a variety

---

[1]The examiner asks production items first (i.e., items for which children need to produce the answer). If these tasks are performed correctly, the examiner does not need to administer comprehension tasks on the same topic.

of standard sources, and the trial-and-error results obtained during the course of administering the evaluation to a population of approximately 500 children" (Compton, 1999, p. 11).

Adaptations or Instructions for Use with Individuals with Disabilities

No information is provided in the manual.

FUNCTIONAL CONSIDERATIONS

Measure Development

The first prototype of the Compton Speech and Language Screening Evaluation of Children was developed in 1975 at the Institute of Child Language and Phonology. The measure "has undergone several revisions during the course of administering it to a population of approximately 500 children from a wide range of socio-economic and ethnic backgrounds" (Compton, 1999, p. ii). The latest publication was in 1999. Specific information regarding the development and revision of items, however, is not provided within the manual.

Standardization Sample

Although the manual describes administering the measure to approximately 500 children, there is no explicit discussion of standardization (such as the characteristics of these children or the results of the tryouts).

Norming

Criterion referenced

Reliability

Test–Retest Reliability

No information is provided in the manual.

Internal Consistency

No information is provided in the manual.

Interrater Agreement

No information is provided in the manual.

Other Forms of Reliability (e.g., Equivalent Forms)

No information is provided in the manual.

Validity

Face and Content

Although the measure appears to assess the areas it purports to, no information about the sources for the items is provided in the manual.

Internal Construct

No information is provided in the manual.

External Construct
No information is provided in the manual.

Criterion
No information is provided in the manual.

RELEVANT STUDIES USING THE MEASURE

A brief literature search using PsycINFO and Google Scholar did not yield any studies that mentioned using the most recent version of the measure. However, an older version has been utilized. It is also possible that the most recent measure has been utilized in studies that could not be located.

ADDITIONAL REFERENCES

None

Compton Speech and Language Screening Evaluation of Children: Spanish Adaptation

Information pertaining specifically to the Spanish version of the measure is in bold and italics. The remainder is equivalent information provided in the English review.

Manual

Compton, A.J., & Kline, M. (2005). *Compton Speech and Language Screening Evaluation of Children: Spanish Adaptation.* San Francisco, CA: Carousel House.

Publisher

Carousel House
212C Arguello Boulevard
San Francisco, CA 94118
http://www.carouselhouse.com

Type of Measure

Direct assessment

Intended Age Range

3 years to 6 years

Key Constructs/Domains

- Expressive/receptive language (e.g., articulation, vocabulary, fluency, and voice)
- Cognitive skills (e.g., auditory-visual memory span)

Cost

Complete kit: $63

Description of Measure

"This screening evaluation is designed to provide a quick estimate of the speech and language development of preschool, kindergarten, and first-grade children (ages 3–6 years). It is intended to be used as a means of selecting out those children with potential speech and language handicaps, thereby alerting the tester and parents that a more extensive evaluation is warranted" (Compton & Kline, 2005, p. 1).

According to Compton and Kline, the Spanish version of the Compton Speech and Language Screening Evaluation of Children was developed to untangle children's growing English language proficiency from potential language disorders or lack of exposure to English.

Available Languages and Formats

An English version is available.

Strengths

The measure examines multiple components of speech and language.

The nature of the tasks (i.e., the use of objects) is likely appealing to young children.

The assessment takes less than 10 minutes to administer, according to Compton and Kline (2005).

The differences between the English and Spanish version suggest that the latter is not a basic translation. Rather, attention was paid to capturing key linguistic differences between the languages, such as gender in the Spanish language.

This measure is also referred to as the Pre-Schoolers Screening Evaluation.

(continued)

Weaknesses

There is very little information regarding how scoring guidelines were developed, although more than 250 bilingual children were involved in tryouts of the measure.

Limited information related to the reliability and validity of the Spanish version is presented in the manual, as is limited information about the method used to adapt the measure from English to Spanish.

ADMINISTRATION

Procedure

Compton and Kline explained that the assessment is "object oriented" in that activities center around a small number of toy objects (2005, p. 1). *They indicated that the examiner should begin by speaking Spanish with the child, as the child may feel uncomfortable using his or her primary language outside of home at the outset of the examination. "So far as the child is concerned, you only speak and understand Spanish, and you should not give him/her the option of speaking English" (p. 5). Children's code-switching from Spanish to English should be noted but not penalized.*

Time Needed

6–10 minutes (a hearing screening can be added, resulting in an additional 5–8 minutes)

The examiner begins by opening the test's carrying case (i.e., a lunchbox) full of toys and inviting the child to come see them. These objects are then used in a series of tasks. Specifically, the administrator covers items across nine broad sections:

- *Articulation and language.* The child is asked to name objects presented to him or her. "To conserve time in testing for articulation, the objects have been chosen so that initial, intervocalic, and final consonants can be checked at the same time with each item" (Compton & Kline, 2005, p. 2).

- *Color recognition.* The administrator names each colored block and then asks the child to point to the target color. In the English version of the measure, the child is asked to name the colors. *During the development of the Spanish version, Compton and Kline (2005) found that Spanish-speaking children could recognize but not independently identify colors in Spanish. Usually children would provide the color names in English instead. The test developers therefore modified the task.*

- *Shape recognition.* The child is asked to point to blocks of various shapes.

- *Auditory-visual memory span.* The examiner places certain objects (selected according to the child's age) within the test carrying case, showing and saying each item first. The child is then asked to recall which items were placed in the case.

- *Language.*[1] The child completes various tasks, including

  - *Creating plural forms for objects; contrasting opposites (e.g.,* chiquito *versus* grande*)*
  - Completing ideas using progressive or past tense forms of verbs
  - Using appropriate prepositions
  - Following multiple commands
  - Using object and reflexive pronouns
  - *Using appropriate gender, which is a key feature of the Spanish language*

---

[1]The examiner asks production items first (i.e., items for which children need to produce the answer). If these tasks are performed correctly, the examiner does not need to administer comprehension tasks on the same topic.

- *Spontaneous language sample.* The child is asked to describe one of the pictures for the examiner (who has his or her eyes closed). The examiner then guesses which picture the child has described. The examiner is asked to make a mental note of the average number of words per utterance as well as the intelligibility of the utterance. This task can be omitted, according to the manual, if the administrator has already obtained a sufficient sample of the child's conversational speech.

- *Fluency and voice.* The administrator should note any concerns about the child's fluency or voice quality based on his or her observations during the assessment thus far.

- *Oral mechanisms.* The administrator should note any concerns about the child's oral mechanisms (i.e., structural or functional problems such as poor tongue mobility that may interfere with speech) based on his or her observations during the assessment thus far.

Administration and Interpretation

"Either a bilingual speech pathologist or a trained bilingual aide working under the direction of a speech pathologist" (Compton & Kline, 2005, p. 1) may administer the measure.

"No special preparation is required for administration other than familiarity with the test materials and several practice trials to become acquainted with procedures for giving the evaluation" (Compton & Kline, 2005, p. 1). Nonetheless, given the focus on speech and language, individuals with training in this area (e.g., speech-language pathologists) are especially well suited to administer the Compton Speech and Language Screening Evaluation of Children.

Scoring Method

Administrators utilize a record sheet to document children's responses. For the Articulation and Vocabulary sections of the measure, administrators with training in speech-language pathology are encouraged to record the sound substitutions or distortions made by children. *In addition, administrators are asked to note whether children use the correct pronoun (la or el) within their responses.* The total number of correct and incorrect responses is then tallied.

Guidelines are provided for characterizing children as 1) passing, 2) in need of rescreening, or 3) in need of a speech evaluation. These guidelines "are based upon several years of extensive research on normal and abnormal linguistic development, information available from a variety of standard sources, and the trial-and-error results obtained during the course of administering this evaluation and the English counterpart to a population of approximately 500 monolingual (English) children *and 250 bilingual (Spanish) children representing 15 different Spanish speaking countries" (Compton & Kline, 2005, p. 11).*

Adaptations or Instructions for Use with Individuals with Disabilities

No information is provided in the manual.

FUNCTIONAL CONSIDERATIONS

Measure Development

The first prototype of the Compton Speech and Language Screening Evaluation of Children was developed in 1975 at the Institute of Child Language and Phonology. *The Spanish adaptation "parallels the English counterpart" (Compton & Kline, 2005, p. ii) as much as possible, allowing for comparisons of children's responses in English and Spanish for most items (when children are administered both versions).*

The Spanish adaptation may be used with monolingual Spanish-speaking children or bilinguals. When both the Spanish and English versions are administered, Compton and Kline stress that the Spanish version should be given before the English version (2005). However, there is no explanation for why this should be done.

Content Equivalence of Items and Measure

No information is provided in the manual about the process undertaken to create the Spanish version. However, some differences between the Spanish and English forms appear to capture key linguistic differences between the languages, such as gender in Spanish. It would be helpful, though, if the manual explained the rationale for the examiners' understanding.

Semantic Equivalence of Translations

No information is provided in the manual about the translation process undertaken, though most of the translations appear consistent and accurate.

Structural Consistency Across the English and Spanish Versions

There are some structural differences between the two forms, suggesting that the authors took the linguistic difference between the English and Spanish languages into account:

- The English form has a Possessive Pronouns Section for Item 6, and the Spanish form has an Object Pronouns Section. The Spanish items make reference to feminine and masculine pronouns and the English items ask about Possessive Pronouns, such as hers, mine, and yours.

- The Spanish form has two additional sections that assess children's linguistic skills with reflexive pronouns and with gender agreement with Spanish nouns, adverbs, and adjectives.

- The Spontaneous Language Sample section has one additional item on the English form that asks about the intelligibility of the child's conversational speech.

- The Spanish section for color recognition asks the child to recognize colors instead of naming them. The rationale for this difference is that during the development of the test, most bilingual children were able to recognize the colors in Spanish but could not name them in Spanish. However, the manual indicates that monolingual Spanish-speaking children are administered a color-naming task instead of a recognition one, which can be confusing to examiners.

Standardization Sample

According to the manual, the prototype for the **Compton Speech and Language Screening Evaluation of Children:** Spanish Adaptation was field-tested over 5 years with 250 children from Spanish-speaking families living in the San Francisco Bay Area. "Virtually all Latin America countries of origin were represented" within this sample (Compton & Kline, 2005, p. ii). There is, however, no explicit description of the standardization sample or the results of these tryouts.

Norming

Criterion referenced

Reliability

Test–Retest Reliability

No information is provided in the manual.

Internal Consistency

No information is provided in the manual.

Interrater Agreement

No information is provided in the manual.

Other Forms of Reliability (e.g., Equivalent Forms)

No information is provided in the manual.

Validity

Face and Content

Although the measure appears to assess the areas it purports to, no information about the sources for the items is provided in the manual. However, the test developers demonstrated a sound knowledge of the Spanish language.

Internal Construct

No information is provided in the manual.

External Construct

No information is provided in the manual.

Criterion

No information is provided in the manual.

Comparison of Psychometric Properties Between English and Spanish Versions

Technical Equivalence in Reliability

Not available, because neither the English nor Spanish version has been standardized.

Technical Equivalence in Validity

Not available, because neither the English nor Spanish version has been standardized.

RELEVANT STUDIES USING THE MEASURE

A brief literature search using PsycINFO and Google Scholar did not result in citations to any studies whose abstracts specified using the Compton Speech and Language Screening Evaluation of Children: Spanish. However, it is possible that this measure has been utilized in studies.

ADDITIONAL REFERENCES

None

Developmental Indicators for the Assessment of Learning–Fourth Edition (DIAL-4): English

Manual

Mardell, C., & Goldenberg, D.S. (2011). *Developmental Indicators for the Assessment of Learning–Fourth Edition Manual.* Bloomington, IL: Pearson Assessments.

Publisher

Pearson, Inc.
19500 Bulverde Road
San Antonio, TX 78259-3701
http://www.pearsonassessments.com

Cost

DIAL-4 kit: $625. Speed DIAL-4 (English and Spanish): $275.

Description of Measure

The DIAL-4 "is an individually administered developmental screener designed to identify children ages 2:6 through 5:11 who are in need of intervention or diagnostic assessment in the following areas: motor, concepts, language, self-help, and social-emotional skills" (Mardell & Goldenberg, 2011, p. 1). The DIAL-4 (2011) is an updated version of the DIAL-3 published in 1998 (see "Measure Development" for additional details).

Type of Measure

Direct child assessment, behavioral observations, Parent Questionnaire, and Teacher Questionnaire

Intended Age Range

2;6 years to 5;11 years

Key Constructs/Domains

- Motor
- Language
- Concepts
- Self-Help Development (questionnaires)
- Social-Emotional Development (questionnaires)

Available Languages and Formats

The DIAL-4 is also available in Spanish (updated concurrently with the English version). A shorter Speed DIAL-4 is also available. It consists of a subset of 10 of the 20 items on the full DIAL-4 and can be completed in approximately 20 minutes.

Strengths

The DIAL-4 helps educators to efficiently screen a large number of children who might be at risk for school failure resulting from developmental delays.

Clinical analyses were utilized to maximize and study the DIAL-4's ability to identify children with delays.

The measure, particularly the behavioral observations and Parent/Teacher Questionnaires that assess social skills and self-help skills, generally has solid reliability and validity, whereas other measures have weaker psychometrics.

The theoretical and empirical bases for each item were extensively examined and presented in the manual.

The tryout and standardization phases were conducted well.

Weaknesses

The motor scale may not solely reflect physical development. The Motor Area of the DIAL-4 correlates more highly with cognitive subtests of other measures than with motor tasks, which is not surprising as it includes items that are used as cognitive tasks on other measures.

Because the DIAL-4 is a screener, it is primarily analyzed with cutoff scores based on weighted scores. The use of percentiles and standard scores is secondary. Thus, there are gaps in the distribution of percentiles and standard scores, which may be important for some examiners.

ADMINISTRATION

Procedure

Items are presented one at a time using manipulatives or prompts. The direct assessment components of the Motor, Concepts, and Language Areas utilize either movable dials that allow the examiner to present a single stimulus at a time or other manipulatives such as wooden blocks or plastic chips. After the direct assessment, the examiner completes behavioral observations. Children's self-help and social-emotional skills are examined through parent and teacher report.

Time Needed
DIAL-4: About 30–45 minutes total (10–15 minutes for each of the three direct child assessment areas)
Speed DIAL-4: About 20 minutes total

The following are examples of items assessed within each domain:

Motor Area (7 items)

- Gross motor activities include throwing, hopping, and skipping. Fine motor activities include building with blocks, cutting, copying, and writing one's name.

Concepts Area (7 items)

- Concepts activities include pointing to body parts, naming or identifying colors, rote counting, counting blocks, and sorting shapes. The DIAL-4 also has an item that assesses rapid naming.

Language Area (6 items)

- Language activities include answering personal questions (e.g., name, age), articulating, and naming (i.e., expressive) or identifying (i.e., receptive) objects and actions. The DIAL-4 also includes phonemic awareness tasks such as rhyming and letter–sound correspondence.

Behavioral Observations

- After completing each domain, the child is rated by the operator in the following areas: separation from adult, crying/whining, verbal response to questions, persistence (nonverbal), attention, activity level, participation, impulsivity, ability to understand directions, and intelligibility.

Self-Help Development (22-item Parent Questionnaire and 10-item Teacher Questionnaire)

- Parents are asked to report on their child's personal care skills related to dressing, eating, and grooming. The Teacher Questionnaire also includes a number of self-help questions, though fewer than the Parent Questionnaire.

Social-Emotional Development (28-item Parent Questionnaire and 34-item Teacher Questionnaire)

- Parents and teachers are asked to report on the child's development of social skills with other children and adults (e.g., sharing, self-control, and empathy) as well as his or her emotional functioning (e.g., acts sad/withdrawn, whines/pouts).

Overall Development

- An open-ended question asks parents about the nature of development concerns (if any) that they may have.

Administration and Interpretation

A unique feature of the DIAL-4 is its flexibility in terms of administration. It can be administered by one operator to one child or in a group format. In the latter scenario, three examiners set up stations in each of the areas in a large room. Children then circulate to each of the stations, where they are asked to respond to questions or perform tasks related to one of the domains assessed.

The DIAL-4 manual suggests calling the examiners or assessors *operators.* Mardell and Goldenberg recommended that those using or supervising operators be competent in the use of the DIAL-4 and have an "ability to relate to young children of any linguistic or cultural background" (2011, p. 15). The coordinator of the assessments should be a "professional in special education, early childhood education, psychology, speech and language, school nursing, or another closely related Area" (p. 15). The manual details a list of responsibilities for the coordinator and operators.

A variety of training materials are available, including the manual, a training packet (including written and performance tests and role-playing scripts), and a video.

A discussion about interpreting potential delay results while considering socioeconomic, cultural, and linguistic characteristics is presented in the manual. Bilingual development in particular is reviewed.

Finally, it is recommended that the Parent Questionnaire be completed prior to testing.

Scoring Method

Children can respond in either English or Spanish to receive credit.

- *Motor, Concepts, and Language.* All of the tasks within an item are summed and then converted to an item weighted score. (For example, the alphabet song, letter naming, and letter–sound correspondence tasks are combined to create a weighted score for the fourth item, Letters and Sounds.) The weighted scores are on a 6-point scale, with 0 as the lowest and 5 as the highest. They are summed to obtain a total score for each domain. The Motor, Concepts, and Language Total Scores are then summed to obtain the DIAL-4 Total Score.
- *Behavioral Observations.* Children are rated on a 3-point scale on nine behaviors demonstrated during each of the Motor, Concepts, and Language assessments. For example, Understands Directions is rated 0 for easily understands, 1 for needs some repetition, or 2 for unable to understand. Scores on the nine items are summed to obtain a Total Score for each domain, and these domain scores are then added together for a Behavioral Observations Total Score. The children are also rated in their level of intelligibility, but this rating does not contribute to the score.
- *Self-Help Development and Social-Emotional Development.* Parents' and teachers' responses to questionnaire items are added to obtain a raw score for each area.

Cutoff scores for identifying children who may be experiencing delays (e.g., okay versus potential delay) are available for the DIAL-4 Total Score, each of the domain Total Scores, the Speed DIAL-4, the Parent Questionnaire, the Teacher Questionnaire, and the Behavioral Observations Total Score. Mardell and Goldenberg (2011) strongly advise that children who are identified as potentially delayed be referred to a professional for further assessment. For most domains, the examiner may choose one of five cutoff levels depending upon his or her needs and community factors: 1, 1.3, 1.5, 1.7, or 2 SD below the mean. In his review of the DIAL-3, Cizek (2001) noted that the manual had few suggestions to help examiners decide which cutoff to use. The DIAL-4 manual states that the cutoff is often made at the school or organization level and is related to the base rate in the community. For the Behavioral Observations domain, the cutoff score is 1.5 SD below the mean for the child's age. Contributing to this score were analyses that examined Behavioral Observations Total Scores with DIAL-4 Area scores and the questionnaires.

Percentile ranks and their corresponding standard scores are also available for DIAL-4 Total Score, each of the domain Total Scores, the Speed DIAL-4, the Parent Questionnaire, and the Teacher Questionnaire (but not the Behavioral Observations Total Score).

Adaptations or Instructions for Use with Individuals with Disabilities

No specific adaptations for use with children with special needs are indicated in the manual.

FUNCTIONAL CONSIDERATIONS

Measure Development

The DIAL was first developed as a developmental screening measure for young children in 1975, with assistance from an advisory board. This initial version was revised first in 1983 and then in 1990. Test items in the DIAL-3 (1998) were adapted based on the current research literature on screening of the five developmental areas (Motor, Concepts, Language, Self-Help Development, and Social-Emotional Development). At that point, the manual did not detail the use of additional advisory or expert panels. The DIAL-3 was used with children ages 3;0–6;11 years, and an abbreviated version (the Speed DIAL) was created from it (Fairbank, 2001). A Spanish version of the DIAL-3 was also created at this time.

The DIAL-4 was published in 2011 with a variety of changes. These include updated norms, a new Teacher Questionnaire, 21 new or revised items, new enter/exit rules, an expanded response scale, a new visual presentation (e.g., art, size format), simplified instructions, additional examples, and new training tools. In addition, the assessment of developmental domains across the five areas has been expanded, and the manual documents the alignment of the DIAL-4 content areas with domains that have been identified by early childhood organizations as important for child development. Furthermore, the English and Spanish versions were concurrently developed. Finally, the intended age range is now 2;6–5;11 years.

Development of the DIAL-4 included a concept development stage, a pilot stage, a tryout stage, and a standardization stage. Specifically, results from studies using previous versions of the DIAL were reviewed. A literature review was conducted on each of the items, along with a review focused on identifying the skills most predictive of school success. "In addition, new items were developed to include content that was identified as important by a variety of sources, including early-childhood experts, relevant state and federal legislation, and research" (Mardell & Goldenberg, 2011, p. 7). Early childhood professionals were invited to complete a survey, and 85 of about 800 completed it.

The pilot stage aimed to provide a preliminary analysis of the new items, the functioning of the items among the youngest children, the comparability of English and Spanish items, and the utility of administration and scoring procedures. At this stage, 100 children were assessed in English, and 27 children were assessed in Spanish. At this point, some items were dropped because of issues with administration, scoring, or insufficient item-level variability.

A total of 1,574 children participated in the DIAL-4 tryout stage, with 924 assessed in English and 650 assessed in Spanish. Additional data were collected for the items added to the Language Area after the start of the tryout stage, with 234 children assessed in English and 236 in Spanish. Children with delays and impairments were included in the sample to examine clinical utility and item adequacy. The aims of this stage were to examine items by difficulty, validity, and bias as well as to examine reliability, validity, and score distributions of subtest scores across age groups. Furthermore, continued attention was placed on artwork and examiner directions. "During this stage, all DIAL-4 items and tasks were reviewed by experts for their relevance, importance, and possible bias (with respect to sex and culture/ethnicity)" (Mardell & Goldenberg, 2011, p. 32). In additional, half of the sample was assigned to the individual assessment approach, whereas the other half was administered the test using the stations approach. Parents also completed the Parent Questionnaire. Comprehensive analyses were then undertaken, including item response theory analyses; differential item functioning analyses at the item and task levels to identify potential biases; exploratory and confirmatory factor analyses of the Parent Questionnaires within the English and Spanish versions; and Total Score analyses with attention to reliability, age variations, and level of difficulty. The analytic results were coupled with operator feedback to provide the final adjustments to the DIAL-4 prior to the standardization stage. Chapter 2 in the manual provided theoretical and empirical support for each of the final items on the DIAL-4.

Standardization Sample

A sample of 1,400 children was selected to norm the Motor, Concepts, and Language scales, with 182 completing the Spanish version and 1,218 completing the English version. The sample was stratified by gender, race/ethnicity, geographic region, chronological age, and socioeconomic status. The sample was created to be representative of 2008 Census results. Data collection occurred in the United States and Puerto Rico. The sample included children with clinical/educational diagnoses (7%), premature birth (12%), alcohol/drug abuse during pregnancy (5%), and low birth weight (8%). In addition, an effort was made to include children from multiple settings (child care, Head Start, preschool, home school), as the tryout results had found that younger children in child care or preschool settings scored higher than children who were not attending any program. Exclusionary criteria included impairments that precluded the use of the standard administration procedures, medication use that would impair performance, and a primary language other than English or Spanish.

During the standardization stage, a new Teacher Questionnaire was developed and examined using a combination of item analyses (e.g., classical test theory and IRT) and teacher and expert reviews for bias, relevance, and overall quality. Subsequently, 700 parents and 700 teachers completed their respective questionnaires. About 30% of the sample completed both Teacher and Parent Questionnaires.

Item analyses of the direct assessment items led to a reduction of tasks in the Concepts Area. Rasch-model analyses also led to the development of item scoring rules by optimizing the utility of items and tasks to differentiate children's performance by ability level. Weights were developed using a combination of content/age expectations, performance differentiation, reliability examination, and clinical group performances. Furthermore, the standardization data were subjected to logistic regression to identify the 10 items with the most clinical predictability for the Speed DIAL-4. Finally, the English–Spanish equating process occurred during this stage, as discussed in the separate Spanish review.

Norming

Norm referenced

Reliability

Test–Retest Reliability

The DIAL-4 was administered twice to 93 English-speaking children, with the amount of time between administrations not reported in the manual. The sample generally approximated the U.S. population. Results presented in the manual are organized into two age samples (2;6–3;11 and 4;0–5;11 years). The test–retest reliability coefficients were adequate for both groups. For example, the younger group obtained a .83 for the DIAL-4 Total Score, whereas the older group obtained a .88. The coefficients were slightly lower for the younger group on the direct assessment, though they were slightly higher on the questionnaires. The Parent Questionnaire's Self-Help Development section test–retest reliabilities were in the .65–.68 range, which is low. This may reflect rapid change in this area over time or a measurement issue.

Internal Consistency

The DIAL-4 Total Score has an average split-half reliability of .95, and the Speed DIAL has one of .91. The standard error of measurement (SEM) for the DIAL-4 Total Score is 2.8, whereas that for the Speed DIAL is 1.9. For each domain, the manual reports median reliability coefficients across age groupings that fall in the moderate to strong range. Corresponding median SEMs range from 1.2 to 1.9 for the direct assessment scores and from 1.3 to 2.6 for the questionnaires. As Cizek (2001) noted with the DIAL-3, the relatively weaker area is the Motor domain. However, this domain in the DIAL-4 is markedly improved from the prior version, which had reliability coefficients in the .59–.74 range. Now the Motor Area has reliability coefficients in the .74–.88 range. The questionnaires have moderate internal consistency (ranging from .83 for both the Parent and Teacher Questionnaires' Self-Help Development section to .93 for the Teacher Questionnaire's Social-Emotional Development section).

Interrater Agreement

Items that were subjective in terms of scoring were examined in interscorer reliability studies. Two individuals scored these items for 52–80 English cases. The average coefficients were high, ranging from .89 for the Writing Name task to .98 for Cutting.

Other Forms of Reliability (e.g., Equivalent Forms)

Not applicable

Validity

Face and Content

The face and content validities of the DIAL-4 are solid. Both developmental theory and empirical research findings on young children's development were taken into consideration in the revision. Expert panelists were involved throughout the revision. In addition, items were analyzed using examiner feedback and classical and IRT methods for both the tryout and standardization phases. Finally, bias reviews were conducted.

Internal Construct

For the Parent Questionnaire, "exploratory and confirmatory factor analyses were conducted on the English and Spanish versions to evaluate the two-factor model (i.e., self-help and social-emotional development) and to identify tasks that were weak indicators of the factors" (Mardell & Goldenberg, 2011, p. 33). Although a three-factor model may also have been supported, many items had cross-loadings. The two-factor structure was retained, and tasks with loadings less than .30 and tasks that did not function similarly across the English and Spanish versions were dropped.

Factor analyses were not conducted on the specific items across the Motor, Concepts, and Language Areas to examine their distribution across these areas. As may be expected, the areas are somewhat intercorrelated (.44–.68). Two articles have been published about the factor structure of the DIAL-3. Anthony, Assel, and Williams (2007) first reported that a different factor structure composed of Verbal Ability, Nonverbal Ability, and Achievement better described the performance of a low-income sample attending Head Start. What is interesting is that Assel and Anthony (2009) utilized the DIAL-3 full standardization sample to find that both the theoretical model presented in the DIAL-3 (Motor, Concepts, and Language) and the empirical model (Verbal Ability, Nonverbal Ability, and Achievement) fit equally well. Thus, there was support for the use of both approaches to the DIAL-3 in a nationally representative sample, though the empirical structure is a better fit within the Head Start sample examined (Assel & Anthony, 2009). The authors noted that this may reflect unique features of the low-income population or the shared experiences these children have in the Head Start program (Assel & Anthony, 2009).

External Construct

The manual presents analyses examining the validity of the DIAL-4 with children with special needs. As may be expected, children with a clinical diagnosis (including autism, developmental delay, physical impairment, speech-language impairment) scored lower than matched children with no clinical diagnosis in the pattern expected. For example, children with a speech-language impairment scored much lower in the Language Area and somewhat lower on concepts and the Parent Questionnaire.

The sensitivity, specificity, and agreement index of the DIAL-4 were examined to assess the clinical utility of this measure as a screener. The manual suggests that the results may be lower than expected for two reasons. First, children had to have been able to attempt every test item to be part of these analytic studies. Thus, the results may have differed if the sample had included children with more severe impairments. Second, children in the clinical samples were receiving remediation and treatment, which likely was beneficial and helped to improve their performance on the DIAL-4.

Although the results are presented at the 1 *SD* and 0.67 *SD* level, the focus of this review is at the 1 *SD* level because 0.67 *SD* is not one of the optional cutoff levels in the screener. Across the clinical groups, the sensitivity ranges from .49 to .74, the specificity from .82 to .89, and the agreement index from .66 to .78. At this basic cutoff (1 *SD*), these are generally acceptable for demonstrating that the DIAL-4 can be used as a screener (as intended) though not for full diagnostic purposes.

Finally, children's performance on the DIAL-4 was compared with their scores on the cognitive composite of the Differential Ability Scales–Second Edition (DAS-II). Sensitivity was .33, specificity was .95, and the agreement value was .92. As reported in the manual, "These results support the referral efficiency of the DIAL-4 total score" (Mardell & Goldenberg, 2011, p. 71).

Support for the convergent and discriminant validity of the DIAL-4 is also indicated by some the correlational studies described in "Criterion."

Criterion

Correlations among the different assessment modes on the DIAL-4 support its validity. For example, children scored lower on the direct assessment components as they exhibited more behavior difficulties. Furthermore, the correlation between the Parent and Teacher Questionnaires was higher within a domain (e.g., comparing Self-Help Development scores) than across domains (e.g., comparing teacher reports of self-help with parent reports of socioemotional development). Overall the correlations between the Parent and Teacher Questionnaires were at the level expected.

Concurrent criterion validity of the DIAL-4 was assessed via comparisons with various screening profiles, including the DIAL-3, the Early Screening Profiles (ESP), the Battelle Developmental Inventory–Second Edition (BDI-2), the DAS-II, and the parent and teacher versions of the Vineland–II Adaptive Behavior Scales. The sample size, geographic distribution, and intervals in test administration varied across studies.

As may be expected, high correlations were evidenced between the DIAL-4 and DIAL-3 (total adjusted score correlation = .85). In terms of its correspondence with other measures, strong support exists for the DIAL-4 Total Score and the Language score across all studies. Because language is incorporated into many of the DIAL-4 Concepts items, it is not surprising that this domain correlates highly with language subscales on other measures, sometimes even more than with cognitive or nonverbal subscales. Furthermore, the DIAL-4 Motor Area corresponds just as highly or even higher with the cognitive subscales of other measures, as it does with the motor subscales of other measures. This likely reflects the presence of both cognitive and motor skills in some tasks, such as block building and name writing. The manual also indicates that motor and cognitive development are highly connected in the early years, though this does not explain why the motor scales themselves correlated less well across measures.

Correlations of DIAL-4 scores with those from other measures were moderate in nature and generally supported the criterion validity of the DIAL-4, particularly when it came to the Total Score. For example, the adjusted correlation of the DIAL-4 Total Score with the ESP Cognitive/ Language Profile score was .68, with the BDI-2 Total score was .61, and with the DAS-II General Conceptual Ability score was .73. Concurrent validity was also demonstrated for many of the domain scores.

Lastly, the Parent and Teacher Questionnaires have also undergone examination. DIAL-4 Total Scores have moderate correlations with the Vineland Scales across both the parent and teacher versions, indicating that children scoring higher on this direct assessment are functioning at higher levels at home and school. As may be expected, the parent report on the DIAL-4 Self-Help Development scale correlated well with the parent report of Daily Living Skills on the Vineland. However, the parent report comparison of the DIAL-4's Social-Emotional Development and the Vineland's Socialization scale (and its subscales) was weak. The opposite pattern was seen among the Teacher Questionnaires. A solid correlation was present between the Teacher Questionnaires across the DIAL-4 Socio-Emotional Development and the Vineland's Socialization scale. Teacher scores on the Self-Help Development component of the DIAL-4 correlated highly with the Vineland's Daily Skills (.56) but even more highly with its Socialization scale (.69). These patterns indicate stronger validity for parent reports of daily living skills and for teacher reports of socioemotional skills.

RELEVANT STUDIES USING THE MEASURE

A brief literature search using PsycINFO and Google Scholar did not find any articles that mentioned using the DIAL-4, as it had not yet been published at the time of this review. However, the DIAL-3 was used by preschools in a statewide survey (Pretti-Frontczak, Kowalski, & Brown, 2002). It has also been utilized in dissertation studies. Older versions of the DIAL have also been utilized in studies.

ADDITIONAL REFERENCES

Anthony, J.L., & Assel, M.A. (2007). A first look at the validity of the Spanish version of the DIAL-3. *Journal of Psychoeducational Assessment, 25,* 165–179.

Anthony, J.L., Assel, M.A., & Williams, J. (2007). Exploratory and confirmatory factor analyses of the DIAL-3: What does this "screener" really measure? *Journal of School Psychology, 45,* 423–438.

(continued)

Assel, M.A., & Anthony, J.L. (2009). Factor structure of the DIAL-3: A test of the theory-driven conceptualization versus an empirically driven conceptualization in a nationally representative sample. *Journal of Psychoeducational Assessment, 27,* 113–124.

Chen, T.-H., Wang, J.-J., Mardell-Czudnowski, C., Goldenberg, D.S., & Elliott, C. (2000). The development of the Spanish version of the Developmental Indicators for the Assessment of Learning–Third Edition (DIAL-3). *Journal of Psychoeducational Assessment, 18,* 316–343.

Cizek, G.J. (2001). Test review of the Developmental Indicators for the Assessment of Learning, Third Edition. In B.S. Plake & J.C. Impara (Eds.), *The fourteenth mental measurements yearbook.* Retrieved from the Buros Institute's *Test Reviews Online* web site: http://www.unl.edu/buros

Fairbank, D.W. (2001). Test review of the Developmental Indicators for the Assessment of Learning, Third Edition. In B.S. Plake & J.C. Impara (Eds.), *The fourteenth mental measurements yearbook.* Retrieved from the Buros Institute's *Test Reviews Online* web site: http://www.unl.edu/buros

Pretti-Frontczak, K., Kowalski, K., & Brown, R.D. (2002). Preschool teachers' use of assessments and curricula: A statewide examination. *Exceptional Children, 69,* 109–123.

Developmental Indicators for the Assessment of Learning–Fourth Edition (DIAL-4): Spanish

Information pertaining specifically to the Spanish version of the measure is in bold and italics. The remainder is equivalent information provided in the English review.

Manual

Mardell, C., & Goldenberg, D.S. (2011). *Developmental Indicators for the Assessment of Learning–Fourth Edition Manual.* Bloomington, IL: Pearson Assessments.

Publisher

Pearson, Inc.
19500 Bulverde Road
San Antonio, TX 78259-3701
http://www.pearsonassessments.com

Cost

Complete Basic Kit: $625. *Spanish Administration Forms: $85.*

Type of Measure

Direct child assessment, behavioral observations, Parent Questionnaire, and Teacher Questionnaire

Intended Age Range

2;6 years to 5;11 years

Key Constructs/Domains

- Motor
- Language
- Concepts
- Self-Help Development (questionnaires)
- Social-Emotional Development (questionnaires)

Description of Measure

The DIAL-4 "is an individually administered developmental screener designed to identify children ages 2:6 through 5:11 who are in need of intervention or diagnostic assessment in the following areas: motor, concepts, language, self-help, and social-emotional skills" (Mardell & Goldenberg, 2011, p. 1). The DIAL-4 (2011) is an updated version of the DIAL-3 published in 1998 (see "Measure Development" for additional details).

Available Languages and Formats

The DIAL-4 is also available in English (updated concurrently with the Spanish version). A shorter Speed DIAL-4 is also available. It consists of a subset of 10 of the 20 items on the full DIAL-4 and can be completed in approximately 20 minutes.

Strengths

The DIAL-4 helps educators to efficiently screen a large number of children who might be at risk for school failure resulting from developmental delays.

The theoretical and empirical bases for each item were extensively examined *for the Spanish version* and are presented in the manual.

The tryout and standardization phases were conducted well.

Like the English version, the Spanish DIAL-4, particularly the Social-Emotional Development and Self-Help Development, generally has solid reliability and validity, whereas other measures have weaker psychometrics.

The development and norming of the DIAL-4 Spanish were conducted concurrently. Furthermore, the approaches used to develop the Spanish version were generally solid and are well documented in the manual.

The Spanish version of the DIAL-4 was statistically equated with the English version, which allows for a direct comparison of children's results on each measure.

Conceptual scoring is allowed for some of the direct assessment items.

Weaknesses

The external construct and criterion validity of the Spanish DIAL-4 likely should be separately examined.

Data from studies of the English version suggest that the Motor Area may not solely reflect physical development. No studies were available for the Spanish version to examine this. However, the equating studies suggested direct equivalence between the Motor subtests across languages. Thus, this potential weakness of the English version may be applicable to the Spanish version.

Because the DIAL-4 is a screener, it is primarily analyzed with cutoff scores based on weighted scores. The use of percentiles and standard scores is secondary. Thus, there are gaps in the distribution of percentiles and standard scores, which may be important for some examiners.

ADMINISTRATION

Procedure

Items are presented one at a time using manipulatives or prompts. The direct assessment components of the Motor, Concepts, and Language areas utilize either movable dials that allow the examiner to present a single stimulus at a time or other manipulatives such as wooden blocks or plastic chips. After the direct assessment, the examiner completes behavioral observations. Children's self-help and social-emotional skills are examined through parent and teacher report.

Time Needed
DIAL-4: About 30–45 minutes total (10–15 minutes for each of the three direct child assessment areas)
Speed DIAL-4: About 20 minutes total

The following are examples of items assessed within each domain:

Motor Area (7 items)

- Gross motor activities include throwing, hopping, and skipping. Fine motor activities include building with blocks, cutting, copying, and writing one's name.

Concepts Area (7 items)

- Concepts activities include pointing to body parts, naming or identifying colors, rote counting, counting blocks, and sorting shapes. The DIAL-4 also has an item that assesses rapid naming.

Language Area (6 items)

- Language activities include answering personal questions (e.g., name, age), articulating, and naming (i.e., expressive) or identifying (i.e., receptive) objects and actions. The DIAL-4 also includes phonemic awareness tasks such as letter–sound correspondence.

- *Rhyming questions are not included in the Spanish version because a growing body of literature does not support their use as a linguistic or academic indicator among Spanish speakers. Two other differences in the items include Articulation and I Spy, for which different words and phonemes are used.*

Behavioral Observations

- After completing each domain, the child is rated by the operator in the following areas: separation from adult, crying/whining, verbal response to questions, persistence (nonverbal), attention, activity level, participation, impulsivity, ability to understand directions, and intelligibility.

Self-Help Development (22-item Parent Questionnaire and 10-item Teacher Questionnaire)

- Parents are asked to report on their child's personal care skills related to dressing, eating, and grooming. The Teacher Questionnaire also includes a number of self-help questions, though fewer than the Parent Questionnaire.

Social-Emotional Development (28-item Parent Questionnaire and 34-item Teacher Questionnaire)

- Parents and teachers are asked to report on the child's development of social skills with other children and adults (e.g., sharing, self-control, and empathy) as well as his or her emotional functioning (e.g., acts sad/withdrawn, whines/pouts).

Overall Development

- An open-ended question asks parents about the nature of development concerns (if any) that they may have.

Administration and Interpretation

A unique feature of the DIAL-4 is its flexibility in terms of administration. It can be administered by one operator to one child or in a group format. In the latter scenario, three examiners set up stations in each of the areas in a large room. Children then circulate to each of the stations, where they are asked to respond to questions or perform tasks related to one of the domains assessed.

The DIAL-4 manual suggests calling the examiners or assessors *operators*. Mardell and Goldenberg recommended that those using or supervising operators be competent in the use of the DIAL-4 and have an "ability to relate to young children of any linguistic or cultural background" (2011, p. 15). The coordinator of the assessments should be a "professional in special education, early childhood education, psychology, speech and language, school nursing, or another closely related Area" (p. 15). The manual details a list of responsibilities for the coordinator and operators. *Coordinators should be fluent in Spanish and English or be able to work with qualified interpreters in order to be able to monitor the competency levels of team members in both languages and to be able to provide training workshops.*

A variety of training materials are available, including the manual, a training packet (including written and performance tests and role-playing scripts), and a video.

A discussion about interpreting potential delay results while considering socioeconomic, cultural, and linguistic characteristics is presented in the manual. Bilingual development in particular is reviewed.

Finally, it is recommended that the Parent Questionnaire be completed prior to testing.

For the prior DIAL-3, Fairbanks (2003) estimates that approximately four hours of training is required for the English and Spanish version together.

Scoring Method

Children can respond in either English or Spanish to receive credit.

- *Motor, Concepts, and Language.* All of the tasks within an item are summed and then converted to an item weighted score. (For example, the alphabet song, letter naming, and letter–sound correspondence tasks are combined to create a weighted score for the fourth item, Letters and Sounds.) The weighted scores are on a 6-point scale, with 0 as the lowest and 5 as the highest. They are summed to obtain a total score for each domain. The Motor, Concepts, and Language Total Scores are then summed to obtain the DIAL-4 Total Score.

- *Behavioral Observations.* Children are rated on a 3-point scale on nine behaviors demonstrated during each of the Motor, Concepts, and Language assessments. For example, Understands Directions is rated 0 for easily understands, 1 for needs some repetition, or 2 for unable to understand. Scores on the nine items are summed to obtain a Total Score for each domain, and these domain scores are then added together for a Behavioral Observations Total Score. The children are also rated in their level of intelligibility, but this rating does not contribute to the score.

- *Self-Help Development and Social-Emotional Development.* Parents' and teachers' responses to questionnaire items are added to obtain a raw score for each Area.

Cutoff scores for identifying children who may be experiencing delays (e.g., okay versus potential delay) are available for the DIAL-4 Total Score, each of the domain Total Scores, the Speed DIAL-4, the Parent Questionnaire, the Teacher Questionnaire, and the Behavioral Observations Total Score. Mardell and Goldenberg (2011) strongly advised that children who are identified as potentially delayed be referred to a professional for further assessment. For most domains, the examiner may choose one of five cutoff levels depending upon his or her needs and community factors: 1, 1.3, 1.5, 1.7, or 2 *SD* below the mean. In his review of the DIAL-3, Cizek (2001) noted that the manual had few suggestions to help examiners decide which cutoff to use. The DIAL-4 manual states that the cutoff is often made at the school or organization level and is related to the base rate in the community. For the Behavioral Observations domain, the cutoff score is 1.5 *SD* below the mean for the child's age. Contributing to this score were analyses that examined Behavioral Observations Total Scores with DIAL-4 Area scores and the questionnaires.

Percentile ranks and their corresponding standard scores are also available for the DIAL-4 Total Score, each of the domain Total Scores, the Speed DIAL-4, the Parent Questionnaire, and the Teacher Questionnaire (but not the Behavioral Observations Total Score).

Adaptations or Instructions for Use with Individuals with Disabilities

No specific adaptations for use with children with special needs are indicated in the manual.

FUNCTIONAL CONSIDERATIONS

Measure Development

The DIAL was first developed as a developmental screening measure for young children in 1975, with assistance from an advisory board. This initial version was revised first in 1983 and then in 1990. Test items in the DIAL-3 (1998) were adapted based on the current research literature on screening of the five developmental areas (Motor, Concepts, Language, Self-Help Development, and Social-Emotional Development). At that point, the manual did not detail the use of additional advisory or expert panels. The DIAL-3 was used with children ages 3;0–6;11 years, and an abbreviated version (the Speed DIAL) was created from it (Fairbank, 2001). *A Spanish version of the DIAL-3 was also created at this time.*

(continued)

The DIAL-4 was published in 2011 with a variety of changes. These include updated norms, a new Teacher Questionnaire, 21 new or revised items, new enter/exit rules, an expanded response scale, a new visual presentation (e.g., art, size format), simplified instructions, additional examples, and new training tools. In addition, the assessment of developmental domains across the five areas has been expanded, and the manual documents the alignment of the DIAL-4 content areas with domains identified by early childhood organizations as important for child development. *Furthermore, the English and Spanish versions were concurrently developed*. Finally, the intended age range is now 2;6–5;11 years.

Development of the DIAL-4 included a concept development stage, a pilot stage, a tryout stage, and a standardization stage. Specifically, results from studies using previous versions of the DIAL were reviewed. A literature review was conducted on each of the items, along with a review focused on identifying the skills most predictive of school success. "In addition, new items were developed to include content that was identified as important by a variety of sources, including early-childhood experts, relevant state and federal legislation, and research" (Mardell & Goldenberg, 2011, p. 7). Early childhood professionals were invited to complete a survey, and 85 of about 800 completed it.

The pilot stage aimed to provide a preliminary analysis of the new items, the functioning of the items among the youngest children, *the comparability of English and Spanish items,* and the utility of administration and scoring procedures. At this stage, 100 children were assessed in English, and *27 children were assessed in Spanish.* At this point, some items were dropped because of issues with administration, scoring, or insufficient item-level variability.

A total of 1,574 children participated in the DIAL-4 tryout stage, with 924 assessed in English and *650 assessed in Spanish.* Additional data were collected for the items added to the Language Area after the start of the tryout stage, with 234 children assessed in English *and 236 in Spanish.* Children with delays and impairments were included in the sample to examine clinical utility and item adequacy. The aims of this stage were to examine items by difficulty, validity, and bias as well as to examine reliability, validity, and score distributions of subtest scores across age groups. Furthermore, continued attention was placed on artwork and examiner directions. "During this stage, all DIAL-4 items and tasks were reviewed by experts for their relevance, importance, and possible bias (with respect to sex and culture/ethnicity). *In addition, bilingual experts reviewed the English and Spanish items and tasks and the appropriateness of translations" (Mardell & Goldenberg, 2011, p. 32). This included particular attention to the articulation, phonemic awareness, and rhyming tasks. Attention was paid to variations in culture and dialects through intensive expert reviews.*

Furthermore, half of the sample was assigned to the individual assessment approach whereas the other half was administered the test using the stations approach. Parents also completed the Parent Questionnaire. Comprehensive analyses were then undertaken *separately for both the English and the Spanish versions.* These included item response theory analyses and differential item functioning analyses at the item and task levels to identify potential biases, *with attention being paid to comparing identical items across the English and Spanish forms.* Furthermore, *exploratory and confirmatory factor analyses were conducted of the Parent Questionnaires within the English and Spanish versions.* Total Score analyses attended to reliability, age variations, and level of difficulty. The analytic results were coupled with operator feedback to provide the final adjustments to the DIAL-4 prior to the standardization stage. Chapter 2 in the manual provides theoretical and empirical support for each of the final items on the DIAL-4, *including the Spanish items.*

As with the DIAL-3, the DIAL-4 used a statistical equating procedure for the English and Spanish versions (versus engaging in separate norming procedures). Thus, the same norm tables are used, and a direct comparison of children's performance on the two language versions can be made in reference to a common normative sample. The

DEVELOPMENTAL INDICATORS FOR THE ASSESSMENT OF LEARNING–FOURTH EDITION (DIAL-4): SPANISH *equating procedures for the Motor, Concepts, and Language areas were conducted with IRT analyses. Common items identified through qualitative and quantitative procedures were used to link the scores (Chen, Wang, Mardell-Czudnowski, Goldenberg, & Elliott, 2000). Attention was also paid to items that differed across language groups. For example, the Language question about actions is harder for English-speaking children than Spanish-speaking children, whereas the Concepts question about body parts is harder for Spanish speakers. Thus, these items have different weights for the English and Spanish versions, as evidenced in comparing the English and Spanish record forms.*

"For the Parent and Teacher Questionnaires, the English and Spanish versions were not equated because bias analyses showed the most tasks on these areas performed similarly across forms" (Mardell & Goldenberg, 2011, p. 40). The manual does not identify which or how many items differed in their functioning across the questionnaires. The manual does not discuss the Behavioral Observations scores or cutoffs for the Spanish version.

Content Equivalence of Items and Measure

The English and Spanish versions of the DIAL-4 were developed simultaneously, which increases the content equivalence of the measures. As noted in the Measure Development section, multiple steps were taken to examine the appropriateness of the items across the languages.

Semantic Equivalence of Translations

As described, the items were translated and reviewed for their accuracy and utility with the Spanish-speaking population, including people speaking dialectical variations. This part of the test development included both qualitative and quantitative examination.

Structural Consistency Across the English and Spanish Versions

The English and Spanish versions are structurally similar. The only differences are the omission of the Rhyming task in the Spanish version because of its limited applicability and utility as well as adjustments made to the Articulation and I Spy items based upon expert input. These differences are accounted for in score weighting procedures across the English and Spanish versions.

Standardization Sample

A sample of 1,400 children was selected to norm the Motor, Concepts, and Language scales, *with 182 completing the Spanish version* and 1,218 completing the English version. The sample was stratified by gender, race/ethnicity, geographic region, chronological age, and socioeconomic status. The sample was created to be representative of 2008 Census results. Data collection occurred in the United States and Puerto Rico, *with the majority of the Spanish forms collected in Puerto Rico.* The sample included children with clinical/educational diagnoses (7%), premature birth (12%), alcohol/drug abuse during pregnancy (5%), and low birth weight (8%). In addition, an effort was made to include children from multiple settings (child care, Head Start, preschool, home school), as the tryout results had found that younger children in child care or preschool settings scored higher than children who were not attending any program. Exclusionary criteria included impairments that precluded the use of standard administration procedures, medication use that would impair performance, and a primary language other than English or Spanish.

During the standardization stage, the Teacher Questionnaire was developed and examined using a combination of item analyses (e.g., classical test theory and IRT) and teacher and expert reviews for bias, relevance, and overall quality. Subsequently, 700 parents and 700 teachers completed the respective questionnaires. About 30% of the sample completed both Teacher and Parent Questionnaires.

Furthermore, a Spanish-speaking calibration sample for the equating procedures was created from Spanish-speaking cases drawn from either the larger standardization or equating samples. A total of 502 children from all regions of the United States and Puerto Rico participated. The sample was stratified by socioeconomic status, gender, Hispanic country of origin, and clinical status. In contrast to the greater representation of Spanish-speaking children from Puerto Rico in the normative sample, the final Spanish-speaking calibration sample included 62% Mexicans, 21% Caribbeans, and 16% people of other Hispanic origin/descent.

Item analyses of the direct assessment items led to a reduction of tasks in the Concepts Area. Rasch-model analyses also led to the development of item scoring rules by optimizing the utility of items and tasks to differentiate children's performance by ability level. Weights were developed using a combination of content/age expectations, performance differentiation, reliability examination, and clinical group performances. Furthermore, the standardization data were subjected to logistic regression to identify the 10 items with the most clinical predictability for the Speed DIAL-4.

Norming

Norm referenced

Reliability

Test–Retest Reliability

The Spanish DIAL-4 was administered twice to 81 children, with the amount of time between administrations not reported in the manual. The sample generally approximated the U.S. population. Results presented in the manual are organized into two age samples (2;6–3;11 and 4;0–5;11 years). The test–retest reliability coefficients of the Spanish version were strong for both groups, even higher than for the English version. For example, the younger group obtained a .91 for the DIAL-4 Total Score, whereas the older group obtained a .92. The coefficients were similar across age groups for the direct assessment tasks and the questionnaires.

Internal Consistency

The DIAL-4 Total Score for the Spanish version has an average split-half reliability of .96, and the Speed DIAL has one of .95, which is similar to those of the English version. The standard error of measurement (SEM) for the DIAL-4 Total Score is 2.8, whereas that for the Speed DIAL is 1.7. For each domain, the manual reports median alpha reliabilities across age groupings that fall in the moderate to strong range for the direct assessments (.86–.96). The questionnaires have moderate internal consistency (ranging from .79 on the Parent Questionnaire's Social-Emotional Development section to .90 on the Teacher Questionnaire's Social-Emotional Development section). Corresponding median SEMs range from 1.2 to 1.7 for the direct assessment scores and from 1.3 to 2.7 for the questionnaires.

Interrater Agreement

Items that were subjective in terms of scoring were examined in interscorer reliability studies, in which two individuals both scored each of these items for 46–47 Spanish cases. The average coefficients were high for the three items from the Motor area that were scored using a random sample of 60–80 English- and Spanish-speaking cases from the normative sample, ranging from .89 for the Writing Name task to .98 for Cutting. Among the two Spanish language items scored with a sample of just 46–47 Spanish-speaking cases, the coefficients were .90 for Problem Solving and .94 for Expressive Objects and Actions.

Other Forms of Reliability (e.g., Equivalent Forms)

Not applicable

Validity

Face and Content

The face and content validities of the Spanish DIAL-4 are solid. The measure was developed concurrently with the English version, and the two are statistically equated. Theoretical and empirical research findings on young Spanish-speaking children's development were used to guide the revision. Experts on Spanish speakers and bilingual development were involved. In addition, items were analyzed using examiner feedback and classical and IRT methods for both the tryout and standardization phases. Finally, bias reviews were conducted at multiple levels.

Internal Construct

For the Parent Questionnaire, "exploratory and confirmatory factor analyses were conducted on the English and Spanish versions to evaluate the two-factor model (i.e., self-help and social-emotional development) and to identify tasks that were weak indicators of the factors" (Mardell & Goldenberg, 2011, p. 33). Although a three-factor model may also have been supported, many items had cross-loadings. The two-factor structure was retained, and tasks with loadings less than .30 and tasks that did not function similarly across the English and Spanish versions were dropped.

Factor analyses were not conducted on the specific items across the Motor, Concepts, and Language areas to examine their distribution across these domains. *As may be expected, the areas are somewhat intercorrelated (.52–.74). Factor analyses were conducted by Anthony and Assel (2007) on the Spanish DIAL-3 using two samples. Similar to their results for the English version (Anthony, Assel, & Williams, 2007), a different factor structure composed of Verbal Ability, Nonverbal Ability, and Achievement better described the performance of Spanish-speaking children attending Head Start. As noted in the English review, subsequent analyses with the full English standardization sample found support for the original DIAL-3 theoretical model (Assel & Anthony, 2009). It is unknown whether these findings would extend to a national sample of Spanish-speaking children. The findings by Anthony and Assel (2007) suggested a different structure among Spanish-speaking Head Start children that may reflect unique features of the low-income population or the shared experiences these children have in the Head Start program (Assel & Anthony, 2009).*

External Construct

The ability of the Spanish DIAL-4 to identify Spanish-speaking children with disabilities remains to be examined, although the statistical equating approach utilized suggests that this ability is likely similar to that of the English version.

Criterion

The criterion validity of the Spanish DIAL-4 needs to be examined separately given that some of the comparison measures are available in Spanish and themselves have varying psychometric properties in Spanish.

Comparison of Psychometric Properties Between English and Spanish Versions

Technical Equivalence in Reliability

Overall, the reliability results of the English and Spanish versions are similar and even slightly more solid for the Spanish version.

Technical Equivalence in Validity

The validity of the English and Spanish versions is generally equivalent. However, the external construct and criterion validities of the Spanish version could benefit from additional examination.

RELEVANT STUDIES USING THE MEASURE

A brief literature search using PsycINFO and Google Scholar did not result in any citations for the Spanish version of the DIAL-4, as it had not yet been published at the time of this review. However, it is possible that prior versions of the measure have been utilized in studies.

ADDITIONAL REFERENCES

Anthony, J.L., & Assel, M.A. (2007). A first look at the validity of the Spanish version of the DIAL-3. *Journal of Psychoeducational Assessment, 25,* 165–179.

Anthony, J.L., Assel, M.A., & Williams, J. (2007). Exploratory and confirmatory factor analyses of the DIAL-3: What does this "screener" really measure? *Journal of School Psychology, 45,* 423–438.

Assel, M.A., & Anthony, J. L. (2009). Factor structure of the DIAL-3: A test of the theory-driven conceptualization versus an empirically driven conceptualization in a nationally representative sample. *Journal of Psychoeducational Assessment, 27,* 113–124.

Chen, T.-H., Wang, J.-J., Mardell-Czudnowski, C., Goldenberg, D.S., & Elliott, C. (2000). The development of the Spanish version of the Developmental Indicators for the Assessment of Learning-Third Edition (DIAL-3). *Journal of Psychoeducational Assessment, 18,* 316–343.

Cizek, G.J. (2001). Test review of the Developmental Indicators for the Assessment of Learning, Third Edition. In B.S. Plake & J.C. Impara (Eds.), *The fourteenth mental measurements yearbook*. Retrieved from the Buros Institute's *Test Reviews Online* web site: http://www.unl.edu/buros

Early Literacy Skills Assessment (ELSA): English

Manual

DeBruin-Parecki, A. (2005). *Early Literacy Skills Assessment User Guide.* Ypsilanti, MI: High/Scope Press.

Publisher

High/Scope Press
600 North River Street
Ypsilanti, MI 48198-2898
http://www.highscope.org

Cost

Complete kit: $149.95 (featuring either *Violet's Adventure* or *Dante Grows Up*). Items sold separately.

Type of Measure

Direct child assessment

Intended Age Range

3;0 years to 5;11 years

Key Constructs/Domains

- Comprehension
- Phonological awareness
- Alphabetic principle
- Concepts about print

Description of Measure

The purpose of this assessment is to "provide preschool programs and teachers with an authentic and meaningful way to assess young children's early literacy" (DeBruin-Parecki, 2005, p. 1).

Available Languages and Formats

A Spanish version is also available. The ELSA book-reading session has two forms (e.g., books): *Violet's Adventure* and *Dante Grows Up.*

Strengths

The ELSA format resembles an activity that is familiar to children (i.e., one-to-one reading).

The factor structure of the ELSA is well established, and three of the four Content Areas (Phonological Awareness, Alphabetic Principle, and Concepts About Print) generally have good psychometric properties.

Having alternative story forms (*Dante Grows Up* and *Violet's Adventure*) decreases the chance that children will improve on a measure because of previous experience (e.g., test–retest effects) rather than their own development in the domains assessed.

Weaknesses

The criterion validity of the Comprehension Content Area has not yet been established. This is because of the paucity of available assessments in this domain (A. DeBruin-Parecki, personal communication, June 18, 2009). Analyses also suggest that the Comprehension Content Area may not differentiate well among children of varying ages and abilities.

According to Cheadle (2007), there may be some floor effects on the ELSA, and the ELSA may work better with children older than 45 months, particularly if it is being used for a one-time assessment.

Raw scores can be transformed to a three-level skill designation (Level 1: Early Emergent, Level 2: Emergent, Level 3: Competent Emergent), though the process for creating the levels is not well described in the manual. The validity of the levels has not been examined. The levels were designed to match the Growing Readers Curriculum (A. DeBruin-Parecki, personal communication, June 18, 2009). However, the use of the raw scores is suggested by DeBruin-Parecki.

ADMINISTRATION

Procedure

The ELSA assesses early literacy skills during a book-reading interaction with children. Two assessment books (*Violet's Adventure* and *Dante Grows Up*) were developed for the ELSA. The administrator begins by saying to the child: "(Name of Child), today we are going to read a book together called *Violet's Adventure* (or *Dante Grows Up*). While we are reading the book I will be writing down some of the wonderful things you tell me about the story" (DeBruin-Parecki, 2005, p. 5). After the instructions are explained, the examiner begins to read the assessment book and asks the child items as they appear in the story. For example, the examiner asks the child questions assessing the extent of comprehension, phonological awareness, alphabet knowledge, and concepts about print throughout the storytelling activity.

Time Needed
15–20 minutes

Though the instrument looks like a children's book that can be kept in the classroom and read for leisure, using the instrument in such a way "would diminish the integrity of the assessment, due to practice effects" (DeBruin-Parecki, 2005, p. 1).

Administration and Interpretation

It is recommended that a teacher or adult familiar with the child administer the measure. The manual also suggests that the examiner be familiar with the ELSA, practice reading it several times out loud, and practice it with a child who will not be given the measure. It is recommended that first-time ELSA users undergo a training session through High/Scope. In addition, a DVD (*Scoring the ELSA: Establishing Reliability*) is available to increase the interrater reliability of the measure.

Scoring Method

There are three score sheets for the ELSA (ELSA Score Sheet, ELSA Child Summary form, ELSA Class Summary form). The ELSA Score Sheet is used to document responses during the assessment. The Child Summary is used to transform children's raw scores into their developmental level (Level 1: Early Emergent, Level 2: Emergent, Level 3: Competent Emergent) for each of the four early literacy areas, following the manual's directions. These levels were determined using ELSA sample data, though the method used is not described. Standard scores are not provided. Finally, the Class Summary represents the level (or raw) scores for all children in a class. Scoring is conducted manually.

Adaptations or Instructions for Use with Individuals with Disabilities

The measure can be completed in two sessions for children with special needs and/or whose primary language is not English. Before beginning the second session, the examiner needs to summarize the part of the story completed during the first session through a picture walk (DeBruin-Parecki, 2005).

FUNCTIONAL CONSIDERATIONS

Measure Development

The ELSA was designed to assess early literacy skills through an authentic assessment (i.e., "one that engages children in a task that is personally meaningful, takes place in real life context, and is grounded in naturally occurring instructional activity," DeBruin-Parecki, 2005,

p. 1). It was developed to assess four key areas of early literacy identified in the reading research. Additional information about how the items were developed, refined, and selected is not provided in the manual.

Standardization Sample

According to an ELSA psychometric report (Cheadle, 2007), more than 1,000 children are in the sample. As Eigenbrood noted, the manual does not present information about how the sample was selected, though the sample matched U.S. demographics in terms of race/ethnicity and gender (2007).

A total of 535 children in the sample were administered the *Dante* form, and 505 used the *Violet* form. "Averaging over both samples, the average child was approximately 52 months old at the first assessment and 57.7 months old at the second, so that the average child was assessed 5.5 months after the initial assessment" (Cheadle, 2007, p. 16). About 60% of children in both samples attended subsidized programs (such as Head Start). In general, the *Dante* sample (26% white, 34% African American, 26% Hispanic) was more diverse than the *Violet* sample (71% white, 12% African American, 3% Hispanic).

Norming

Criterion referenced

Reliability

Test–Retest Reliability

This information is not provided in the manual.

Internal Consistency

The pilot data presented in the manual are indicative of weaker reliability in some domains, particularly when the measure was administered in the fall of an academic year when preschool children were younger. Eigenbrood noted, "The reliability coefficients were higher for each of the subscales for the spring administration for each of the four areas with large differences for Comprehension (.69 [*fall*]–.83[*spring*]) and Phonological Awareness (.57[*fall*]–.67[*spring*])" (2007, emphasis added).

Stronger statistics were found in a follow-up ELSA psychometric report (Cheadle, 2007): pretest: Comprehension = .89, Phonological Awareness = .81, Alphabetic Principle = .96, and Concepts About Print = .82; posttest: Comprehension = .91, Phonological Awareness = .80, Alphabetic Principle = .93, and Concepts About Print = .85.

These results suggest that the ELSA has medium to high internal consistency. Particularly strong is the Alphabetic Principle Content Area; the Phonological Awareness Content Area is the least consistent, though still quite acceptable.

Interrater Agreement

This information is not provided in the manual, though the author recalls high interrater reliability during the measure's development (A. DeBruin-Parecki, personal communication, June 18, 2009).

Other Forms of Reliability (e.g., Equivalent Forms)

The ELSA has two forms: *Dante Grows Up* and *Violet's Adventure*. Cheadle (2007) found that they are statistically equivalent.

Validity

Face and Content

"The content validity of the ELSA was first established by linking all items to four key principles of early literacy measured by ELSA and identified in the scientifically based research literature: comprehension, phonological awareness, alphabetic principle, and concepts about print" (DeBruin-Parecki, 2005, p. 24). The procedure for deciding which items to assess in these areas is not described, which Eigenbrood (2007) has also noted. Overall, the measure appears to measure the intended constructs.

Internal Construct

Factor analyses were conducted by Cheadle, who found the following: "Factor structures for both the English and Spanish-speaking versions across the ELSA instruments adequately reproduced the observed variation in the data; factor loadings were typically high, indicating that the items had adequate discrimination; factor structures were similar over time, indicating that the instrument factor models were largely invariant, suggesting that the same constructs are measured on both the pre- and posttests" (2007, p. 8).

External Construct

According to the manual, older children scored higher on *Violet's Adventure* than younger children. Comprehension scores did not improve, though, between 3- and 4-year-olds. Also, children with disabilities scored lower on all Content Areas except for Comprehension.

According to Cheadle (2007), there may be some floor effects on the ELSA, and the ELSA may work better with children older than 45 months, particularly if it is being used for a one-time assessment.

Support for the measure's convergent and discriminant validity is indicated by some the correlational studies described in "Criterion."

Criterion

According to Cheadle (2007), correlations between the ELSA Alphabetic Principle Content Area and related subscales from the Woodcock-Johnson and Preschool Comprehensive Test of Phonological & Print Processing (Pre-CTOPP) are moderate to strong (rs = .74 and 1.00, respectively). The ELSA's Phonological Awareness and Concepts About Print Content Areas correlated moderately with the Pre-CTOPP (rs = .64 and .65, respectively).

Violet's Adventure was administered with the Get Ready to Read! (GRR) measure. The total correlation between the ELSA and the GRR was .67, which is moderate. Among the Content Areas, ELSA's Phonological Awareness Content Area has a .53 correlation with GRR's Linguistic Awareness subscale; ELSA's Alphabetic Principle Content Area has a .64 correlation with GRR's Emergent Writing subscale; and ELSA's Concepts About Print Content Area had a .43 correlation with GRR's Print Knowledge subscale, which is lower than expected.

No studies have examined the criterion validity of ELSA's Comprehension Content Area.

RELEVANT STUDIES USING THE MEASURE

A brief literature search using PsycINFO and Google Scholar did not result in citations to any studies whose abstracts specified using the ELSA English. However, it is possible that this measure has been utilized in studies.

ADDITIONAL REFERENCES

Cheadle, J.E. (2007). *The Early Literacy Skills Assessment (ELSA): Psychometric report for both English and Spanish versions.* Ann Arbor, MI: High/Scope.

Eigenbrood, R. (2007). Test review of the Early Literacy Skills Assessment. In K.F. Geisinger, R.A. Spies, J.F. Carlson, & B.S. Plake (Eds.), *The seventeenth mental measurements yearbook.* Retrieved from the Buros Institute's *Test Reviews Online* web site: http://www.unl.edu/buros

Early Literacy Skills Assessment (ELSA): Spanish

Information pertaining specifically to the Spanish version of the measure is in bold and italics. The remainder is equivalent information provided in the English review.

Manual

DeBruin-Parecki, A. (2005). *Early Literacy Skills Assessment User Guide.* Ypsilanti, MI: High/Scope Press.

Publisher

High/Scope Press
600 North River Street
Ypsilanti, MI 48198-2898
http://www.highscope.org

Type of Measure
Direct child assessment

Intended Age Range
3;0 years to 5;11 years

Key Constructs/Domains
• Comprehension • Phonological awareness • Alphabetic principle • Concepts about print

Cost

ELSA kit: $149.95 (featuring either La Aventura de Violeta or El Cambio en Dante). Items sold separately.

Description of Measure

The purpose of this assessment is to "provide preschool programs and teachers with an authentic and meaningful way to assess young children's early literacy" (DeBruin-Parecki, 2005, p. 1).

Available Languages and Formats

An English version is also available. The ELSA book-reading session has two forms (e.g., books): *La Aventura de Violeta* (*Violet's Adventure*) and *El Cambio en Dante* (*Dante Grows Up*).

Strengths

The ELSA format resembles an activity that is familiar to children (i.e., one-to-one reading).

Having alternative story forms (*Dante Grows Up* and *Violet's Adventure*) decreases the chance that children will respond differently to the measure as a result of having previously seen the material (e.g., test–retest effects).

The factor structure of the Spanish ELSA has been examined and is supported by the data.

Weaknesses

According to Cheadle (2007), there may be some floor effects on the ELSA, and the ELSA may work better with children older than 45 months, particularly if it is being used for a one-time assessment.

Limited information is presented in the manual about the content validity of the Spanish version or its creation. This may relate to some psychometric weaknesses evidenced in the Phonological Awareness and Concepts About Print Content Areas. On a positive note, the Comprehension Content Area appears to function better in the Spanish version than in the English one.

The criterion validity of the ELSA Spanish needs to be examined.

Raw scores can be transformed to a three-level skill designation (Level 1: Early Emergent, Level 2: Emergent, Level 3: Competent Emergent), though the process for creating the levels is not well described in the manual. The validity of the levels has not been examined, *particularly for Spanish-speaking children.* The levels were designed to match the Growing Readers Curriculum (A. DeBruin-Parecki, personal communication, June 18, 2009). However, the use of the raw scores is suggested by DeBruin-Parecki.

ADMINISTRATION

Procedure

The ELSA assesses early literacy skills during a book-reading interaction with children. Two assessment books (*La Aventura de Violeta* and *El Cambio en Dante*) were developed in Spanish for the ELSA.

Time Needed
15–20 minutes

The administrator begins by saying to the child (*in Spanish*): "(Name of Child), today we are going to read a book together called *Violet's Adventure* (or *Dante Grows Up*). While we are reading the book I will be writing down some of the wonderful things you tell me about the story" (DeBruin-Parecki, 2005, p. 5). After the instructions are explained, the examiner begins to read the book naturally and asks the child items as they appear in the story. For example, the examiner asks the child questions assessing the extent of comprehension, phonological awareness, alphabet knowledge, and concepts about print throughout the storytelling activity.

Though the instrument looks like a children's book that can be kept in the classroom and read for leisure, using the instrument in such a way "would diminish the integrity of the assessment, due to practice effects" (DeBruin-Parecki, 2005, p. 1).

Administration and Interpretation

It is recommended that a teacher or adult familiar with the child administer the measure. The manual also suggests that the examiner be familiar with the ELSA, practice reading it several times out loud, and practice it with a child who will not be given the measure. It is recommended that first-time ELSA users undergo a training session through High/Scope. In addition, a DVD (*Scoring the ELSA: Establishing Reliability*) is available to increase the interrater reliability of the measure.

Scoring Method

There are three score sheets for the ELSA (ELSA Score Sheet, ELSA Child Summary form, ELSA Class Summary form). The ELSA Score Sheet is used to document responses during the assessment. The Child Summary is used to transform children's raw scores into their developmental level (Level 1: Early Emergent, Level 2: Emergent, Level 3: Competent Emergent) for each of the four early literacy areas, following the manual's directions. These levels were determined using ELSA sample data, though the method used is not described *and their applicability to Spanish speakers is unknown.* Standard scores are not provided. Finally, the Class Summary represents the level (or raw) scores for all children in a class. Scoring is conducted manually.

Adaptations or Instructions for Use with Individuals with Disabilities

The measure can be completed in two sessions for children with special needs and/or whose primary language is not Spanish. Before beginning the second session, the examiner needs to summarize the part of the story completed during the first session through a picture walk (DeBruin-Parecki, 2005).

FUNCTIONAL CONSIDERATIONS

Measure Development

The ELSA was designed to assess early literacy skills through an authentic assessment (i.e., "one that engages children in a task that is personally meaningful, takes place in real life context, and is grounded in naturally occurring instructional activity," DeBruin-Parecki, 2005, p. 1). It was developed to assess four key areas of early literacy identified in the reading research. Additional information about how the items were developed, refined, and selected is not provided in the manual.

Content Equivalence of Items and Measure

Overall, the Spanish and English versions appear to measure similar domains. The manual does not specifically discuss how the four early literacy domains are indicative of early literacy development among Spanish-speaking children, though there is some research to support this. It would be helpful, though, if the manual explained the rationale behind this assumption.

Semantic Equivalence of Translations

The ELSA was translated and adapted into Spanish by an individual with a background in both early childhood development and English as a second language instruction. Consideration was given to Spanish dialectal differences by incorporating feedback from across the country during standardization (A. DeBruin-Parecki, personal communication, June 18, 2009).

Structural Consistency Across the English and Spanish Versions

The structures of the English and Spanish versions are consistent with each other, though it is unknown whether some changes may have been necessary to account for underlying differences in literacy development among Spanish and English speakers.

Standardization Sample

According to an ELSA psychometric report (Cheadle, 2007), 307 children from 15 centers are represented in the Spanish-speaking sample. "Age at assessment is nearly 54 months, which is slightly older than the English sample studies in the previous sections, and the average time between assessments is about 5.6 months. Nearly 10% of children qualify for having special needs. In addition, nearly 80% of children have no or little understanding of English" (Cheadle, 2007, p. 44). According to DeBruin-Parecki (2006a), **La Aventura de Violeta** *was tested with children from Mexican, Puerto Rican, and South and Central American heritages, but the specific backgrounds of the Spanish-speaking children who were administered the* **Dante** *story is unknown.*

Norming

Criterion referenced

Reliability

Test–Retest Reliability

This information is not provided in the manual, though researchers in Mexico have been examining this area (A. DeBruin-Parecki, personal communication, June 18, 2009).

Internal Consistency

According to a recent ELSA psychometric report (Cheadle, 2007), the following internal consistency results (using item response theory) were found for the Spanish-language assessments conducted in both the fall and spring of an academic year: pretest: Comprehension = .91, Phonological Awareness = .63, Alphabetic Principle = .92, and Concepts About Print = .65; posttest: Comprehension = .93, Phonological Awareness = .72, Alphabetic Principle = .92, and Concepts About Print = .72.

These results suggest that the Spanish ELSA has low to high internal consistency. Particularly strong are the Comprehension and Alphabetic Principle Content Areas; the Phonological Awareness and Concepts About Print Content Areas are the least consistent.

Interrater Agreement

This information is not provided in the manual.

Other Forms of Reliability (e.g., Equivalent Forms)

The ELSA Spanish has two forms: **El Cambio en Dante** *and* **La Aventura de Violeta.** *Because of the small sample of Spanish-speaking children, Cheadle (2007) could not examine whether they were statistically equivalent.*

Validity

Face and Content

"The content validity of the ELSA was first established by linking all items to four key principles of early literacy measured by ELSA and identified in the scientifically based research literature: comprehension, phonological awareness, alphabetic principle, and concepts about print" (DeBruin-Parecki, 2005, p. 24). The procedure for deciding which items to assess in these areas is not described, which Eigenbrood (2007) has also noted. Overall, the measure appears to measure the intended constructs. *The extent to which the literacy literature was reviewed for Spanish speakers is not discussed, though the measure appears generally consistent with the literature.*

Internal Construct

Factor analyses on the Spanish version were conducted by Cheadle, who found the following: "Factor structures for both the English and Spanish-speaking versions across the ELSA instruments adequately reproduced the observed variation in the data; factor loadings were typically high, indicating that the items had adequate discrimination; factor structures were similar over time, indicating that the instrument factor models were largely invariant, suggesting that the same constructs are measured on both the pre- and posttests" (2007, p. 8).

For the Spanish version, there is also evidence that the Content Areas can be combined to create a total emergent literacy score and that the Phonological Awareness Content Area may be weaker than the others.

External Construct

According to Cheadle (2007), there may be some floor effects on the ELSA Spanish (as for the English version), and the ELSA may work better with children older than 45 months, particularly if it is being used for a one-time assessment.

Data on convergent and discriminant validity with other measures are not presented in the manual.

Criterion

The criterion validity of the Spanish version has not yet been examined.

Comparison of Psychometric Properties Between English and Spanish Versions

Technical Equivalence in Reliability

Overall, the reliability of the English and Spanish versions is similar, though the internal reliability results of the Phonological Awareness and Concepts About Print Content Areas are lower for the Spanish version. The two forms of the ELSA (El Cambio en Dante and La Aventura de Violeta) were equivalent in English but could not be examined for the Spanish version because of the sample size.

Technical Equivalence in Validity

Overall, the validity of the English and Spanish versions is similar. Criterion validity has not yet been examined for the Spanish version. Both versions evidence similar factor structures, though the Phonological Awareness Content Area may be weaker in the Spanish version and the Comprehension Content Area may be weaker in the English version. Both Content Areas evidence floor effects for young children.

RELEVANT STUDIES USING THE MEASURE

A brief literature search using PsycINFO and Google Scholar did not result in citations to any studies whose abstracts specified using the ELSA Spanish. However, it is possible that this measure has been utilized in studies.

ADDITIONAL REFERENCES

Cheadle, J.E. (2007). *The Early Literacy Skills Assessment (ELSA): Psychometric report for both English and Spanish versions.* Ann Arbor, MI: High/Scope.

DeBruin-Parecki A. (2006a, Spring). Early Literacy Skills Assessment for Spanish speaking preschoolers: Filling a need. *High/Scope Resource,* pp. 21–23. Available at http://www.highscope.org/file/NewsandInformation/ReSourceReprints/Spring06pdfs/EarlyLiteracyAssess.pdf

Early Screening Inventory•Revised (ESI•R)
2008 Edition: English

Manual

Meisels, S.J., Marsden, D.B., Wiske, M.S., & Henderson, L.W. (2008). *Early Screening Inventory•Revised (ESI•R) 2008 Edition, Examiner's Manual.* Minneapolis, MN: NCS Pearson.

Publisher

Pearson, Inc.
19500 Bulverde Road
San Antonio, TX 78259-3701
http://www.pearsonassessments.com

Cost

ESI•Preschool (ESI•P) or ESI•Kindergarten (ESI•K) toolkit: $139.50 per kit. Items also sold separately.

Description of Measure

"The Early Screening Inventory Revised (ESI•R) 2008 Edition is a brief developmental screening instrument that is individually administered to children ages 3 years through 5 years. It samples performance in the areas of speech, language, cognition, perception, and motor coordination. The ESI•R 2008 Edition is designed to identify children who may need special educational services in order to perform successfully in school" (Meisels, Marsden, Wiske, & Henderson, 2008, p. 2).

Available Languages and Formats

A Spanish version, the *Inventario para la Detección Temprana–Revisado,* is available. In addition, the ESI•R 2008 Edition is composed of two forms: the Preschool version (ESI•P) and the Kindergarten version (ESI•K).

Strengths

A generally thorough and solid set of psychometric data, including predictive validity, is presented in the manual. In addition, local reliability statistics are presented that examine the accuracy of cutoff points and thus the referral implications of the screening measure.

The ESI•R 2008 Edition appears to be a fairly quick and accurate screening tool that is likely to appeal to young children

Weaknesses

The test–retest reliability among the older children in the ESI•K sample from the 1993 standardization was lower than for the other age groups.

ADMINISTRATION

Procedure

The measure assesses the following domains:

- *Visual-Motor/Adaptive.* Tasks include drawing, building with blocks, and visual memory tasks (e.g., remembering which overturned card matches the target image).

Type of Measure

Direct child assessment

Intended Age Range

3;0 years to 5;11 years

Key Constructs/Domains

- Visual-Motor/Adaptive
- Language and Cognition
- Gross Motor

Time Needed

15–20 minutes

- *Language and Cognition.* Tasks include counting, describing objects, verbal analogies, and number recall.
- *Gross Motor.* Tasks include jumping, walking, balancing, and hopping.

The Parent Questionnaire includes five sections that provide information about 1) the child, 2) the child's family, 3) the family's school history (e.g., parent education level, child's previous preschool/child care experiences), 4) the child's medical history, and 5) the child's overall development. Meisels et al. (2008) advise parents to complete the questionnaire before administering the developmental screening. Though the Parent Questionnaire has been correlated to ESI scores (Henderson & Meisels, 1994), Meisels et al. "recommend that the Parent Questionnaire be used only as supplementary information, rather than making explicit screening decisions. Such decisions are best made in the basis of objective, reliable performance measures such as the ESI•R 2008 Edition" (p. 15).

Administration and Interpretation

According to Meisels et al. (2008), examiners may be early education teachers, paraprofessionals, or individuals studying child development. Supervision by an individual with formal training in early childhood assessment is needed. A training manual and videos are available. The training involves three steps:

- Studying the manual
- Observing an experienced examiner administer the test (including observing examiners administer the test on the training video)
- Engaging in supervised practice administering the test

Scoring Method

Examiners hand-score children's responses during the test. Specifically, they circle the number of points earned for each item and document observations and behavioral responses by the children. These comments, along with the Parent Questionnaire, help to determine the extent to which the children's scores on the ESI•R 2008 Edition are an accurate reflection of their ability.

After the assessment is administered, points are totaled and compared with charts detailing cutoff scores by age and language (English versus Spanish). Examiners then circle the screening decision (*refer, rescreen,* or *okay*). The cutoff scores were initially established for the ESI•P and the ESI•K with cost-matrix analyses to identify optimal cutoff points to predict whether children would later score more than 1 *SD* below the mean on the McCarthy Scales of Children's Abilities (MCSA). The 2008 standardization examined the cutoff scores. As similar percentages of children continued to be identified for referral, the cutoff scores for the English version remained the same.

Adaptations or Instructions for Use with Individuals with Disabilities

No specific information is provided in the manual.

FUNCTIONAL CONSIDERATIONS

Measure Development

The ESI•R 2008 Edition was introduced in 1975 as the Eliot-Pearson Screening Inventory (EPSI). Most of the EPSI items were developed independently. A small number of items, however, were adapted from other measures (e.g., the Stanford-Binet Intelligence Scale, Denver Developmental Screening Test). ESI items were selected based on the ease, speed, and reliability with which they could be administered and scored (Meisels et al., 2008).

Attention was paid to typical norms, tasks that represent an area of development well, and the manipulatives used with the children. The test was renamed the *Early Screening Inventory* in 1983 and subsequently underwent five major revisions. Further details regarding ESI's revisions and psychometric properties over time can be found in the numerous articles cited in the manual.

In 1993, the ESI was heavily revised and renormed. The ESI•P was studied with a standardization sample of approximately 1,000 children, the majority of whom were attending Head Start programs. The ESI•K was standardized with 5,034 children, roughly half of whom were attending public school programs. The manual presents solid psychometric properties for the ESI•R 2008 Edition across interrater reliability and internal construct, external construct, and predictive validities. These are discussed later in this review.

The ESI•R 2008 Edition's 2008 edition is equivalent to the 1993 version in its item content, administration, and scoring approach. Differences include updated formatting and additional text. Furthermore, the 2008 version was normed on a nationally representative sample, and the cutoff scores were reexamined.

Standardization Sample

A nationally representative sample was used to renorm the ESI•R 2008 Edition in the fall of 2007. A total of 1,200 children were included in the sample, with 200 per each 5-month age span between 3;0–3;5 and 5;6–5;11 years. Most children were drawn from programs and schools already using the ESI•R 2008 Edition. Additional cases were sought to create a nationally representative sample matched to 2006 U.S. Census data across sex, race/ethnicity, maternal education, and region.

In addition, prevalence rates were matched to primary language use (English versus Spanish). As stated in the manual, "Because many Hispanic children of preschool age speak Spanish as their primary language, and because the ESI•R 2008 Edition has both English and Spanish versions, the norm sample for the ESI•R 2008 Edition includes both versions in order to accurately represent the U.S. population.... Spanish language forms make up about 14% of the norm sample" (Meisels et al., 2008, p. 188). As described in the Spanish review, the Spanish and English items underwent statistical equating procedures.

Norming

Norm referenced

Reliability

Test–Retest Reliability

Although the temporal stability was not reexamined in the 2008 edition, coefficients from the previous standardization are applicable, as the items and scoring remained the same. A small sample (*n* = 5) was readministered the ESI•P during a 7- to 10-day interval. The correlation between test and retest scores was greater than .98. In turn, 174 children were readministered the ESI•K during a similar interval. The weighted average correlation coefficient was .72 for the entire sample. It was lower among children in the 5;6–5;11 years range (.67) and higher among children in the 4;6–4;11 years range (.84).

Internal Consistency

Split-half reliabilities were calculated by age for the English version. Overall, the mean for the ESI•P was .80 and the mean for the ESI•K was .79, which is generally in the medium range.

Local reliabilities and related standard errors of measurement are described in "Other Forms of Reliability."

Interrater Agreement

Although the interrater reliability was not reexamined in the 2008 edition, coefficients from the previous standardization are applicable, as the items and scoring remained the same. For the ESI•P, agreement between 35 tester-observer pairs was high, with correlations greater than .99. For the ESI•K, agreement between 586 tester-observer pairs was high, with correlations greater than .97.

Other Forms of Reliability (e.g., Equivalent Forms)

An additional statistic, *local* or *conditional reliability,* was also calculated. This coefficient examines the accuracy of the cutoff points (Meisels et al., 2008). The mean local reliability for the English version was .88 for refer versus rescreen, ranging from .81 for children 3;0–3;5 years to .91 among 5-year-olds. The mean local reliability for the English version was .88 for rescreen versus okay, ranging from .86 for children 3;0–3;5 years to .90 for children 5;0–5;5 years.

Validity

Face and Content

The majority of test items were developed by Meisels et al., though a small number of items were adapted from commonly used instruments (e.g., the Stanford-Binet Intelligence Scale; Meisels et al., 2008). The criteria for these items are described in the Measure Development section of this review. The use of expert consultants is not explicitly described in the manual.

Internal Construct

Not applicable, as the ESI•R 2008 Edition uses only the total score in interpretation rather than subdomain scores.

External Construct

A table presented in the manual demonstrated that older children score higher than young children on each of the forms.

Although differences among groups of children with potential disabilities were not reexamined in the 2008 edition, the following coefficients from the previous standardization are applicable, as the items and scoring remained the same. Statistical analyses in 1993 indicated that the ESI•P and ESI•K were able to discriminate in two ways children identified as needing a referral versus those who passed the screening. First, both of the age forms underwent item analysis to examine whether individual items differentiated children who were later referred based on the total score. Second, sensitivity and specificity indexes were developed based on the ESI•R 2008 Edition's ability to predict whether children scored low (1.5 *SD* below the mean) on the MCSA at a later point in time. The sensitivity of the ESI•P was .93 and its specificity was .80. These coefficients were .93 and .80, respectively, for the ESI•K.

Support for the convergent validity of the ESI•R 2008 Edition is also indicated by a correlational study described in "Criterion."

Criterion

Although the criterion validity was not reexamined in the 2008 edition, coefficients from the previous standardization are applicable, as the items and scoring remained the same. In the previous standardization, 130 children were administered the MCSA approximately 4–6 months after being administered the ESI-P. Correlations ranged from .69 to .77 across the age ranges, "showing that the instrument is a good predictor of future cognitive test performance" (Meisels et al., 2008, p. 175).

A similar approach was used to examine the ESI•K. A total of 251 children were administered the MCSA approximately 7–9 months after being administered the ESI•K. Correlations ranged from .74 to .76 across the age ranges of the ESI•K.

The relationship between the ESI•R 2008 Edition and other screening measures has not been examined.

RELEVANT STUDIES USING THE MEASURE

A brief literature search using PsycINFO and Google Scholar did not yield any published studies that mentioned using the ESI•R 2008 Edition English version. Older versions of the measure have been utilized in studies, though.

ADDITIONAL REFERENCES

Henderson, L.W., & Meisels, S.J. (1994). Parental involvement in the developmental screening of their young children: A multiple-source perspective. *Journal of Early Intervention, 18*(2), 141–154.

Inventario para la Detección Temprana•Revisado (IDT•R) 2008

Information pertaining specifically to the Spanish version of the measure is in bold and italics. The remainder is equivalent information provided in the English review.

Manual

Meisels, S.J., Marsden, D.B., Wiske, M.S., & Henderson, L.W. (2008). *Early Screening Inventory–Revised (ESI•R) 2008 Edition, Examiner's Manual.* Minneapolis, MN: Pearson Education.

Publisher

Pearson, Inc.
19500 Bulverde Road
San Antonio, TX 78259-3701
http://www.pearsonassessments.com

Cost

IDT•Preschool (IDT•P) or IDT•Kindergarten (IDT•K) toolkit: $139.50 per kit. Items also sold separately.

Description of Measure

Though a description of the IDT•R was not presented in the manual, the following one of its English counterpart applies: "The Early Screening Inventory-Revised (ESI•R) 2008 Edition is a brief developmental screening instrument that is individually administered to children ages 3 years through 5 years. It samples performance in the areas of speech, language, cognition, perception, and motor coordination. The ESI•R 2008 Edition is designed to identify children who may need special educational services in order to perform successfully in school" (Meisels, Marsden, Wiske, & Henderson, 2008, p. 2).

Available Languages and Formats

An English version, the Early Screening Inventory–Revised (ESI•R) 2008 Edition, is available. In addition, there are two versions of the IDT•R based on age: the Preschool version (IDT•P) and the Kindergarten version (IDT•K).

Strengths

The ESI•R 2008 Edition appears to be a fairly quick and accurate screening tool that is likely to appeal to young children.

Careful attention was paid to the standardization sample and the equating process. Thus, equated cutoff scores were created for the English and Spanish versions. This allows for a direct comparison of children's results on each measure.

Local reliability statistics are presented that examine the accuracy of the cutoff points for the Spanish version and thus the referral implications of the screening measure.

Type of Measure

Direct child assessment

Intended Age Range

3;0 years to 5;11 years

Key Constructs/Domains

- Visual-Motor/Adaptive
- Language and Cognition
- Gross Motor

Weaknesses

Little discussion is presented in the manual about the Spanish translation process, though the procedure was clarified through direct communication with the publisher.

The criterion validity of the IDT•R likely may need to be separately examined from that of the ESI•R 2008 Edition.

ADMINISTRATION

Procedure

The measure assesses the following domains:

Time Needed
15–20 minutes

- *Visual-Motor/Adaptive.* Tasks include drawing, building with blocks, and visual memory tasks (e.g., remembering which overturned card matches the target image).
- *Language and Cognition.* Tasks include counting, describing objects, verbal analogies, and number recall.
- *Gross Motor.* Tasks include jumping, walking, balancing, and hopping.

The Parent Questionnaire includes five sections that provide information about 1) the child, 2) the child's family, 3) the family's school history (e.g., parent education level, child's previous preschool/child care experiences), 4) the child's medical history, and 5) the child's overall development. Meisels et al. (2008) advise parents to complete the questionnaire before administering the developmental screening. Though the Parent Questionnaire was correlated to ESI scores (e.g., Henderson & Meisels, 1994), Meisels et al. "recommend that the Parent Questionnaire be used only as supplementary information, rather than making explicit screening decisions. Such decisions are best made in the basis of objective, reliable performance measures such as the ESI•R 2008 Edition" (p. 15).

Administration and Interpretation

According to Meisels et al. (2008), examiners may be early education teachers, paraprofessionals, or individuals studying child development. Supervision by an individual with formal training in early childhood assessment is needed. A training manual is available, as are videos. The training involves three steps:

- Studying the manual
- Observing an experienced examiner administer the test (including observing examiners administer the test on the training video)
- Engaging in supervised practice administering the test

Scoring Method

Examiners hand-score children's responses during the test. Specifically, they circle the number of points earned for each item and document observations and behavioral responses by the children. These comments, along with the Parent Questionnaire, help to determine the extent to which the children's scores on the ESI•R 2008 Edition are an accurate reflection of their ability.

After the assessment is administered, points are totaled and compared with charts detailing cutoff scores by age and language (English versus Spanish). Examiners then circle the screening decision (*refer, rescreen,* or *okay*). The cutoff scores were initially established for the English version of the ESI•Preschool (ESI•P) and the ESI•Kindergarten (ESI•K) with cost-matrix analyses to identify optimal cutoff points to predict whether children would later score more than 1 *SD* below the mean on the McCarthy Scales of Children's Abilities.

The 2008 standardization examined the cutoff scores for both the English and Spanish versions. As similar percentages of English-speaking children continued to be identified for referral, the cutoff scores for the English version remained the same. The cutoff scores for the Spanish version were adjusted based on Rasch calibration analyses.

Adaptations or Instructions for Use with Individuals with Disabilities

No specific information is provided in the manual.

FUNCTIONAL CONSIDERATIONS

Measure Development

The ESI•R 2008 Edition was introduced in 1975 as the Eliot-Pearson Screening Inventory (EPSI). Most of the EPSI items were developed independently. A small number of items, however, were adapted from other measures (e.g., the Stanford-Binet Intelligence Scale, Denver Developmental Screening Test). ESI items were selected based on the ease, speed, and reliability with which they could be administered and scored (Meisels et al., 2008). Attention was paid to typical norms, tasks that represent an area of development well, and the manipulatives used with the children. The test was renamed the *Early Screening Inventory* in 1983 and subsequently underwent five major revisions. Further details regarding ESI's revisions and psychometric properties over time can be found in the numerous articles cited in the manual.

In 1993, the ESI was heavily revised and renormed. The ESI•P was studied with a standardization sample of approximately 1,000 children, the majority of whom were attending Head Start programs. The ESI•K was standardized with 5,034 children, roughly half of whom were attending public school programs. The manual presents solid psychometric properties for the ESI•R 2008 Edition across interrater reliability and internal construct, external construct, and predictive validities. These are discussed later in this review. *In 1993, a Spanish translation became available for the ESI•R 2008 Edition.*

The ESI•R 2008 Edition's 2008 edition is equivalent to the 1993 version in its item content, administration, and scoring approach. Differences include updated formatting and additional text. Furthermore, the 2008 version was normed on a nationally representative sample and the cutoff scores were updated.

Content Equivalence of Items and Measure

It appears that the content of the Spanish version is the same as that of the English version. As described in "Scoring Method," Rasch analyses examined potential differences in Spanish-speaking children's scores on the IDT•R and adjusted the cutoff scores accordingly.

Semantic Equivalence of Translations

Though no information is specifically provided in the manual about the translation of the measure, personal communication with the publisher clarified the translation process (G. Perkins, June 29, 2009). A group of Spanish-speaking professionals developed the Spanish version, which was subsequently "tried out" with Spanish-speaking teachers over a several-year period. As issues, questions, or errors were identified, a "consensus committee" composed of Spanish speakers from a variety of backgrounds was convened to decide on the final text. A note at the beginning of the IDT•R instructions also indicates that careful attention was paid to the use of masculine and feminine articles in the translation process.

Structural Consistency Across the English and Spanish Versions

The number and order of the items is similar across the English and Spanish versions, thus making the versions structurally similar.

Standardization Sample

A nationally representative sample was used to renorm the ESI•R 2008 Edition in the fall of 2007. A total of 1,200 children were included in the sample, with 200 per each 5-month age span between 3;0–3;5 and 5;6–5;11 years. Most children were drawn from programs and schools already using the ESI•R 2008 Edition. Additional cases were sought to create a nationally representative sample matched to 2006 U.S. Census data across sex, race/ethnicity, maternal education, and region.

In addition, prevalence rates were matched to primary language use (English versus Spanish). As stated in the manual, "Because many Hispanic children of preschool age speak Spanish as their primary language, and because the ESI•R 2008 Edition has both English and Spanish versions, the norm sample for the ESI•R 2008 Edition includes both versions in order to accurately represent the U.S. population .... Spanish language forms make up about 14% of the norm sample" (Meisels et al., 2008, p. 188). The children's country of origin is not presented in the manual.

The Spanish and English items underwent statistical equating procedures. The manual presents the following rationale: "The question of the equivalence of the English and Spanish versions had practical as well as theoretical significance. Because the English and Spanish versions are often used in the same programs and are interpreted and applied in the same way, it would be appropriate for the national ESI•R 2008 Edition norm sample to represent the entire population of preschool-age children who speak either English or Spanish, so that every child's score can be compared with the same national sample" (Meisels et al., 2008, p. 189). This process was conducted using Rasch modeling, with details described in the manual. Overall, the Spanish version was a little more difficult at each ability level. Thus, the cutoff scores for the Spanish version were adjusted.

Norming

Norm referenced

Reliability

Test–Retest Reliability

Although the temporal stability was not reexamined in the 2008 edition, coefficients from the previous standardization could be applicable as the items and scoring remained the same and the language versions are equated. Spanish-speaking children were not engaged in this substudy.

Internal Consistency

Split-half reliabilities were calculated by age for the Spanish version. Overall, the mean for the IDT-P was .83, and the mean for the IDT-K was .73, which is generally in the low-to-medium range.

Local reliabilities and related standard errors of measurement are described in "Other Forms of Reliability."

Interrater Agreement

Although the interrater reliability was not reexamined in the 2008 edition, coefficients from the previous standardization could be applicable as the items and scoring remained the same. Although the language versions are equated, Spanish-speaking children did not participate in the initial study.

Other Forms of Reliability (e.g., Equivalent Forms)

An additional statistic, local or conditional reliability, *was also calculated. This coefficient examines the accuracy of the cutoff points (Meisels et al., 2008). The mean local reliability for the Spanish version was .86 for refer versus rescreen, ranging from .80 for children 3;0–3;5 years to .90 for children 5;6–5;11 years. The mean local reliability for the Spanish version was .87 for rescreen versus okay, ranging from .85 for children 3;0–3;5 years to .90 for children 5;6–5;11 years.*

Validity

Face and Content

The majority of test items were developed by Meisels et al., though a small number of items were adapted from commonly used instruments (e.g., the Stanford-Binet Intelligence Scale; Meisels et al., 2008). The criteria for these items are described in the English review, and the items are the same in the Spanish version. Overall, the items in Spanish appear applicable for the purposes described. As described in the Standardization Sample section of this review, the items were also statistically examined.

Internal Construct

Not applicable, as the IDT•R uses only the total score in interpretation rather than subdomain scores.

External Construct

A table presented in the manual demonstrates that older children score higher than young children on each of the forms. This table presents data from the combined (English and Spanish) norm samples after the Spanish raw data was statistically equated.

Although the manual presents specificity and sensitivity data for the English standardization from 1993, these are not likely applicable to the Spanish version because differences in difficulty level were identified.

Support for the convergent validity of the IDT•R is also indicated by a correlational study described in "Criterion."

Criterion

The manual presents criterion validity data for the English standardization from 1993, which provide some indication of the relationship of the IDT•R with developmental measures, as the IDT•R and ESI•R 2008 Edition are statistically equated. However, the relationship between the IDT•R and a Spanish-language measure still needs examination. The relationships between the ESR-I/IDT•R and other screening measures are not reported.

Comparison of Psychometric Properties Between English and Spanish Versions

Technical Equivalence in Reliability

The internal consistency reliabilities across the English and Spanish versions are similar, as are the local reliabilities, which examine the accuracy of the cutoff scores.

(continued)

Past studies of temporal and interrater reliabilities conducted with the English version may be applicable given the equating procedure utilized. However, updated studies that include Spanish-speaking children may be preferable.

Technical Equivalence in Validity

Though little discussion is presented in the manual about the creation of the Spanish measure as compared to the English version, personal communication with the publisher clarified the process. In addition, statistical analyses examined item functioning for both measures. Although age-related performance results are shown in the manual for the whole norm group, the sensitivity and specificity of the Spanish version need to be examined, as they were for the English version. Additional studies with Spanish-language criterion measures may also be needed.

RELEVANT STUDIES USING THE MEASURE

A brief literature search using PsycINFO and Google Scholar did not yield any study abstracts that specified using the IDT•R. However, it is possible that this measure has been utilized in studies.

ADDITIONAL REFERENCES

Henderson, L.W., & Meisels, S.J. (1994). Parental involvement in the developmental screening of their young children: A multiple-source perspective. *Journal of Early Intervention, 18*(2), 141–154.

Expressive One-Word Picture Vocabulary Test–Fourth Edition (EOWPVT-4): English

Manual

Martin, N., & Brownell, R. (2010). *Expressive One-Word Picture Vocabulary Test-4: Manual.* Novato, CA: Academic Therapy Publications.

Publisher

Academic Therapy Publications
20 Commercial Boulevard
Novato, CA 94949-6191
http://www.academictherapy.com

Cost

Complete kit: $175. Items sold separately.

Description of Measure

"The EOWPVT-4 offers a quick and reliable measure of English expressive vocabulary, utilizing a picture-naming paradigm: An individual is asked to name (in one word) the objects, actions, and concepts pictured in color illustrations" (Martin & Brownell, 2010, p. 8).

Intended purposes of the measure include assessing a person's ability to generate words, documenting expressive vocabulary development, assessing reading skills, screening for early language delay, examining word/concept retrieval in people with expressive aphasia, obtaining an indirect indication of some cognitive skills, and evaluating intervention programs.

Available Languages and Formats

A related measure, the Receptive One-Word Picture Vocabulary Test–Spanish-Bilingual Edition, examines vocabulary comprehension (i.e., receptive vocabulary) across the Spanish and English languages. It is based on the 2000 edition of the EOWPVT, though a newer bilingual version linked to the EOWPVT-4 is in development.

In addition, both English and bilingual versions are available to assess receptive vocabulary (i.e., the ability to identify and comprehend the meaning of words). (See separate reviews of the Receptive One-Word Picture Vocabulary Test–Fourth Edition [ROWPVT-4]: English and Receptive One-Word Picture Vocabulary Test–Spanish-Bilingual Edition in this book.)

Strengths

The EOWPVT-4's reliability is generally strong.

The large colorful illustrations, the nature of the task, and fact that a verbal response is not required can make it appealing to young children and easy to administer.

The EOWPVT-4 includes more items for younger children than prior editions.

Weaknesses

Smaller preschool sample sizes were included in the most recent norming of the EOWPVT, though the measure included more items at a lower range to be examined.

Fewer validity studies are presented for the EOWPVT-4 than the 2000 edition, with barely any at the preschool range. Because much of the measure remained the same at the child level, prior research likely extends to support the EOWPVT. At the geriatric level, validity research is needed.

Type of Measure
Direct child assessment

Intended Age Range
2;0 years to 80+ years

Key Constructs/Domains
Expressive vocabulary

ADMINISTRATION

Procedure

After establishing rapport and recording background information on the record sheet, the examiner explains the directions. Essentially, the child is presented with four pictures, and the examiner says

Time Needed
15–20 minutes

a word. The child then selects the picture corresponding to the word. Next, example items are presented. These items are intended to show the child how to give a response. Example items can be used as many times as necessary before starting the main part of the assessment.

Children begin the EOWPVT-4 at different starting points depending on their age. The examiner presents one picture at a time, providing recommended cues as necessary.

It is recommended that the examiner turn the pages and provide about 20–30 seconds for a response.

Administration and Interpretation

"The EOWPVT-4 was developed to be used by professionals in speech-language, occupational therapy, rehabilitation psychology, neuropsychology, clinical psychology, and education who have training to understand both the psychometric and cognitive developmental aspects of such an assessment" (Martin & Brownell, 2010, p. 8). It can be administered by individuals who are familiar with administration and scoring procedures and who have conducted trial administrations. Results are interpreted by those with formal psychometric training and an understanding of derived scores and testing limitations.

Scoring Method

This measure is scored by hand. The total number of correct responses below the basal level (eight consecutive correct responses) is added to the number of correct responses between the basal and ceiling levels (six consecutive errors[1]). This raw score is then converted to standard scores using tables in the manual. In addition, the appendix provides a table that can be utilized to examine the relevance of performance differences on the EOWPVT-4 and ROWPVT-4.

Adaptations or Instructions for Use with Individuals with Disabilities

Specific suggestions are not provided for adapting the EOWPVT-4 for use with individuals with disabilities, though the previous manual included such suggestions (Brownell, 2000).

FUNCTIONAL CONSIDERATIONS

Measure Development

The EOWPVT was previously nationally normed through early adulthood (18;11 years). The EOWPVT-4 extends the "utility of this popular test by providing national norms through geriatric ages (80 and older). New words were added to reflect the extended age range and the current emphasis on early screening. The EOWPVT-4 is co-normed with the ROWPVT-4" (Martin & Brownell, 2010, p. 6).

---

[1]This is a slightly different criterion than that used for the ROWPVT-4, in which the ceiling level is determined by six errors made within eight consecutive items.

An initial normative edition of 194 images was examined compared to 174 items in the 2000 edition. Twenty-eight new items were added, and the remainder stemmed from the 2000 version. Eight items were dropped between the 2000 and 2010 editions. All new items for the younger ages were administered to all examinees younger than 13 during the norming process for item analysis purposes. Similarly, all new items for the older ages were administered to all teenagers and adults in the sample. All items retained from the 2000 version remained in their existing order.

In line with classical test theory and item response theory, all items were examined for their functioning and for potential biases. In addition to examining item difficulty levels and item statistics, test developers conducted differential item functioning analysis to identify potential items that were biased along the following dimensions: gender, residence (urban/rural), and race/ethnicity. Further input into item selection was provided by item reviews and other item bias studies during the standardization study. The final version of the EOWPVT-4 contains 190 items.

Standardization Sample

The measure was standardized with 2,394 individuals from an original pool of more than 2,400. To remain in the standardization sample, individuals must also have been administered the ROWPVT-4 and provided complete and useable data. Testing sites were sought by contacting everyone in a contact directory of speech-language pathologists and those who had previously purchased the EOWPVT or similar tests. A total of 106 examiners participated across 84 sites in 26 states. Sites included private practices as well as private, public, and parochial schools. Examiners were instructed to randomly select classrooms and settings for participation as well as to include individuals with a wide range of disabilities. No mention is made in the manual about primary language at home and school, though primary language had been a criterion for inclusion in the norming sample in the prior version of the EOWPVT. Smaller sample sizes of 3- to 5-year-olds were noted in the EOWPVT-4 normative sample ($n = 86–117$) than in the 2000 version ($n = 105–209$). Given the variability in vocabulary development at this age, larger sample sizes could be needed. For example, the normative sample included only 86 children age 5. With norms provided at 2-month intervals, this is about 14 children per age subgroup.

The final standardization sample generally matched the demographics of the U.S. population on key characteristics such as region, race/ethnicity, gender, education, and residence. A slightly higher representation of people of Hispanic heritage, people living in rural areas, and people with postgraduate degrees was noted.

Norming

Norm referenced

Reliability

Test–Retest Reliability

A total of 78 examinees were retested by the same examiner after a period of about 19 days. The test–retest correlation was .98 for raw scores and .97 for standard scores. It is unknown whether the sample included preschoolers, as it did for the 2000 version.

Internal Consistency

The internal consistency of this test was determined by calculating Cronbach's coefficient alpha at each age level; the median value was .95, which is in the high range. The values at the preschool-age level (3- to 5-year-olds) were also strong at .94–.95.

The average standard error of measurement (SEM) was 3.29. Among preschoolers, the SEM ranged from 3.29 to 3.79.

Interrater Agreement

No information is provided on the EOWPVT-4's interrater agreement.

Other Forms of Reliability (e.g., Equivalent Forms)

Not applicable

Validity

Face and Content

Primarily nouns are included in the EOWPVT-4 because nouns are generally acquired prior to verbs and are more prevalent in many languages. Moreover, their production involves less interaction between neural areas and is more robust to the effects of brain damage and aging. The source of the new items is not discussed in the EOWPVT-4 manual, though most of the items (all but the 28 new items) were included in the prior version. At that time, the items were selected from a variety of sources to represent words that individuals at any age could be expected to understand at the given age range, and difficult items were included for children with strong vocabularies. Only words that could be illustrated were represented. Item analysis was also utilized to remove problematic items from the measure. Furthermore, the utilization of feedback from a range of users and the cultural panel for the 2000 version contributes to the face and content validity of this measure.

Internal Construct

Not applicable because the EOWPVT-4 examines one construct (i.e., expressive vocabulary).

External Construct

External construct validity was indicated in analyses that examined chronological age and exceptional group differences. First, a table provided suggests that older children with a more developed vocabulary will demonstrate greater proficiency on the EOWPVT-4. No correlation is provided.

Second, the scores of 208 individuals with disabilities were examined. Some children in the preschool age range appear to have been included in this sample. Children experiencing the following difficulties scored significantly lower than a matched subsample: autism ($n = 28$), specific language impairment ($n = 14$), learning disability ($n = 74$), attention disability ($n = 39$), and reading disability ($n = 53$). This supports the expectation that individuals identified as having cognitive or learning-related difficulties will perform significantly worse on the EOWPVT-4 than their typically developing counterparts.

Support for the measure's convergent and discriminant validity is also indicated by some of the correlational studies described in "Criterion."

Criterion

Correlations of the EOWPVT-4 with other individually administered expressive vocabulary tests are not reported. As may be expected given their similarity in format, the EOWPVT-4 correlated well with its receptive vocabulary counterpart (the ROWPVT-4). The standard score correlation was .69 and the raw score correlation was .86.

The EOWPVT-4 was also correlated with nonpreschool tests of general cognitive ability and reading development. Weak to moderate relationships with Wechsler Intelligence Scale for

Children–Fourth Edition (WISC-IV) Full Scale IQ scores and Verbal Comprehension Index scores (.35 and .43, respectively) were found in a preliminary sample of 24 students. These scores are not surprising given that the WISC-IV generally includes expressive reasoning tasks rather than solely vocabulary. A stronger relationship was obtained between the EOWPVT-4 and STAR Reading standard scores (.69) in a sample of 33 children, supporting the relationship between vocabulary and reading skills.

RELEVANT STUDIES USING THE MEASURE

A brief literature search using PsycINFO and Google Scholar did not yield any published studies that mentioned using the EOWPVT-4. Older versions have been used. It is possible, though, that the EOWPVT-4 is being used in ongoing studies.

ADDITIONAL REFERENCES

Brownell, R. (2000). *Expressive One-Word Picture Vocabulary Test: Manual.* Novato, CA: Academic Therapy Publications.

Expressive One-Word Picture Vocabulary Test–Spanish-Bilingual Edition (EOWPVT-SBE)

Information pertaining specifically to the Spanish version of the measure is in bold and italics. The remainder is equivalent information provided in the English review.

Manual

Brownell, R. (2001). *Expressive One-Word Picture Vocabulary Test–Spanish-Bilingual Edition.* Novato, CA: Academic Therapy Publications.

Publisher

Academic Therapy Publications
20 Commercial Boulevard
Novato, CA 94949-6191
http://www.academictherapy.com/

Cost

Complete kit: $151. Items sold separately.

Description of Measure

This assessment "provides a measure that reflects the extent of an individual's vocabulary that can be accessed and retrieved from memory and used to produce a meaningful speech in Spanish or English" (Brownell, 2001, p. 12).

Intended purposes of the measure include assessing a person's ability to generate words, documenting overall expressive vocabulary development (across both English and Spanish), assessing reading skills, screening for early language delay, examining word/concept retrieval in people with expressive aphasia, obtaining an indirect indication of some cognitive skills, and evaluating intervention programs.

Available Languages and Formats

A related measure, the Expressive One-Word Picture Vocabulary Test–Fourth Edition examines English vocabulary production (i.e., expressive vocabulary). The EOWPVT-SBE is based on the 2000 edition of the EOWPVT, though a newer bilingual version linked to the EOWPVT-4 is in development.

In addition, both English and bilingual versions are available to assess receptive vocabulary (i.e., the ability to identify and comprehend the meaning of words). (See separate reviews of the Receptive One-Word Picture Vocabulary Test–Fourth Edition [ROWPVT]: English and Receptive One-Word Picture Vocabulary Test–Spanish-Bilingual Edition [ROWPVT-SBE] in this book.)

Strengths

This measure examines a child's overall ability to label items regardless of language by accepting answers in both English and Spanish. The measure was normed with a Spanish–English bilingual sample in the United States. Thus, the measure assesses bilinguals' overall expressive vocabulary rather than their English or Spanish development exclusively. Few other measures have this feature.

Type of Measure
Direct child assessment

Intended Age Range
4;0 years to 12;11 years

Key Constructs/Domains
Expressive vocabulary

Careful attention was paid during development to both the psychometric and linguistic/cultural properties of the measure, which are generally strong.

Weaknesses

The EOWPVT-SBE is based on the 2000 edition of the EOWPVT, though a newer bilingual version linked to the EOWPVT-4 is in development.

If an examiner is interested in learning specifically about a child's Spanish expressive vocabulary or English expressive vocabulary compared to that of a monolingual child, another measure will need to be utilized.

The interrater reliability of the EOWPVT-SBE remains in need of examination, as does its criterion validity in the preschool age range.

Although the English edition has been normed for individuals between ages 2 and 80+, the EOWPVT-SBE is normed for children between ages 4 and 12. Thus, norms are not available for young preschoolers.

ADMINISTRATION

Procedure

In general, the child is first asked to name pictures in his or her dominant language. If the child does not know a word in his or her dominant language, he or she is asked to give it in his or her nondominant language. The child's dominant language is determined by asking him or her to answer the questions that appear on the record form. Once determined, the dominant language is used to deliver the instructions, prompts, and cues to the examinee to minimize difficulties in understanding directions due to language. If necessary, the nondominant language can also be utilized with the examinee.

Time Needed

10–15 minutes

*The administrator begins with examples at the suggested starting point for the examinee's chronological age. The main part of the measure is then started. Equal points are given whether the child knows the word in English or Spanish. All exact responses are recorded on the record form on the line corresponding to that item. The specific language used to answer each item correctly is documented. For example, if the child answers an item correctly in Spanish, a slash is placed through the **S** on the record form. If the child answers correctly in English, a slash is placed through the **E** on the record form.*

The same picture book is used for the EOWPVT-SBE and its English counterpart. However, certain items are skipped on the EOWPVT-SBE because of identified linguistic and/or cultural difficulties associated with those items.

Administration and Interpretation

As with the 2000 edition of the EOWPVT, the examiner need not have training in assessment to administer the EOWPVT-SBE but must be trained under the supervision of someone who is familiar with the principles of psychological assessment and interpretation. The examiner must be fluent in both English and Spanish, or an assistant must be present who is fluent in the language not spoken by the examiner.

As with the 2000 edition of the EOWPVT, the examiner should become very familiar with the administration and scoring of the measure and should perform several trials. Results should be interpreted by someone familiar with psychometrics and statistics. This measure can be used by speech-language pathologists; psychologists; counselors;

learning specialists; physicians; occupational therapists; or other educational, psychological, and medical professionals (Brownell, 2001).

Scoring Method

This measure is scored by hand. The total number of correct responses below the basal level (eight consecutive correct responses) is added to the number of correct responses between the basal and ceiling levels (six consecutive errors). This raw score is then converted to standard scores using tables in the manual. In addition, the appendix provides a table that can be utilized to examine the relevance of performance differences on the EOWPVT-SBE and ROWPVT-SBE.

As with the 2000 edition of the EOWPVT, the use of slashes instead of circles to record correct responses on the record form may cause administration error initially because slashes may be incorrectly interpreted as incorrect responses. Training and experience will assist in avoiding this potential problem.

Adaptations or Instructions for Use with Individuals with Disabilities

None indicated

FUNCTIONAL CONSIDERATIONS

Measure Development

This is the first edition of the EOWPVT-SBE. It is based on the 2000 English edition of the EOWPVT. A newer version based on the newer EOWPVT-4 is in development. Earlier editions of the EOWPVT had optional Spanish record forms. Their reliability and validity were questionable because 1) the items were a direct translation from the English version, 2) content screening or item analysis based on the Spanish responses was not conducted, and 3) normative information for the Spanish-speaking population was not available (Brownell, 2001).

In the early development of the EOWPVT-SBE, a survey was conducted with professionals engaged in examining the language skills of Spanish-speaking students. The results indicated that the greatest concern among these professionals was accounting for bilingualism, because the majority of Spanish-speaking students in the United States are bilingual. Respondents to the survey indicated that their primary goal was to assess their students' general vocabulary competence regardless of the particular language. As a result, it was decided that this measure would examine overall expressive vocabulary development by accepting responses in Spanish and English and by using a standardization sample of Spanish–English bilingual students living in the United States (Brownell, 2001).

When developers were revising the 2000 edition of the EOWPVT, a Spanish translation was created for the bilingual edition by an independent firm that specialized in developing educational materials in Spanish. The items were selected from a variety of sources to represent words that individuals could be expected to know at each age range (Brownell, 2001). However, only words that could be illustrated were represented. Any items that did not translate accurately either from English to Spanish or between different Spanish dialects were eliminated from the test. Next, the translated items were sent to leaders in bilingual education across four states who were asked to critique the items and make recommendations.

The measure was then revised and administered to a sample of 1,050 individuals. Item-level analyses using both item response theory and classical test theory approaches were then conducted to statistically identify items that did not function well. Qualitative analysis was also conducted based on the individuals' feedback on the items. After this process, six items were eliminated (Brownell, 2001).

The final item analysis found that the median correlation of item difficulty to item order was .95, indicating that the item discrimination was quite high. It was also strong among the preschool population (.92–.95). The median item discrimination index was .82–.83 among preschoolers and .84 across the whole sample. Together, these findings suggest that each item presented to bilingual children provides significant information on their expressive vocabulary development (Brownell, 2001).

Content Equivalence of Items and Measure

The constructs and operationalization are appropriate for this test, as items seem to be able to transcend both English- and Spanish-speaking cultures (Brownell, 2001). The use of qualitative and quantitative methods throughout the creation of the two language versions contributes to their content equivalence.

Semantic Equivalence of Translations

Translation, feedback, and item analysis were utilized. Attention was paid to dialectical issues.

Structural Consistency Across the English and Spanish Versions

The instrument structure between the English and bilingual versions is no longer identical, as the 2000 edition was updated to the EOWPVT-4 and the EOWPVT-SBE is still being updated. The EOWPVT-SBE and the 2000 edition of the EOWPVT use the same picture book. Yet Spanish language knowledge was taken into account, and thus certain items are skipped on the EOWPVT-SBE because of identified linguistic and/or cultural difficulties associated with those items. Lastly, although the EOWPVT-4 has been normed for individuals between ages 2 and 80+, the EOWPVT-SBE is normed for children between ages 4 and 12.

Standardization Sample

The sample included 1,050 children who generally matched the demographic characteristics of the U.S. Hispanic population. Overrepresented in this sample were individuals from the Western region whose dialect was Mexican; other categories of region and Hispanic origin were underrepresented. Details can be found in the manual (Brownell, 2001).

Only individuals who spoke at least some Spanish were included in the norms groups. Because type of language dominance (e.g., Spanish dominant, balanced bilingual, English dominant) did not significantly relate to performance, a single set of norms is appropriate for this measure (Brownell, 2001).

The EOWPVT-SBE and its counterpart the ROWPVT-SBE were co-normed together.

Norming

Norm referenced

Reliability

Test–Retest Reliability

A total of 32 examinees were retested by the same examiner within about a 20-day interval. This sample included children as young as 4;1 years, though the median age was 6;10 years. The corrected test–retest correlation was .91. These coefficients suggest that the EOWPVT-SBE is stable over time.

Internal Consistency

On average, Cronbach's alpha was .95. Among preschoolers, the alpha was in the .92–.93 range, which is high. Corresponding standard errors of measurement for preschoolers' standard scores were 4.24 among 4-year-olds and 3.97 among 5-year-olds.

The correlation between the scores derived from the odd-numbered items and the scores derived from the even-numbered items was also examined. The median corrected split-half coefficient was also high at .96 (.93–.95 for preschoolers).

Interrater Agreement

This information is not provided in the manual.

Other Forms of Reliability (e.g., Equivalent Forms)

Not applicable

Validity

Face and Content

The utilization of feedback from a range of expert consultants and users contributes to the face validity of this measure. Furthermore, this measure appears to assess bilingual expressive vocabulary as it purports to do. In addition, items that could not be translated accurately and consistently across Spanish dialects, that had item difficulties in both English and Spanish, that might be culturally biased, or that might present other problems were eliminated through quantitative and qualitative procedures. However, because the EOWPVT-SBE began with the list of words already in the EOWPVT, the full range (e.g., content) of potentially appropriate words in Spanish was not initially examined.

Internal Construct

Not applicable, as the EOWPVT examines one construct (i.e., expressive vocabulary).

External Construct

External construct validity was first evidenced in analyses by chronological age. First, there was an uncorrected correlation of .75 of raw scores to chronological age, which indicates that older individuals with a more developed vocabulary will demonstrate greater proficiency on the EOWPVT-SBE than younger individuals. Second, individuals with intellectual disability, a language disorder, or a learning disorder all showed a significant difference in performance from the normative group, whereas individuals with articulation difficulties did not show a significant difference. These results highlight the fact that articulation is a disorder of speech production, not language comprehension or usage (Brownell, 2001). Each of the samples of exceptional children included preschool-age children.

Support for the convergent and discriminant validities of the EOWPVT-SBE among preschoolers remains in need of investigation.

Criterion

The EOWPVT-SBE shows a corrected correlation of .75 with the Language Achievement subtest of the Stanford Achievement Tests (SAT-9), which is an

English group-administered exam. The EOWPVT-SBE's correlation with the Reading Achievement subtest was .67 and its correlation with the SAT-9 receptive vocabulary task was 57. These correlations indicate that English academic achievement relates significantly to children's vocabulary across English and Spanish as measured by the EOWPVT-SBE. Although this is a start at examining criterion validity among older children, criterion validity still needs to be examined among preschoolers.

In addition, the EOWPVT-SBE and the ROWPVT-SBE are correlated at .43, which is not as strong a correlation as may be expected given that they both examine bilingual vocabulary—one expressive and the other receptive. The manual suggests that this may relate to the greater linguistic variability seen in bilingual samples (Brownell, 2001). It appears then that these two measures test overlapping but distinct features of bilingual vocabulary (receptive and expressive).

Comparison of Psychometric Properties Between English and Spanish Versions

Technical Equivalence in Reliability

The reliability statistics of the EOWPVT-4 and the EOWPVT-SBE are quite high, in the .90s. The interrater reliability has not been examined for either version.

Technical Equivalence in Validity

The validity statistics of the EOWPVT-4 and EOWPVT-SBE are similar. However, the relationship between the EOWPVT and ROWPVT is stronger (.69) than that between the EOWPVT-SBE and ROWPVT-SBE (.43). That is, the expressive and receptive vocabularies of English speakers are more strongly related than the expressive and receptive vocabularies of Spanish speakers/bilinguals. Although this may relate to measurement issues, it may also reflect bilingual development, as Brownell (2001) states. Receptive and expressive abilities across two languages may not be as closely connected as these same skills within a single language. This weaker correlation should be considered when one is interpreting data on individuals and groups using both the ROWPVT-SBE and the EOWPVT-SBE.

RELEVANT STUDIES USING THE MEASURE

A brief literature search using PsycINFO and Google Scholar identified the use of the EOWPVT-SBE in studies or preschoolers. Older versions of the measure have also been utilized.

Lugo-Neris, Jackson, and Goldstein (2010) compared the language development of young bilingual migrant children participating in English-only vocabulary instruction with that of children also receiving Spanish bridging. The EOWPVT-SBE, among other measures, was utilized, with a positive outcome.

ADDITIONAL REFERENCES

Jenkins, J.A. (2005). Test review of the Expressive One-Word Picture Vocabulary Test, Spanish-Bilingual Edition. In R.A. Spies & B.S. Plake (Eds.), *The sixteenth mental measurements yearbook*. Retrieved from the Buros Institute's *Test Reviews Online* web site: http://www.unl.edu/buros

Lugo-Neris, M.J., Jackson, C.W., & Goldstein, H. (2010). Facilitating vocabulary acquisition of young English language learners. *Language, Speech, and Hearing Services in Schools, 41*, 314–327.

FirstSTEp: Screening Test for Evaluating Preschoolers: English

Manual

Miller, L.J. (1993). *FirstSTEp Screening Test for Evaluating Preschoolers.* San Antonio, TX: Harcourt Assessment.

Publisher[1]

Pearson, Inc.
19500 Bulverde Road
San Antonio, TX 78259-3701
http://www.pearsonassessments.com

Cost

Complete kit: $278.35. Items are also sold separately.

Description of Measure

FirstSTEp is "an individually administered screening test designed to identify young children (aged 2 years, 9 months to 6 years, 2 months) who may have mild to severe school-related problems. FirstSTEp is also designed to serve as a short, but effective, companion to the Miller Assessment for Preschoolers (MAP, 1988, 1982), which is used to assess a child's nonverbal, cognitive, verbal, neuromaturational, and integrated abilities" (Miller, 1993, p. 1)

Available Languages and Formats

A Spanish version (*PrimerPASO* Screening Test for Evaluating Preschoolers) is available.

Strengths

Thorough reliability and validity studies were conducted, and the resulting psychometrics are solid.

The child assessment is composed of game-like activities, potentially making the process more engaging for children.

Weaknesses

FirstSTEp was last published in the early 1990s. Thus, the norms are becoming outdated.

Internal reliability coefficients were weaker among 5- and 6-year-olds' scores on the Motor domain, which may indicate a ceiling effect.

Type of Measure

Direct child assessment, parent report, and examiner observation

Intended Age Range

2;9 years to 6;2 years

Key Constructs/Domains

- Cognition
- Communication
- Motor
- Social-Emotional (observation)
- Adaptive Behavior (questionnaire)

ADMINISTRATION

Procedure

FirstSTEp assesses three domains (i.e., Cognitive, Communication, and Motor), with each domain containing four subtests. The Social-Emotional Scale

Time Needed

15 minutes

---

[1]FirstSTEp is now distributed by Pearson.

163

and Adaptive Behavior Checklist are optional components of the measure whose scores are not included in the composite score.

In FirstSTEp, the child engages in various game-like activities with the administrator. For example, they play the "What's Missing?" game or picture completion task, in which the child is asked to identify what is missing from the picture (e.g., a tire is missing from a car). Some items are designated for particular age groups.

Activities (and primary abilities measured) include the following:

- Money Game (quantitative reasoning)
- What's Missing? Game (picture completion)
- Which Way? Game (visual position in space)
- Put Together Game (problem solving)
- Listen Game (auditory discrimination)
- How Many Can You Say? Game (word retrieval)
- Finish Up Game (association)
- Copy Me Game (sentence and digit repetition)
- Drawing Game (visual-motor integration)
- Things with Strings Game (fine motor planning)
- Statue Game (balance)
- Jumping Game (gross motor planning)

For the Adaptive Behavior Checklist, the examiner asks a parent or caregiver questions regarding the child's daily living, self-management and social interaction, and functioning within the community. The Parent/Teacher Scale allows for those individuals most closely involved with the child to provide supplemental information about typical behaviors in areas assessed. Finally, the Social-Emotional Scale is an examiner rating form of the child's behavior during the administration of FirstSTEp.

Administration and Interpretation

A wide range of individuals working with young children can administer the measure, including early childhood educators, speech and language therapists, psychologists, physicians, and aides in all of these professions (Miller, 1993). A training video is available for purchase.

Scoring Method

Responses are recorded by hand, and there are different record forms for different age groups. The scoring template guides calculations of composite or scaled scores for each of the areas assessed. In addition, "FirstSTEp utilizes a red/yellow/green system to indicate whether a child is functioning in the normal or delayed range" (Miller, 1993, p. 108). Cut points between the yellow, red, and green sections are empirically derived (e.g., a cut point is in the center of the yellow zone, 1 SD from the mean). These cut points were established with a double cross-validation design.

Adaptations or Instructions for Use with Individuals with Disabilities

No specific adaptations or special instructions are provided for adapting the measure for use with children with disabilities.

FUNCTIONAL CONSIDERATIONS

Measure Development

A longer standardized developmental measure, the Miller Assessment for Preschoolers (MAP; Miller, 1982, 1988), influenced the development of FirstSTEp. Specifically, the initial item pool for FirstSTEp was derived from prior MAP research. There were five phases in developing FirstSTEp's item content: two pilot studies, a larger tryout study, a standardization study, and a final edition phase. The pilot studies included the administration of criterion measures. Furthermore, the questionnaires' psychometrics were also examined. The manual provides detailed descriptions for each of these phases.

Within this process, items were analyzed for potential cultural, ethnic, and gender biases; age-level trends; and discrimination in performance between typically developing children and those with clinical diagnoses. In addition, content experts were involved in item modifications. Field researchers also provided feedback regarding the measure (e.g., ease of administration, children's enjoyment of activities, reliability in scoring).

Standardization Sample

The FirstSTEp standardization sample consisted of 1,433 children, with roughly 100 boys and 100 girls represented in seven age groupings between 2;9 and 6;2 years of age. Using a random, stratified sampling plan, researchers selected the sample to represent the similarly aged population of U.S. children in 1988 across a range of variables, including region, race/ethnicity, and parent education level. For example, the sample consisted of 68% white, 13% African American, 14% Hispanic, and 5% other children (Asians were not identified). Only children who spoke English as their first language were included in the sample (Miller, 1993).

Norming

Norm referenced

Reliability

Test–Retest Reliability

A total of 86 children were randomly selected from the standardization sample to assess test–retest reliability. FirstSTEp was administered on two different occasions within a 1- or 2-week interval. The stability coefficients were indicative of medium to high temporal stability and were as follows: Cognitive = .85, Communication = .91, Motor = .85, Social-Emotional = .82, Composite = .93.

Internal Consistency

The reliability coefficient for the composite score was .89 on average across age groups, which falls at the top of the medium range. The lowest composite score alpha (.86) was found in the 3;3–3;8-year range and the highest (.91) was in the 4;3–4;8- and 4;9–5;2-year ranges. Composite score standard errors of measurement ranged from 2.99 to 3.68.

Among the domain scores, the average Communication coefficient was .87 (range = .83–.89). The average Cognitive coefficient was .75 (range = .72–.79). The average Motor coefficient was .71; lower reliabilities (range = .65–.69) were found among the older children and higher ones (range = .74–.75) were found among the younger ones. A ceiling effect may be present on the Motor scale.

The split-half reliability coefficients for the subscales were consistent with the alphas. The average coefficients across the age groups were as follows: Cognitive = .75, Communication = .87, Motor = .71, Social-Emotional = .92.

The average reliability coefficients were in the medium to high range for the optional measures and were generally similar across the age groups (Social-Emotional, $r = .92$; Adaptive Behavior, $r = .85$; and Parent/Teacher, $r = .89$).

Interrater Agreement

Two independent raters assessed 43 children, with one rater administering the assessment while the other observed. The correlation coefficients for the scaled scores indicated a fairly high level of consistency between the two raters, though they were lower for the Social-Emotional examiner observation scale (Composite = .94, Cognitive = .96, Communication = .96, Motor = .88, Social-Emotional = .77).

Other Forms of Reliability (e.g., Equivalent Forms)

No information provided

Validity

Face and Content

FirstSTEp was reviewed by a range of consultants and experts during its development and appears to assess what it purports to. Furthermore, the manual describes three approaches used to ensure adequate content coverage. First, the original item pool was reviewed by more than 50 consultants, who evaluated how representative the items were of the domains. Second, examiners participating in the pilot, tryout, and standardization phases completed evaluation forms asking for feedback, such as the appropriateness of administration and scoring rules and perceived item discrimination between typical children and those with clinical diagnoses. Third, FirstSTEp was reviewed by an expert panel that examined the appropriateness of "content and…breadth of coverage" (Miller, 1993, p. 118). According to the manual, if experts felt an area was lacking, additional items were added to the instrument.

Internal Construct

Confirmatory and exploratory factor analyses were conducted to examine the fit of the theoretical model presented as well as to assess whether another factor structure may be present. Broadly speaking, these analyses supported the existence of three factors—Motor, Communication, and Cognitive. Within the exploratory factor analyses, the Quantitative Reasoning and Visual Position in Space subtests loaded more highly on the Communication than the Cognitive factor. Miller speculates that this slight mismatch between empirical and theoretical factors may be due to the fact that the subtests in question are "verbally mediated and thus may reflect a child's language as well as cognitive skills" (1993, p. 119). It is important to note that forcing these two subtests to load on the Communication factor in the confirmatory factor analysis did not improve model fit. Thus, they remained on the Cognitive factor in the final version.

External Construct

Optimal cut points for each domain and composite score were examined using a double cross-validation design. The standardization sample ($n = 1,443$) and a clinical sample of children who had been diagnosed with cognitive, language, or motor delays ($n = 372$) were included. Sensitivity values across the different special needs areas ranged from .74 (language and motor delay groups) to .84 (cognitive delay group) for domain scores. Specificity values across the different special needs areas ranged from .76 (language delay) to .82 (cognitive delay) for domains scores. Additional information is available in the manual. Findings suggest that the percentage of false negatives is fairly low (1%–3%), whereas the percentage of false positives is substantially higher (15%–21%; Miller, 1993). Given that this is a screener, a decision is often made to err on the side of referring more children for a full evaluation (i.e., false positive) than to miss children with a true disability (i.e., false negative).

Support for the measurer's convergent and discriminant validities is also indicated by some the correlational studies described in "Criterion."

Criterion

Children's performance on FirstSTEp was compared to their performance on six other measures. The interval between tests ranged from 7 to 30 days, with generally acceptable correlations ranging from fair to adequate (Overton, 1998). Presented here are coefficients related to the FirstSTEp Composite Score. Specific correlations with the domain scores, which are of the magnitude expected, are also presented in the manual. Some of the studies also examined correlations with the questionnaires.

- MAP (n = 226): r = .71
- Wechsler Preschool and Primary Scale of Intelligence–Revised (n = 127): r = .82
- Bruininks-Oseretsky Test of Motor Proficiency (n = 89): r = . 63.
- Test of Language Development–Primary: Second Edition (n = 109): r = .57–.75
- Walker Problem Behavior Identification Checklist–Revised (n = 135): r = −.24 (Note that because the Walker Problem Behavior Identification Checklist–Revised is scored in the opposite direction of FirstSTEp, with higher scores indicating more problem behaviors, all correlations are negative.)

The Adaptive Behavior questionnaire was also examined in a correlational study with the Vineland Adaptive Behavior Scales (n = 134). The correlation with the Vineland's Adaptive Behavior scale was .57, which suggests moderate overlap between the two measures.

RELEVANT STUDIES USING THE MEASURE

A brief literature search using PsycINFO and Google Scholar yielded the use of FirstSTEp in the following studies. It is also possible that the measure has been utilized in additional studies.

Clift, Stagnitti, and DeMello (1998) utilized the FirstSTEp Communication domain in a validation study of another measure, the Test of Pretend Play. They found a significant relationship between the language and play measures.

Helfritch and Beer (2007) found the FirstSTEp screening tool to be effective for measuring the behavior, developmental, and emotional changes of 19 preschoolers who experienced homelessness and witnessed domestic violence.

ADDITIONAL REFERENCES

Clift, S., Stagnitti, K., & DeMello, L. (1998). A validational study of the Test of Pretend Play using correlational and classificational analyses. *Child Language Teaching and Therapy, 14*(2), 199–209.

Emmons, M.R., & Alfonso, V.C. (2005). A critical review of the technical characteristics of preschool screening batteries. *Psychoeducational Assessment, 23,* 111–127.

Helfritch, C.A., & Beer, D.W. (2007). Use of the FirstSTEp screening tool with children exposed to domestic violence and homelessness: A group case study. *Physical & Occupational Therapy in Pediatrics, 27*(5), 63–76.

Miller, L.J. (1988, 1982), *Miller Assessment for Preschoolers (MAP).* San Antonio, TX: The Psychological Corporation.

Overton, T. (1998) Test review of the FirstSTEp Screening Test for Evaluating Preschoolers. In J.C. Impara & B.S. Plake (Eds.), *The thirteenth mental measurements yearbook.* Retrieved from the Buros Institute's *Test Reviews Online* web site: http://www.unl.edu/buros

PrimerPASO Screening Test for Evaluating Preschoolers: Spanish

Information pertaining specifically to the Spanish version of the measure is in bold and italics. The remainder is equivalent information provided in the English review.

Manual

Miller, L.J. (2003). *PrimerPASO Screening Test for Evaluating Preschoolers.* San Antonio, TX: Harcourt Assessment.

Publisher[1]

Pearson, Inc.
19500 Bulverde Road
San Antonio, TX 78259-3701
http://www.pearsonassessments.com

Cost

Complete PrimerPASO kit: $340.55. An upgrade kit is also available for $160.35 for those who already own FirstSTEp. Individuals can buy a combination kit of both language versions for $516.55. Items are also sold separately.

Type of Measure

Direct child assessment, caregiver report, and examiner observation

Intended Age Range

2;9 years to 6;2 years

Key Constructs/Domains

- Cognitive
- Communication
- Motor
- Social-Emotional (questionnaire)
- Adaptive Behavior (questionnaire)

Description of Measure

"PrimerPASO was developed for Spanish-speaking children who are at risk for developmental and learning problems. Derived from FirstSTEp (Miller, 1993), PrimerPASO is an individually administered, 15-minute preschool screening scale for Spanish-speaking children between 2 years, 9 months to 6 years, 2 months. PrimerPASO includes three subtests that measure performance: Cognitive Abilities, Communication Abilities and Motor Abilities. The administration directions and many of the test items from FirstSTEp have been translated and blind-back translated for the PrimerPASO adaptation" (Miller, 2003, p. 1).

Available Communications and Formats

An English version (FirstSTEp: Screening Test for Evaluating Preschoolers) is available.

Strengths

Multiple options for some of the words in Spanish are provided in the measure (e.g., alternatives for **centavos** *include* **kilos, chavitos, priestos,** *and* **pennies***).*

More recently standardized than the English version, **PrimerPASO** *included in its development methods of translation such as using a bilingual psychologist as the translator, using back-translation procedures, and engaging a review panel of bilingual psychologists.*

The child assessment is composed of game-like activities, potentially making the process more engaging for children.

---

[1]*PrimerPASO is now distributed by Pearson.*

168

Weaknesses

PrimerPASO *has limited psychometric information available beyond internal consistency data.*

Although the internal consistency is generally good for the Composite and Communication score reliabilities, the **PrimerPASO's** *Cognitive score reliability is low, particularly among older children. In addition, the Motor score coefficient is low for both the English and Spanish versions. The manual suggests that small sample sizes and restricted ranges in abilities may have affected the coefficients (Miller, 2003).*

ADMINISTRATION

Procedure

As with FirstSTEp, *PrimerPASO* assesses three domains (i.e., Cognitive, Communication, and Motor), with each domain containing four subtests. The Social-Emotional Scale and Adaptive Behavior Checklist) are optional components of the measure whose scores are not included in the composite score.

Time Needed
15–20 minutes

On *PrimerPASO,* the child engages in various game-like activities with the administrator. For example, they play the "What's Missing?" game or picture completion task, in which the child is asked to identify what is missing from the picture (e.g., a tire is missing from a car).

Activities (and primary abilities measured) include the following:

- Money Game (quantitative reasoning)
- What's Missing? Game (picture completion)
- Which Way? Game (visual position in space)
- Put Together Game (problem solving)
- Listen Game (auditory discrimination)
- How Many Can You Say? Game (word retrieval)
- Finish Up Game (association)
- Copy Me Game (sentence and digit repetition)
- Drawing Game (visual-motor integration)
- Things with Strings (fine motor planning)
- Statue Game (balance)
- Jumping Game (gross motor planning)

For the Adaptive Behavior Checklist, the examiner asks a parent or caregiver questions regarding the child's daily living, self-management and social interaction, and functioning within the community. The Parent/Teacher Scale allows for those individuals most closely involved with the child to provide supplemental information about typical behaviors in areas assessed. Finally, the Social-Emotional Scale is an examiner rating form of the child's behavior during the administration of *PrimerPASO.*

Administration and Interpretation

A wide range of individuals working with young children can administer the measure, including early childhood educators, speech and language therapists, psychologists, physicians and aides in all of these professions (Miller, 2003). A training video is available for purchase.

Scoring Method

Responses are recorded by hand, and there are different record forms for different age groups. The scoring template guides calculations of composite or scaled scores for each of the areas assessed. In addition, "FirstSTEp utilizes a red/yellow/green system to indicate whether a child is functioning in the normal or delayed range" (Miller, 2003, p. 108). Cut points between the yellow, red, and green sections are empirically derived (e.g., a cut point is in the center of the yellow zone, 1 *SD* from the mean). These cut points were established with a double cross-validation design with the English version. Thus, their applicability to the Spanish version is unknown.

Adaptations or Instructions for Use with Individuals with Disabilities

No specific adaptations or special instructions are provided for adapting the measure for use with children with disabilities.

FUNCTIONAL CONSIDERATIONS

Measure Development

PrimerPASO *was developed from FirstSTEp. A bilingual linguist and a bilingual psychologist translated the FirstSTEp's research edition. The linguist also completed a blind back translation of the Cognitive and Motor domain sections. Items for the Communication domain were created to match the language items from FirstSTEp. The completed Spanish version was reviewed by three additional psychologists from the bilingual division of the American Psychological Association. The review took into consideration Spanish dialects from Mexico, Puerto Rico, and Cuba (Miller, 2003).*

PrimerPASO *underwent field testing with 75 bilingual children from six sites in the United States. After this testing, the items that had the best item-to-total subtest correlations and adequate equivalence between the two languages were selected (Miller, 2003).*

Content Equivalence of Items and Measure

Numerous reviewers examined the equivalence of the measures. In addition, quantitative methods were used to examine item statistics with a small field-test sample.

Semantic Equivalence of Translations

*There was an effort to consider different dialects by including alternative words for the assessor to use when asking the questions (e.g., **llanta, goma, rueda neumatico**). This allows children to understand the basic meaning of the questions and provides a greater chance to assess the specific ability or domain. In addition, the prompts are quite equivalent, though some vary slightly.*

Structural Consistency Across the English and Spanish Versions

Overall, the structures of the English and Spanish versions are quite similar.

Standardization Sample

The **PrimerPASO** *standardization sample consisted of 566 children in seven age groupings between 2;9 and 6;2 years. Children were tested in three different sites: Orange County, California; Longmont, Colorado; and Puerto Rico. All of the evaluators were native Spanish speakers. The sample was selected to represent the* *similarly aged population of Hispanic children living in the United States according to 2000 U.S. Census data. The sample included monolingual Spanish speakers and bilingual children (18.7% spoke Spanish only, 74.2% spoke mostly Spanish, and 2.7% spoke English and Spanish fluently; Miller, 2003).*

Norming

Norm referenced

Reliability

Test–Retest Reliability

No information is provided.

Internal Consistency

The reliability coefficient for the **PrimerPASO** *composite score was .84 on average for 3- to 5-year-olds, which is in the medium range. The manual reports that the small sample sizes precluded similar analyses for the other age groups (Miller, 2003). The lowest composite score alpha coefficient (.80) was found in the 5-year-old age range and the highest (.87) was in the 3-year-old age range. Composite score standard errors of measurement ranged from 1.09 to 1.34.*

Among the domain scores, the average Communication coefficient was .82 (range = .81–.82). The average Motor coefficient was .73 (range = .52–.79); lower reliabilities (.60) were found among 5-year-olds and higher ones (.80) were found among 3-year-olds. Thus, a ceiling effect may be present on the Motor scale. Lower reliability coefficients were also reported for the Cognitive domain (average = .61; highest among 3-year-olds at .68 and lowest among 5-year-olds at .52). The manual indicates that small sample sizes and restricted ranges in abilities may have affected the coefficients (Miller, 2003).

Although split-half reliability coefficients for the subscales and reliability coefficients for the optional measures are presented for FirstSTEp, these are not presented in the **PrimerPASO** *manual.*

Interrater Agreement

No information is provided.

Other Forms of Reliability (e.g., Equivalent Forms)

Not applicable

Validity

Face and Content

Bilingual expert reviews and item analyses were conducted. Attention was also paid to dialectical variations in Spanish. However, because **PrimerPASO** *began with the items already in the FirstSTEp version, the full range (e.g., content) of potentially appropriate items in Spanish was not initially examined.*

Internal Construct

No information is provided.

External Construct
No information is provided.

Criterion
No information is provided.

Comparison of Psychometric Properties Between English and Spanish Versions

Technical Equivalence in Reliability
*The internal consistency is generally similar to that of the FirstSTEp, with good Composite and Communication score reliabilities. The Cognitive score reliability is lower for the **PrimerPASO,** particularly among older children. In addition, the Motor score coefficient is low for both the English and Spanish versions. Other forms of reliability could not be compared because they have not yet been examined for the **PrimerPASO.***

Technical Equivalence in Validity
*Though a good effort was obviously made on the development and standardization of the measure, there is little information on **PrimerPASO's** statistical validity.*

RECENT STUDIES USING THE MEASURE

A brief literature search using PsycINFO and Google Scholar did not yield any published studies whose abstracts specified using *PrimerPASO*. However, it is possible that this measure has been utilized in studies.

ADDITIONAL REFERENCES

Miller, L.J. (1993). *FirstSTEp Screening Test for Evaluating Preschoolers.* San Antonio, TX: Harcourt Assessment.

Get Ready to Read! Screening Tool (GRTR): English

Manual

Whitehurst, G.J. (2001). *The NCLD Get Ready to Read! Screening Tool Technical Report.* Retrieved from http://www.getreadytoread.org

Publisher

Pearson, Inc.
19500 Bulverde Road
San Antonio, TX 78259-3701
http://www.pearsonassessments.com

Cost

Print copies: $42.50. Literacy manual: $30.50. Training video: $25. A free version is available at http://www.getreadytoread.org/screening/grtr_directions.php

Type of Measure

Direct child assessment

Intended Age Range

4;0 years to 4;11 years (though it has also been used in research with younger and older preschoolers). *(Note: The enhanced English version released by Pearson is standardized up to 5;11 years; S. Horowitz, personal communication, June 29, 2009.)*

Key Constructs/Domains

- Print knowledge
- Phonological awareness

Description of Measure

"The National Center for Learning Disabilities (NCLD), in collaboration with researchers involved in early literacy and literacy research, developed a screening tool to gauge preschool children's development in reading-related skills. This measure, the Get Ready to Read! Screening Tool (GRTR), was designed for English-speaking four-year-old children. GRTR is a 20-item multiple choice measure that provides information on children's early literacy skills, primarily in the areas of print knowledge (letter knowledge, print concepts) and phonological awareness" (Lonigan, 2003, p. 2).

(Note: The enhanced English version consists of 25 items.)

Available Languages and Formats

A Spanish version is also available.

Strengths

The development of the GRTR incorporated a variety of empirical approaches, including attention to items that would best predict reading outcomes.

A body of published literature is accruing that supports both the concurrent and predictive validities of the GRTR.

The GRTR is a quick, easily administered tool designed to be used by teachers and parents.

A free version is available.

Weaknesses

The test–retest and interrater reliabilities have not yet been examined. But given that the measure does not include subjective scoring, high interrater agreement may be anticipated.

This review focuses on the original version of the Get Ready to Read! Screening Tool. An enhanced English measure was released by Pearson after this review was nearly finalized. Changes in the measure are briefly highlighted here, but readers interested in the new version should carefully review the new version by Pearson.

The internal consistency of the English version appears lower among Latinos than for other racial/ethnic communities (alpha = .55), which may relate to greater variability in English proficiency levels within the Latino population. Though reliability coefficients are important considerations for researchers and clinicians, it is important to note that scores on the English GRTR significantly predict outcomes for Latino children (e.g., Farver, Nakamoto, & Lonigan, 2007; Whitehurst, 2001).

ADMINISTRATION

Procedure

Children are presented with four pictures and asked to select a response based on questions posed by the examiner. The GRTR begins with an example, which

Time Needed
10 minutes

is followed by the 20 items that tap print knowledge, emergent writing, and phonological sensitivity (Molfese, Molfese, Modglin, Walker, & Neamon, 2004).

Data from national demonstrations conducted between 2001 and 2003 indicated that children engaged well with the GRTR (NCLD, n.d.-a). More than 96% of children completed the whole measure, and solid ratings were evidenced across engagement, enjoyment, responsiveness, resistance, and difficulty.

Administration and Interpretation

A major impetus for the development of the GRTR was the desire to create a measure that could be administered by nonprofessionals, such as parents and teachers (Whitehurst, 2001). Thus, a multiple-choice format was selected to simplify administration and scoring. Instructions are provided for the administrator, and little training is needed. In addition, a training video is available.

Scoring Method

The total number of items answered correctly is automatically tallied in the online version. An answer sheet can be downloaded to record answers, though the wording of the example item differed slightly between the online version and the hard copy answer sheet.

Whitehurst (2001) provided the following guidelines for interpretation: Very Weak Skills (0–6 correct), Weak Skills (6–9), Average Skills (9–12), Strong Skills (12–16), and Very Strong Skills (16–20). These guidelines were created using analyses predicting high versus low scores on the Developing Skills Checklist (DSC) from the GRTR, as well as a number of additional considerations described in Whitehurst (2001).

(Note: The enhanced English version was standardized. Thus, standard scores and age equivalents will be available; S. Horowitz, personal communication, June 29, 2009.)

Adaptations or Instructions for Use with Individuals with Disabilities

Specific instructions for using the GRTR with children with disabilities are not presented. However, as the measure involves simple responses from children, it is likely adaptable for use with children with various types of disabilities.

FUNCTIONAL CONSIDERATIONS

Measure Development

The GRTR was first developed in English in 2001, using past theoretical and empirical findings. The primary authors (Drs. Grover Whitehurst and Christopher Lonigan) are well-known researchers in the field. Item development began by identifying children who were good or poor readers at the end of second grade. The DSC was administered in preschool and had a predictive classification accuracy of 78% (with 85% correct classification of poor readers). Items from the DSC were then statistically examined to see which types best predicted these classifications. Items were also examined from other measures developed by Dr. Lonigan for their predictive ability.

An initial set of about 100 multiple-choice items was created, which was reduced to 60 based on a variety of factors. These items were then administered to 342 children (described in "Standardization Sample") along with the DSC within a 2-week period. A total of 200 children were also administered additional language and literacy measures. A variety of statistical approaches yielded somewhat different sets of 20 items, though these were highly correlated (.89–.96). The statistical approaches utilized were item difficulty level, reliability alpha coefficient, and external validity (as demonstrated through item correlations with the DSC). In deciding upon the final set of items, the test developers also paid attention to item coverage. In the final decision-making process, external validity results were given more weight than internal reliability results.

(Note: The enhanced English version includes additional items designed to increase the ceiling of the measure; S. Horowitz, personal communication, June 29, 2009.)

Standardization Sample

A total of 342 children across two states were involved in the development of the GRTR. Of these, 139 children from New York were attending Head Start. Nearly half of this sample was Latino (20% dual language learners), and a little more than a third was African American. Children also participated from three types of sites in Florida: Head Start, state-sponsored prekindergarten, and private centers. The first two groups of Florida children were composed primarily of African Americans, whereas the final group was composed primarily of Caucasians. Whitehurst (2001) presented various rationales for including a high percentage of low-income and minority children in the sample, including their higher representation among children with later reading problems. As described in "Internal Consistency" and "Criterion," the middle-class sample was utilized to examine potential effects of this sampling approach.

The children ranged in age from 3 to just over 5. A total of 273 were in the 4-year-old range, with an approximately equal distribution across the 12 months within this age group.

(Note: The enhanced English version was standardized on a nationally representative sample of more than 850 children; S. Horowitz, personal communication, June 29, 2009.)

Norming

Criterion referenced. *(Note: The enhanced English version is criterion and norm referenced.)*

Reliability

Test–Retest Reliability

This information is not provided in the manual.

Internal Consistency

For the full sample, the GRTR's coefficient alpha was .78 and its split-half reliability was .80. These generally fall near the medium range, which is positive for a short measure.

Reliability coefficients were also calculated for various subgroups. Similar coefficients were found for the middle-class and Head Start samples (range = .78–.80). Similar results were also evidenced between the African American and Caucasian samples. The Latino sample's coefficients were lower (alpha = .55, split-half reliability = .67). This may relate to Latino children's varying levels of English proficiency (Whitehurst, 2001), though subanalyses were not conducted. It is important to note that Whitehurst refers to a prior validity study in which performance on the DSC better predicted second-grade reading levels for Hispanic children than for African Americans or Caucasians, suggesting "that measures similar to those used in the Screening Tool, administered in English, can still be valid for children from Hispanic homes" (2001, p. 12). This is positive, though reliability coefficients still remain important considerations for researchers and clinicians.

Interrater Agreement

This information is not provided in the manual. But given that the measure does not include subjective scoring, high interrater agreement may be anticipated.

Other Forms of Reliability (e.g., Equivalent Forms)

Not applicable

Validity

Face and Content

As described in "Measure Development," item and content selection incorporated both theoretical and empirical approaches. Internal reliability and external validity analyses were conducted to identify the final set of 20 items. Overall, these approaches contributed to the face and content validities of the English GRTR.

Internal Construct

A factor analysis was conducted. The results provided support for a one-factor model and the use of the total score for interpretation. According to Whitehurst, additional subscales may become apparent if the scale is made longer: "A longer assessment designed explicitly to identify profiles of emergent literacy skills will be necessary to differentiate specific areas of emergent literacy in which a child needs help. The Screening Tool itself only allows inferences to the child's general level of emergent literacy readiness" (2001, p. 12).

External Construct

Across the 3- to 5-year-old range, a relationship between age and GRTR score exists. It is important to note that no age-related differences were evidenced within the 4-year-old range, indicating that the GRTR can be interpreted similarly for children at the younger and lower ends of this continuum.

Results from national demonstrations conducted between 2001 and 2003 also support the external construct validity of the GRTR (NCLD, n.d.-a). In these demonstrations, 1,200 preschoolers attending a variety of early education and care programs across three states were administered the screening tool in the fall and spring. Gains were demonstrated from fall to spring across all children. Greater gains were evidenced among children who participated in a broader GRTR program (18.7%) than those who did not (3.7%). The broader GRTR program included "print- and Web-based resources (www.getreadytoread.org), such as learning activities that can be used by early educators, child care professionals, and parents to help children further develop and strengthen specific pre-reading skills."

No data are presented related to how children with various disabilities perform on the measure.

Support for the measure's convergent and discriminant validities is also indicated by some of the correlational studies described in "Criterion."

(continued)

Criterion

As described in "Measure Development," the whole standardization sample was administered the DSC within 2 weeks of having been administered the GRTR. The roughly 200 children in the Florida sample were also administered additional language and literacy measures. Solid correlations were found, supporting the validity of the GRTR. For example, its correlation with the DSC was .69, and the Florida sample's correlations with measures of receptive vocabulary (Peabody Picture Vocabulary Test), letter knowledge, and phonological awareness ranged from .58 to 66. Validity coefficients were also calculated for the various subgroups described in "Internal Consistency." Similar coefficients were generally evidenced for the middle-class and Head Start samples, as well as the African American and Caucasian samples. Latino children's scores on the GRTR correlated at .60 with the DSC, but correlations with other language and literacy measures could not be examined because Latino children made up so little of the Florida sample.

A report published by the NCLD (n.d.-b) provided additional information about the GRTR's concurrent and predictive validities. A variety of other studies found positive concurrent correlations with the Denver Developmental Screening Test–Second Edition, the Ages & Stages Questionnaires, the Early Literacy Skills Assessment, the Peabody Picture Vocabulary Test–Third Edition, and the Wide Range Achievement Test (WRAT). Two studies were presented that describe the GRTR's predictive validity. In a sample of 122 children, fall and spring GRTR scores predicted early kindergarten scores on the Work Sampling System. Of interest is that the GRTR predicted mathematics scores as well as or slightly better than language and literacy scores. As Whitehurst indicates, these correlations "may be explained by young children's abilities to recognize print symbols" (2001, p. 7). In another study (n = 249), the GRTR predicted children's scores on the Georgia Criterion-Referenced Competency Test at the end of first grade. Positive correlations were found between preschool administrations of the GRTR and first-grade reading domain and subscale scores.

(Note: The validity of the enhanced English version has been examined at two time points; Wilson & Lonigan, 2009, 2010; S. Horowitz, personal communication, June 29, 2009.)

RELEVANT STUDIES USING THE MEASURE

A brief literature search using PsycINFO and Google Scholar resulted in a number of articles that mentioned utilizing the GRTR.

Molfese and colleagues published two related studies (Molfese et al., 2006; Molfese, Molfese, Modglin, Walker, & Neamon, 2004). In one study, general cognitive and vocabulary measures were administered in the fall (Molfese et al., 2004). In the spring, the GRTR was administered along with environmental print and phonological sensitivity measures. Among 4-year-olds, correlations were found between the GRTR, vocabulary, rhyming, and environmental print measures but not the Phonological Processing measure from the NEPSY. The authors speculated that different types of phonological processing skills may be assessed by the NEPSY and the GRTR, though this needed further examination. Molfese et al. (2004) also examined predictive models with the GRTR and demonstrated the measure's use with 3-year-olds. Molfese et al. (2006) examined differences between children who made literacy gains during their prekindergarten years and those who did not. They found that the GRTR correlated with gain score differences on the WRAT Letter Identification task.

Farver et al. (2007) examined both the English and Spanish versions of the GRTR. About half of their sample of 540 children from a Head Start–state preschool program was composed of dual language learners. The children were a mix of Latinos and African Americans, though the relative proportions were not described. The alpha coefficient for the English version was .63, which is similar to that found for the Latino sample in Whitehurst (2001). However, the English GRTR version was found to predict both English and Spanish early literacy skills. (For results for the Spanish version, see the Spanish GRTR review.)

Phillips, Lonigan, and Wyatt (2009) examined the GRTR's predictive validity over a short-term follow-up (6 months) and a long-term follow-up (16 and 37 months). Data for these analyses came from three longitudinal studies. The GRTR alpha coefficient they reported was similar to the full sample coefficient reported by Whitehurst (2001). Included in the study were vocabulary, decoding, print awareness, phonological awareness, rapid naming, and reading tasks. In general, significant relationships were found that supported both the concurrent and predictive validities of the GRTR.

ADDITIONAL REFERENCES

Farver, J.M., Nakamoto, J., & Lonigan, C.J. (2007). Assessing preschoolers' emergent literacy skills in English and Spanish with the Get Ready to Read! Screening Tool. *Annals of Dyslexia, 57,* 161–178.

Lonigan, C.J. (2003). *Technical report on the development of the NCLD Spanish-language Get Ready to Read! Screening Tool.* Retrieved from http://www.getreadytoread.org

Molfese, V.J., Modglin, A.A., Beswick, J.L., Neamon, J.D., Berg, S.A., Berg, C.J., & Molnar, A. (2006). Letter knowledge, phonological processing, and print knowledge: Development in nonreading preschool children. *Journal of Learning Disabilities, 39,* 296–304.

Molfese, V.J., Molfese, D.L., Modglin, A.T., Walker, J., & Neamon, J. (2004). Screening early reading skills in preschool children: Get ready to read. *Journal of Psychoeducational Assessment, 22,* 136–150.

National Center for Learning Disabilities. (n.d.-a). *Evaluation findings from national demonstrations: 2001–2003. Executive summary.* Retrieved from http://www.getreadytoread.org/index.php?option=com_content&task=view&id=175&Itemid=429

National Center for Learning Disabilities. (n.d.-b). *A guide for researchers.* Retrieved from http://www.getreadytoread.org/index.php?option=com_content&view=article&id=80:background-research&catid=43

Phillips, B.M., Lonigan, C.J., & Wyatt, M.A. (2009). Predictive validity of the Get Ready to Read! Screener: Concurrent and long-term relations with reading-related skills. *Journal of Learning Disabilities, 42,* 133–147.

Wilson, S B., & Lonigan, C.J. (2009). An evaluation of two emergent literacy screening tools for preschool children. *Annals of Dyslexia, 59,* 115–131.

Wilson, S.B., & Lonigan, C.J. (2010). Identifying preschool children at risk of later reading difficulties: Evaluation of two emergent literacy screening tools. *Journal of Learning Disabilities 43,* 62–76.

Get Ready to Read! Screening Tool (GRTR): Spanish

Information pertaining specifically to the Spanish version of the measure is in bold and italics. The remainder is equivalent information provided in the English review.

Manual

Lonigan, C.J. (2003). *Technical Report on the Development of the NCLD Spanish-Language Get Ready to Read! Screening Tool.* Retrieved from http://www.getreadytoread.org

Publisher

Pearson, Inc.
19500 Bulverde Road
San Antonio, TX 78259-3701
http://www.pearsonassessments.com

Type of Measure

Direct child assessment

Intended Age Range

4;0 years to 4;11 years (though it has also been used in research with younger and older preschoolers)

Key Constructs/Domains

* Print knowledge
* Phonological awareness

Cost

Print copies: $40.50. Literacy manual: $31.50. Training video: $25. A free version is available at http://www.getreadytoread.org.

Description of Measure

The Spanish version of the GRTR is an adaptation of the English version, which is described in the following statement: "The National Center for Learning Disabilities (NCLD), in collaboration with researchers involved in early literacy and literacy research, developed a screening tool to gauge preschool children's development in reading-related skills. This measure, the Get Ready to Read! Screening Tool (GRTR), was designed for English-speaking four-year-old children. GRTR is a 20-item multiple choice measure that provides information on children's early literacy skills, primarily in the areas of print knowledge (letter knowledge, print concepts) and phonological awareness" (Lonigan, 2003, p. 2).

Available Languages and Formats

An English version is also available.

Strengths

The GRTR is a quick, easily administered tool designed to be used by teachers and parents.

A free version is available online.

The development of the Spanish GRTR incorporated a variety of empirical approaches, including attention to items that would best relate to other language and literacy measures. The analyses utilized were generally similar to those utilized for the English version.

The utility of the Spanish GRTR is beginning to be examined.

The Spanish GRTR has a coefficient alpha of .76, which is similar to that of the English version (.78). This falls within the lower range for internal consistency, following the convention of Emmons and Alfonso (2005). However, this reflects the measure's short length and the range of items asked on the GRTR. As noted by Whitehurst (2001) and Lonigan (2003), greater emphasis was given to items' predictive ability than their internal consistency.

Weaknesses

The test–retest and interrater reliabilities remain in need of examination. But given that the measure does not include subjective scoring, high interrater agreement may be anticipated.

As the Spanish GRTR was developed and examined within low-income samples of primarily Mexican descent in California, additional studies will likely need to examine its properties among other samples.

ADMINISTRATION

Procedure

Children are presented with four pictures and asked to select a response based on questions posed by the examiner. The GRTR begins with an example, which is followed by the 20 items that tap print knowledge, emergent writing, and phonological sensitivity (Molfese, Molfese, Modglin, Walker, & Neamon, 2004). *The distribution of items composing the Spanish version differs from that of the English version. Based on the procedures described in "Measure Development," a print concepts item and both letter naming items were eliminated. These were substituted with three sound blending (Lonigan, 2003).*

Time Needed
10 minutes

Data from national demonstrations conducted between 2001 and 2003 indicate that children engage well with the GRTR (NCLD, n.d.-a). More than 96% of children completed the whole measure, and solid ratings were evidenced across engagement, enjoyment, responsiveness, resistance, and difficulty. *Because the Spanish version was not created until 2003, it was not likely utilized in these national demonstrations.*

Administration and Interpretation

A major impetus for the development of the GRTR was the desire to create a measure that could be administered by nonprofessionals, such as parents and teachers (Whitehurst, 2001). Thus, a multiple-choice format was selected to simplify administration and scoring. Instructions are provided for the administrator, and little training is needed. In addition, a training video is available.

Scoring Method

The total number of items answered correctly is automatically tallied in the online version. *An answer sheet can be downloaded to record answers, though slight differences were noted in the wordings of the Spanish items online and on the answer sheets. For instance, in the example item, the word* mono *is used online for* monkey *whereas the answer sheet lists* chango.

Whitehurst (2001) provided the following guidelines for interpretation: Very Weak Skills (0–6 correct), Weak Skills (6–9), Average Skills (9–12), Strong Skills (12–16), and Very Strong Skills (16–20). These guidelines were created using analyses predicting high versus low scores on the Developing Skills Checklist (DSC) from the English GRTR, as well as a number of additional considerations described in Whitehurst (2001). *Lonigan (2003) suggested that the interpretation key developed for the English version is applicable to the Spanish version because the average performance is generally similar in the average range ($M_{Spanish}$ = 11.30, SD = 3.96; $M_{English}$ = 9.14; SD = 4.31). Overall, the mean of the Spanish version is more consistent with the findings on the English version for Caucasians (M = 11.23) than for blacks (M = 9.03). Lonigan also noted the following: "Unlike the development sample for the E-GRTR [English GRTR] in which Hispanic children scored* *significantly lower than other children (i.e., mean score of 6.86; see Whitehurst, 2001), these results suggest that S-GRTR [Spanish GRTR] provides a relatively unbiased means to assess Spanish-speaking children's emergent literacy skills. Consequently, the same interpretive scale for scores developed for the E-GRTR should be used for the S-GRTR for Spanish-speaking four-year-old children (see Table 7)" (2003, p. 16).*

Adaptations or Instructions for Use with Individuals with Disabilities

Specific instructions for using the GRTR with children with disabilities are not presented. However, as the measure involves simple responses from children, it is likely adaptable for use with children with various types of disabilities.

FUNCTIONAL CONSIDERATIONS

Measure Development

The GRTR was first developed in English in 2001, using past theoretical and empirical findings. The primary authors (Drs. Grover Whitehurst and Christopher Lonigan) are well-known researchers in the field. Item development began by identifying children who were good or poor readers at the end of second grade. The DSC was administered in preschool and had a predictive classification accuracy of 78% (with 85% correct classification of poor readers). Items from the DSC were then statistically examined to see which types best predicted these classifications. Items were also examined from other measures developed by Dr. Lonigan for their predictive ability.

An initial set of about 100 multiple-choice items was created, which was reduced to 60 based on a variety of factors. These items were then administered to 342 children along with the DSC within a 2-week period. A total of 200 children were also administered additional language and literacy measures. A variety of statistical approaches yielded somewhat different sets of 20 items, though these were highly correlated (.89–.96). The statistical approaches utilized were item difficulty level, reliability alpha coefficient, and external validity (as demonstrated through item correlations with the DSC). In deciding upon the final set of items, the test developers also paid attention to item coverage. In the final decision-making process, external validity results were given more weight than internal reliability results.

Taking dual language learner literacy research into consideration, experts developed the Spanish version to be an adaptation of the English version with a stated goal of remaining parallel to the English version. The first Spanish version created had a similar item order and similar proportions of print knowledge and phonological awareness items as the English version. The Spanish translation of the initial pilot version was examined by native speakers for accuracy, clarity, and bias. The first Spanish version was field-tested with 82 children (details presented in "Standardization Sample"). Results from the initial field test indicated low item-total correlations for a few items. For example, the elision task had an item-total correlation of .00, which likely reflects the lower prevalence of compound words in Spanish preschoolers' vocabularies (Lonigan, 2003).

As the elision item was a phonological awareness task, six new phonological awareness items that assessed blending skills were created as a replacement. These were field-tested along with the initial 20 items among a final sample of 222 Spanish-speaking children. Additional measures were administered, including the Preschool Language Scale–Fourth Edition (PLS-4) in English and Spanish and the Spanish-language version of the Preschool Comprehensive Test of Phonological and Print Processing (Pre-CTOPP). The 26 Spanish items were examined for their item-total correlations, difficulty level, and validity. Analysis of the samples led to the elimination of the letter naming items and one print concepts item and the addition of three blending items. Though these changes were made, the original and final versions of the Spanish GRTR correlate at .96. Tables reporting item results are presented in Lonigan (2003).

Content Equivalence of Items and Measure

The Spanish version of the GRTR was developed after the English GRTR was created. Attention was paid to remaining consistent in content; however, Spanish-language considerations led to the adaptation of specific types of items, which is positive. Language and literacy development among Spanish speakers was taken into consideration.

Semantic Equivalence of Translations

The initial translation process used is not specified. After the original version was translated, "native speakers of Spanish reviewed these 20 items for accuracy and clarity, as well as to identify any potential source of bias in the items when used with a Spanish-speaking population" (Lonigan, 2003, p. 4). This description suggests that dialectical differences may have been taken into consideration. For example, a noun that is often used in Mexican dialects appears on the answer sheets for one question, while the actual screener includes another term widely used by other Spanish-speaking communities.

Structural Consistency Across the English and Spanish Versions

The Spanish version of GRTR is very similar to the English version. As reported in "Measure Development," attention was paid to keeping the same types of items, length, and format. Field testing led to the inclusion of a greater proportion of phonological awareness items in the Spanish version. This may have been the result of only field testing new phonological awareness items in the final sample because the focus was originally on replacing an elision task. Other items were then found to warrant replacement. It is important to note that these items appear to function well. Furthermore, the strong correlation between the original structure in Spanish and the final version was quite high (.96).

Standardization Sample

Two samples were involved in the field tests for the Spanish GRTR. A total of 82 Spanish-speaking 4- and 5-year-olds attending Head Start in Los Angeles were involved in the initial field test. Their mean age was 58.82 months (**SD** = 4.72), and their English language ability ranged from limited to conversationally competent. More than half of the children's mothers had been born in Mexico, with the remaining mothers hailing from Central America or the United States.

A total of 222 Spanish-speaking children from Los Angeles Head Start centers completed the expanded field test. This sample included a wider age range (3.5–5 years of age; **M** = 52.34 months, **SD** = 5.16 months). Parent interview data with 71% of the mothers revealed that 67% of the mothers had been born in Mexico, with the remaining mothers hailing from Central America (14%) or the United States. (9%). The average length of time in the United States among the immigrant mothers was 17.7 years. Children's English language ability was reported to range from limited to conversationally competent. Children scored in the average range on the Spanish PLS and below average on the English version, "consistent with the Spanish-language dominant designation of these bilingual children" (Lonigan, 2003, p. 6).

Norming

Criterion referenced

Reliability

Test–Retest Reliability

This information is not provided in the manual.

Internal Consistency

The Spanish GRTR has a coefficient alpha of .76, which was reproduced with a random split of the sample. This falls within the lower range for internal consistency, following the convention of Emmons and Alfonso (2005). However, this reflects the measure's short length and the inclusion of various types of items on the GRTR. As noted by Whitehurst (2001) and Lonigan (2003), greater emphasis was given to items' predictive ability than their internal consistency.

Interrater Agreement

This information is not provided in the manual. But given that the measure does not include subjective scoring, high interrater agreement may be anticipated.

Other Forms of Reliability (e.g., Equivalent Forms)

Not applicable

Validity

Face and Content

As described in "Measure Development," item and content selection for the Spanish GRTR incorporated both theoretical and empirical approaches. Both internal reliability and external validity analyses were conducted to identify the final set of 20 items. Overall, these approaches contributed to the face and content validities of the Spanish GRTR.

Internal Construct

A factor analysis of the Spanish GRTR was conducted. The results provided support for a one-factor model and the use of the total score for interpretation.

External Construct

Across the 3- to 5-year-old range, a relationship between age and Spanish GRTR score exists (.31). As with the English version, minimal age-related differences were evidenced within the 4-year-old range, indicating that the GRTR can be interpreted similarly for children at the younger and lower ends of this continuum. Girls were reported to score about 1 point higher than boys on the Spanish GRTR.

No data are presented related to how children with various disabilities perform on the measure.

Support for the measure's convergent and discriminant validities is also indicated by some of the correlational studies described in "Criterion."

Criterion

As described in "Measure Development," the Spanish GRTR was administered along with the Spanish Pre-CTOPP and the English and Spanish versions of the PLS in the expanded field test. Significant correlations were found among all comparisons with the CTOPP (range = .68 for the Print subscale to .37 for the Blending subscale). Significant correlations between the Spanish GRTR and the Pre-CTOPP were found even after age and linguistic ability were controlled. "These results convincingly indicate that S-GRTR measures reliable variance related to emergent literacy skills in the domains that it is intended to measure" (Lonigan, 2003, p. 13). Children's performance on the Spanish GRTR was also correlated with the PLS (Spanish PLS = .31; English PLS = .39). The slightly stronger correlation of the Spanish GRTR with the English PLS than the Spanish PLS may reflect the greater use of English for instructional purposes in California classrooms (Farver, Nakamoto, & Lonigan, 2007).

Comparison of Psychometric Properties Between English and Spanish Versions

Technical Equivalence in Reliability

The Spanish GRTR has a coefficient alpha of .76, which is similar to that of the English version (.78). Neither test–retest nor interrater reliability is reported for the Spanish or English version, though high interrater agreement may be anticipated given the objective scoring approach used.

Technical Equivalence in Validity

Strong attention was paid to validity in the development of both the English and Spanish GRTR. Literacy research was taken into consideration in their development, and analyses were conducted on both language versions to identify items that could work across three dimensions: item-total correlations, difficulty level, and external validity. Factor analyses were also conducted on both versions. In general, the criterion validity of the Spanish version has been examined to a lesser degree.

RELEVANT STUDIES USING THE MEASURE

A brief literature search using PsycINFO and Google Scholar resulted in the following article. *The Spanish GRTR may be in use in other studies as well.*

Farver et al. (2007) examined both the English and Spanish versions of the GRTR. About half of their sample of 540 children from a Head Start–state preschool program were dual language learners. The children were a mix of Latinos and African Americans, though the relative proportions were not described. The alpha for the Spanish version was .56, which is lower than that found in Lonigan (2003). It is unknown whether the inclusion of young 3-year-olds in the sample affected this average coefficient or whether it was also low among 4-year-olds. It is important to note that the Spanish GRTR was found to predict both English and Spanish early literacy skills among dual language learners. (For results for the English version, see the English GRTR review).

ADDITIONAL REFERENCES

Emmons, M.R., & Alfonso, V.C. (2005). A critical review of the technical characteristics of preschool screening batteries. *Psychoeducational Assessment, 23*, 111–127.

(continued)

Farver, J.M., Nakamoto, J., & Lonigan, C.J. (2007). Assessing preschoolers' emergent literacy skills in English and Spanish with the Get Ready to Read! Screening Tool. *Annals of Dyslexia, 57,* 161–178.

Molfese, V.J., Molfese, D.L., Modglin, A.T., Walker, J., & Neamon, J. (2004). Screening early reading skills in preschool children: Get ready to read. *Journal of Psychoeducational Assessment, 22,* 136–150.

National Center for Learning Disabilities. (n.d.-a). *Evaluation findings from national demonstrations: 2001–2003. Executive summary.* Retrieved from http://www.getreadytoread.org/index.php?option=com_content&task=view&id=175&Itemid=429

National Center for Learning Disabilities. (n.d.-b). *A guide for researchers.* Retrieved from http://www.getreadytoread.org/index.php?option=com_content&view=article&id=80:background-research&catid=43

Whitehurst, G.J. (2001). *The NCLD Get Ready to Read! Screening Tool technical report.* Retrieved from http://www.getreadytoread.org

Merrill-Palmer–Revised Scales of Development (M-P-R): English

Manual

Roid, G.H., & Sampers, J. (2004). *Merrill-Palmer-Revised Scales of Development (M-P-R)*. Wood Dale, IL: Stoelting.

Publisher

Stoelting Co.
620 Wheat Lane
Wood Dale, IL 60191
http://www.stoeltingco.com

Cost

Complete kit: $925. Items sold separately.

Description of Measure

"The Merrill-Palmer-Revised Scales of Development (M-P-R; Roid & Sampers, 2004) was developed for use with infants and children between the ages of 1 month and 78 months. M-P-R meets the needs of infant and early childhood assessments, as required by federal and state legislation for early identification of developmental delays and learning difficulties in children ([Individuals with Disabilities Education Act of 1990])" (Roid & Sampers, 2004, p. 1). Recommended uses of the M-P-R, according to Roid and Sampers (2004), include assessing general development in English- and Spanish-speaking children; screening for developmental delays or disabilities; assessing children with hearing impairments/deafness, autism, or other disabilities who have limited language skills; and reevaluating individuals previously identified as developmentally delayed.

Type of Measure

Direct child assessment, parent report, and examiner report

Intended Age Range

1 month to 6;6 years

Key Constructs/Domains

- Cognitive (including General Cognitive, Memory, Speed of Cognition, Receptive Language, Visual Motor, and Fine Motor)
- Gross Motor
- Expressive Language (through parent and examiner report)
- Self-help/adaptive (questionnaires)
- Social-emotional (questionnaires)

Available Languages and Formats

Spanish translations of the directions, prompts, and questionnaires are available, except for the Expressive Language scale.

Strengths

The M-P-R provides growth scores and is able to capture relatively small increments of growth between assessment periods.

Information can be gathered from multiple sources (e.g., direct child assessments, parent reports, examiner reports) to provide insight on children's development.

Thorough reliability and validity studies were conducted.

Attention was paid during both the tryout and standardization phases to item- and group-level differences among specific ethnic, language, and special needs groups.

Weaknesses

Because it is a comprehensive battery, new examiners will need to allow for adequate time to read the manual and learn the procedures.

Information about interrater reliability is not presented in the manual, though personal communication with the first author (G. Roid, June 19, 2009) yielded the rationale for its exclusion.

ADMINISTRATION

Procedure

The M-P-R is organized into four batteries: the Cognitive Battery, the Gross Motor Development Battery, Parent Rating forms, and Examiner Scales. According to Roid and Sampers (2004), the standard order of administration involves conducting the Cognitive Battery first, followed by the Gross Motor Battery. The remaining scales can be administered according to the examiner's preference.

Time Needed
Approximately 45 minutes for the full battery

- *Cognitive Battery.* Subscales examine general cognitive skills, receptive language abilities, and fine motor abilities. The examiner can additionally examine memory, speed of cognition, and visual-gross motor skills. Expressive language is assessed through a combination of parent and examiner report.

- *Gross Motor Development Battery.* Children are asked to perform physical movements such as jumping and throwing a ball. General gross motor development, along with unusual movements and atypical movement patterns, are assessed.

- *Self-Help/Adaptive and Social-Emotional.* Three parent-report questionnaires examine social-emotional development and self-help/adaptive skills: the Social-Emotional Developmental Scale, the Social-Emotional Temperament Scale, and the Self-Help/ Adaptive Behavior Scale. Examiners can also complete the Social-Emotional Problem Indicators form when there are possible behavioral concerns. In addition, examiners use the Examiner Observation Form for Testing Behaviors to describe the frequency with which various types of behavior were observed during the assessment session.

Administration and Interpretation

Roid and Sampers (2004) suggest that the examiner have a degree in psychology, counseling, or a closely related field from an accredited 4-year college or university in addition to having satisfactorily completed coursework in test interpretation, psychometrics and measurement theory, educational statistics, or a closely related area. Examiners who have a license or certification from an agency that requires appropriate training and experience in the use of psychological tests are also able to administer the measure. A training video is available for purchase from the publisher.

Scoring Method

Examiners and parents record children's responses on the M-P-R record forms by hand. There are different start points for different age groups.

Raw scores from all Cognitive Battery scales and the rating scales from the parent and examiner forms are transformed into normalized scores. Percentiles and age equivalents are also available. In addition, the manual provides growth scores for the rating scales, Gross Motor Battery, and other developmental measures completed by the examiner and/or the parent. More detailed explanations for calculating scores are provided within the manual.

Adaptations or Instructions for Use with Individuals with Disabilities

The M-P-R manual provides a list of suggested accommodations that may be used when administering the measure to children with severe disabilities, including allowing for extra time on nonspeeded or untimed sections and allowing for alternative response modes (e.g., gestures; Roid & Sampers, 2004).

FUNCTIONAL CONSIDERATIONS

Measure Development

The M-P-R allows examiners to assess children from birth, whereas the prior version (the M-P) began at 18 months. The M-P-R was developed after 6 years of extensive research. In creating the measure, test developers interviewed experts from various fields, including neuropsychology and special education, who had experience using the M-P.

There were five phases to the measure's development: 1) research, 2) pilot-testing, 3) field testing of tryout items, 4) norming of the standardized edition, and 5) performing of statistical analyses prior to publication. Some of the items on the Cognitive Battery were adapted from another assessment (the Leiter International Performance Scale–Revised [Leiter-R]). Age trends were also examined. Namely, "items not showing sensitivity to age were inspected closely and most were discarded unless they served a function of introducing or concluding a task" (Roid & Sampers, 2004, p. 145). The manual also provides a brief description of the theoretical basis for the M-P-R, namely the use of the Cattell-Horn-Carroll (C-H-C) model of cognitive abilities. Loew (2007) suggested that more theoretical description would have been preferable, including the rationale for utilizing some rather than all of the constructs in the C-H-C model. However, personal communication with Dr. Roid (June 19, 2009) provided the rationale for including only a portion of the factors in C-H-C theory: "(a) the lack of research on C-H-C theory in infancy (where many theorists have suggested fewer factors of cognition due to the delay in brain-function differentiation), and (b) the impracticality of attempting to assess 8–10 factors in long test sessions with very young children."

Standardization Sample

"The scales were standardized on a nationally representative sample of 1,068 children selected on the basis of gender, ethnicity, parental education level, and geographical region to match the 2000 Census" (Roid & Sampers, 2004, p. 1). Generally speaking, the sample reflects Census data within a percentage point, as detailed in manual charts. In addition, efforts were made to capture communities of different sizes.

The Cognitive Battery, Gross Motor Battery, and Examiner Observation Form for Testing Behaviors were standardized with the full sample of 1,068 children, whereas the remaining components were standardized on "systematic sub-samples" of approximately 650–850 children (Roid & Sampers, 2004, p. 121). Comparison samples of children with exceptionalities, Native American children, and Spanish-speaking children were also included in the standardization (as well as tryout) phase in order to examine hypothesized differences between groups and examine how the items worked for the various groups. A total of 56 Spanish-speaking children were included in the Cognitive Battery standardization sample and presented with translated items.

Content experts from diverse backgrounds, as well as psychologists and examiners, participated in the tryout and standardization phases and reviewed each item for potential bias and clarity. Differential item functioning results for pairs of subgroups (e.g., boys and girls, Caucasians and African Americans) were also plotted. "Only a very small number of items were detected as falling outside the confidence zones of these scatterplots" (Roid & Sampers, 2004, p. 137). Most of these items were subsequently removed from the test. Furthermore, Floyd, Gathercoal, and Roid (2004) conducted differential item functioning analyses to examine the cultural validity of the M-P-R. Their findings indicated that the M-P-R is not biased toward African American, Euro-American, or Hispanic children.

Norming

Norm referenced, as well as "criterion-referenced, change-sensitive growth scores," according to the publisher's web site (Stoelting Company, n.d.)

Reliability

Test–Retest Reliability

A total of 41 children ages 3–70 months (median = 33 months) completed the Cognitive Battery twice within a 3-week interval on average. Test–retest correlations were all in the medium to high range (range = .84–.90). Spenciner and Appl (2007) suggested that the other components of the measure also require examination.

Internal Consistency

Internal consistency reliability coefficients are provided by age bands for the Cognitive Battery, Gross Motor Battery, social-emotional, self-help/adaptive and language scales. Reliability coefficients for only two cognitive subscales—Memory and Speed—were in the moderate range (average = .77). All other domains demonstrated high reliability coefficients, with averages ranging from .91 to .98 across all age bands. Corresponding standard errors of measurement (SEMs) were also provided. As with the alphas, the Memory and Speed domains had higher SEMs (6.00–8.26) than other subtests (2.12–6.36).

Internal consistency alphas for the examiner-administered Social-Emotional Temperament Scale are also provided. Alphas for children younger than 18 months range from .49 to .73; alphas for older children range from .78 to .90. "As one would expect, these reliabilities are not terribly high for the very young children, but much higher for children 18 months of age and older" (Roid & Sampers, 2004, p. 129).

Interrater Agreement

No information is provided in the manual. However, personal communication with Dr. Roid (June 19, 2009) yielded the following: "The M-P-R performance tests (Cognitive, receptive language, Gross Motor) are objective measures of specific behavioral responses (pointing to pictures, placement of objects) and such tests do not require inter-rater reliability in cognitive and achievement testing realms as judged by most psychometric experts such as Dr. Roid."

Other Forms of Reliability (e.g., Equivalent Forms)

Not applicable

Validity

Face and Content

The utilization of a range of expert consultants and careful qualitative and quantitative steps in development contribute to the face and content validities of this measure.

Internal Construct

Exploratory factor analyses were conducted (first at the item level using principal component and maximum-likelihood factor analyses, followed by principal-axis factor analyses of subscales). These analyses were used to identify and drop problematic items from the measure as well as empirically support the use of subscales in the measure.

External Construct

As may be expected, M-P-R performance was lower among special groups (e.g., children with cognitive delays, deafness, or autism spectrum disorder).

In addition, the classification accuracy of M-P-R scores was also examined. Among children with a cognitive delay, specificity and sensitivity scores were examined for the Cognitive, Fine

(continued)

Motor, and Receptive Language scales. These were high (about 99% for specificity and about 92%–95% for sensitivity). The specificity and sensitivity of the Receptive Language scale was also examined in a sample of children with speech-language delays. The sensitivity was low (57%), but the specificity was high (92%). The ability of this scale to identify premature infants was lower (specificity = 82%, sensitivity = 39%), which is not a great concern because prematurity is diagnosed according to children's gestational age at birth rather than their scores on a measure.

Data on convergent and discriminant validity with other measures are also presented in the manual. These studies are described in "Criterion."

Criterion

Children's performance on the M-P-R was correlated with their performance on various measures using relatively small samples of children. For example, a small sample across a large age range (24 children ages 1–39 months) was administered the Bayley Scales of Infant Development–Second Edition (BSID-2). As may be expected, BSID-2 Mental scores correlated well with M-P-R scores related to cognition and language (range = .76–.98), whereas BSID-2 Motor scores had low to moderate correlations with these same scores (range = .36–.61). Similarly, correlations between M-P-R Memory and BSID-2 Mental and Motor Scores were strong (.85 and .76, respectively). Finally, Roid and Sampers (2004) speculate that the relatively high correlation between BSID-2 Gross Motor and M-P-R Receptive Language Scores (.61) may be due to the verbal instructions in the Gross Motor section.

Forty children ages 37–78 months were also administered the Brief IQ of the Leiter-R. Generally speaking, M-P-R scores and Leiter-R Rasch scores were moderately to highly correlated, with higher correspondence in the expected subdomains, such as between the Leiter-R Developmental Index and M-P-R's Cognitive Battery. Similar findings were found for a study using the Stanford-Binet Intelligence Scales–Fifth Edition.

RELEVANT STUDIES USING THE MEASURE

A literature review using PsycINFO, the Education Resources Information Center database, and Google Scholar found that the M-P-R has been utilized in the following study. It has also been used in dissertations and discussed in school district–related documents.

Floyd et al. (2004) conducted differential item functioning analyses to examine the cultural validity of the M-P-R. Their findings indicated that the M-P-R is not biased toward African American, Euro-American, or Hispanic children.

ADDITIONAL REFERENCES

Floyd, R.L., Gathercoal, K., & Roid, G. (2004). No evidence for ethnic and racial bias in the tryout edition of the Merrill-Palmer Scale-Revised. *Psychological Reports, 94,* 217–220.

Loew, S. (2007). Test review of the Merrill-Palmer-Revised Scales of Development. In K.F. Geisinger, R.A. Spies, J.F. Carlson, & B.S. Plake (Eds.), *The seventeenth mental measurements yearbook.* Retrieved from the Buros Institute's *Test Reviews Online* web site: http://www.unl.edu/buros

Spenciner, L., & Appl, D. (2007). Test review of the Merrill-Palmer- Revised Scales of Development. In K.F. Geisinger, R.A. Spies, J.F. Carlson, & B.S. Plake (Eds.), *The seventeenth mental measurements yearbook.* Retrieved from the Buros Institute's *Test Reviews Online* web site: http://www.unl.edu/buros

Stoelting Company (n.d.). *Merrill-Palmer–Revised (M-P-R).* Retrieved from https://www.stoeltingco.com/stoelting/productlist13c.aspx?catid=1944&home=&CatIDPrevA=&CatIDPrevB=1488

Merrill-Palmer–Revised Scales of Development (M-P-R): Spanish

Information pertaining specifically to the Spanish version of the measure is in bold and italics. The remainder is equivalent information provided in the English review.

Manual

Roid, G.H., & Sampers, J. (2004). *Merrill-Palmer– Revised Scales of Development.* Wood Dale, IL: Stoelting.

Publisher

Stoelting Co.
620 Wheat Lane
Wood Dale, IL 60191
http://www.stoeltingco.com

Cost

Complete kit: $925. Packages of each of the parent-report forms can be purchased separately for $20. Items sold separately.

Type of Measure

Direct child assessment, parent report, and examiner report

Intended Age Range

1 month to 6;6 years

Key Constructs/Domains

- Cognitive (including General Cognitive, Memory, Speed of Cognition, Receptive Language, Visual Motor, and Fine Motor)
- Gross Motor
- Expressive Language (through examiner report)
- Self-help/adaptive (questionnaires)
- Social-emotional (questionnaires)

Description of Measure

"The Merrill-Palmer-Revised Scales of Development (M-P-R; Roid & Sampers, 2004) was developed for use with infants and children between the ages of 1 month and 78 months. M-P-R meets the needs of infant and early childhood assessments, as required by federal and state legislation for early identification of developmental delays and learning difficulties in children ([Individuals with Disabilities Education Act of 1990])" (Roid & Sampers, 2004, p. 1). Recommended uses of the M-P-R, according to Roid and Sampers (2004), include assessing general development in English- and Spanish-speaking children; screening for developmental delays or disabilities; assessing children with hearing impairments/deafness, autism, or other disabilities who have limited language skills; and reevaluating individuals previously identified as developmentally delayed.

Available Languages and Formats

The M-P-R is available in English.

Strengths

The M-P-R provides growth scores and is able to capture relatively small increments of growth between assessment periods.

Information can be gathered from multiple sources (e.g., direct child assessments, parent reports, examiner reports) to provide insight on children's development.

Attention was paid during both the tryout and standardization phases to item- and group-level differences among specific ethnic, language, and special needs groups.

Item- and group-level analyses with 56 Spanish-speaking children were conducted for the Cognitive Battery but not the supplemental measures.

Weaknesses

The Expressive Language subscale is not available in Spanish.

As data for 56 Spanish-speaking children were included in the overall standardization sample for the Cognitive Battery, separate examination of reliability and validity is not possible.

The M-P-R's criterion validity in Spanish may need to be examined separately given that some of the comparison measures are available in Spanish and themselves have varying psychometric properties in Spanish.

Because it is a comprehensive battery, new examiners will need to allow for adequate time to read the manual and learn the procedures.

ADMINISTRATION

Procedure

The M-P-R is organized into four batteries: the Cognitive Battery, the Gross Motor Battery, Parent Rating forms, and Examiner Scales. According to Roid and Sampers (2004), the standard order of administration involves conducting the Cognitive Battery first, followed by the Gross Motor Battery. The remaining scales can be administered according to the examiner's preference.

Time Needed

Approximately 45 minutes for the full battery

- *Cognitive Battery.* Subscales examine general cognitive skills, receptive language abilities, and fine motor abilities. The examiner can additionally examine memory, speed of cognition, and visual-motor skills. *Expressive language is assessed through examiner report.*

- *Gross Motor Battery.* Children are asked to perform physical movements such as jumping and throwing a ball. General gross motor development, along with unusual movements and atypical movement patterns, are assessed.

- *Self-Help/Adaptive and Social-Emotional.* Three parent-report questionnaires examine social-emotional development and self-help/adaptive skills: the Social-Emotional Developmental Scale, the Social-Emotional Temperament Scale, and the Self-Help/ Adaptive Behavior Scale. Examiners can also complete the Social-Emotional Problem Indicators form when there are possible behavioral concerns. In addition, examiners use the Examiner Observation Form for Testing Behaviors to describe the frequency with which various types of behavior were observed during the assessment session.

Administration and Interpretation

Roid and Sampers (2004) suggested that the examiner have a degree in psychology, counseling, or a closely related field from an accredited 4-year college or university in addition to having satisfactorily completed coursework in test interpretation, psychometrics and measurement theory, educational statistics, or a closely related area. Examiners who have a license or certification from an agency that requires appropriate training and experience in the use of psychological tests are also able to administer the measure. A training video is available for purchase from the publisher.

Scoring Method

Examiners and parents record children's responses on the M-P-R record forms by hand. There are different start points for different age groups.

Raw scores from all Cognitive Battery scales and the rating scales (i.e., parent and examiner forms) are transformed into normalized scores. Percentiles and age equivalents are also available. In addition, the manual provides growth scores for the rating scales, Gross Motor

Battery, and other developmental measures completed by the examiner and/or the parent. More detailed explanations for calculating scores are provided within the manual.

Adaptations or Instructions for Use with Individuals with Disabilities

The M-P-R manual provides a list of suggested accommodations that may be used when administering the M-P-R to children with severe disabilities, including allowing for extra time on nonspeeded or untimed sections and allowing for alternative response modes (e.g., gestures).

FUNCTIONAL CONSIDERATIONS

Measure Development

The M-P-R allows examiners to assess children from birth, whereas the prior version (the M-P) began at 18 months. The M-P-R was developed after 6 years of extensive research. In creating the measure, test developers interviewed experts from various fields, including neuropsychology and special education, who had experience using the M-P.

There were five phases to the measure's development: 1) research, 2) pilot-testing, 3) field testing of tryout items, 4) norming of the standardized edition, and 5) performing of statistical analyses prior to publication. Some of the items on the Cognitive Battery were adapted from another assessment (the Leiter International Performance Scale–Revised [Leiter-R]). Age trends were also examined. Namely, "items not showing sensitivity to age were inspected closely and most were discarded unless they served a function of introducing or concluding a task" (Roid & Sampers, 2004, p. 145). The manual also provides a brief description of the theoretical basis for the M-P-R, namely the use of the Cattell-Horn-Carroll (C-H-C) model of cognitive abilities. Loew (2007) suggested that more theoretical description would have been preferable, including the rationale for utilizing some rather than all of the constructs in the C-H-C model. However, personal communication with Dr. Roid (June 19, 2009) provided the rationale for including only a portion of the factors in C-H-C theory: "(a) the lack of research on C-H-C theory in infancy (where many theorists have suggested fewer factors of cognition due to the delay in brain-function differentiation), and (b) the impracticality of attempting to assess 8–10 factors in long test sessions with very young children."

Spanish translations of the directions, prompts, and questionnaires are available, except for the Expressive Language scale (Spenciner & Appl, 2007). Once the standardization edition was developed in English, a nationally recognized expert in test translation developed an initial Spanish translation with an emphasis on meaning versus literalness. A panel of school psychologists and educational diagnosticians from different Spanish-language backgrounds was then consulted.

Content Equivalence of Items and Measure

Except for the expressive language questionnaires, it appears that the content of the Spanish version is the same as that of the English version. Multiple consultants were utilized, though the degree to which the literature on Spanish child development was consulted is not described in the manual.

Semantic Equivalence of Translations

As noted, the translation was focused on meaning and was reviewed by individuals who spoke various dialects. Item- and group-level analyses with 56 Spanish-speaking children were conducted for the Cognitive Battery but not the supplemental measures.

Structural Consistency Across the English and Spanish Versions

Overall, the structures are consistent, except for the exclusion of the Expressive Language Parent Response Form in Spanish.

Standardization Sample

"The scales were standardized on a nationally representative sample of 1,068 children selected on the basis of gender, ethnicity, parental education level, and geographical region to match the 2000 Census" (Roid & Sampers, 2004, p. 1). Generally speaking, the sample reflects Census data within a percentage point, as detailed in manual charts. In addition, efforts were made to capture communities of different sizes.

The Cognitive Battery, Gross Motor Battery, and the Examiner Observation Form for Testing Behaviors were standardized with the full sample of 1,068 children, whereas the remaining components were standardized on "systematic sub-samples" of approximately 650–850 children (Roid & Sampers, 2004, p. 121). *Comparison samples of children with exceptionalities, Native American children, and Spanish-speaking children were also included in the standardization (as well as tryout) phase in order to examine hypothesized differences between groups and examine how the items worked for the various groups. A total of 56 Spanish-speaking children were included in the standardization sample and presented with translated items. A separate standardization of the Spanish version does not appear to have been conducted.*

Content experts from diverse backgrounds, as well as psychologists and examiners, participated in the tryout and standardization phases and reviewed each item for potential bias and clarity. Differential item functioning results for pairs of subgroups (e.g., boys and girls, Caucasians and African Americans) were also plotted. "Only a very small number of items were detected as falling outside the confidence zones of these scatterplots" (Roid & Sampers, 2004, p. 137). Most of these items were subsequently removed from the test. Furthermore, Floyd, Gathercoal, and Roid (2004) conducted differential item functioning analyses to examine the cultural validity of the M-P-R. Their findings indicated that the M-P-R is not biased toward African American, Euro-American, or Hispanic children.

Norming

Norm referenced

Reliability

Test–Retest Reliability

Spanish-speaking children do not appear to have participated in the test–retest reliability substudy.

Internal Consistency

This information is not provided in the manual for the Spanish version. As indicated in "Standardization Sample," data for 56 Spanish-speaking children were included in the overall standardization sample for the Cognitive Battery.

Interrater Agreement

No information on interrater agreement is provided in the manual for either language version. However, personal communication with Dr. Roid (June 19, 2009) yielded the following: "The M-P-R performance tests (Cognitive, receptive language, gross motor) are objective measures of specific behavioral responses (pointing to pictures, placement of objects) and such tests do not require inter-rater reliability in cognitive and achievement testing realms as judged by most psychometric experts such as Dr. Roid."

Other Forms of Reliability (e.g., Equivalent Forms)

Not applicable

Validity

Face and Content

Bilingual experts reviewed the measure and item analyses were conducted. Attention was also paid to dialectical variations in Spanish. Because the Spanish version began with the items already included in the English version, the full range (e.g., content) of potentially appropriate items in Spanish was not likely examined initially.

Internal Construct

This information is not provided in the manual for the Spanish version. Spanish data appear to have been mixed with English data in the M-P-R's norming. Furthermore, only 56 Spanish speakers were included in the standardization sample.

External Construct

This information is not provided in the manual for the Spanish version. As indicated in "Standardization Sample," data for 56 Spanish-speaking children were included in the overall standardization sample for the Cognitive Battery.

Criterion

The M-P-R's criterion validity in Spanish may need to be examined separately given that some of the comparison measures are available in Spanish and themselves have varying psychometric properties in Spanish.

Comparison of Psychometric Properties Between English and Spanish Versions

Technical Equivalence in Reliability

The reliability statistics for the English and Spanish versions could not be compared as Spanish data are not presented separately in the manual.

Technical Equivalence in Validity

The validity statistics for the English and Spanish versions could not be compared as Spanish data are not presented in the manual.

RELEVANT STUDIES USING THE MEASURE

A brief literature search using PsycINFO and Google Scholar did not result in any published studies whose abstracts specified using the Spanish version of the M-P-R. However, it is possible that this measure has been utilized in studies.

ADDITIONAL REFERENCES

Floyd, R.L., Gathercoal, K., & Roid, G. (2004). No evidence for ethnic and racial bias in the tryout edition of the Merrill-Palmer Scale–Revised. *Psychological Reports*, 94, 217–220.

Loew, S. (2007). Test review of the Merrill-Palmer–Revised Scales of Development. In K.F. Geisinger, R.A. Spies, J.F. Carlson, & B.S. Plake (Eds.), *The seventeenth mental measurements yearbook*. Retrieved from the Buros Institute's *Test Reviews Online* web site: http://www.unl.edu/buros

Spenciner, L., & Appl, D. (2007). Test review of the Merrill-Palmer–Revised Scales of Development. In K.F. Geisinger, R.A. Spies, J.F. Carlson, & B.S. Plake (Eds.), *The seventeenth mental measurements yearbook*. Retrieved from the Buros Institute's *Test Reviews Online* web site: http://www.unl.edu/buros

Peabody Picture Vocabulary Test–Fourth Edition (PPVT-4): English

Manual

Dunn, L.M., & Dunn, D.M. (2007). *Peabody Picture Vocabulary Test, 4th Edition: Manual.* Minneapolis, MN: Pearson Assessments.

Publisher

Pearson, Inc.
19500 Bulverde Road
San Antonio, TX 78259-3701
http://www.pearsonassessments.com

Cost

Form A or Form B kit: $224. Complete kit (Forms A and B): $414. PPVT-4/Assist CD-ROM kit: $150. Items sold separately.

Type of Measure

Direct assessment

Intended Age Range

2;6 years to 90+ years

Key Constructs/Domains

Receptive vocabulary (specifically, the ability to understand vocabulary words in English)

Description of Measure

The purpose of this assessment is to measure English receptive vocabulary (i.e., the degree to which words are understood) in both children and adults. The "PPVT-4 scale is an untimed power test of vocabulary, rather than a speed test" (Dunn & Dunn, 2007, p. 5). Although examinees are not given a time limit, those who do not respond to an item within 10 seconds should be reminded to give a response.

Available Languages and Formats

A Spanish version, the *Test de Vocabulario en Imágenes Peabody* (TVIP), is available. As the PPVT is in its fourth edition and the TVIP is a Spanish adaptation of the 1981 revised version of the PPVT, the TVIP and PPVT-4 are not direct comparisons. In addition, short forms of the PPVT have been created using advanced statistics, and these are utilized in national studies.

Strengths

The PPVT-4 was thoroughly standardized across a wide age range of individuals and has generally good reliability and validity.

The large colorful illustrations, the nature of the task, and the fact that it does not require a verbal response can make it appealing to young children and easy to administer.

Weaknesses

Interrater reliability needs to be examined, though it is likely quite high given how easy the PPVT-4 is to administer.

ADMINISTRATION

Procedure

After establishing rapport with the child and recording background information on the record sheet, the examiner presents the training items. These items are intended to introduce the child to the measure and also to determine whether the child is capable of responding to the items

Time Needed

10–15 minutes

on the PPVT-4. To qualify to take the test, the child must respond correctly without any help to at least two training items.

Children begin the PPVT-4 at different starting points depending on their age. The examiner presents a page with four pictures and the vocabulary word and asks the child to point to, or say the number of, the picture that shows the meaning of the word. Some examinees (especially younger children) may respond more easily by pointing to the picture rather than saying the number.

Administration and Interpretation

The manual does not specify who is qualified to administer the PPVT-4 but emphasizes that no matter how much experience the examiner has had with the previous three versions of this assessment, it is important that he or she have a thorough understanding of the administration of the PPVT-4. Examiners should practice administering the test, paying particularly close attention to the training items, the basal and ceiling rules, and the pronunciation of the most challenging stimulus words (pronunciation guides are provided). The test may be administered and scored by people with a range of educational backgrounds.

Scoring Method

Examiners are instructed to record the examinees' responses on the scoring sheet as the PPVT-4 is being administered and then convert the responses to a raw score (this can also be done electronically if the CD-ROM kit is purchased).

This measure has two types of normative scores: deviation and developmental. Deviation-type normative scores include standard scores, percentiles, normal curve equivalents, and stanines. Developmental-type normative scores include age equivalents and grade equivalents. Furthermore, growth score values (GSVs) can be calculated. "The GSV score is useful for measuring change in PPVT-4 performance over time. The GSV is not a normative score, because it does not involve the comparison with a norm group. Rather, it is a transformation of the raw score and is superior to raw scores for making statistical comparisons" (Dunn & Dunn, 2007, p. 18). The manual includes the procedures for obtaining these types of scores as well as an explanation of the calculation and interpretation of confidence intervals.

Adaptations or Instructions for Use with Individuals with Disabilities

Some examinees, such as those with extreme physical disabilities or impaired motor coordination, cannot make a pointing or oral response. With these examinees, the examiner may point to each of the pictured response options and ask the examinee to use a headshake or a coded message (e.g., one blink for yes, two for no) to indicate his or her response. A communication board or other forms of nonverbal communication may be used as well. All of these changes must be noted on the scoring sheet.

The manual also includes an article by Dr. Margery Miller titled "Considerations for Use of the PPVT Instrument with Children Who Are Deaf or Hard of Hearing" (Dunn & Dunn, 2007, p. 203). In addition, the manual indicates that the publishers are "planning a study to provide preliminary norms for children who are deaf or hard of hearing, using a modified version of the PPVT-4 scale" (p. 204).

FUNCTIONAL CONSIDERATIONS

Measure Development

The first edition of the PPVT began development in the 1950s with an examination of all entries in the 1953 edition of *Webster's New Collegiate Dictionary* in order to determine possible stimulus words. After multiple rounds of field testing and revision, the original PPVT was published. Development of the PPVT–Revised (PPVT-R) took place in the 1970s with an increased pool of possible stimulus words. Repeated field testing and item revision were again conducted and two forms (Forms L and M) were normed on a nationally representative sample (4,200 individuals ages 2;6 years through 40 years). The third edition of the PPVT included more of both the very easy and very difficult items on each form. Rational item analysis was conducted by a bias panel, a national user survey by mail and telephone, and focus groups. 300 individuals who used the PPVT-R identified problems with stimulus words and illustrations, administration procedures, and scoring procedures.

The PPVT-4 was created to achieve two primary goals: to increase the number of very easy items for more accurate assessment at low ability levels and to replace all of the black-and-white pictures with full-color illustrations. In addition, the illustrations were made more reflective of the population, with the inclusion of people of multiple ethnicities and a more equal gender balance, and attention was paid to minimize potential issues with color blindness. A larger easel format is used as well.

In addition, the PPVT-4's vocabulary was modernized following a review of various written and pictorial dictionaries. The stimulus words were selected from a pool of words that could be illustrated by drawings (in color) and that fairly represented 20 different content areas. Numerous expert panel reviews were conducted with individuals representing frequent users, different English-speaking nations, and diverse communities across the United States. Item-level difficulties were also statistically examined across the sample and by different communities. Minority communities and communities with disabilities were oversampled in order to allow for such an examination (Kush, 2009). GSVs were added as a way of recording progress over time.

Standardization Sample

Standardization of the PPVT-4 took place from the fall of 2005 through the spring of 2006 on a sample of U.S. residents age 2;6 years and older who were proficient in English and who did not meet any of the exclusionary criteria. For each age and grade, the sample was intended to match the U.S. population with regard to sex, race/ethnicity, socioeconomic status, geographic region, and special education status. For the age norms, the sample consisted of 3,540 people ages 2;6 years through 90 years and older divided into 28 age groups, with the goal of obtaining 100–200 people in each age group. For the grade norms, individuals ages 5–18 years were divided into 26 groups by education level.

Testing was conducted at 320 sites nationwide with more than 450 examiners, including speech-language pathologists, psychologists, educational diagnosticians, and graduate students. The manual includes multiple tables describing the standardization sample by sex, age, race/ethnicity, education level, geographic region, and parents' education level.

Norming

Norm referenced

Reliability

Test–Retest Reliability

During standardization, 340 examinees in five different age groups were retested using the same PPVT-4 form an average of 4 weeks after the first administration of the test. Approximately half took Form A and half took Form B. The average test–retest correlation was .93 (range = .92–.96), suggesting that this test has high stability over time.

Internal Consistency

The coefficient alpha was consistently high across all ages and grades, with averages of .97 (Form A) and .96 (Form B). The split-half reliabilities were also high across the age and grade ranges, with averages of .94 or .95, respectively, on each form.

Interrater Agreement

This information is not provided in the manual.

Other Forms of Reliability (e.g., Equivalent Forms)

Alternate-form reliability was examined with 508 examinees taking both forms of the measure up to 7 days apart. When adjusted for age restrictions, these reliabilities were in the moderate to high range (range = .87–.93, M = .89).

Validity

Face and Content

Overall, the face and content validities of the PPVT-4 are solid. Activities performed to examine the face and content validities included a review of modern dictionaries, utilization of examiner feedback, and conducting of multiple panel reviews. Furthermore, item-level analyses were conducted to examine general properties and potential biases.

Internal Construct

Not applicable because the PPVT-4 examines one construct (i.e., receptive vocabulary).

External Construct

During standardization, data were collected on various groups with clinical diagnoses or special education status. These groups included individuals with speech impairment, language delay, language disorder, hearing impairment, learning disability (reading), intellectual disability, giftedness, emotional/behavior disturbance, and attention-deficit/hyperactivity disorder. The language delay and hearing impairment groups contained preschoolers. The manual includes detailed tables of the differences between the general population and the clinical samples (differences that are statistically significant at the .001 level when sex, race/ethnicity, and education level are controlled). The groups performed differently on the PPVT-4 in the expected directions.

Support for the measure's convergent and discriminant validities is also indicated by some the correlational studies described in "Criterion."

Criterion

Multiple studies have correlated the PPVT-4 with other measures, though none of these were other receptive vocabulary tests. One study reported the results of the PPVT's co-norming with the Expressive Vocabulary Test–Second Edition, which is the expressive vocabulary counterpart to the PPVT-4. Results were in the medium range, from .80 to .84 (M = .82), across age groups (including preschoolers). A sample of about 66 preschoolers was also administered the Comprehensive Assessment of Spoken Language (CASL). Correlations with the CASL's Basic Concepts, Antonyms, and Sentence Completion subtests ranged from .41 to .54, which shows a relationship between receptive vocabulary skills and other language skills among preschoolers. The manual presents other studies that included elementary and high school students and that showed results in the expected direction.

RELEVANT STUDIES USING THE MEASURE

A brief literature search using PsycINFO and Google Scholar did not result in any peer-reviewed studies that specified using the PPVT-4. However, the previous three versions of this measure have been used in many studies, and it is possible that the PPVT-4 is already in use in studies.

(continued)

ADDITIONAL REFERENCES

Kush, J. (2009). Test review of the Peabody Picture Vocabulary Test, Fourth Edition. In R.A. Spies, J.F. Carlson, & K.F. Geisinger (Eds.), *The eighteenth mental measurements yearbook*. Retrieved from the Buros Institute's *Test Reviews Online* web site: http://www.unl.edu/buros

Shaw, S.R. (2009). Test review of the Peabody Picture Vocabulary Test, Fourth Edition. In R.A. Spies, J.F. Carlson, & K.F. Geisinger (Eds.), *The eighteenth mental measurements yearbook*. Retrieved from the Buros Institute's *Test Reviews Online* web site: http://www.unl.edu/buros

Test de Vocabulario en Imágenes Peabody (TVIP)

Information pertaining specifically to the Spanish version of the measure is in bold and italics. The remainder is equivalent information provided in the English review.

Manual

Dunn, L.M., Padilla, E.R., Lugo, D.E., & Dunn, L.M. (1986). *Test de Vocabulario en Imágenes Peabody: Examiner's Manual.* Circle Pines, MN: American Guidance Service.

Publisher[1]

Pearson, Inc.
19500 Bulverde Road
San Antonio, TX 78259-3701
http://www.pearsonassessments.com

Cost

Test kit: $181. Items sold separately.

Description of Measure

"This psychometric test measures an individual's receptive or hearing vocabulary of single Spanish words spoken by the examiner" (Dunn, Padilla, Lugo, & Dunn, 1986, p. 3).

Available Languages and Formats

An English version of the TVIP (the Peabody Picture Vocabulary Test [PPVT]) is available. *As the PPVT is in its fourth edition and the TVIP is a Spanish adaptation of the 1981 revised version of the PPVT, the TVIP and PPVT-4 are not direct comparisons. In addition, the TVIP has been normed for children and adolescents, whereas the PPVT-4 has been normed for adults 90 years of age or older.*

Short forms of the TVIP have been created using advanced statistics, and these are utilized in national studies.

Strengths

The measure is relatively easy to administer and does not require high levels of language use during the assessment, which is particularly useful when assessing young children.

The TVIP's manual presents good split-half reliability and criterion validity results for preschoolers, though the applicability of these dated results is unknown.

Weaknesses

The normative data are out of date (1981–1983), because the TVIP is based on an older version of the PPVT. In addition, the TVIP has been normed for children and adolescents, whereas the PPVT-4 has been normed for adults 90 years of age or older.

The psychometrics of the TVIP have not been examined to the same extent as those of the PPVT-4.

Type of Measure
Direct assessment

Intended Age Range
2;6 years to 17;11 years

Key Constructs/Domains
Receptive vocabulary (specifically, the ability to understand vocabulary words in Spanish)

The TVIP is an *adaptation* of the 1981 version of the Peabody Picture Vocabulary Test–Revised.

[1]Pearson Assessments, Inc., now distributes the TVIP.

ADMINISTRATION

Procedure

After establishing rapport with the examinee and recording background information on the record sheet, the examiner presents the training items. These items are intended to introduce the child to the measure and to determine whether the child is capable of responding to the items.

Time Needed
10–15 minutes

Children begin the measure at different starting points depending on their age. The examiner presents a page with four pictures and the vocabulary word and asks the child to point to, or say the number of, the picture that shows the meaning of the word. Some examinees (especially younger children) may respond more easily by pointing to the picture rather than saying the number. *If the child gives a verbal response, he or she can be asked to identify the picture by the printed number on the picture. Because articles (el/la) can provide hints to the child about the correct response given their feminine and masculine indicators, the examiner is asked not to utilize articles when presenting the word, although this is not grammatically correct in a question. Alternatively, and especially as the assessment progresses, the examiner may present the word alone when showing the picture.*

Administration and Interpretation

The examiner should be thoroughly familiar with the test materials and instruction manual. He or she should also practice administering the test and using the scoring materials, preferably with a trained examiner. It is extremely important that the examiner be proficient in correctly pronouncing each stimulus word. Formal training in psychometrics is not required to administer this assessment. The manual suggests that individuals who are interpreting results have a background in psychological testing and statistics as well as familiarity with the research literature on the language and cognitive development of Spanish-speaking Latino children.

Scoring Method

Using several tables, examiners can convert raw scores into different types of age-adjusted standardized scores using Mexican norms, Puerto Rican norms, or norms for a composite group. One table is used to convert the raw score into a standard score. A second table is used to convert the standard score into percentile rank, decile, or stanine. Finally, a third table is used to convert the examinee's raw score into an age-equivalent score.

Adaptations or Instructions for Use with Individuals with Disabilities

Because no reading or writing is required, the TVIP can be administered to many individuals with disabilities without any changes. However, the manual does not specifically describe if or how the TVIP can be adapted or modified.

FUNCTIONAL CONSIDERATIONS

Measure Development

The TVIP was adapted from the PPVT–Revised (PPVT-R) and includes 125 translated items that are used to assess the vocabulary of Spanish-speaking and bilingual children. The 125 stimulus words that make up the TVIP were carefully selected from an original pool of 350 stimulus words contained in the two different forms (Forms L and M) of the PPVT-R (Dunn & Dunn, 1981). The original pool of 350 PPVT-R items was selected to ensure coverage across 18 categories of vocabulary, though the PPVT-4 covers 20 categories.

Each of the 350 PPVT-R items was translated into Spanish by a Spanish professor and a Spanish teacher. The manual indicates that they attempted to provide items in Spanish that were equal in level of difficulty to the original English items and that were considered to be universal to the various Spanish-speaking communities. The resulting list of translated items was then reviewed and edited by psychologists in Mexico. In addition, translated items were dropped from the original 350-item pool based on data from Mexican and Puerto Rican participants using item response theory analyses, Rasch-Wright item calibration during the standardization process, and a qualitative analysis of the frequency of word usage. This yielded a final set of 125 stimulus words.

Content Equivalence of Items and Measure

Given that the TVIP is translated and adapted from the PPVT-R rather than the PPVT-4, the contents of the TVIP and the PPVT-4 are discrepant in terms of both items and categories.

Semantic Equivalence of Translations

The manual reports the utilization of various translators and the statistical examination of data stemming from Mexico and Puerto Rico. Dunn et al. assert that "subjective and empirical methods were used to ensure that [the]...stimulus words were universal Spanish, not words of other origins indigenous to a particular Spanish-speaking country" (1986, p. 78).

Structural Consistency Across the English and Spanish Versions

When it was developed, the TVIP generally approximated the structure of the PPVT-R. However, the PPVT has undergone two revisions since then, and the PPVT-4 differs significantly from the TVIP in terms of items, length, and format. For example, the TVIP's pictures are black and white, whereas the PPVT-4's are in color. In addition, the TVIP has been normed for children and adolescents, whereas the PPVT-4 has been normed for adults 90 years of age or older.

Standardization Sample

The norming samples consisted of two sets of monolingual Spanish-speaking students from Mexico and Puerto Rico. Testing in Mexico took place between September 1981 and November 1982 and included 1,219 children from the Federal District of Mexico. Testing in Puerto Rico took place between September 1982 and February 1983 and included 1,488 children from Puerto Rico (62.2% from the San Juan metropolitan area, where 53% of Puerto Rico's residents lived at that time). To correct for the uneven representation by socioeconomic status (SES), test developers used a weighting system to increase or decrease the contributions of each individual's score at each age so as to fit the SES ratios established by U.S. Census statistics.

Norming

Norm referenced. (Norms are available for the separate Mexican and Puerto Rican standardization samples as well as the combined sample.)

Reliability

Test–Retest Reliability
No information is provided in the manual.

Internal Consistency
The median split-half correlation coefficient, corrected using the Spearman-Brown formula, was .93, which is high. For 2-year-olds, the split-half coefficient was .80, which is in the medium range. The manual further indicates that "the lower value for very young children is expected because the TVIP lacks sufficient 'bottom' (very easy items)" (Dunn et al., 1986, p. 45). Among older preschoolers it was higher (.92–.94). Standard errors of measurement were 4–5 standard score points among preschoolers and 7 among 2-year-olds. The TVIP's alpha coefficients are not presented in the manual.

Interrater Agreement
No information is provided in the manual.

Other Forms of Reliability (e.g., Equivalent Forms)
Not applicable

Validity

Face and Content
The utilization of a range of expert consultants and careful qualitative and quantitative development contributed to this measure's face and content validities at the time it was developed. However, the pictures and norms are dated.

Internal Construct
Not applicable because the TVIP examines one construct (i.e., receptive vocabulary).

External Construct
The manual reports that a criterion for construct validity was fulfilled, as the percentage of subjects completing an item correctly increased with age (Dunn et al., 1986). No studies are presented that have examined how children with exceptionalities perform on the TVIP.

Support for the measure's convergent and discriminant validities is also indicated by some the correlational studies described in "Criterion."

Criterion
Criterion validity was examined with the Kaufman Assessment Battery for Children (K-ABC) using a young subsample (3–6 years old) of the Mexican standardization sample. Correlations ranged from .25 to .59 between scores on the TVIP and the Spanish K-ABC global scales and from .28 to .69 between the TVIP and the Spanish K-ABC Achievement scale subtests. This indicates weak to moderate relationships with the general subtests of the Kaufman batteries. The stronger relationship with the academic battery is expected given the important role of vocabulary in academic learning. As may be expected, correlations of the TVIP with the Expressive Vocabulary subtest were moderate (.57 for combined preschool groups). Studies were also conducted with school-age children.

In addition, the manual presents correlations of the English PPVT with other vocabulary tests to provide an indication of the degree of concurrent validity. However, it is unknown whether these correlations also pertain to the TVIP.

Comparison of Psychometric Properties Between English and Spanish Versions

Technical Equivalence in Reliability

Overall, the split-half coefficients of the TVIP and PPVT-4 are similar (in the .90s). However, there is a basal effect with the TVIP that is not apparent with the PPVT, given that the PPVT includes more items at the lower range. Furthermore, other types of reliability have been investigated more thoroughly for the PPVT-4 (e.g., test–rest reliabilities, internal consistency).

Technical Equivalence in Validity

The validity indicators examined to date suggest that the TVIP was a generally valid measure when developed, though has become dated. In general, more validity research is available for the PPVT, including external validity studies.

RELEVANT STUDIES USING THE MEASURE

A brief literature search using PsycINFO and Google Scholar yielded evidence of the use of the TVIP in a number of studies since its publication. For example, Umbel, Pearson, Fernandez, and Oller (1992) utilized the TVIP to investigate bilingual development among first graders. A study by Farver, Xu, Eppe, and Lonigan (2006) found that Latino preschoolers' interest in literacy mediated the relationship between parents' literacy and children's PPVT/TVIP scores. Furthermore, greater improvement was evidenced on the TVIP among Spanish- and English-dominant children attending a two-way bilingual preschool than an English-immersion program (Barnett, Yarosz, Thomas, Jung, & Blanco, 2006).

ADDITIONAL REFERENCES

Barnett, W.S., Yarosz, D.J., Thomas, J., Jung, K., & Blanco, D. (2006). *Two-way and monolingual English immersion in preschool education: An experimental comparison.* Rutgers, NJ: National Institute for Early Education Research.

Dunn, L.M., & Dunn, L.M. (1981). *Peabody Picture Vocabulary Test–Revised.* Circle Pines, MN: American Guidance Service.

Farver, J.A.M., Xu, Y., Eppe, S., & Lonigan, C.J. (2006). Home environments and young Latino children's school readiness. *Early Childhood Research Quarterly, 21,* 196–212.

Umbel, V.M., Pearson, B.Z., Fernandez, M.C., & Oller, D.K. (1992). Measuring bilingual children's receptive vocabularies. *Child Development, 63,* 1012–1020.

Xu, Y., Eppe, S., & Lonigan, C.J. (2006). Home environments and young Latino children's school readiness. *Early Childhood Research Quarterly, 21*(2), 196–212.

*pre*LAS 2000: English

Manuals

Duncan, S.E., & De Avila, E.A. (1998). *pre*LAS 2000*: Examiner's Manual. English Forms C and D.* Monterey, CA: CTB/McGraw-Hill.

De Avila, E.A., & Duncan, S.E. (2000). *pre*LAS 2000*: English and Spanish Technical Notes.* Monterey, CA: CTB/McGraw-Hill.

De Avila, E.A., & Duncan, S.E. (2005). *pre*LAS 2000*: English and Spanish Technical Notes Supplement.* Monterey, CA: CTB/McGraw-Hill.

Publisher

CTB McGraw-Hill Companies, Inc.
20 Ryan Ranch Road
Monterey, CA 93940-5703
http://www.ctb.com

Cost

*pre*LAS 2000 examiner's kit for each form: $265.25. Items are also available separately.

Type of Measure

Direct child assessment

Intended Age Range

The Oral Language Component is intended for children ages 4 to 6 years, whereas the Pre-Literacy Component is appropriate for children ages 5 to 6 years.

Key Constructs/Domains

- Oral Language (4- to 6-year-olds)
- Pre-Literacy (5- to 6-year-olds)

Description of Measure

"*pre*LAS 2000 assesses both receptive language (comprehension or the process of apprehending the 'meaning of something: a word, a phrase, an idea, a sentence, or a longer discourse') and expressive language (linguistic output, which requires all the processing capabilities of comprehension plus cognitive organization and the performance of appropriate motor behavior to make the requisite speech sounds)" (De Avila & Duncan, 2000, p. 4). A primary purpose of the measure is to determine the most appropriate placements for dual language learners (DLLs) in classroom settings. The publisher reports that "*pre*LAS 2000 continues to be used by thousands of young learners in the US, who participate in different [English language learner] programs" (L. Houston, personal communication, July 8, 2009).

Available Languages and Formats

The measure is also available in Spanish (*pre*LAS 2000 *Español*). There are two alternative versions of the measure in English (Forms C and D) based on the 2000 standardization. One form is available in Spanish (Form C).

Strengths

The subtests are likely quite appealing to young children, particularly those in the Oral Language Component. Two of these subtests (i.e., Say What You Hear and Let's Tell Stories) assess spontaneous-like speech samples.

Samples of both English speakers and DLLs were drawn from the same schools in an effort to control for experiences aside from language proficiency.

A measure that helps identify children by proficiency level is helpful for instructional decision making. Standardized scores in the form of normal curve equivalents (NCEs) and percentiles are also available in the 2005 supplement.

Item development and selection involved a wide range of qualitative and quantitative activities, from classroom observations to item-level analyses, that contributed to the measure's face and content validities. However, Ward (2003) questioned the type of items utilized in the Pre-Literacy Component.

Weaknesses

Limited information is provided on the criterion validity of the measure.

The publishers do not describe how the different subscale weights or proficiency cutoff levels were determined for the various subscales.

In one study, the *preLAS 2000* was found to have inadequate levels of sensitivity for those children with the lowest levels of English language proficiency (Siders, 2003). This may relate to the low number (< 9%) of 4-year-olds in the original sample, which was used to create the proficiency-level cutoff scores. It is important to note that a larger sample was used to create the English norming tables for NCE and percentile scores in 2005.

ADMINISTRATION

Procedure

The *preLAS 2000* contains 11 individual subtests that are divided into an Oral Language Component and a Pre-Literacy Component.

The *Oral Language Component* consists of five subtests:

- *Simon Says.* In a manner similar to the popular game, children's receptive understanding is assessed with action-oriented prompts.

- *Art Show.* Children are asked to identify or describe items that the examiner points to in the Cue Picture Book.

- *Say What You Hear.* Children repeat phrases or sentences from an audio recording. "This sentence imitation subscale assesses the child's receptive and expressive ability with morphological and syntactical features. It is based on the results of many researchers who have reported that when children are given adult sentences for imitation too long to be retained in immediate memory, they invariably alter them to fit the grammar of the moment, and that young children's spontaneous imitations mimic their spontaneous productions" (De Avila & Duncan, 2000, p. 12).

- *The Human Body.* Children are asked to verbally label or identify different parts of the body that the examiner points to in the Cue Picture Book.

- *Let's Tell Stories.* Children are asked to listen to a story (either read by the examiner or played on an audio recording) and look at the accompanying pictures in the Cue Picture Book. After the story has been read, the examiner asks the children to tell what happened in the story. In a manner similar to Say What You Hear, children's responses are examined for their complexity and accuracy. The technical manual states, "Because of cultural, ethnic, and regional differences and preferences, alternate stories are provided. To counteract any possible cultural bias or personal interest, each child is given two stories and the holistic scores are added together" (De Avila & Duncan, 2000, p. 12).

The Pre-Literacy Component consists of six subtests:

- *Letters.* Children are asked to verbally identify letters.
- *Numbers.* Children are asked to verbally identify numbers.
- *Colors.* Children are asked to verbally identify colors.
- *Shapes and Spatial Relationships.* Children are asked to verbally identify shapes and relationships.
- *Reading.* Children are asked to read simple words.
- *Writing.* Children are asked to write their name, their age, and simple words.

Time Needed

The Oral Language Component is generally administered in 10–15 minutes and the Pre-Literacy Component in 5–10 minutes.

Each subtest has its own administration procedures, which can be found in the examiner's manual. All of the subtests, except the Let's Tell Stories subtest, have practice items. According to the manual, the subtests can be administered across multiple sessions and in any order as may be necessary (Duncan & De Avila, 1998).

Administration and Interpretation

The manual recommends the following of those administering the measure (Duncan & De Avila, 1998):

- Examiners should be proficient English speakers who have experience working with young children and are able to accurately write the children's responses.
- Testers should be familiar with the testing materials and have been adequately trained.
- Individuals who score the holistic language samples in the Let's Tell Stories subtest should have attained a consistent level of 90% reliability during training, as outlined in the manual (Duncan & De Avila, 1998).

Scoring Method

The individual subtests can either be scored by the optional LASscore computerized scoring program or be hand-scored following the guidelines in the examiner's manual (Duncan & De Avila, 1998). All subtests (except for Let's Tell Stories) are scored by summing the total number of correct responses and then multiplying this number by a weight that has been created by the publisher for each respective subtest.

The manual suggests scoring the responses for the Let's Tell Stories subtest separately for each age group of 4-year-olds, 5-year-olds, and 6-year-olds (Duncan & De Avila, 1998). Responses are scored by comparing each child's response with the set of age-appropriate response descriptions provided in the manual as well as a corresponding set of specific, illustrative samples of responses for children from each of the age groups.

Once each of the subtests is scored and weighted, the total scores for the Oral Language Component and Pre-Literacy Component are calculated by summing the total weighted subtest scores. NCEs and percentile ranks became available in 2005 through the *Technical Notes Supplement*.

Cutoff scores are also available by age group (4-year-olds versus 5- and 6-year-olds). Five levels are provided for the Oral Language Component: 1 = non-English speaker, 2 = limited English speaker, 3 = limited English speaker, 4 = fluent (proficient) English speaker, and 5 = fluent (proficient) English speaker. Three levels are provided for the Pre-Literacy Component: 1 = low, 2 = mid-level, and 3 = high. As noted in reviews by Pratt (2003) and Ward (2003), the manual does not describe how either the weights or levels were established. For example, the decision to weight Let's Tell Stories by 4 and Say What You Hear by 2 may have been made based on either theory or empirical data, or perhaps both. It is also possible that score differences among the subsamples of proficient English speakers and English learners were utilized to create the levels. However, this is not described in the manual.

Adaptations or Instructions for Use with Individuals with Disabilities

No information is provided in the manual.

FUNCTIONAL CONSIDERATIONS

Measure Development

The *preLAS 2000* is a revision of the 1985 version of the *pre*LAS. The following subtests were dropped from the 1985 version: What's in the House? and Finishing Stories. As described by Ward, "[The original] PreLAS English is used only to assess English-language proficiency of ESL

[English as a second language] children. preLAS 2000 goes beyond this objective to assess language proficiency and preliteracy skills of both speakers of English as a first language and ESL speakers" (2003). Thus, the preLAS 2000 added the Pre-Literacy Component. As described in "Standardization Sample," English-proficient children were also included in the standardization sample.

According to the technical manual, the items for the *pre*LAS 2000 were created "based on reviews of the literature of child language, kindergarten readiness skills, bilingualism, assessment of immigrant children, expert opinion, and extended observations of language instruction and discourse" (De Avila & Duncan, 2000, pp. 4–5). The manual does not indicate which items if any were retained from the 1985 version and which were new additions. Professional writers, primarily teachers, wrote the items with attention to difficulty and length. Furthermore, the manual describes matching the Let's Tell Stories passages from the 1985 version along a number of dimensions.

The items were subsequently examined in a pilot study of about 100 mainstream and language-minority children. Item analyses led to the deletion or editing of some items, which were additionally examined in a larger tryout study. Following the tryout, items were further refined and Forms C and D were created. The technical manual describes the criteria used in the item selection process, including "level of difficulty, discriminant validity, inter-item and inter-scale reliability, age- and grade-level appropriateness, cultural bias, and representation of gender" (De Avila & Duncan, 2000, p. 5).

Standardization Sample

Two normative samples contributed to the *pre*LAS 2000. Normative data for the creation of the proficiency-level designations were collected in 1997 from 956 children living in six states and the District of Columbia. Samples of both English speakers and DLLs were drawn from the same schools in an effort to control (to some degree) for experiences aside from language proficiency. About 26% of children spoke English in the home, 42% spoke Spanish, and 22% spoke two languages (primarily Spanish and English). The remainder of the sample (about 10%) spoke one or more of 23 other languages. Pratt (2003) noted, "The standardization process was reasonable for the purposes of the test and the target population, although the test may be more appropriate for children from middle and low SES [socioeconomic status] Spanish- and English-speaking environments than for children from other non-English-speaking or high-SES backgrounds" (2003). Only about 9% of children were younger than 5, and about 11% were in prekindergarten. Finally, 54% of the children were attending kindergarten, whereas 35% attended first grade.

The normative data for the development of the NCEs and percentile ranks stemmed from children who had been administered the exam between 2000 and 2004 across 55 school districts and 286 schools across the country. As may be expected, a larger number of children completed the English form ($n = 7,584$) than the Spanish form ($n = 2,233$). Among those completing the English form, about 65% were administered the long form.

Norming

Criterion and norm referenced

Reliability

Test–Retest Reliability

The technical manual presents the data comparing Forms C and D as test–retest reliability, though it can be considered alternate-form reliability (De Avila & Duncan, 2000). These two forms were created after all of the items were presented to participants in the tryout sample. Data for about 900 children were collected for both forms. Thus, the results indicate the correspondence of children's performance on these sets of items when the items were presented at about the same time. Temporal stability across a few weeks was not examined.

According to a table on p. 35 of the technical manual (De Avila & Duncan, 2000), the interform correlation coefficients for Oral Language Component were .99 (total score) and .95 (proficiency level), and those for the Pre-literacy Component were .97 (total score) and .87 (proficiency level). The examiner's manual notes that 94% of children scored at the same proficiency level on the two forms (Duncan & De Avila, 1998). The data are not broken down by age or grade level in order to allow for the examination of results for the preschool subsample.

Internal Consistency

In general, internal consistency for the *pre*LAS 2000 is in the medium to high range across the subtests. Within the Oral Language Component, standardized Cronbach's alphas range from .86 (The Human Body) to .90 (Simon Says, Art Show, and Say What You Hear). Within the Pre-Literacy Component, standardized Cronbach's alphas range from .76 (Shapes and Spatial Relationships) to .91 (Letters). Cronbach's alphas are not provided for the Let's Tell Stories subtest.

In addition, subscale-to-total score correlations are .79 and greater for both Forms C and D. Finally, both item and subscale descriptive statistics are presented for the overall standardization sample as well as separately by language subgroups (English only vs. language-minority households). These item and subscale descriptive statistics are reasonably consistent across both forms as well as across language subgroups. The data are not broken down by age or grade level in order to allow for the examination of results for the preschool subsample.

In the examiner's manual, the standard errors of measurement are presented as 2 points for the Oral Language Component and 1 point for the Pre-Literacy Component (Duncan & De Avila, 1998). The appendix describes the importance of considering additional information about children who score within these points near critical cut points that are used for instructional purposes.

Interrater Agreement

Interrater reliabilities are presented for the more subjective portions of the *pre*LAS 2000: Let's Tell Stories (.88) and Writing (.90).

Other Forms of Reliability (e.g., Equivalent Forms)

The manual presents interform correlations as test–retest reliabilities (see "Test–Retest Reliability"). The examiner's manual also presents information about the interform correspondence between the 1985 and 2000 versions of the *pre*LAS. Of 55 students, 89% were identified at the same proficiency levels (Duncan & De Avila, 1998).

Validity

Face and Content

As described in "Strengths," item development and selection involved a wide range of qualitative and quantitative activities, from classroom observations to item-level analyses, that contributed to its face and content validities. However, Ward (2003) questioned the type of items utilized in the Pre-Literacy Component.

The publishers report that "external expert reviews have also been conducted and overall these reviewers find the *pre*LAS 2000 an engaging and useful instrument for young learners" (L. Houston, personal communication, July 8, 2009).

Internal Construct

Factor analyses are not reported in the technical manual. The correlation between the Oral Language and Pre-Literacy Components was .70. Examinations of the scale intercorrelations for the Oral Language Component generally ranged from .71 between Simon Says and Say What You Hear to .79 between The Human Body and Art Show. However, the intercorrelations between Let's Tell Stories and the other subtests were lower, ranging from .61 to .67. In terms of the Pre-Literacy Component, intercorrelations ranged from .52 between Letters and Writing to .85 between Numbers and Reading.

External Construct

Age- and grade-related differences were evidenced on the *preLAS 2000*, suggesting that older children perform better on the measure. The manual also presents data to demonstrate that children from English-speaking homes score higher on the measure than language-minority children (Duncan & De Avila, 1998). Furthermore, potential interactions among age, grade, and language were examined and presented in the technical manual (De Avila & Duncan, 2000).

Score differences among children with exceptionalities are not presented. In addition, concurrent and discriminant validities in comparison to other measures are not described.

Criterion

As noted by Pratt (2003) and Ward (2003), no information on criterion validity is provided in the examiner's manual or technical manuals. A comparison of the *preLAS 2000* and the PreIPT-2 was conducted by Siders (2003) and is described in "Examples of Relevant and/or Recent Studies."

RELEVANT STUDIES USING THE MEASURE

Shorter forms of the *preLAS 2000* have been utilized in a series of studies. One of the most common forms is the Oral Language Development Scale (OLDS) developed for the Early Childhood Longitudinal Study–Kindergarten (ECLS-K) cohort as a short English proficiency screener (Rock & Pollack, 2002). The OLDS comprised three of the *preLAS* subtests: Simon Says, Art Show, and Let's Tell Stories. Two of the subtests (Simon Says and Art Show) were used in the Head Start Family and Child Experiences Survey (Administration on Children, Youth, and Families, 2001). These federal studies examined the psychometric properties of the subtests for their respective samples. The *preLAS 2000* was also used in this manner by Boller et al. (2008) for a program evaluation.

López and Greenfield (2004) utilized the English and Spanish versions of the *preLAS 2000* to examine cross-language transfer among preschool-age children in Head Start. Both English and Spanish total scores from the *preLAS 2000* predicted English phonological ability.

Siders (2003) compared the utility of the *preLAS 2000* to that of the PreIPT-2 for ESL preschool children and found that although the measures were comparable in terms of qualitative elements, the *preLAS* lacked sensitivity for low-performing children and younger children (younger than 5 years of age). The correlation between the two tests was .63. Only 14% of the subjects had the same language proficiency level for both subtests, a problem seen most commonly at the lowest level of language proficiency. The *preLAS* rated language proficiency lower than either the PreIPT-2 or teacher ratings of language proficiency. It was concluded that the *preLAS 2000* might underestimate the language abilities of young children, which may be because of the relatively small number of children younger than 5 in the standardization sample (approximately 10%).

ADDITIONAL REFERENCES

Administration on Children, Youth, and Families. (2001). *Head Start FACES: Longitudinal findings on program performance, third progress report.* Washington, DC: U.S. Department of Health and Human Services.

Boller, K., Paulsell, D., Aikens, N., Potamites, L., Carlson, B., & Kovak, M. (2008). *A profile of kindergarten readiness in White Center: Fall 2007.* Princeton, NJ: Mathematica Policy Research. Retrieved from http://www.mathematica-mpr.com/publications/redirect_PubsDB.asp?strSite=PDFs/readiness_WhiteCenter.pdf

López, L.M., & Greenfield, D.B. (2004). The cross-language transfer of phonological skills to Hispanic Head Start children. *Bilingual Research Journal, 28,* 1–18.

Pratt, S. (2003). Test review of the *pre*LAS 2000. In B.S. Plake, J.C. Impara, & R.A. Spies (Eds.), *The fifteenth mental measurements yearbook.* Retrieved from the Buros Institute's *Test Reviews Online* web site: http://www.unl.edu/buros

Rock, D.A. & Pollack, J.M. (2002). *Early Childhood Longitudinal Study–Kindergarten Class of 1998-1999 (ECLS-K): Psychometric report for kindergarten through first grade.* Washington, DC: U.S. Department of Education, Office of Educational Research and Improvement, National Center for Education Statistics.

Siders, J.J. (2003). *A comparative evaluation of the preLAS 2000 English and the PRE-IPT Oral English, Second Edition for use with preschool children.* Retrieved from http://www.uwstout.edu/lib/thesis/2003/2003sidersj.pdf

Ward, A.M. (2003). Test review of the *pre*LAS 2000. In B.S. Plake, J.C. Impara, & R.A. Spies (Eds.), *The fifteenth mental measurements yearbook.* Retrieved from the Buros Institute's *Test Reviews Online* web site: http://www.unl.edu/buros

*pre*LAS 2000: Español

Information pertaining specifically to the Spanish version of the measure is in bold and italics. The remainder is equivalent information provided in the English review.

Manuals

Duncan, S.E., & De Avila, E.A. (1998). *pre*LAS 2000: *Manual para Examinadores. Español Forma C.* Monterey, CA: CTB/McGraw-Hill.

De Avila, E.A., & Duncan, S.E. (2000). *pre*LAS 2000 : *English and Spanish Technical Notes.* Monterey, CA: CTB/McGraw-Hill.

De Avila, E.A., & Duncan, S.E. (2005). *pre*LAS 2000: *English and Spanish Technical Notes Supplement.* Monterey, CA: CTB/McGraw-Hill.

Publisher

CTB McGraw-Hill Companies, Inc.
20 Ryan Ranch Road
Monterey, CA 93940-5703
http://www.ctb.com

Cost

preLAS examiner's kit (Spanish): $265.25. Items also available separately.

Description of Measure

According to the technical manual, the *pre*LAS 2000 Español is essentially identical to the English version, although it is not a direct translation of the English version. Thus, the "*pre*LAS 2000 assesses both receptive language (comprehension or the process of apprehending the 'meaning of something: a word, a phrase, an idea, a sentence, or a longer discourse') and expressive language (linguistic output, which requires all the processing capabilities of comprehension plus cognitive organization and the performance of appropriate motor behavior to make the requisite speech sounds)" (De Avila & Duncan, 2000, p. 4). A primary purpose of the measure is to determine the most appropriate placements for dual language learners (DLLs) in classroom settings. The publisher reports that "*PreLAS 2000* continues to be used by thousands of young learners in the US, who participate in different [English language learner] programs" (L. Houston, personal communication, July 8, 2009).

Available Languages and Formats

The measure is available in English, with two forms (Forms C and D).

Strengths

The subtests are likely quite appealing to young children, particularly those in the Oral Language Component. Two of these subtests (i.e., *Repetición* and *Contando cuentos*) assess spontaneous-like speech samples.

A measure that helps identify children by proficiency level is helpful for instructional decision making. Standardized scores in the form of normal curve equivalents (NCEs) and percentiles are also available in the 2005 supplement.

Type of Measure

Direct child assessment

Intended Age Range

The Oral Language Component is intended for children ages 4 to 6 years, whereas the Pre-Literacy Component is appropriate for children ages 5 to 6 years.

Key Constructs/Domains

- Oral Language (4- to 6-year-olds)
- Pre-Literacy (5- to 6-year-olds)

214

Samples were drawn from various Spanish-speaking countries as well as the United States. Thus, the preLAS 2000 Español was developed for use with bilingual and/or native Spanish speakers.

The preLAS 2000 Español's item development and selection involved a wide range of qualitative and quantitative activities, from classroom observations to item-level analyses, that contributed to the measure's face and content validities. However, Ward (2003) questioned the type of items utilized in the Pre-Literacy Component for the English version. This critique may also be applicable to the Spanish version.

The Spanish version is not a direct translation of the English version but rather was designed to have an identical format and administration procedure.

Internal consistency coefficients were generally adequate for the Oral Language Component subtests, except for **El cuerpo humano** *(.66). Similarly, the* **Letras, Lectura,** *and* **Escritura** *subtest alpha coefficients were solid on the Spanish version, though those for* **Números, Colores,** *and* **Formas geométricas y relaciones espaciales** *were lower. This may relate to differences in the experiences of children from across the countries assessed or to measurement.*

Weaknesses

Limited information is provided on the criterion validity of the measure.

De Avila and Duncan (2005) cautioned against the use of the Spanish norming data for younger children. A limited sample size was available for 4-year-olds. The norming sample used for the creation of the NCEs and percentile ranks on the Spanish version was generally adequate for older children.

The publishers do not describe and/or justify how either the different subscale weights or proficiency cutoff levels were determined for the various subscales. *Furthermore, because the weights and levels reported in the technical report for the Spanish version are identical to those for the English version, it is unknown whether they were simply applications from the English version, concurrently derived with the English version, or found to be statistically equivalent across the forms.*

The test–retest reliability of the Spanish version is not reported in the manuals.

The Let's Tell Stories subtest correlates less strongly with the other Oral Proficiency subtests. This is particularly the case for the Spanish version, with correlations in the .30 range. It is interesting that this subtest is then weighted highly on the total score. Such correspondence issues were also noted in MacSwan, Rolstad, and Glass's (2002) examination of the prior version of the preLAS.

Older children apparently do not score higher on some subtests of the Spanish Oral Language Component, though they do on the English version.

ADMINISTRATION

Procedure

The preLAS 2000 Español contains 11 individual subtests that are divided into an Oral Language Component and a Pre-Literacy Component.

The Oral Language Component consists of five subtests:

- *Símon dice (Simon Says). In a manner similar to the popular game, children's receptive understanding is assessed with action-oriented prompts.*

Time Needed

The Oral Language Component is generally administered in 10–15 minutes and the Pre-Literacy Component in 5–10 minutes.

- *Muestra de arte (Art Show). Children are asked to verbally label or identify items that the examiner points to in the Cue Picture Book.*
- *Repetición (Say What You Hear). Children repeat phrases or sentences from an audio recording. "This sentence imitation subscale assesses the child's receptive and expressive ability with morphological and syntactical features. It is based on the results of many researchers who have reported that when children are given adult sentences for imitation too long to be retained in immediate memory, they invariably alter them to fit the grammar of the moment, and that young children's spontaneous imitations mimic their spontaneous productions" (De Avila & Duncan, 2000, p. 12).*
- *El cuerpo humano (The Human Body). Children are asked to verbally label or identify different parts of the body that the examiner points to in the Cue Picture Book.*
- *Contando cuentos (Let's Tell Stories). Children are asked to listen to a story (either read by the examiner or played on an audio recording) and look at the accompanying pictures in the Cue Picture Book. After the story has been read, the examiner asks the children to tell what happened in the story. In a manner similar to Say What You Hear, children's responses are examined for their complexity and accuracy. The technical manual states, "Because of cultural, ethnic, and regional differences and preferences, alternate stories are provided. To counteract any possible cultural bias or personal interest, each child is given two stories and the holistic scores are added together" (De Avila & Duncan, 2000, p. 12).*

The *Pre-Literacy Component* consists of six subtests:

- Letras *(Letters).* Children are asked to verbally identify letters.
- Números *(Numbers).* Children are asked to verbally identify numbers.
- Colores *(Colors).* Children are asked to verbally identify colors.
- Formas geométricas y relaciones espaciales *(Shapes and Spatial Relationships).* Children are asked to verbally identify shapes and relationships.
- Lectura *(Reading).* Children are asked to read simple words.
- Escritura *(Writing).* Children are asked to write their name, their age, and simple words.

Each subtest has its own administration procedures, which can be found in the examiner's manual. All of the subtests except the Let's Tell Stories subtest have practice items. The subtests can be administered across multiple sessions and in any order as may be necessary (Duncan & De Avila, 1998).

Administration and Interpretation

The manual recommends the following of those administering the measure (Duncan & De Avila, 1998):

- *Examiners should be proficient Spanish speakers who have experience working with children 4–6 years of age and are able to accurately write the children's responses.*
- Examiners should be familiar with the testing materials and have been adequately trained, either by attending a seminar or engaging in self-training with extensive progress.
- Individuals who score the holistic language samples in the Let's Tell Stories subtest should have attained a consistent level of 90% reliability, as outlined in the manual (Duncan & De Avila, 1998).

Scoring Method

The individual subtests can either be scored by the optional LASscore computerized scoring program or be hand-scored following the guidelines in the examiner's manual. All subtests (except for **Contando cuentos**) are scored by summing the total number of correct responses and then multiplying this number by a weight that has been created by the publisher for each respective subtest.

The manual suggests scoring the responses for the **Contando cuentos** subtest separately for each age group of 4-year-olds, 5-year-olds, and 6-year-olds (Duncan & De Avila, 1998). Responses are scored by comparing each child's response with the set of age-appropriate response descriptions provided in the manual as well as a corresponding set of specific, illustrative samples of responses for children from each of the age groups.

Once each of the subtests is scored and weighted, the total scores for the Oral Language Component and Pre-Literacy Component are calculated by summing the total weighted subtest scores. NCEs and percentile ranks became available in 2005 through the *Technical Notes Supplement*. *Although the norming sample was generally adequate (as described in "Standardization Sample"), the authors caution against the use of the norming data for younger children: "Note in Table 2 that the available case count for the Spanish Oral total score for 48–59 month olds was only 213. Caution should be exercised when referring to the Spanish norms for this group of students due to the extremely low sample size" (De Avila & Duncan, 2005, pp. 1–2).*

Cutoff scores are also available by age group (4-year-olds versus 5- and 6-year-olds). *Five levels are provided for the Oral Language Component: 1 =* **no fluente en español** *(non-Spanish speaker), 2 =* **limitado en español** *(limited Spanish speaker), 3 =* **limitado en español** *(limited Spanish speaker), 4 =* **fluente en español** *(proficient Spanish speaker), and 5 =* **fluente en español** *(proficient Spanish speaker). Three levels are provided for the Pre-Literacy Component: 1 =* **bajo** *(low), 2 =* **mediano** *(mid-level), and 3 =* **alto** *(high).*

As noted in reviews by Pratt (2003) and Ward (2003), the manual does not describe how either the weights or levels were established. For example, the decision to weight **Contando cuentos** by 4 and **Repetición** by 2 may have been based on either theory or empirical data, or perhaps both. It is also possible that score differences among the subsamples of proficient English speakers and English learners were utilized to create the levels. However, this was not described in the manual. *Furthermore, because the weights and levels for the Spanish version are identical to those for the English version, it is unknown whether they were simply applications from the English version, concurrently derived with the English version, or found to be statistically equivalent across the forms.*

Adaptations or Instructions for Use with Individuals with Disabilities

No information is presented in the manual.

FUNCTIONAL CONSIDERATIONS

Measure Development

The *pre*LAS 2000 Español is a revision of the 1985 version of the *pre*LAS, to which the Pre-Literacy Component was added. The following subtests were dropped from the 1985 version: What's in the House? and Finishing Stories.

According to the technical manual (De Avila & Duncan, 2000), the preLAS 2000 **Español** *is essentially identical in many respects to the English version, although it is not a direct translation of the English version. The Spanish version is similar in structure, format, administration, and scoring methods and techniques, but given the differences across languages it differs in content, the specific words for items, syntax, and even artwork.*

The items for the *pre*LAS 2000 were created "based on reviews of the literature of child language, kindergarten readiness skills, bilingualism, assessment of immigrant children, expert opinion, and extended observations of language instruction and discourse" (De Avila & Duncan, 2000, pp. 4–5). The manual does not indicate which items if any were retained from the 1985 version and which were new additions. Professional writers, primarily teachers, wrote the items with attention to difficulty and length. Furthermore, the manual describes matching the Let's Tell Stories passages from the 1985 version along a number of dimensions. *It appears that these procedures were conducted for both the English and Spanish versions (Duncan & De Avila, 1998).*

Thus, it appears that the pilot study with about 100 mainstream and language-minority children also included the preLAS **Español**. Item analyses led to the deletion or editing of some items, which were additionally examined in a larger tryout study. The technical manual describes the criteria used in the item selection process, including "level of difficulty, discriminant validity, inter-item and inter-scale reliability, age- and grade-level appropriateness, cultural bias, and representation of gender" (De Avila & Duncan, 2000, p. 5).

Content Equivalence of Items and Measure

The English and Spanish versions of the **preLAS 2000** *were developed concurrently using similar qualitative and quantitative processes. The result is "language parity" in structure, format, methods, and techniques rather than a direct translation (De Avila & Duncan, 2000, p. 50).*

Semantic Equivalence of Translations

The preLAS 2000 **Español** *is not a direct translation of the English version but rather varies along "the content, the words, the syntax, and the artwork" (De Avila & Duncan, 2000, p. 50). The specific translation process used is not described in the manual.*

Structural Consistency Across the English and Spanish Versions

The format and number of items used for both the English and Spanish forms are identical.

Standardization Sample

Two normative samples contributed to the *preLAS 2000*. *Normative data for the creation of the proficiency-level designations were collected in 1997 for 397 children living in five countries (Colombia, Mexico, Panama, Puerto Rico, and the United States). A total of 261 children were from Latin America, and the remaining 136 were from California and Texas. It should be noted that 25% of the sample came from one Head Start program in Texas. The overall sample consisted of 192 girls and 205 boys. Of the children sampled from Latin America, 245 spoke Spanish as their primary language and 21 spoke English as their primary language. Because of the schooling differences across countries, it is difficult to make comparisons by grade. Across the Spanish sample, represented grades in the sample are generally in the* **pre-kinder** *(21%) to* **sercero** *(11%) range.*

Compared to the English version, a greater proportion of younger children were included in the Spanish sample in this original sample (though not for the norming sample described next). About 52% of the children were younger than 5. What is interesting is that the sample included children between 3 and 8 years of age, although the preLAS is only used with children between 4 and 6. The prevalence of 3-, 7-, and 8-year-old children in the Spanish sample is unknown.

The normative data for the development of the NCEs and percentile ranks stemmed from children who had been administered the exam between 2000 and 2004 across 55 school districts and 286 schools across the country. As may be expected, a larger number of children completed the English form ($n = 7,584$) than the Spanish form ($n = 2,233$). *Among those completing the Spanish form, about 81% were administered the long form. As noted in "Scoring Method," the norming data for 48–59-month-olds were limited.*

Norming

Criterion and norm referenced

Reliability

Test–Retest Reliability

This information is not presented in the Spanish examiner's manual or the technical manuals.

Internal Consistency

*In general, the internal consistency for the pre*LAS 2000 **Español** *ranges from medium to high across the subtests. Within the Oral Language Component, standardized Cronbach's alphas range from .66 (**El cuerpo humano**) to .88 (**Muestra de arte**). Within the Pre-Literacy Component, standardized Cronbach's alphas range from .55 (**Formas geométricas y relaciones espaciales**) to .96 (**Lectura**). Cronbach's alpha scores are not provided for the **Contando cuentos** subtest.*

*In addition, subscale-to-total score correlations range from .60 for **Muestra de arte** to .83 for the first story in **Contando cuentos**. Finally, both item and subscale descriptive statistics are presented for the overall standardization sample as well as separately by country subgroup (Latin American and U.S. language minority). These item and subscale descriptive statistics are reasonably consistent across both forms as well as across language subgroups. The data are not broken down by age or grade level in order to allow for the examination of results for the preschool subsample.*

In the examiner's manual, the standard errors of measurement (SEMs) are presented as 2 points for the Oral Language Component and 1 point for the Pre-Literacy Component (Duncan & De Avila, 1998). The appendix describes the importance of considering additional information about children who score within these points near critical cut points that are used for instructional purposes. The SEM data presented in the Spanish manual are exactly the same as those for the English version, which is surprising given the statistical differences between the two samples.

Interrater Agreement

*This information is provided for 2 of the 11 subtests: **Contando cuentos** and **Escritura**. Interrater agreement is good for both (.87 and .88, respectively).*

Other Forms of Reliability (e.g., Equivalent Forms)

The Oral Language Component of Spanish Forms A and C was administered to 64 students over a 4-week period. (Note that Form A was designed in 1985, whereas Form C was created in 2000. A Form B does not exist.) A total of 92% of the students fell into the same level of oral language proficiency using the two forms. Of the remaining five students who fell into different categories based on which form they were administered, none differed by more than one proficiency category.

Validity

Face and Content

*As described in "Strengths," item development and selection for the pre*LAS 2000 **Español** *involved a wide range of qualitative and quantitative activities, from classroom observations to item-level analyses, that contributed to its face and content validities. Yet in her review of the English version, Ward (2003) questioned* *the type of items utilized in the Pre-Literacy Component. This critique may also be applicable to the Spanish version.*

The publishers report that "external expert reviews have also been conducted and overall these reviewers find the *preLAS 2000* an engaging and useful instrument for young learners" (L. Houston, personal communication, July 8, 2009).

Internal Construct

Factor analyses for the preLAS 2000 **Español** *are not reported in the technical manual. The correlation between the Oral Language and Pre-Literacy Components was .25, which is much lower than for the English version. The manual speculates that this may reflect the varied instructional approaches in other countries. In addition, it is important to note that the English and Spanish samples varied in their inclusion of younger children.*

Examination of the scale intercorrelations for the Oral Language Component raises some questions about the correspondence of the **Contando cuentos** *subtest with the other subtests. For example, data were presented for Stories 1, 3, and 5. These correlated between .27 and .35 with the other Oral Language Component subscales. The intercorrelations among these other subscales were higher, at about .41–.63. In terms of the Pre-Literacy Component, intercorrelations ranged from .25 between* **Lectura** *and* **Formas geométricas y relaciones espaciales** *to .78 between* **Lectura** *and* **Escritura.**

External Construct

Age-related differences were evidenced only on the preLAS 2000 **Español's Contando cuentos** *subtest and the Oral Proficiency total score (which is weighted heavily with the* **Contando cuentos** *subtest). There were no differences between children younger than 5 and those older than 5.*

Data demonstrate that children from Spanish-speaking countries score higher than language-minority children in the United States (Duncan & De Avila, 1998).

Potential interactions between age and language were not examined for the Spanish version as they had been for the English version. Score differences among children with exceptionalities are not presented. In addition, data examining concurrent and discriminant validities in comparison to other measures are not described.

Criterion

No information on criterion validity is provided in the examiner's manual or technical manual.

Comparison of Psychometric Properties Between English and Spanish Versions

Technical Equivalence in Reliability

The Cronbach's alpha was higher for the Spanish **Lectura** *subtest (.96) than the English Reading subtest (.86), which is quite acceptable. However, the alpha coefficients were lower on the Spanish version for two of the Oral Proficiency subtests (i.e.,* **Simón dice** *and* **El cuerpo humano***) and three of the Pre-Literacy Component subtests (i.e.,* **Números, Colores,** *and* **Formas geométricas y relaciones espaciales***). This may relate to differences in the experiences of children from across the countries assessed or to measurement. Other subtests (e.g.,* **Muestra de arte, Repetición de frases, Letras,** *and* **Escritura***) had generally equivalent alphas. The SEM data presented in the Spanish manual are exactly the same as those for the English* *version, which is surprising given the statistical differences between the two samples. The test–retest reliability of the Spanish version has not been reported. Interrater reliability for both language versions is similar.*

Technical Equivalence in Validity

Face and content validities were well established in and across both versions. Factor analyses have not been conducted for either version. The Let's Tell Stories subtest correlates the least strongly with all the other Oral Proficiency subtests. This is particularly the case for the Spanish version, with correlations in the .30 range. What is interesting is that this subtest is then weighted highly on the total score, though the rationale for this is not provided. In terms of external construct validity, both versions distinguish between language groups, which is positive. However, older children apparently do not score higher on some subtests of the Spanish Oral Proficiency Component than younger children. Finally, criterion-related validity is in need of examination for both the English and Spanish versions.

RELEVANT STUDIES USING THE MEASURE

A few studies have utilized the Spanish version of the preLAS (either the 1985 version or the preLAS 2000). For example, López and Greenfield (2004) used the English and Spanish versions of the preLAS 2000 to examine cross-language transfer among preschool-age children in Head Start. Both English and Spanish total scores from the preLAS 2000 predicted English phonological ability.

*MacSwan et al. (2002) examined the construct validity of the 1985 preLAS Spanish version. Although some of the scales differ, some of the results may be applicable to the 2000 version. In a factor analysis, they noted that **Contando historias** (similar to the **Contando cuentos**) and another former subtest (**Terminando cuentitos**) did not converge statistically with the other subtests. This is similar to the interscale correlations noted above in the "Technical Equivalence in Validity" section. MacSwan et al. were also concerned about the more subjective scoring approaches for these subtests. Based on their analyses, they indicated that it was likely that the older version of the preLAS may result in high number of false negatives (i.e., children wrongly classified as non-Spanish speakers).*

ADDITIONAL REFERENCES

López, L.M., & Greenfield, D.B. (2004). The cross-language transfer of phonological skills to Hispanic Head Start children. *Bilingual Research Journal, 28,* 1–18.

MacSwan, J., Rolstad, K., & Glass, G.V. (2002). Do some school age children have no language? Some problems of construct validity in the preLAS Espanol. *Bilingual Research Journal, 26,* 213–238.

Pratt, S. (2003). Test review of the *preLAS 2000*. In B.S. Plake, J.C. Impara, & R.A. Spies (Eds.), *The fifteenth mental measurements yearbook*. Retrieved from the Buros Institute's *Test Reviews Online* web site: http://www.unl.edu/buros

Ward, A.M. (2003). Test review of the *preLAS 2000*. In B.S. Plake, J.C. Impara, & R.A. Spies (Eds.), *The fifteenth mental measurements yearbook*. Retrieved from the Buros Institute's *Test Reviews Online* web site: http://www.unl.edu/buros

Preschool Language Scale–Fifth Edition (PLS-5): English

Manual

Zimmerman, I.L., Steiner, V.G., & Pond, R.E. (2011). *Preschool Language Scales Fifth Edition: Examiner's Manual.* Bloomington, MN: NCS Pearson.

Publisher

Pearson, Inc.
19500 Bulverde Road
San Antonio, TX 78259-3701
http://www.pearsonassessments.com

Cost

PLS-5 complete kit (with manipulatives): $300; PLS-5 basic kit (without manipulatives): $248; PLS-4 upgrade kit: $49.

Type of Measure

Direct child assessment, examiner observation, and parent report

Intended Age Range

Birth to 7;11 years

Key Constructs/Domains

Auditory Comprehension, Expressive Communication, Articulation

Description of Measure

The PLS-5 is "an individually administered test used to identify children who have a language delay or disorder" (Zimmerman, Steiner, & Pond, 2011, p. 13). In addition, it is used to determine children's language skills in a number of discrete areas and to determine service eligibility for early intervention or speech and language services. It is also used as a measure of treatment efficacy. The PLS-5 (2011) is an updated version of the PLS-4 (2002; see "Measure Development" for additional details).

Available Languages and Formats

The PLS-5 has been available in Spanish since 2011. The fifth edition of the Spanish version is scheduled to come out in 2012.

Strengths

The reliability coefficients are very strong, and all aspects of the PLS-5 (e.g., administration, elicitation, interpretation, recording, scoring, and child comprehension) were examined and improved to ensure its validity.

Dialectical variations are included in the norming process and scoring criteria for selected items on the Expressive Communication scale. These variations include African American English, Spanish-influenced English, Southern English, Appalachian English, and Chinese-influenced English.

The standardization sample and procedures are solid.

The PLS-5 differentiates children with language disorders and children with autism spectrum disorder (ASD) from the general population.

The standardized scoring method allows for three methods of item completion (elicited response to a question, caregiver report, observations of spontaneous behavior) for children younger than 3, which may provide a more complete picture of very young children's development.

Weaknesses

Factor analyses could have been conducted to verify the distribution of items across the two scales.

ADMINISTRATION

Procedure

The PLS-5 has two scales, either of which can be administered first:

- *Auditory Comprehension (AC).* Among younger children, this scale assesses precursors to language, such as attention to the environment and people. Among older children, it assesses the ability to understand receptive vocabulary, morphology, syntax, investigative language skills, emergent literacy skills, and a variety of additional concepts.

Time Needed
• Birth to 11 months: 25–35 minutes
• 12 months to 2;11 years: 45–55 minutes
• 3 years to 4;11 years: 50–60 minutes
• 5 years to 7;11 years: 40–50 minutes

- *Expressive Communication (EC).* Among younger children, this scale assesses children's vocal development and social communication. Among older children, it assesses vocabulary, morphology, syntax, integrative language, phonological ability, and a variety of additional concepts.

In addition, three optional supplemental measures may be used with the PLS-5:

- The Language Sample Checklist assesses children's spontaneous speech. It provides a summary profile of utterances, enables calculation of mean length of utterance, and enables recording of dialect and intelligibility.

- The Articulation Screener assesses children's ability to pronounce different speech sounds. It is designed for use with children 2;6 years to 7;11 years. It provides "research-based criterion scores that a clinician can use to determine if further articulation testing is warranted" (Zimmerman et al., 2011, p. 14).

- The Home Communication Questionnaire (HCQ) is recommended for use by caregivers of children younger than 2;11 years. It allows the examiner to gain a broader perspective on children's communication skills in home and child care settings. It is important to note that responses on the HCQ can be used to provide credit for items on the AC and EC scales. It is suggested that the HCQ be completed prior to the testing session so that the examiner is aware of children's strengths and areas of concern.

Three additional forms are also available to assist the examiner in examining success and error patterns in children's language development:

- The Item Analysis Checklist organizes all of the items across the AC and EC scales by age level.

- The PLS-5 Profile organizes the items across the AC and EC scales by type of language skill.

- The Clinician's Worksheet is used to "summarize information about the child's language ability, prepare for his or her program planning meeting, and include information relevant to development of the Individualized Family Service Plan" (Zimmerman et al., 2011, p. 15).

Administration and Interpretation

The PLS-5 can be administered by the following individuals: "Speech and language pathologists, early childhood specialists, psychologists, educational diagnosticians, and other professionals who have experience working with children of this age and training in individual assessment" (Zimmerman et al., 2011, p. 17). Although paraprofessionals can administer the PLS-5, scoring and interpretation should be conducted by clinicians trained and experienced in diagnostic assessment.

Recommendations for assessing children in general at various age ranges and from nonmainstream cultures are provided in the manual. Caregivers are often involved in working with the youngest children.

Scoring Method

The PLS-5 is hand-scored.

A child younger than 3 can be considered to have successfully completed a task based on one of three types of assessment:

- Elicitation—the child performs the task when cued
- Observation—the child performs the task at some point during the session but not when cued
- Caregiver report—the caregiver is able to provide the tester with specific examples of when the child engaged in the task that meet the criteria for successful completion of the task

The Total Language Score is the raw score from the AC scale plus the raw score from the EC scale. After scoring is complete, the examiner can convert the child's scores on the scales and the Total Language Score to standard scores, percentile ranks, growth scale values, and age equivalents.

The examiner's manual provides scoring guidelines for children with the following dialectical variations: African American English, Southern English, Appalachian English, English influenced by Spanish, and English influenced by Chinese. In addition, suggestions for identifying and working with such children are provided.

Criterion-based cutoff scores are presented in the manual for the Articulation Screener. The HCQ and Language Sample Checklist are subjectively reviewed by the examiner.

Adaptations or Instructions for Use with Individuals with Disabilities

The HCQ can be used to identify an appropriate starting point on the PLS-5.

Accommodations and modifications can be made to the PLS-5, though those that change the stimuli or procedures will compromise the examiner's ability to utilize the normative scores. The manual presents a range of examples of norm-referenced alterations that can be used to allow the use of norms (such as adjusting stimulus placement for children with physical impairments) as well as criterion-referenced alterations that preclude the use of norms (such as placing manipulatives on contrasting colored paper for children with visual impairments). Accommodations and modifications are presented for children with severe developmental delays, hearing impairments, visual impairments, or autism and children who utilize sign language.

FUNCTIONAL CONSIDERATIONS

Measure Development

The PLS was first developed in 1969 and is now in its fifth edition. Three principal differences exist between the PLS-4 (2002) and the PLS-5 (2011): 1) Items were added or adjusted to assess gestural communication, theory of mind, emergent literacy, and other areas; 2) multistep items or procedures were eliminated and the number of practice items was diminished when appropriate; and 3) the intended age range was extended from 6;11 years for the PLS-4 to 7;11 years for the PLS-5. About 25% of the PLS-5 items are identical to those on the PLS-4, 25% are new items, and 50% are adapted items.

The development or refinement of items followed established criteria and approaches for children at each of the age levels. For example, preschool items had to "engage the child in a variety of interactive behaviors (e.g., responding to questions, manipulating objects, pointing to pictures)" and had to "show diversity in cultural groups, lifestyles, age groups, and physical attributes, while depicting everyday contexts and routines that are familiar to a diverse population of children" (Zimmerman et al., 2011, p. 52).

New items were also developed according to prevailing research and literature, trends in young child assessment (e.g., caregiver report, observation), clinician feedback, and input from experts in language development. Particular attention was paid in the literature review to identifying skills and abilities that distinguish children with typical and atypical language development. The addition of new items related to joint attention, gestural communication, theory of mind, and emergent literacy in particular was prompted by clinician feedback.

Feedback from practicing speech-language pathologists in a variety of settings across the country was utilized as the new items were developed and finalized. Furthermore, a panel of experts in assessment, cultural/linguistic diversity, and/or regional issues provided a bias review at various stages in the development of the PLS-5.

Pilot research was subsequently conducted with two studies. First, all items that were added or significantly modified were examined among 42 children. As part of the pilot-testing, an analysis of children's response processes was conducted by asking some of the children to try and explain why they gave certain responses in order to gauge whether the items were eliciting the desired responses. Results prompted the revision of items for the older children. Second, 35 children age 7 were administered these items, and final modifications were made for the full tryout edition.

Two samples participated in the tryout research activities: 455 children without language disorders, certain types of articulation disorders, or a history of hearing difficulties who could be assessed without modifications (birth to 7;11 years) and 169 children with a language disorder (2 years to 7;11 years). The nonclinical sample was generally representative of the U.S. population. African American and Latino children were oversampled to provide an adequate sample for bias analyses.

Scoring guidelines were developed and the correspondence between the caregiver report and the examiner elicitation and observation was examined for children younger than 3. Item-level analyses were also conducted between the clinical and nonclinical samples, and items were eliminated if they did not differentiate between the samples. Results were also utilized to examine items for fairness, ease of scoring, and difficulty.

Although the Language Sample Checklist remained the same from the PLS-4, the HCQ was modified based on input from parents, speech-language pathologists, and an advisory board. The Articulation Screener was adapted by adding visual stimuli. It was administered to all children older than 2 years during standardization, and cutoff scores were established based on standard deviations.

Standardization Sample

Based on U.S. Census information from 2008, a sample of 1,400 children (with boys and girls equally represented) was selected for the PLS-5 standardization.

The sample was stratified by age, sex, race/ethnicity, geographic region, and primary caregiver's education level. Three-month age ranges were utilized for children younger than 1, and 6-month age ranges were utilized for older children.

Inclusion criteria were the ability to take the PLS-5 without modifications, primary receptive and expressive abilities in English for verbal children, and exposure to primarily English for younger nonverbal children. About 1% of the sample also spoke Spanish at home, and another 1% spoke another non-English language. The sample was also examined by type of English dialect (i.e., 79% mainstream English; 4.2% African American English; 6% Spanish-influenced English; 4% Southern English; and less than 1% for each of the following: Appalachian/Ozark, Central Midland, Chinese influenced, Eastern New England, Middle Atlantic, New York City, Western Pennsylvania, and other). Scoring rules were developed based on statistical analysis and expert review for the following dialects: African American English, Spanish-influenced English, Southern English, Appalachian English, and Chinese-influenced English.

Norming

Norm referenced (AC and EC scales) and criterion referenced (Articulation Screener)

Reliability

Test–Retest Reliability

A total of 195 children from the standardization sample were used to assess the test–retest reliability (*M* = 7.8 days). They ranged in age from birth to 7;11 years. The average corrected stability coefficients were strong for the Total Language Score across the age groups (.91–.95) and were in the medium to strong range for the scales (.86–.91).

Internal Consistency

Internal consistency was examined with split-half coefficients. Cronbach's alphas are not reported in the manual. Overall, the Total Language Scale yielded a split-half reliability coefficient of .95, the AC scale yielded .91, and the EC scale yielded .93.

The corresponding standard errors of measurement for the full sample were as follows: Total Language Score = 3.4, AC scale = 4.7, and EC scale = 4.2.

In general, stronger alphas were present among the older age groups. Among preschoolers, alphas for the Total Language Scale were generally in the high range (.96–.97), as were those for the AC scale (.91–.94) and the EC scale (.94–.95).

Split-half reliability was also examined among 23 children with a language delay (ages birth to 2;11 years) and 79 children diagnosed with a language disorder (ages 3 years to 7;11 years). Strong coefficients (.93–.98) indicate that the PLS-5 is as reliable for children with language difficulties as it is for the general population.

Interrater Agreement

Interrater reliability was examined with 54 children. Two examiners were present at each assessment, one of whom administered and scored while the other observed and scored. Strong reliability coefficients (.96–.99) were evidenced.

For the interscorer reliability assessment, 200 completed protocols from the standardization sample were randomly selected and scored by a trained scorer. An additional 10% were then selected to be scored by a second trained scorer. The results showed that there was a .92–.99 correlation between test scorers on items that required scoring judgments.

Other Forms of Reliability (e.g., Equivalent Forms)

Not applicable

Validity

Face and Content

The comprehensive literature review, item reviews, examiner feedback, children's responses, and bias reviews contribute to the face and content validities of the PLS-5. Detailed descriptions of content relevance and coverage are in the manual, as are the theoretical and empirical bases for the new items that were added. Attention was paid to all aspects of the PLS-5 (e.g., administration, elicitation, interpretation, recording, scoring, and child comprehension).

Internal Construct

The correlation between the AC scale and the EC scale was calculated to assess internal construct validity. There was a moderate relationship between receptive and expressive skills, with a coefficient at .75 at all ages. A factor analysis was not conducted to examine whether the items on each of the scales fit best on those scales.

External Construct

The percentage of children passing each task was examined to verify that it increased with age.

Four comparisons were made to examine the ability of the PLS-5 to distinguish between children with and without identified language difficulties. Children from the nonclinical sample were matched to children with one of the following conditions based on age, sex, ethnicity, and parent education: 1) developmental language delay, 2) receptive language disorder, 3) expressive language disorder, or 4) receptive/expressive language disorder. Sample sizes ranged from 23 to 84. Overall, children with language difficulties scored lower on the PLS-5 than children without such difficulties. In addition, the sensitivity of correctly identifying a child with a language disorder with the Total Language Score was .83 and the specificity was .80. Among children with a language delay, sensitivity was .91 and specificity was .78 when a Total Language Score of 85 or less (1 *SD* below the mean) was used. These values improve if one takes into account the referral base rate, though they also suggest that that PLS-5 should not be used in isolation.

The manual also presents a study of the PLS-4 in which 44 children diagnosed with ASD were compared with matched controls. Differences were evidenced in performance. The PLS-5 was used to compare five children with ASD to five typically developing children. About 25–30 standard score differences were evidenced on the scales. Finally, specific responses to items such as the theory of mind item were examined, with differences evidenced. All children in either the language-disordered or non–language-disordered samples with a diagnosis of ASD were included in the item analysis.

Support for the measurer's convergent and discriminant validities is also indicated by some of the correlational studies described in "Criterion."

Criterion

The manual presents correlations between the PLS-5, PLS-4, and the Clinical Evaluation of Language Fundamentals®–Preschool–Second Edition (CELF® Preschool-2). In the first study, which had 134 children, the PLS-4 and PLS-5 were moderately correlated with each other. Overall, the correlation between the Total Language Scores was .85 and that between the scales was .80.

A second study was conducted with a sample of 97 children to examine the relationship between the PLS-5 and the CELF® Preschool-2. A moderate relationship was evidenced between the two, with correlations between the PLS-5 Total Language Score and the CELF® Core Language Score of .79, the PLS-5 Receptive Language Score and the CELF® Auditory Comprehension Score of .70, and the PLS-5 EC Score and the CELF® Expressive Language Score of .82. Thus, generally similar results will likely be evidenced on the two measures.

The manual does not present any other correlational studies, perhaps because few existed at the time of publication.

RELEVANT STUDIES USING THE MEASURE

A brief literature search using PsycINFO and Google Scholar did not yield any published studies that mentioned using the PLS-5 as it was released in 2011. Many studies have utilized prior versions of the PLS.

ADDITIONAL REFERENCES

None

Preschool Language Scale–Fourth Edition (PLS-4): Spanish

Information pertaining specifically to the Spanish version of the measure is in bold and italics. The remainder is equivalent information provided in the English review.

Manual

Zimmerman, I.L., Steiner, V.G., & Pond, R.E. (2002). *Preschool Language Scale Fourth Edition Spanish: Examiner's Manual.* San Antonio, TX: The Psychological Corporation.

Publisher[1]

Pearson, Inc.
19500 Bulverde Road
San Antonio, TX 78259-3701
http://www.pearsonassessments.com

Type of Measure

Direct child assessment, examiner observation, and parent report

Intended Age Range

Birth to 6;11 years

Key Constructs/Domains

Linguistic (Auditory Comprehension, Expressive Communication, Articulation)

Cost

PLS-4 Spanish edition basic kit (without manipulatives): $254; PLS-4 Spanish edition basic kit (with manipulatives) $310.

Description of Measure

The PLS-4 Spanish is "used to identify monolingual or bilingual Spanish speaking children who have a language disorder or delay" (Zimmerman, Steiner, & Pond, 2002, p. 2). In addition, the PLS-4 authors strove to reflect "the important developmental milestones for children who speak Spanish, as well as to develop a test with sound psychometric properties" (p. 5).

Available Languages and Formats

The fifth edition of the PLS (PLS-5) is available in English, and a screener is also available. The Spanish version of the PLS-5 will be published in 2012.

Strengths

The PLS-4 Spanish is one of the few measures to be concurrently developed with its English version (rather than translated or adapted) and has gone through the vast majority of the same development and standardization activities as the PLS-4 English. Thus, the content and psychometric validity of this measure for Spanish-speaking children is generally high.

The standardized scoring method allows for three methods of item completion (elicited response to a question, caregiver report, spontaneous behavior), which may provide a more complete picture of very young children's development.

Weaknesses

The criterion validity of the PLS-4 Spanish needs further investigation.

Although the independent development and norming of the Spanish version improves its content validity, scores from the Spanish and English versions are not directly comparable because of the different standardization samples (Zimmerman et al., 2002).

---

[1]Pearson Assessments now distributes the PLS-4.

In general, the Total Language Scale and Expressive Communication scale have higher internal reliability statistics than the Auditory Comprehension scale.

ADMINISTRATION

Procedure

The PLS-4 has two scales, either of which can be administered first:

- *Auditory Comprehension.* Among younger children, this scale assesses children's attention to the environment and people. Among older children, it assesses the ability to understand receptive vocabulary, morphology, syntax, investigative language skills, phonological awareness, and a variety of additional concepts.

Time Needed
• Birth to 11 months: 20–40 minutes
• 12 months to 3;11 years: 30–40 minutes
• 4 years to 6;11 years: 25–40 minutes

- *Expressive Communication.* Among younger children, this scale assesses children's vocal development. Among older children, it assesses the ability to express oneself with social communication, vocabulary, morphology, syntax, integrative language, phonological ability, and a variety of additional concepts.

In addition, three optional supplemental measures may be used with the PLS-4 Spanish.

- *The* Cuestionario para los Padres *is recommended for use by caregivers of children younger than 2;11 years. It allows the examiner to gain a broader perspective on the children's communication background and takes an average of 15–20 minutes to complete.*

- *The Articulation Screener assesses Spanish-speaking children's ability to pronounce different speech sounds. It is designed for use with children 2;6 years to 6;11 years. It consists of 40 items and takes approximately 2 minutes for the examiner to administer.*

- *The Language Sample Checklist assesses children's spontaneous speech in Spanish. It has three versions: brief (about 15 minutes), average, and lengthy (about 60 minutes). Results on the Language Sample Checklist can be directly compared to those on the Expressive Communication scale.*

- The manual recommends the presence of the caregiver for children younger than 2;11 years or children with developmental delays. As described in "Scoring Method," items may be scored as correct if a caregiver reports the presence of a skill outside of the assessment session.

Administration and Interpretation

The PLS-4 can be administered by the following individuals: speech-language pathologists, early childhood specialists, psychologists, educational diagnosticians, and *professionals who have experience and training in administering assessments with Hispanic children. Test administers must be proficient in Spanish to administer the test, or someone who is proficient in Spanish must administer the test with them (Zimmerman et al., 2002).* Scoring should be conducted by clinicians experienced in diagnostic assessment.

Scoring Method

The PLS-4 Spanish is hand-scored.

A child can be considered to have successfully completed a task based on one of three types of assessment:

- Elicited—the child performs the task when cued
- Spontaneous—the child performs the task at some point during the session but not when cued
- Caregiver—the caregiver is able to provide the tester with specific examples of when the child engaged in the task that meet the criteria for successful completion of the task

The Total Language Score is the raw score from the Auditory Comprehension scale plus the raw score from the Expressive Communication scale. After scoring is complete, the examiner can convert the child's raw scores using the norm-referenced tables to standard scores, rank, and percentile.

Criterion-based cutoff scores are presented in the manual for the Articulation Screener. The **Cuestionario para los Padres** *and Language Sample Checklist are subjectively reviewed by the examiner.*

The examiner's manual encourages scorers to take into consideration dialect differences and code-switching when scoring and encourages administers to get background information about the child from teachers and caregivers, including but not limited to the developmental level of the child and the Latin/Spanish culture with which the child most identifies. Examiners may also consider modifying the manipulatives; however, if such modifications are made, the assessment can no longer be used as a norm-referenced measure (Zimmerman et al., 2002).

Adaptations or Instructions for Use with Individuals with Disabilities

If a child has mild or moderate developmental disabilities, the examiner is prompted to begin the PLS-4 at 1 year below the child's chronological age. If a child has severe developmental disabilities, consultation with the child's teacher or caregiver is recommended to get a better understanding of the child's abilities and potential starting points.

Modifications can be made to the PLS-4, though those that change the stimuli or procedures will compromise the examiner's ability to utilize the normative scores. The manual presents a range of examples of norm-referenced alterations that can be used to allow the use of norms (such as adjusting stimulus placement for children with physical impairments) as well as criterion-referenced alterations that preclude the use of norms (such as placing manipulatives on contrasting colored paper for children with visual impairments). Norm- and criterion-referenced alterations are also included for children with severe developmental delays, hearing impairments, or autism and children who utilize sign language.

FUNCTIONAL CONSIDERATIONS

Measure Development

The PLS was first developed in 1969 and was initially available only in English. In 1979, a Spanish version of the PLS became available. This version received criticism for its limited attention to lexical variations across Spanish dialects and for grammatical errors on the record form. A revised version (the PLS-3) was published in 1993, featuring new task items, information on different dialects in the directions, and research with Spanish-speaking children in the United States and Puerto Rico. The PLS-3 did not have separate Spanish norms.

The PLS-4 Spanish was created concurrently with the English version of the PLS-4, but it is not simply a straight translation. As stated in the manual, "Some test tasks appear only in the Spanish edition, and all test tasks and subitems are ordered to reflect developmental order in Spanish" (Zimmerman et al., 2002, p. 2). In creating the PLS-4 Auditory Comprehension and Expressive Communication scales, test developers first conducted a literature review on Spanish language development, assessment approaches, and curricula. Feedback from clinicians who had previously purchased the PLS-3 was also utilized. In addition, a bias review was conducted at multiple points by expert consultants to determine whether the measure was appropriate for use with diverse Spanish-speaking children. Furthermore, a tryout edition was piloted with a national sample of 218 children to examine modified and new tasks, develop criteria, and statistically examine item order and difficulty level. The final edition was then standardized, as described below in the section entitled "Standardization Sample."

The Articulation Screener for use with the Spanish-speaking population was also adapted based on feedback from PLS-3 Spanish users. It was administered to the whole standardization sample and criterion-based cutoff scores created. Less detail about the creation of the **Cuestionario para los Padres** is available in the manual. The Language Sample Checklist was generally based on English language research, as the manual notes that less research is available on Spanish spontaneous language sampling.

Content Equivalence of Items and Measure

Although the "initial development phase of the PLS-4 Spanish was conducted in conjunction with that for the English edition, the two editions are not identical in terms of components, test tasks, scoring, or research design" (Zimmerman et al., 2002, p. 6). The independent development and norming of the Spanish version improve the content validity of the measure, as the measure does not solely adapt items from the English version. Rather, the whole spectrum of the Spanish language was considered for the domains assessed, just as the whole spectrum of the English language was considered for items developed for the English version of the PLS-4.

Semantic Equivalence of Translations

Translated items were reviewed by panelists with expertise in different dialects. Feedback from past PLS-3 examiners and those participating in the tryout study was also incorporated.

Structural Consistency Across the English and Spanish Versions

Overall, the structure is consistent, though some differences reflect the linguistic differences between English and Spanish. There are differences in item order, subitems (e.g., the types of plurals are different in English and Spanish), and standardization samples (Zimmerman et al., 2002).

Standardization Sample

Based on information from the 2000 U.S. Census, a sample of 1,334 children was selected for the PLS-4 Spanish. The sample contained children from 15 states across the Northeast, North Central, South, and West regions. Primary caregiver's education level was utilized to stratify the sample. A total of 99.2% of the sample was Hispanic, and the remaining participants were identified as of either Native American or European ancestry. Countries/areas of origin were Mexico (81.2%), the southwestern United States (6.3%), Puerto Rico (3%), Cuba (2%), and a variety of other countries (less than 1% for each). Flowerday (2005) noted that the predominance of Mexican Spanish in the norming may cause difficulties in assessing children with other Spanish dialects. Information on the children's Spanish environment was also recorded, and it was found that about 60% of the sample was almost always exposed to Spanish and about 40% were often exposed to Spanish on a daily basis.

Norming

Norm referenced (Auditory Comprehension and Expressive Communication scales) and criterion referenced (Articulation Screener)

Reliability

Test–Retest Reliability

A total of 188 children randomly selected from the standardization sample were used to assess the test–retest reliability. They ranged in age from 2 years to 5;11 years (M = 4;2 years). Correlations were in the medium range for the Total Language Score across the age groups (.80–.89) and in the low to medium range for the scales (.73–.86).

Internal Consistency

Overall, the Total Language Scale yielded a Cronbach's alpha of .89, the Auditory Comprehension scale yielded a Cronbach's alpha of .79, and the Expressive Communication scale yielded a Cronbach's alpha of .83. The corresponding standard errors of measurement (SEMs) were as follows: Total Language Score = 5.27, Auditory Comprehension = 7.11, and Expressive Communication = 6.36.

In general, stronger alphas were present among the older age groups. Among preschoolers, the Total Language Scale was generally in the high range (.89–.94), with Auditory Comprehension yielding coefficients in the low to medium range (.77–.89) and Expressive Communication yielding coefficients in the medium to high range (.86–.90). The corresponding SEMs were as follows: Total Language Score = 3.67–4.97, Auditory Comprehension = 4.97–7.19, and Expressive Communication = 4.74–5.61.

In general, the Total Language Scale and Expressive Communication scale have higher internal reliability statistics than the Auditory Comprehension scale.

Interrater Agreement

For the interrater reliability assessment, 100 completed tests were randomly selected from the study and scored by two trained scorers "under the supervision of the test developers" (Zimmerman et al., 2002, p. 192). Only the Expressive Communication scale was examined for interrater reliability. The results showed that there was a .99 correlation between test scorers, indicating high interrater reliability for the Expressive Communication scale, which necessitates more subjective scoring than the Auditory Comprehension scale.

Other Forms of Reliability (e.g., Equivalent Forms)

Not applicable

Validity

Face and Content

The comprehensive literature review, survey, item reviews, examiner feedback, and bias reviews for a Spanish-speaking population contribute to the face and content validities of the PLS-4.

Internal Construct

The correlation between the Auditory Comprehension scale and the Expressive Communication scale was calculated to assess internal construct validity. It was .66. This suggests the scales are moderately similar, which is to be expected because the domains they assess overlap. A factor analysis was not conducted to examine whether the items on each of the scales fit best on those scales.

External Construct

The percentage of children passing each task was examined to verify that it increased with age. In addition, PLS-4 scale and Total Language Scale scores of 94 children from the standardization sample who resided in Puerto Rico or Peru were compared to those of 94 children in the U.S. norming sample. Participants living in Peru or Puerto Rico scored higher on the scales for all but one age group (1–3 years old). This may suggest that children with more exposure to Spanish will score higher on the measure, though other factors may also be influencing this difference. The manual indicates that the PLS-4 Spanish can be used with a child who recently immigrated from a native Spanish-speaking country.

To examine the ability of the PLS-4 to distinguish between children with and without an identified language disorder, researchers matched 70 children with a language disorder with 70 typically developing children from the standardization sample. The mean age was 4;5 years. Overall, those with a language disorder scored lower on the PLS-4. In addition, the sensitivity of correctly identifying a Spanish-speaking child with a language disorder with the Total Language Score was .91 and the specificity was .63. These values may relate to the low performance of the typical children matched on demographics, who scored below the mean in the 80s (Zimmerman et al., 2002).

Support for the measure's convergent and discriminant validities is also indicated by some of the correlational studies described in "Criterion."

Criterion

The manual presents a correlational study between the PLS-4 Spanish and the PLS-3 Spanish. The correlation between the Auditory Comprehension scales was .67, whereas that between the Expressive Communication scales was .71. These lower correlations reflect the standardization differences between the two versions. The PLS-3 did not have separate Spanish norms, whereas the PLS-4 does. Thus, "it is probably not clinically useful to attempt to compare a child's scores on PLS-4 Spanish with PLS-3 Spanish" (Zimmerman et al., 2002, p. 213).

The manual does not present any other correlational studies, perhaps because few existed at the time of publication.

Comparison of Psychometric Properties Between English and Spanish Versions

Technical Equivalence in Reliability

In general, the reliability properties of the English and Spanish versions are comparable. The test–retest reliability and internal consistency for the Spanish version are just slightly lower than those of the English version, whereas the interrater agreement is equivalent.

Technical Equivalence in Validity

Overall, the validity of the PLS-4 is similar for the Spanish and English versions.

RELEVANT STUDIES USING THE MEASURE

A brief literature search using PsycINFO and Google Scholar yielded Zimmerman and Castilleja (2005), which describes the development of the PLS-4 Spanish. Older versions of this measure have been used in studies. The PLS-4 Spanish was utilized in the following study and may have been used in others as well.

Bunta and Ingram (2007) utilized the PLS-4 Spanish to examine the speech rhythm acquisition of bilingual Spanish–English-speaking children. The following results are described in their abstract: "Bilingual children show distinct speech rhythm patterns for their target languages but with some early equal timing bias that diminishes over time, on the basis of the vocalic measurements" (p. 999).

ADDITIONAL REFERENCES

Bunta, F., & Ingram, D. (2007). The acquisition of speech rhythm by bilingual Spanish- and English-speaking 4- and 5-year-old children. *Journal of Speech, Language, and Hearing Research, 50,* 999–1014.

Flowerday, T. (2005). Test review of the Preschool Language Scale–Fourth Edition. In R.A. Spies & B.S. Plake (Eds.), *The sixteenth mental measurements yearbook.* Retrieved from the Buros Institute's *Test Reviews Online* web site: http://www.unl.edu/buros

Suen, H. K. (2005). Test review of the Preschool Language Scale–Fourth Edition In R.A. Spies & B.S. Plake (Eds.), *The sixteenth mental measurements yearbook.* Retrieved from the Buros Institute's *Test Reviews Online* web site: http://www.unl.edu/buros

Zimmerman, I.L., & Castilleja, N.F. (2005). The role of a language scale for infant and preschool assessment. *Mental Retardation and Development, 11,* 238–246.

Receptive One-Word Picture Vocabulary Test–Fourth Edition (ROWPVT-4): English

Manual

Martin, N., & Brownell, R. (2010). *Receptive One-Word Picture Vocabulary Test-4: Manual.* Novato, CA: Academic Therapy Publications.

Publisher

Academic Therapy Publications
20 Commercial Boulevard
Novato, CA 94949
http://www.academictherapy.com

Type of Measure
Direct child assessment

Intended Age Range
2;0 years to 80+ years

Key Constructs/Domains
Receptive vocabulary

Cost

Complete kit: $175. Items sold separately.

Description of Measure

"The ROWPVT-4 offers a quick and reliable measure of English receptive vocabulary, utilizing a picture-matching paradigm: On hearing a word spoken, an individual is asked to choose the one of four color illustrations that matches the word" (Martin & Brownell, 2010, p. 8). Individuals are asked to identify objects, actions, and concepts that correspond to vocabulary words presented orally by the examiner.

The intended purposes of the measure include assessing a person's ability to comprehend the meaning of words, diagnosing reading difficulties, diagnosing word/concept retrieval in people with expressive aphasia, screening preschool and kindergarten children, assessing vocabulary with a nonverbal response, evaluating an English learner's receptive vocabulary, indirectly assessing cognitive ability, monitoring growth, and evaluating program effectiveness.

Available Languages and Formats

A related measure, the Receptive One-Word Picture Vocabulary Test–Spanish-Bilingual Edition, examines vocabulary comprehension (i.e., receptive vocabulary) across the Spanish and English languages. It is based on the 2000 edition of the ROWPVT, though a newer bilingual version linked to the ROWPVT-4 is in development.

In addition, both bilingual and English versions are available to assess expressive vocabulary (i.e., the ability to verbalize words). (See the Expressive One-Word Picture Vocabulary Test–Fourth Edition [EOWPVT-4]: English and Expressive One-Word Picture Vocabulary Test–Spanish-Bilingual Edition reviews for additional information.)

Strengths

The ROWPVT-4's reliability is generally strong.

The large colorful illustrations, the nature of the task, and the fact that a verbal response is not required can make the test appealing to young children and easy to administer.

The ROWPVT-4 includes more items for younger children than were included in the 2000 edition of the ROWPVT.

Weaknesses

Smaller preschool sample sizes were included in norming of the ROWPVT-4 than had been used in the past for the ROWPVT, though the measure examines more items at the lower range.

Fewer validity studies are presented for the ROWPVT-4 than the 2000 edition, with barely any at the preschool range. Because much of the measure remained the same at the child level, prior research likely extends to support the ROWPVT-4. At the geriatric level, validity research is needed.

ADMINISTRATION

Procedure

After establishing rapport with the child and recording background information on the record sheet, the examiner explains the directions.

Time Needed
15–20 minutes

Essentially, the child is presented with four pictures, and the examiner says a word. The child then selects the picture corresponding to the word. Example items are first presented. These items are intended to show the child how to give a response. Example items can be used as many times as necessary before starting the main part of the assessment.

Children begin the ROWPVT-4 at different starting points depending on their age. The examiner presents a page with four pictures, orally presents the vocabulary word, and then asks the child to point to, or say the number of, the picture that shows the meaning of the word. It is recommended that the examiner turn the pages and provide about 20–30 seconds for a response.

Administration and Interpretation

"The ROWPVT-4 was developed to be used by professionals in speech-language, occupational therapy, rehabilitation psychology, neuropsychology, clinical psychology, and education who have training to understand both the psychometric and cognitive developmental aspects of such an assessment" (Martin & Brownell, 2010, p. 8). It can be administered by individuals who are familiar with administration and scoring procedures who have conducted trial administrations. Results are interpreted by those with formal psychometric training and an understanding of derived scores and testing limitations.

Scoring Method

This measure is scored by hand. The total number of correct responses below the basal level (eight consecutive correct responses) is added to the number of correct responses between the basal and ceiling levels (six errors made within eight consecutive items). This raw score is then converted to a standard score using tables in the manual. In additional, the appendix provides a table that can be utilized to examine the relevance of performance differences on the ROWPVT-4 and EOWPVT-4.

Adaptations or Instructions for Use with Individuals with Disabilities

Specific suggestions are not provided for adapting the ROWPVT-4 for use with individuals with disabilities, though the previous manual included such suggestions (Brownell, 2000).

FUNCTIONAL CONSIDERATIONS

Measure Development

The ROWPVT was previously nationally normed through early adulthood. The ROWPVT-4 extends the "norms into geriatric ages, includes new words for both younger and older examinees, and presents the words in a new developmental sequence. The ROWPVT-4 is co-normed with the EOWPVT-4" (Martin & Brownell, 2010, p. 6).

An initial normative edition of 194 images was examined, compared to 174 items in the 2000 edition. A total of 28 new items were added and 8 items were dropped between the 2000 and 2010 editions. Brownell (2000) states that items were balanced in their representation of gender and race/ethnicity. In addition, images of individuals with disabilities and older adults were included.

All new items for the younger ages were administered to all examinees younger than 13 during the norming process for item analysis purposes. Similarly, all new items for the older ages were administered to all teenagers and adults in the sample. All items retained from the 2000 version remained in their existing order.

In line with classical test theory and item response theory, all items were examined for their functioning and for potential biases. In addition to examining item difficulty levels and item statistics, test developers conducted differential item functioning analysis to identify potential items that were biased along the following dimensions: gender, residence (urban/rural), and race/ethnicity. Further input into item selection was provided by item reviews and other item bias studies during the standardization study. The final version of the ROWPVT-4 contains 190 items.

Though the 2000 edition included information about item order and item difficulties and medial item discrimination indexes, such information is not provided in the ROWPVT-4 manual.

Standardization Sample

The measure was standardized with 2,394 individuals from an original pool of more than 2,400. To remain in the standardization sample, individuals must also have been administered the EOWPVT-4 and provided complete and useable data. Testing sites were sought by contacting everyone in a contact directory of speech-language pathologists and those who had previously purchased the ROWPVT or similar tests. A total of 106 examiners participated across 84 sites in 26 states. Sites included private practices as well as private, public, and parochial schools. Examiners were instructed to randomly select classrooms and settings for participation as well as include individuals with a wide range of disabilities. No mention is made in the manual about primary language at home and school, though primary language had been a criterion for inclusion in the norming sample in the previous version of the ROWPVT. Smaller sample sizes (n = 86–117) of 3- to 5-year-olds were noted in the ROWPVT-4 normative sample than in the 2000 version normative sample (n = 105–209). Given the variability in vocabulary development at this age, larger sample sizes could be needed. For example, the sample included only 86 children age 5. With norms provided at 2-month intervals, this is about 14 children per age subgroup.

The final standardization sample generally matched the demographics of the U.S. population on key characteristics such as region, race/ethnicity, gender, education, and residence. A slightly higher representation of people of Hispanic heritage, people living in rural areas, and people with postgraduate degrees was noted.

Norming

Norm referenced

Reliability

Test–Retest Reliability

A total of 78 examinees were retested by the same examiner after a period of about 19 days. The test–retest correlation was .97 for raw scores and .91 for standard scores. It is unknown whether the sample included preschoolers, as it did for the 2000 version.

Internal Consistency

The internal consistency of this test was determined by calculating Cronbach's coefficient alpha at each age level; the median value was .97, which is in the high range. The values at the preschool-age level (3- to 5-year-olds) were also strong at .97–.98.

The average standard error of measurement (SEM) was 2.85. Among preschoolers, the SEM ranged from 2.60 to 3.25.

Interrater Agreement

No information is provided on the ROWPVT-4's interrater agreement. As it is fairly easy to administer and 100% agreement was reported in the previous manual, no difficulties are anticipated.

Other Forms of Reliability (e.g., Equivalent Forms)

Not applicable

Validity

Face and Content

Primarily nouns are included in the ROWPVT-4 because nouns are generally acquired prior to verbs and are more prevalent in many languages. Moreover, their production involves less interaction between neural areas and is more robust to the effects of brain damage and aging. The source of the new items is not discussed in the ROWPVT-4 manual, though most of the items (all but the 28 new items) were included in the prior version. At that time, the items were selected from a variety of sources to represent words that individuals at any age could be expected to understand at the given age range, and difficult items were included for children with strong vocabularies. Only words that could be illustrated were represented. Item analysis was also utilized to remove problematic items from the measure. Furthermore, the utilization of feedback from a range of users and the cultural panel for the 2000 version contributes to the face and content validity of this measure.

Internal Construct

Not applicable because the ROWPVT-4 examines one construct (i.e., receptive vocabulary).

External Construct

External construct validity was indicated in analyses that examined chronological age and exceptional group differences. First, a table provided suggests that older children with a more developed vocabulary will demonstrate greater proficiency on the ROWPVT-4. No correlation is provided.

Second, the scores of 208 individuals with disabilities were examined. Some children in the preschool age range appear to have been included in this sample. Children experiencing the following difficulties scored significantly lower than a matched subsample: autism ($n = 28$), specific language impairment ($n = 14$), learning disability ($n = 74$), attention disability ($n = 39$), and reading disability ($n = 53$). This supports the expectation that individuals identified as having cognitive or learning-related difficulties will perform significantly worse on the ROWPVT-4 than their typically developing counterparts.

Support for the measure's convergent and discriminant validities is also indicated by some of the correlational studies described in "Criterion."

Criterion

Correlations of the ROWPVT-4 with other individually administered receptive vocabulary tests (such as the Peabody Picture Vocabulary Test) are not reported. Prior research with the 2000 version suggested corrected correlations in the moderate level.

As may be expected given their similarity in format, the ROWPVT-4 correlated well with its expressive vocabulary counterpart (the EOWPVT-4). The standard score correlation was .69 and the raw score correlation was .86.

The ROWPVT-4 was also correlated with nonpreschool tests of general cognitive ability and reading development. Weak to moderate relationships with Wechsler Intelligence Scale for Children–Fourth Edition (WISC-IV) Full Scale IQ scores and Verbal Comprehension Index scores (.35 and .39, respectively) were found in a preliminary sample of 23 students. These scores are not surprising given that the WISC-IV generally includes more expressive language tasks. A stronger relationship was obtained between the ROWPVT-4 and STAR Reading standard scores (.69) in a sample of 33 children, supporting the relationship between vocabulary and reading skills.

RELEVANT RECENT STUDIES USING THE MEASURE

A brief literature search using PsycINFO and Google Scholar did not yield any published studies that mentioned using the ROWPVT-4. Older versions have been used. It is possible, though, that the ROWPVT-4 is being used in ongoing studies.

ADDITIONAL REFERENCES

Brownell, R. (2000). *Receptive One-Word Picture Vocabulary Test: Manual.* Novato, CA: Academic Therapy Publications.

Receptive One-Word Picture Vocabulary Test–Spanish-Bilingual Edition (ROWPVT-SBE)

Information pertaining specifically to the Spanish version of the measure is in both and italics. The remainder is equivalent information provided in the English review.

Manual

Brownell, R. (2001). *Receptive One-Word Picture Vocabulary Test-Spanish-Bilingual Edition: Manual.* Novato, CA: Academic Therapy Publications.

Publisher

Academic Therapy Publications
20 Commercial Boulevard
Novato, CA 94949
http://www.academictherapy.com

Cost

Complete kit: $151. Items sold separately.

Description of Measure

The ROWPVT-SBE "provides a measure of an individual's hearing vocabulary that reflects the extent of an individual's understanding of single words presented in either Spanish or English" (Brownell, 2001, p. 12). It also is useful for measuring vocabulary without the need for a verbal response. Individuals are asked to identify objects, actions, and concepts that correspond to vocabulary words presented orally by the examiner.

Available Languages and Formats

A related measure, the Receptive One-Word Picture Vocabulary Test–Fourth Edition (ROWPVT-4) solely examines English vocabulary comprehension (i.e., receptive vocabulary). However, note that the ROWPVT-SBE is based on the 2000 edition of the ROWPVT, though a newer bilingual version linked to the ROWPVT-4 is in development.

In addition, both bilingual and English versions are available to assess expressive vocabulary (i.e., the ability to verbalize words). (See the Expressive One-Word Picture Vocabulary Test–Fourth Edition [EOWPVT-4]: English and Expressive One-Word Picture Vocabulary Test–Spanish-Bilingual Edition [EOWPVT-SBE] reviews for additional information.)

Strengths

This measure examines a child's overall ability to label items regardless of language by accepting answers in both English and Spanish. The measure was normed with a Spanish–English bilingual sample in the United States. Thus, the measure assesses bilinguals' overall expressive vocabulary rather than their English or Spanish development exclusively. Few other measures have this feature.

Careful attention was paid during development to both the psychometric and linguistic/cultural properties of the measure, which are generally strong.

Weaknesses

The ROWPVT-SBE is based on the 2000 edition of the ROWPVT, though a newer bilingual version linked to the ROWPVT-4 is in development.

Type of Measure

Direct child assessment

Intended Age Range

4;0 years to 12;11 years

Key Constructs/Domains

Receptive vocabulary (specifically, the ability to understand words)

If an examiner is interested in learning specifically about a child's Spanish expressive vocabulary or English expressive vocabulary compared to that of a monolingual child, another measure will need to be utilized.

The interrater reliability of the ROWPVT-SBE remains in need of examination, as does its criterion validity in the preschool age range.

Although the ROWPVT-4 has been normed for people between ages 2 and 80+, the ROWPVT-SBE is normed for children between ages 4 and 12. Thus, norms are not available for young preschoolers.

ADMINISTRATION

Procedure

In general, the child is first asked to identify pictures in his or her dominant language. If the child does not know a word in his or her

Time Needed
10–15 minutes

dominant language, he or she is asked to give it in his or her nondominant language. The child's dominant language is determined by asking him or her to answer the questions that appear on the record form. Once determined, the dominant language is used to deliver the instructions, prompts, and cues to the examinee to minimize difficulties in understanding directions due to language. If necessary, the nondominant language can also be utilized with the examinee.

*The administrator begins with examples at the suggested starting point for the examinee's chronological age. The main part of the measure is then started. Equal points are given whether the child knows the word in English or Spanish. All exact responses are recorded on the record form on the line corresponding to that item. The specific language used to answer each item correctly is documented. For example, if the child answers an item correctly in Spanish, a slash is placed through the **S** on the record form. If the child answers correctly in English, a slash is placed through the **E** on the record form.*

The same picture book is used for the ROWPVT-SBE and its English counterpart. However, certain items are skipped on the ROWPVT-SBE because of identified linguistic and/or cultural difficulties associated with those items.

Administration and Interpretation

The examiner must be fluent in both English and Spanish, or an assistant must be present who is fluent in the language not spoken by the examiner.

Similar to the 2000 edition of the ROWPVT, the examiner need not have training in assessment to administer the ROWPVT-SBE but must be trained under the supervision of someone who is familiar with the principles of psychological assessment and interpretation. Before administering the test, the examiner should become very familiar with the administration and scoring of the measure and should perform several trials. Results should be interpreted by someone familiar with psychometrics and statistics. This measure can be used by speech-language pathologists; psychologists; counselors; learning specialists; physicians; occupational therapists; or other educational, psychological, and medical professionals.

Scoring Method

Similar to the 2000 edition of the ROWPVT, this measure is scored by hand. The total number of correct responses below the basal level is added to the number of correct responses between the basal and ceiling levels. This raw score is then converted to a standard score using tables in the manual. In addition, the appendix provides a table that can be utilized to examine the relevance of performance differences on the ROWPVT-SBE and EOWPVT-SBE.

The use of slashes instead of circles to record correct responses on the record form may cause administration error initially because slashes may be incorrectly interpreted as incorrect responses. Training and experience will assist in avoiding this potential problem.

Adaptations or Instructions for Use with Individuals with Disabilities

Similar to the 2000 edition of the ROWPVT, the examinee may answer in a simple yes or no fashion if he or she is unable to verbally answer or indicate the answer by pointing. The test examiner presents the test item and then points to each of the four alternatives, asking "Is this [stimulus word]?" as the examinee answers either yes or no to each one. As long as the examinee is capable of answering in this manner, the test may be administered.

FUNCTIONAL CONSIDERATIONS

Measure Development

This is the first edition of the ROWPVT-SBE. It is an adaptation of the 2000 English version of the ROWPVT, which was originally published in 1985. Earlier editions had optional Spanish record forms. Their reliability and validity were questionable because 1) the items were a direct translation from the English version, 2) content screening or item analysis based on the Spanish responses was not conducted, and 3) normative information for the Spanish-speaking population was not available (Brownell, 2001).

In the early development of the ROWPVT-SBE, a survey was conducted with professionals engaged in examining the language skills of Spanish-speaking students. The results indicated that the greatest concern among these professionals was accounting for bilingualism, because the majority of Spanish-speaking students in the United States are bilingual. Respondents to the survey indicated that their primary goal was to assess their students' general vocabulary competence regardless of the particular language. As a result, it was decided that this measure would examine overall receptive vocabulary development by providing words in Spanish and English and by using a standardization sample of Spanish–English bilingual students living in the United States (Brownell, 2001).

When developers were revising the 2000 edition of the ROWPVT, a Spanish translation was created for the bilingual edition by an independent firm that specialized in developing educational materials in Spanish. Any items that did not translate accurately either from English to Spanish or between different Spanish dialects were eliminated from the test. Next, the translated items were sent to leaders in bilingual education across four states who were asked to critique the items and make recommendations. Although these activities were undertaken, Medina-Diaz (2005) noted errors in the directions (switching mid-sentence from formal to informal language) and concern about specific items.

The measure was then revised and administered to a sample of 1,050 individuals. Item-level analyses using both item response theory and classical test theory approaches were then conducted to statistically identify items that did not function well. Qualitative analysis was also conducted based on the individuals' feedback on the items. After this process, 11 items were eliminated (Brownell, 2001).

The final item analysis found that the median correlation of item difficulty to item order was .97, indicating that the item discrimination was quite high. It was also strong among the preschool population (.91–.94). The median item discrimination index was .92 among preschoolers and .91 across the whole sample. Together, these findings suggest that each item presented to bilingual children provides significant information on their receptive vocabulary development (Brownell, 2001).

Content Equivalence of Items and Measure

The constructs and operationalization are appropriate for this test, as items seem to be able to transcend both English- and Spanish-speaking cultures (Brownell, 2001). The use of qualitative and quantitative methods throughout the creation of the two language versions contributes to their content equivalence.

Semantic Equivalence of Translations

Translation, feedback, and item analysis were utilized. Attention was paid to dialectical issues.

Structural Consistency Across the English and Spanish Versions

The instrument structure between the English and bilingual versions is no longer identical, as the ROWPVT is in its 4th edition and the ROWPVT-SBE is in the process of being updated. The ROWPVT-SBE and the 2000 edition of the ROWPVT use the same picture book. Yet Spanish language knowledge was taken into account, and thus certain items are skipped on the ROWPVT-SBE because of identified linguistic and/or cultural difficulties associated with those items. Lastly, although the ROWPVT-4 has been normed for people between ages 2 and 80+, the ROWPVT-SBE is normed for children between ages 4 and 12.

Standardization Sample

The sample included 1,050 children who generally matched the demographic characteristics of the U.S. Hispanic population. Overrepresented in this sample were individuals from the Western region whose dialect was Mexican; other categories of region and Hispanic origin were underrepresented. Details can be found in the manual (Brownell, 2001).

Only individuals who spoke at least some Spanish were included in the norms groups. Because type of language dominance (e.g., Spanish dominant, balanced bilingual, English dominant) did not significantly relate to performance, a single set of norms is appropriate for this measure (Brownell, 2001).

The ROWPVT-SBE and its counterpart the EOWPVT-SBE were co-normed together.

Norming

Norm referenced

Reliability

Test–Retest Reliability

A total of 32 examinees were retested by the same examiner within about a 20-day interval. This sample included children as young as 4;1 years, though the median age was 6;10 years. The corrected test–retest correlation was .92, which is in the high range.

Internal Consistency

On average, Cronbach's alpha was also high at .97. Among preschoolers, alphas were in the .96–.97 range. Corresponding standard errors of measurement for preschoolers' standard scores were 3.00 among 4-year-olds and 2.60 among 5-year-olds.

The correlation between the scores derived from the odd-numbered items and the scores derived from the even-numbered items was also examined. The median corrected split-half coefficient was high at .98 (also .98 for preschoolers).

Interrater Agreement

This information is not provided in the manual.

Other Forms of Reliability (e.g., Equivalent Forms)

Not applicable

Validity

Face and Content

The utilization of feedback from a range of expert consultants and users contributes to the face validity of this measure. Furthermore, this measure appears to assess bilingual receptive vocabulary as it purports to do. In addition, items that could not be translated accurately and consistently across Spanish dialects, that had item difficulties in both English and Spanish, that might be culturally biased, or that might present other problems were eliminated through the quantitative and qualitative procedures described in the "Measure Development" section. However, because the ROWPVT-SBE began with the list of words already in the ROWPVT, the full range (e.g., content) of potentially appropriate words in Spanish was not initially examined.

Internal Construct

Not applicable, as the ROWPVT purports to examine one construct (i.e., receptive vocabulary).

External Construct

*External construct validity was evidenced in analyses by chronological age and exceptional group differences. First, there was an uncorrected correlation of .70 of raw scores to chronological age, which indicates that older individuals with a more developed vocabulary will demonstrate greater proficiency on the ROWPVT-SBE than younger individuals. Second, 13 individuals with intellectual disability scored significantly lower than the norms group (**M** = 70.77, **SD** = 20.40, **p** < .0001). This supports the expectation that individuals identified as having lower cognitive ability will perform significantly worse on the ROWPVT-SBE. Finally, those with language or learning disorders showed a significant difference in performance from the normative group, whereas individuals with articulation difficulties did not show a significant difference. These results highlight the fact that articulation is a disorder of speech production, not language comprehension (Brownell, 2001). Each of the samples of exceptional children included preschool-age children.*

Support for the convergent and discriminant validities of the ROWPVT-SBE is also indicated by some the correlational studies described in "Criterion."

Criterion

The ROWPVT-SBE shows a corrected correlation of .61 with the Language Achievement subtest of the Stanford Achievement Test (SAT)-9, which is an English group-administered exam. The ROWPVT-SBE's correlation with the Reading Achievement subtest was .46 and its correlation with the English vocabulary subtest was .38. These correlations indicate that English academic achievement relates significantly to children's receptive vocabulary across English and Spanish as measured by the ROWPVT-SBE. Although this is a start at examining criterion validity among older children, criterion validity still needs to be examined among preschoolers.

In addition, the ROWPVT-SBE and the EOWPVT-SBE are correlated at .43, which is not as strong a correlation as may be expected given that they both examine bilingual vocabulary—one expressive and the other receptive. The manual suggests that this may relate to the greater linguistic variability seen in bilingual samples (Brownell, 2001). It appears then that these two measures test overlapping but distinct features of bilingual vocabulary (receptive and expressive).

Comparison of Psychometric Properties Between English and Spanish Versions
Technical Equivalence in Reliability
The reliability statistics of the ROWPVT-4 and ROWPVT-SBE are quite comparable. The interrater reliability of each has yet to be examined, though it is likely high given the nature of this task.

Technical Equivalence in Validity
The validity of the ROWPVT-4 and ROWPVT-SBE seems generally similar, with both versions modestly examined. In addition, the relationship between the EOWPVT-4 and ROWPVT-4 is stronger (.69) than that between the EOWPVT-SBE and ROWPVT-SBE (.43). That is, the expressive and receptive vocabularies of English speakers are more strongly related than the expressive and receptive vocabularies of Spanish speakers/ bilinguals. Although this may relate to measurement issues, it may also reflect bilingual development, as Brownell (2001) states. Receptive and expressive abilities across two languages may not be as closely connected as these same skills within a single language. This weaker correlation should be considered when one is interpreting data on individuals and groups using both the ROWPVT-SBE and the EOWPVT-SBE.

RELEVANT RECENT STUDIES USING THE MEASURE

A brief literature search using PsycINFO and Google Scholar yielded the following study that described using the ROWPVT-SBE. It is possible that this measure has been utilized with preschoolers in additional published studies.

Mendelsohn et al. (2001) utilized the ROWPVT-SBE to measure receptive vocabulary in both English- and Spanish-speaking children from the African American and Latino communities. After engaging in a literacy program based on Reach Out and Read, the children evidenced significant improvements on the ROWPVT-SBE.

ADDITIONAL REFERENCES

Krach, S.K. (2005). Test review of the Receptive One-Word Picture Vocabulary Test, Spanish-Bilingual Edition. In R.A. Spies & B.S. Plake (Eds.), *The sixteenth mental measurements yearbook*. Retrieved from the Buros Institute's *Test Reviews Online* web site: http://www.unl.edu/buros

Medina-Diaz, M.D.R. (2005). Test review of the Receptive One-Word Picture Vocabulary Test, Spanish-Bilingual Edition. In R.A. Spies & B.S. Plake (Eds.), *The sixteenth mental measurements yearbook*. Retrieved from the Buros Institute's *Test Reviews Online* web site: http://www.unl.edu/buros

Mendelsohn, A.M., Mogilner, L.N., Dreyer, B.P., Forman, J.A., Weinstein, S.C., Broderick, M.,...Napier, C. (2001). The impact of a clinic-based literacy intervention on language development in inner-city preschool children. *Pediatrics, 107*(1), 130–134.

Woodcock-Muñoz Language Survey–Revised, Normative Update (WMLS-R NU): English

Manuals

Alvarado, C.G., Ruef, M.L., & Schrank, F.A. (2005). *Woodcock-Muñoz Language Survey–Revised: Comprehensive Manual.* Itasca, IL: Riverside.

Schrank, F.A., McGrew, K.S., & Dailey, D.E.H. (2010). *Technical Supplement. Woodcock-Muñoz Language Survey–Revised Normative Update.* Rolling Meadows, IL: Riverside.

Publisher

Riverside Publishing
425 Spring Lake Drive
Itasca, IL 60143-2079
http://www.riversidepublishing.com

Type of Measure

Direct child assessment

Intended Age Range

2 years to 90 years (though not all of the subtests span the whole age range)

Key Constructs/Domains

- Listening
- Oral expression
- Reading
- Writing

Cost

WMLS-R NU English complete kit: $405; *WMLS-R NU Spanish add-on: $215.* Items sold separately.

Description of Measure

The WMLS-R NU (2010) is an updated version of the WMLS-R (2005). It involves a recalculation of the normative data for the WMLS-R to more accurately reflect the characteristics of the U.S. population. The normative data for the WMLS-R were calculated based upon 1996 projections of 2000 Census data, but the WMLS-R NU was based upon calculations using the final 2000 Census data released in 2005. In addition, more advanced statistical procedures were utilized to further improve the precision of the WMLS-R NU.[1]

The purpose of the WMLS-R is to "provide a broad sampling of proficiency in oral language, language comprehension, reading and writing" (Alvarado, Ruef, & Schrank, 2005, p. 1). The manual reports that among other uses, the WMLS-R it can be used to determine eligibility for bilingual education/English as a second language services and the readiness of English language learners for English-only instruction. When both the English and Spanish versions are utilized, the WMLS-R NU can be used to identify the oral language dominance of bilingual (English and Spanish) speakers.

Available Languages and Formats

A Spanish version of the WMLS-R NU is available.

Because of the focus here on language and literacy skills, the WMLS-R NU was reviewed rather than the broader Woodcock-Johnson III batteries (WJ-III). Though both the WMLS-R NU and the WJ-III utilize the same sample, items on some of the subtests differ slightly because the English WMLS-R NU was created to be equivalent to the Spanish WMLS-R. Furthermore, the degree to which information is presented in the manuals differs. As appropriate, information about the WJ-III is provided here. For details, see the reviews by Berry, Bridges, and Zaslow (2004), Cizek (2003), and Sandoval (2003).

[1]Because the WMLS-R NU consists mainly of updated normative data, this review refers to both the 2010 WMLS-R NU *Technical Supplement* and the 2005 WMLS-R *Comprehensive Manual* as necessary.

Strengths

More precise representation and standardization are the result of the stratification of a large sample to a wide range of characteristics and the use of bootstrap-based norm development and other statistical procedures in the WMLS-R NU.

The normative updates reflect continual attention to demographic shifts and their impact on measure development and interpretation. For example, between the development of the WMLS-R in 2005 and the WMLS-R NU in 2010, the weighting for Latinos at the preschool range increased 33% because of even greater shifts in the population than were anticipated by the 1996 Census projections. Furthermore, the WMLS-R NU norms are also stratified to adjust for foreign-born status in addition to the other sampling variables used in the 2005 normative data.

The items selected for the WMLS-R NU have been extensively studied.

In addition to age- and grade-based norms, a variety of results are available for clinicians and researchers to use (e.g., Cognitive-Academic Language Proficiency [CALP], *W* scores, normal curve equivalents [NCEs], Relative Proficiency Index [RPI]). If both the English and Spanish versions are utilized, a Comparative Language Index (CLI) can be used.

Weaknesses

Certain WMLS-R NU psychometric properties (e.g., test–retest and interrater reliabilities, criterion validity) are described less extensively than others (e.g., internal consistency). These properties are more thoroughly described for the fuller Woodcock-Johnson III batteries (WJ-III) in English and Spanish in their manuals.

ADMINISTRATION

Procedure

The WMLS-R NU is composed of the following seven subtests:

- *Picture Vocabulary.* This subtest begins with some receptive vocabulary items, but it is primarily composed of expressive vocabulary items.
- *Verbal Analogies.* This subtest entails listening to three words of an analogy and then completing the analogy with a fourth word.
- *Letter-Word Identification.* This subtest captures alphabet letter knowledge (at the younger ages) and reading of single words (at the older ages).
- *Dictation.* Younger children are assessed on prewriting skills such as tracing and copying letters. Older individuals respond to questions about spelling, capitalization, punctuation, and word usage.
- *Understanding Directions.* Listening skills, word knowledge, and working memory are assessed on this subtest, which presents individuals with increasingly complex directions using an audio player.
- *Story Recall.* Individuals are asked to recall details from a story presented to them via an audio player.
- *Passage Comprehension.* Younger children are asked to identify picture symbols, and older participants read a short passage and respond to questions.

Though the subtests can be individually administered, certain combinations of subtests can be administered in order to obtain the following cluster scores:

Time Needed

The core part of the measure (the first four subtests) takes 15–20 minutes for participants to complete (Alvarado, Ruef, & Schrank, 2005). The full battery (seven subtests) may take approximately 35–45 minutes.

- Oral Language
- Reading–Writing
- Broad English Ability
- Listening
- Oral Expression
- Reading
- Writing
- Language Comprehension
- Applied Language Proficiency
- Oral Language—Total
- Broad English Ability—Total

After administering the selected subtests, the examiner completes the Test Session Observation Checklist to describe cooperation, engagement, attention, and other behaviors that may have influenced the assessment.

Administration and Interpretation

Generally speaking, examiners should be familiar with both the test administration and scoring procedures and should have reviewed the assessment. Those interpreting the WMLS-R NU should have graduate-level training. If administering the measure to English language learners, examiners interpreting the test results should be knowledgeable about the second language acquisition process and about factors influencing second language learning. The manual suggests that examiners be knowledgeable about an individual's amount of exposure to English and Spanish as well as the quality of this exposure (e.g., use of language at school and home, educational history). Cultural and socioeconomic factors should also be considered when interpreting scores (Alvarado, Ruef, & Schrank, 2005).

The manual provides general guidelines for examiners to follow (Alvarado, Ruef, & Schrank, 2005). It also includes exercises that may be completed after the examiner has had a chance to review the manual several times.

Scoring Method

The examiner should score each item while administering the test, though if it is unclear whether a given response is correct or incorrect, the item may be scored later. On the Story Recall subtest, the administrator should check off each part of the story the participant correctly remembers and subsequently count the checkmarks.

After the assessment is administered, a computerized scoring program is used to convert the raw data into standardized scores by either age or grade levels. A variety of results is available, including RPI, NCEs, and percentile ranks. Furthermore, "for the WMLS-R English form, the Number Correct-to-ability level (W score) relationships are based on the English norming sample" (Alvarado, Ruef, & Schrank, 2005, p. 49).

Furthermore, WMLS-R NU rankings can be obtained that indicate the level of proficiency (e.g., CALP) the individual has achieved in English (1 = negligible, 2 = very limited, 3 = limited, 4 = fluent, 5 = advanced, 6 = very advanced).

If both the English and Spanish versions are administered, then a CLI can be produced. This provides the following information: "comparative information revealing which of the two languages is stronger" and "information regarding proficiency in each language compared with that of other subjects at the same age or grade level" (Alvarado, Ruef, & Schrank, 2005, p. 62).

Adaptations or Instructions for Use with Individuals with Disabilities

It is important for the examiner to record any modifications made during testing. The manual has an extensive discussion about how to modify the physical space and create rapport with individuals with disabilities. If an impairment is noted, the written report should include mention of the impairment and describe how it may have affected the individual's score. It also notes that subjects should not be "penalized for articulation difficulties and regional speech patterns" (Alvarado et al., 2005, p. 30).

FUNCTIONAL CONSIDERATIONS

Measure Development

The items on the WMLS-R NU are identical to those on the WMLS-R. The WMLS-R was an extensive revision of the original WMLS created in 1993, with almost all new items and the addition of subtests and clusters. Many of the items stemmed from the pool used to create the Woodcock-Johnson III Tests of Achievement and Cognitive Ability. Though not stated in the WMLS-R manual, the WJ-III tests are based on the Cattell-Horn-Carroll theories of cognitive abilities (see Cizek, 2003; Sandoval, 2003; for details).

After a large set of potential items was created, both classical item selection and Rasch modeling were utilized to select items based on ability levels and then to norm the English WMLS-R. Professionals from across the United States reviewed the items and directions and provided recommendations. "Special attention was directed toward designing items and test instructions that would be deemed appropriate in the skills areas tested and age range covered" (Alvarado, Ruef, & Schrank, 2005, p. 73).

Ochoa (2007) noted that a theoretical influence on the WMLS-R was Cummins' (1994) differentiation of two types of linguistic skills: basic interpersonal communication skill and CALP. "Because the WMLS-R emphasizes academic language tasks and CALP levels, test results more accurately represent and predict the subject's readiness for classroom instruction" (Ochoa, 2007). As noted in "Scoring Method," CALP levels are provided with the WMLS-R NU scores.

Standardization Sample

The WMLS-R was normed using the same data used to standardize its counterpart, the WJ-III. The sample was a nationally representative sample of 8,818 individuals (including 1,143 preschoolers) across more than 100 communities that generally matched 1996 projections for 2000 Census data. Key demographic characteristics used to stratify this weighted and randomly selected sample included race, ethnicity, type of school, gender, education, occupation, community size, and region in the United States. Finally, this sample did not include students with severe disabilities unless they were in a mainstream class for at least part of the school day, and it did not include students who had "less than 1 year of experience in an English-speaking environment" (Alvarado, Ruef, & Schrank, 2005, p. 75).

In 2010, a normative update was released. The WMLS-R NU reflects a recalculation of the data for the WMLS-R based on updated Census data and the application of more advanced statistics. The changes in the resulting standard scores and deviations were considerable, reflecting the importance of consistently updating norms and procedures. For example, the correlation between preschoolers' scores on the WMLS-R and the WMLS-NU is only .58. WMLS-R normative data previously inflated preschoolers' abilities by about 2–5 standard score points on most subtests, though more substantial shifts (5–10 standard score differences) were noted in Passage Comprehension. Thus, examiners who are assessing children or programs with the WMLS-R NU should utilize the most current norms, especially when examining potential developmental changes over time.

Norming

Norm referenced

Reliability

Test–Retest Reliability

This information is not provided in the manual for the WMLS-R. However, such scores are presented for the WJ-III, and they are very strong.

Internal Consistency

Across all age groups, the median split-half internal consistency for the WMLS-R was calculated for each test and corrected for length. Values were in the medium to high range for clusters (.88–.98) and in the low to high range for subtests (.76–.97). Among preschoolers, coefficients were in the high range for the Reading–Writing (.95–.96), Broad English Ability (.95–.96), and Oral Expression (.90–.92) clusters. They were slightly lower for the remaining clusters. Among the subtests, the highest coefficients were found for preschoolers on the Picture Vocabulary subtest (.90–.92) and the lowest were found on Story Recall (.66–.77). Corresponding standard errors of measurement for subtest standard scores ranged from 3.66 for 5-year-olds on Dictation to 8.71 for 3-year-olds on Passage Comprehension.

Overall, the reliability coefficients of the cluster scores are higher. This suggests that the use of multiple subtests to assess an area should be considered, as is typical in assessment. The cluster approach is emphasized in the manual to provide a more valid and stable approach to assessing broad abilities.

Interrater Agreement

This information is not provided in the manual.

Other Forms of Reliability (e.g., Equivalent Forms)

Two forms of the English WMLS-R NU are available, though neither the development nor the intercorrelations between them are described. These are described for the WJ-III in its manual.

Validity

Face and Content

The initial step of developing an extensive set of potential items from which to select for each area contributes to the measure's ability to examine each content area well. This step was followed by a statistical examination of the statistical properties of each item and scale in order to select the most useful items for the measure. Furthermore, expert consultants and professionals from across the United States provided input.

Internal Construct

The WMLS-R manual does not report whether the underlying factor structure was examined, though this information is provided for the WJ-III in its manual. However, intercorrelations among the items and the clusters are reported in the appendices. As may be expected, the intercorrelations are higher among subtests within the same clusters.

External Construct

Growth curves are presented that indicate that "all WMLS-R tests and clusters display average score changes consistent with the developmental growth and decline of cognitive-academic language proficiency across the life span for the monolingual English-speaking population" (Alvarado, Ruef, & Schrank, 2005, p. 91).

The ability of the WMLS-R NU to distinguish children with disabilities was not presented. This information is provided for the WJ-III in its manual.

Support for the convergent and discriminant validity of the WMLS-R NU is also indicated by some of the correlational studies described in "Criterion."

Criterion

A preschool criterion study presented in the manual included a sample of 160 participants (ages 1;9–6;3 years) who were administered the WMLS-R, the Wechsler Preschool and Primary Scale of Intelligence–Revised, and the Differential Ability Scales in a counterbalanced fashion (Alvarado, Ruef, & Schrank, 2005). Overall, there was a moderate correlation between these cognitive tests and the WMLS-R. The weakest relationship between the WMLS-R and these tests was for Passage Comprehension, with correlations in the .20 to .30 range. Thus, the skills involved on this task seem less related to verbal and nonverbal cognitive ability than the skills on the other subtests. Aside from Passage Comprehension, the WMLS-R subtests and domains correlated more strongly with the verbal scales of the cognitive tests (about .42–.69) than the nonverbal scales (.35–.60), as may be expected.

The relationship of the WMLS-R with other measures of preschool language and literacy is not presented in the manual. A bilingual study was conducted with the *original* WMLS with children in kindergarten through Grade 3. In that study, the Spanish and English versions of the IDEA Oral Language Proficiency Test were administered along with either the Language Assessment Scales–Oral Short Form or the *pre*Las 2000 (depending on the child's age). The intercorrelations among the English versions of the WMLS and these tests ranged from .69 to .89. The manual also lists studies conducted with school-age and university students (Alvarado, Ruef, & Schrank, 2005). In these studies, the WMLS-R correlated with academic achievement tests, general intelligence tests, and language tests (university sample only).

RELEVANT STUDIES USING THE MEASURE

A brief literature search using PsycINFO and Google Scholar did not yield any published articles that mentioned using the WMLS-R NU with a preschool population. Older versions of the measure have been utilized.

ADDITIONAL REFERENCES

Berry, D.J., Bridges, L.J., & Zaslow, M.J. (2004). *Early childhood measures profile*. Washington, DC: Child Trends.

Brown, J.D. (2007). Test review of the Woodcock-Muñoz Language Survey–Revised. In K.F. Geisinger, R.A. Spies, J.F. Carlson, & B.S. Plake (Eds.), *The seventeenth mental measurements yearbook*. Retrieved from the Buros Institute's *Test Reviews Online* web site: http://www.unl.edu/buros

Cizek, G.J. (2003). Test review of the Woodcock-Johnson-III. In B.S. Plake, J.C. Impara, & R.A. Spies (Eds.), *The fifteenth mental measurements yearbook*. Retrieved from the Buros Institute's *Test Reviews Online* web site: http://www.unl.edu/buros

Cummins, J. (1984). *Bilingualism and special education: Issues in assessment and pedagogy*. Austin, TX: PRO-Ed.

Ochoa, S.H. (2007). Test review of the Woodcock-Muñoz Language Survey–Revised. In K.F. Geisinger, R.A. Spies, J.F. Carlson, & B.S. Plake (Eds.), *The seventeenth mental measurements yearbook*. Retrieved from the Buros Institute's *Test Reviews Online* web site: http://www.unl.edu/buros

Sandoval, J. (2003). Test review of the Woodcock-Johnson-III. In B.S. Plake, J.C. Impara, & R.A. Spies (Eds.), *The fifteenth mental measurements yearbook*. Retrieved from the Buros Institute's *Test Reviews Online* web site: http://www.unl.edu/buros

Woodcock-Muñoz Language Survey–Revised, Normative Update (WMLS-R NU): Spanish

Information pertaining specifically to the Spanish version of the measure is in bold and italics. The remainder is equivalent information provided in the English review.

Manuals

Alvarado, C.G., Ruef, M.L., & Schrank, F.A. (2005). *Woodcock-Muñoz Language Survey–Revised: Comprehensive Manual.* Itasca, IL: Riverside.

Schrank, F.A., McGrew, K.S., & Dailey, D.E.H. (2010). *Technical Supplement. Woodcock-Muñoz Language Survey–Revised Normative Update.* Rolling Meadows, IL: Riverside.

Publisher

Riverside Publishing
425 Spring Lake Drive
Itasca, IL 60143-2079
http://www.riversidepublishing.com

Cost

WMLS-R NU Spanish complete kit: $405. Items sold separately.

Description of Measure

The WMLS-R NU (2010) is an updated version of the WMLS-R (2005). It involves a recalculation of the normative data for the WMLS-R to more accurately reflect the characteristics of the U.S. population. The normative data for the WMLS-R were calculated based upon 1996 projections of 2000 Census data, but the WMLS-R NU was based upon calculations using the final 2000 Census data released in 2005. In addition, more advanced statistical procedures were utilized to further improve the precision of the WMLS-R NU.[1]

The purpose of the WMLS-R is to "provide a broad sampling of proficiency in oral language, language comprehension, reading and writing" (Alvarado, Ruef, & Schrank, 2005, p. 1). The manual reports that among other uses, the WMLS-R can be used to determine eligibility for bilingual education/English as a second language services and the readiness of English language learners for English-only instruction. When both the English and Spanish versions are utilized, the WMLS-R NU can be used to identify the oral language dominance of bilingual (English and Spanish) speakers.

Type of Measure

Direct child assessment

Intended Age Range

2 years to 90 years (though not all of the subtests span the whole age range)

Key Constructs/Domains

- Listening
- Oral expression
- Reading
- Writing

Because of the focus of here on language and literacy skills, the WMLS-R NU was reviewed rather than the broader *Batería* III Woodcock-Muñoz (*Batería* III). It appears that somewhat different Spanish-speaking samples were utilized, though the rationale for this is unknown. For example, the *Batería* III includes individuals from Spain and the United States. Items on some of the subtests differ slightly because the Spanish WMLS-R NU was created to be equivalent to the English WMLS-R. Furthermore, the degree to which information is presented in the manuals differs. As appropriate, information about the *Batería* III is provided here. For details, see the reviews by Doll and LeClair (2007), Olivarez and Boroda (2007), and Otero (2006).

[1]Because the WMLS-R NU consists mainly of updated normative data, this review refers to both the 2010 WMLS-R NU *Technical Supplement* and the 2005 WMLS-R *Comprehensive Manual* as necessary.

Available Languages and Formats

An English version of the WMLS-R NU is available.

Strengths

The items selected for the WMLS-R NU were extensively studied in both the English and Spanish versions. Thus, its internal reliability statistics are generally solid.

The Spanish version of the WMLS-R was statistically equated with the English version, which allows for a direct comparison of children's results on each measure.

The Spanish version is not simply a translation of the English version. It is composed of original Spanish items along with translated items selected from the English item pool that was used to equate the Spanish and English measures.

More precise representation and standardization are the result of the stratification of a large sample to a wide range of characteristics and the use of bootstrap-based norm development and other statistical procedures.

The normative updates reflect continual attention to demographic shifts and their impact on measure development and interpretation. For example, between the development of the WMLS-R in 2005 and the WMLS-R NU in 2010, the weighting for Latinos at the preschool range increased 33% because of even greater shifts in the population than were anticipated by the 1996 Census projections. Furthermore, the WMLS-R NU norms are also stratified to adjust for foreign-born status in addition to other sampling variables used in the 2005 normative data.

In addition to age- and grade-based norms, a variety of results are available for clinicians and researchers to use (e.g., Cognitive-Academic Language Proficiency [CALP], *W* scores, normal curve equivalents [NCEs], Relative Proficiency Index [RPI]). If both the English and Spanish versions are utilized, a Comparative Language Index (CLI) can be used.

Weaknesses

Certain WMLS-R NU psychometric properties (e.g., test–retest and interrater reliabilities, criterion validity) are described less extensively than others (e.g., internal consistency). These properties are more thoroughly described for the fuller Woodcock-Johnson III batteries (WJ-III) in English and Spanish in their manuals.

The manual does not describe how the standardization sample participants were selected, what their background characteristics were, or what their age distribution was, a fact that has also been noted by Ochoa (2007).

ADMINISTRATION

Procedure

The WMLS-R NU is composed of the following seven subtests:

- **Vocabulario sobre dibujos** *(Picture Vocabulary)*. This subtest begins with receptive vocabulary items, but it is primarily composed of expressive vocabulary items.

- **Analogía verbales** *(Verbal Analogies)*. This subtest entails listening to three words of an analogy and then completing the analogy with a fourth word.

Time Needed

The core part of the measure (the first four subtests) takes 15–20 minutes for participants to complete (Alvarado, Ruef, & Schrank, 2005). The full battery (seven subtests) may take approximately 35–45 minutes.

- **Identificación de letras y palabras** *(Letter-Word Identification)*. This subtest captures alphabet letter knowledge (at the younger ages) and reading of single words (at the older ages).
- **Dictado** *(Dictation)*. Younger children are assessed on prewriting skills such as tracing and copying letters. Older individuals respond to questions about spelling, capitalization, punctuation, and word usage.
- **Comprensión de indicaciones** *(Understanding Directions)*. Listening skills, word knowledge, and working memory are assessed on this subtest, which presents individuals with increasingly complex directions using an audio player.
- **Rememoración de cuentos** *(Story Recall)*. Individuals are asked to recall details from a story presented to them via an audio player.
- **Comprensión de textos** *(Passage Comprehension)*. Younger children are asked to identify picture symbols, and older participants read a short passage and respond to questions.

Though the subtests can be individually administered, certain combinations of subtests can be administered in order to obtain the following cluster scores:

- **Lenguaje Oral** (Oral Language)
- **Lectura-Escritura** (Reading–Writing)
- **Amplia habilidad en español** (Broad Spanish Ability)
- **Habilidad para escuchar** (Listening)
- **Expresión oral** (Oral Expression)
- **Lectura** (Reading)
- **Escritura** (Writing)
- **Comprensión de lenguaje** (Language Comprehension)
- **Proficiencia en el lenguaje aplicado** (Applied Language Proficiency)
- **Lenguaje oral—Total** (Oral Language—Total)
- **Amplia habilidad en español—Total** (Broad Spanish Ability—Total)

After administering the selected subtests, the examiner completes the Test Session Observation Checklist to describe cooperation, engagement, attention, and other behaviors that may have influenced the assessment.

Administration and Interpretation

Generally speaking, examiners should be familiar with both the test administration and scoring procedures and should have reviewed the assessment. ***They should also read, write, and speak Spanish proficiently.*** Those interpreting the WMLS-R NU should have graduate-level training. If administering the measure to English language learners, examiners interpreting the test results should be knowledgeable about the second language acquisition process and about factors influencing second language learning. The manual suggests that examiners be knowledgeable about an individual's amount of exposure to English and Spanish as well as the quality of this exposure (e.g., use of language at school and home, educational history). Cultural and socioeconomic factors should also be considered when interpreting scores (Alvarado, Ruef, & Schrank, 2005).

The manual provides general guidelines for examiners to follow (Alvarado, Ruef, & Schrank, 2005). It also includes exercises that may be completed after the examiner has had a chance to review the manual several times.

Scoring Method

The examiner should score each item while administering the test, though if it is unclear whether a given response is correct or incorrect, the item may be scored later. On the Story

Recall subtest, the administrator should check off each part of the story the participant correctly remembers and subsequently count the checkmarks.

After the assessment is administered, a computerized scoring program is used to convert the raw data into standardized scores by either age or grade levels. A variety of results is available, including RPI, NCEs, and percentile ranks. Furthermore, "for the WMLS-R Spanish, the Number Correct-to-*W* score relationships are based on the Spanish calibration sample" (Alvarado, Ruef, & Schrank, 2005, p. 49).

Furthermore, WMLS-R NU rankings can be obtained that indicate the level of proficiency (e.g., CALP) the individual has achieved in **Spanish** (1 = negligible, 2 = very limited, 3 = limited, 4 = fluent, 5 = advanced, 6 = very advanced).

If both the English and Spanish versions are administered, then a CLI can be produced. This provides the following information: "comparative information revealing which of the two languages is stronger" and "information regarding proficiency in each language compared with that of other subjects at the same age or grade level" (Alvarado, Ruef, & Schrank, 2005, p. 62).

Adaptations or Instructions for Use with Individuals with Disabilities

It is important for the examiner to record any modifications made during testing. The manual has an extensive discussion about how to modify the physical space and create rapport with individuals with disabilities. If an impairment is noted, the written report should include mention of the impairment and describe how it may have affected the individual's score. It also notes that subjects should not be "penalized for articulation difficulties and regional speech patterns" (Alvarado et al., 2005, p. 30).

FUNCTIONAL CONSIDERATIONS

Measure Development

The items on the WMLS-R NU are identical to those on the WMLS-R. The WMLS-R was an extensive revision of the original WMLS created in 1993, with almost all new items and the addition of subtests and clusters. Many of the items stemmed from the pool used to create the Woodcock-Johnson III Tests of Achievement and Cognitive Ability. Though not stated in the WMLS-R manual, the Woodcock-Johnson III batteries are based on the Cattell-Horn-Carroll theories of cognitive abilities (see Doll & LeClair, 2007; Olivarez & Boroda, 2007; for details).

After a large set of potential items was created, both classical item selection and Rasch modeling were utilized to select items based on ability levels and then to norm the Spanish WMLS-R. Professionals from various Spanish-speaking countries as well as Spanish-speaking professionals from across the United States reviewed the Spanish items and directions. "Special attention was directed toward designing items and test instructions that would be deemed appropriate in the skills areas tested and age range covered" (Alvarado et al., 2005, p. 73).

The goal of the Spanish version of the WMLS-R was to create a Spanish measure that was empirically equivalent to, as well as calibrated with, the English version. A pool of potential Spanish items was created first. Part of this pool was a subset of translated items from the English standardization procedures that could be used to statistically connect the Spanish version with the English one. The full set of Spanish items was tested and Rasch calibrated with Spanish-speaking participants from outside of and within the United States. The measure underwent additional statistical examination before being finalized, including the adjustment of the Spanish item difficulties to be equivalent to the English and the creation of Rasch scoring tables for each test.

Ochoa (2007) noted that a theoretical influence on the WMLS-R was Cummins' (1994) differentiation of two types of linguistic skills: basic interpersonal communication skill and CALP. "Because the WMLS-R emphasizes academic language tasks and CALP levels, test results more accurately represent and predict the subject's readiness for classroom instruction" (Ochoa (2007).As noted in "Scoring Method," CALP levels are provided with the WMLS-R NU scores, as they had been for the WMLS-R.

Content Equivalence of Items and Measure

Although the sources used to create the item pools for the two versions are not well described, it is known that an overlapping pool was created in order to equate the English and Spanish forms. English- and Spanish-speaking professionals were involved, and extensive statistical examination of the items was undertaken.

Semantic Equivalence of Translations

*The Spanish version is not simply a translation of the English version. It is composed of original Spanish items along with translated items selected from the English item pool that was used to equate the Spanish and English measures. Problematic items were removed from the list of items that were being used to produce equivalent forms of the WMLS-R across the languages. As with the **Batería III Woodcock-Muñoz (Batería III)**, the translation methods used, including how dialect variations were incorporated, are not well described, though they appear to be adequate (Doll & LeClair, 2007). Otero (2006) noted concerns with a few items in her review of the **Batería III**.*

Structural Consistency Across the English and Spanish Versions

The overall structure of the English and Spanish versions is consistent. The measures, though not exactly the same, are equated across the two versions, allowing for an equivalent interpretation of the two measures.

Standardization Sample

The Spanish WMLS-R standardization sample consisted of 1,157 native Spanish-speaking participants from seven different countries (Mexico, n = 303; Argentina, n = 271; Panama, n = 204; Costa Rica, n = 191; the United States, n = 85; Colombia, n = 79; and Puerto Rico, n = 24). Participants from the United States were monolingual or near-monolingual Spanish speakers. The manual does not describe how the participants were selected, what their background characteristics were, or what their age distribution was, a fact that has also been noted by Ochoa (2007).

In 2010, a normative update was released. The WMLS-R NU reflects a recalculation of the data for the WMLS-R based upon updated census data and the application of more advanced statistics. The changes in the resulting standard scores and deviations were considerable, reflecting the importance of consistently updating norms and procedures. For example, the correlation between preschoolers' scores on the WMLS-R and the WMLS-NU is only .58. WMLS-R normative data previously inflated preschoolers' abilities by about 2–5 standard score points on most subtests, though more substantial shifts (5–10 standard score differences) were noted in Passage Comprehension. Thus, examiners who are assessing children or programs with the WMLS-R NU should utilize the most current norms, especially when examining potential developmental changes over time.

Norming

Norm referenced

Reliability

Test–Retest Reliability
This information is not provided in the manual.

Internal Consistency
Given the statistical calibration procedures used, the following statistics presented in the English review apply to the Spanish version: Across all age groups, the median split-half internal consistency for the WMLS-R was calculated and corrected for length. Values were in the medium to high range for clusters (.88–.98) and in the low to high range for subtests (.76–.97). Among preschoolers, coefficients were in the high range for the Reading–Writing (.95–.96), Broad English Ability (.95–.96), and Oral Expression (.90–.92) clusters. They were slightly lower for the remaining clusters. Among the subtests, the highest coefficients were found for preschoolers on the Picture Vocabulary subtest (.90–.92) and the lowest were found on Story Recall (.66–.77). Corresponding standard errors of measurement for subtest standard scores ranged from 3.66 for 5-year-olds on Dictation to 8.71 for 3-year-olds on Passage Comprehension.

Overall, the reliability coefficients of the cluster scores are higher. This suggests that the use of multiple subtests to assess an area should be considered, as is typical in assessment. The cluster approach is emphasized in the manual to provide a more stable approach to assessing broad abilities.

Interrater Agreement
This information is not provided in the manual.

Other Forms of Reliability (e.g., Equivalent Forms)
Not applicable

Validity

Face and Content
The combination of creating a list of Spanish items as well as examining the initial pool of English items to translate provided a wide range of items to potentially use. This was followed by a statistical examination of the statistical properties of each item and scale in order to select the most useful items for the measure. Furthermore, the WMLS-R's development included the involvement of Spanish-speaking professionals from the United States and other countries.

Internal Construct
The manual does not report whether the underlying factor structure of the WMLS-R was examined, *though this information is provided for the* **Batería** *III in its manual.* However, intercorrelations among the items and the clusters are reported in the appendices. As may be expected, the intercorrelations are higher among subtests within the same clusters.

External Construct
Given the statistical calibration procedures used, the following statistics presented in the English review apply to the Spanish version: Growth curves are presented that indicate that "all WMLS-R tests and clusters display average score changes consistent

with the developmental growth and decline of cognitive-academic language proficiency across the life span for the monolingual English-speaking population" (Alvarado et al., 2005, p. 91).

The ability of the WMLS-R to distinguish children with disabilities was not presented in the WMLS-R manual.

Support for the convergent and discriminant validity of the WMLS-R NU is also indicated by some of the correlational studies described in "Criterion."

Criterion

Although Alvarado et al. (2005) presented studies examining the relationship between the English WMLS-R and English criterion measures, less was presented about the Spanish WMLS-R. A bilingual study was conducted with the *original* WMLS with children in kindergarten through Grade 3. In that study, the Spanish and English versions of the IDEA Oral Language Proficiency Test were administered along with either the Language Assessment Scales–Oral Short Form or the *pre*Las 2000 (depending on the child's age). The intercorrelations among the Spanish versions of the WMLS and these tests ranged from .48 to .76.

Comparison of Psychometric Properties Between English and Spanish Versions

Technical Equivalence in Reliability

Because of the development and calibration approaches taken, the reliabilities of the English and Spanish versions are equivalent. Generally speaking, the internal reliability coefficients are high, and information on interrater and test–retest reliabilities must be sought from another manual.

Technical Equivalence in Validity

Overall, the English and Spanish WMLS-R NU versions are parallel in face, content, internal construct, and external construct validities. Although the WMLS-R manual does not describe whether factor analyses were conducted for either version or how children with exceptionalities performed, both of these examinations have been conducted with the broader Woodcock-Johnson III batteries. Less information is presented about the WMLS-R's criterion validity.

RELEVANT STUDIES USING THE MEASURE

A brief literature search using PsycINFO and Google Scholar did not yield any published studies whose abstracts specified using the WMLS-R NU. However, studies have used the earlier versions of the measure.

ADDITIONAL REFERENCES

Brown, J.D. (2007). Test review of the Woodcock-Muñoz Language Survey–Revised. In K.F. Geisinger, R.A. Spies, J.F. Carlson, & B.S. Plake (Eds.), *The seventeenth mental measurements yearbook*. Retrieved from the Buros Institute's *Test Reviews Online* web site: http://www.unl.edu/buros

Cummins, J. (1984). *Bilingualism and special education: Issues in assessment and pedagogy*. Austin, TX: PRO-ED.

(continued)

Doll, B., & LeClair, C. (2007). Review of the Batería III Woodcock-Muñoz. In K.F. Geisinger, R.A. Spies, J.F. Carlson, & B.S. Plake (Eds.), *The seventeenth mental measurements yearbook*. Retrieved from the Buros Institute's *Test Reviews Online* web site: http://www.unl.edu/buros

Ochoa, S.H. (2007). Test review of the Woodcock-Muñoz Language Survey–Revised. In K.F. Geisinger, R.A. Spies, J.F. Carlson, & B.S. Plake (Eds.), *The seventeenth mental measurements yearbook*. Retrieved from the Buros Institute's *Test Reviews Online* web site: http://www.unl.edu/buros

Olivarez, A.J., & Boroda, A. (2007). Test review of the Batería III Woodcock-Muñoz. In K.F. Geisinger, R.A. Spies, J.F. Carlson, & B.S. Plake (Eds.), *The seventeenth mental measurements yearbook*. Retrieved from the Buros Institute's *Test Reviews Online* web site: http://www.unl.edu/buros

Otero, M. (2006). Test review: Batería III Woodcock-Muñoz (Batería III). *The School Psychologist, 60*(2), 86–88.

Young Children's Achievement Test (YCAT): English

Manual
Hresko, W., Peak, P., Herron, S., & Bridges, D. (2000). *Young Children's Achievement Test.* Austin, TX: PRO-ED.

Publisher
PRO-ED
8700 Shoal Creek Boulevard
Austin, TX 78757
http://www.proedinc.com

Cost
Complete kit: $240. Items sold separately.

Type of Measure
Direct child assessment

Intended Age Range
4;0 years to 7;11 years

Key Constructs/Domains
- General Information
- Reading
- Mathematics
- Writing
- Spoken Language

Description of Measure
The YCAT can be used to identify children who have typical or atypical early academic skills (Hresko, Peak, Herron, & Bridges, 2000). In addition, it can be used to document children's progress in various educational domains.

Available Languages and Formats
The measure is also available in Spanish.

Strengths
The YCAT examines a range of preacademic domains in an interactive manner.

Its reliability and validity have been extensively examined, particularly across gender and racial/ethnic groups.

Weaknesses
Factor analyses of the measure are not presented in the manual to support the distribution of items and subscales. Though the criterion validity data presented are generally supportive of the various subscales, the specificity of the YCAT's subtests may need further examination. According to the Dr. Hresko (personal communication, July 2, 2009), these types of examinations are under way for the forthcoming YCAT–Second Edition (YCAT-2).

There may be some item gradient and floor/ceiling issues for a couple of the subscales, suggesting the need to use caution when interpreting standard scores at the extremes (very young/low functioning and older/high functioning). Otherwise, the subtest scales appear to function well.

ADMINISTRATION

Procedure
The five subtests can be administered in any order as well as independently. If all subtests are administered, then an Early Achievement Composite score (EAC) can be calculated.

Time Needed
25–45 minutes for the full battery, depending upon a child's age and ability

As with many measures, the subtests begin with easier items and become more difficult as the child answers items correctly. Discontinue rules are described. The five subtests are as follows:

- *General Information.* Children are asked questions related to everyday knowledge, colors, routines, and the identification of body parts.
- *Reading.* Children are asked questions ranging from letter identification, to word recognition, to comprehension of short passages read aloud.
- *Mathematics.* Questions include counting, completing simple word problems, adding and subtracting, and working with money (for older children).
- *Writing.* This subtest begins with drawing lines and copying letters for younger children; more difficult items for older children include writing one's name, writing simple words, and writing a letter to a friend.
- *Spoken Language.* In this subtest, children point to a picture within a storybook, repeat a series of numbers, identify beginning sounds, describe how two items are alike, and detect rhymes.

Administration and Interpretation

Formal training in assessment administration and interpretation is recommended (Hresko et al., 2000). In addition, examiners are strongly encouraged to study the manual thoroughly and to practice giving and scoring the test to at least three individuals before using the YCAT.

Scoring Method

The YCAT is hand-scored. It yields raw scores, percentiles, standard scores for the subtests and composite (i.e., EAC), and age equivalents (Hresko et al., 2000). Tables are provided in the manual that allow for the examination of the statistical discrepancy between subscales as well as the use of results such as stanines, normal curve equivalents, z scores, and T scores.

Children scoring less than 90 on the EAC "should be considered at risk for academic failure" (Hresko et al., 2000, p. 35). This cutoff point is based on falling below the typical range. As Carney noted in a review of the YCAT, the manual discusses that "early achievement is based on the interaction of several factors, such as physical/psychological well-being, the child's environmental experiences, informal and formal instruction, and finally, the child's intrinsic curiosity and motivation" (2003). Hresko et al. (2000) recommended that children who score below average on a given subtest be assessed further in that area.

Adaptations or Instructions for Use with Individuals with Disabilities

The manual suggests that modifications may need to be made for children with special needs.

FUNCTIONAL CONSIDERATIONS

Measure Development

Early childhood research and prekindergarten/first-grade curricula were consulted in creating the YCAT (Hresko et al., 2000). Numerous standardized measures were also reviewed (see the manual for a list). These reviews guided the construction of 183 items; 117 of these items were selected for the final version of the YCAT.

Details about the pilot or tryout study design are not presented in the manual. Items underwent statistical analyses, and item discrimination coefficients (corrected for part-whole effect) and item difficulties are reported in the manual. Maller (2003) noted that more description of the rationale for using these specific approaches would have been preferable because there are some potential weaknesses with the approach.

The manual also presents results from bias analyses (i.e., differential item functioning) using logistic regression and delta plots approaches. No differences among the gender and race/ethnicity groups were found when examining performances as a whole. A small proportion of items were identified as having potential gender or ethnicity bias (Turner, 2006). Although the manual does not explicitly describe the rationale for including these items in the YCAT (Maller, 2003; Turner, 2006), Dr. Hresko reported the following (personal communication, July 2, 2009): "As we explicitly noted in the YCAT, statistical findings are not enough (Camili & Shepard, 1994), and subsequent reviews of item content must be undertaken. As noted in the manual, we did such a review, with the help of others, and found no reasons to conclude the items were biased. This led us to conclude that sampling error, unequal or inadequate sample size, etc., could be responsible for the statistical finding. We will provide additional information in the YCAT-2." Indeed, it is a strength of the YCAT that it has been analyzed for item-level biases.

Standardization Sample

Normative data were collected from 1996 to 1999 for 1,224 children living in 32 states. Standardization sites representing the four demographic regions of the United States (Northeast, Midwest, South, and West) were utilized (Hresko et al., 2000). Overall, the sample matched the 1997 U.S. population along various dimensions, including race, ethnicity, gender, region, residence, income, parental education attainment, and disability. In addition, professionals who assisted in the development of the measure or who had the necessary experience administered the YCAT to 20–30 children in their area.

Norming

Norm referenced

Reliability

Test–Retest Reliability

A total of 190 children from Iowa and Texas were given the YCAT twice within a 2-week interval. The (corrected) coefficients for the subtests were all high (.97 or greater), indicating solid test–retest reliability.

Internal Consistency

Coefficient alphas were calculated for four age groupings using the normative sample. The EAC was high (.96) across the whole sample as well as for each of the age groups. Corresponding standard errors of measurement (SEMs) for the EAC were 3 points. The subtests were in the medium range for the sample as well (.80–.89). Among preschoolers, internal consistency coefficients were in the .85–.92 range, with SEMs between 4 and 5 points. Finally, similar coefficients were found across gender, ethnic, and exceptionality groups.

Interrater Agreement

Two examiners independently scored 100 completed protocols drawn at random from the normative sample. The interrater reliability across the two raters was high, with all subtest coefficients greater than .97.

Other Forms of Reliability (e.g., Equivalent Forms)

Not applicable

Validity

Face and Content

The YCAT was developed based on a mix of curricular and assessment reviews and empirical analyses. For example, item-level difficulties were statistically examined across the sample and by different communities. The manual does not specify whether experts were involved in this process, though it appears that they were.

Internal Construct

Factor analyses are not presented in the manual. Intercorrelations for subtest scores from the normative sample range from .57 to .71, suggesting moderate correlations. These correlations suggest that the subtests relate to the same construct of early academic skills (Hresko et al., 2000).

External Construct

Children's performance on the YCAT subtests is highly correlated with their age (correlations range from .71 to .83), suggesting that the measure taps young children's changing academic abilities. In his review, Turner (2006) noted potential floor and ceiling effects, particularly such that the oldest children (7-year-olds) may not be able to score above 103–118 on a particular subtest. Also, item gradients were large for the General Information, Reading, and Mathematics subtests (Turner, 2006). Use of the global EAC standard scores is less likely to result in these difficulties.

Children's performance was also analyzed by various characteristics (i.e., gender, ethnicity, developmental disabilities or special needs). As expected, children with developmental disabilities or special needs did less well than their typically developing peers, but there were no differences by gender or ethnicity.

Support for the measure's convergent and discriminant validity is also indicated by some the correlational studies described in "Criterion."

Criterion

A number of studies are generally supportive of the YCAT's criterion validity. For example, the composite score of the Metropolitan Readiness Tests correlated at .75 with the YCAT's EAC (n = 33 children ages 4–7). Results for the Slosson Intelligence Test–Revised were also as expected. In another small study (n = 34), children between the ages of 4 and 7 were administered the Kaufman Survey of Early Academic and Language Skills. A solid correlation (.76) was found between the YCAT's EAC and the Kaufman Composite Score. In general, the subtest scores interrelated in the manners expected, though the Kaufman's Number Skills subtest related more to the Reading and Writing subtests of the YCAT than the Mathematics subtest. A similar type of relationship was seen in the subtest correlations in a study of 6- to 7-year-olds (n = 75) who were administered the Comprehensive Scales of Student Abilities. However, the Reading, Writing, and Mathematics subtests generally related as expected with a specific reading measure (Gates-MacGintie Reading Diagnostic Tests; n = 43 children ages 4–7).

RELEVANT STUDIES USING THE MEASURE

A brief literature search using PsycINFO and Google Scholar did not result in any published studies whose abstracts specified using the YCAT. However, it is possible that this measure has been utilized in studies.

ADDITIONAL REFERENCES

Camili, G., & Shepard, L.A. (1994). Methods for identifying item biased test items. *Measurement Methods for the Social Sciences* (Vol. 4). Thousand Oaks, CA: Sage.

Carney, R.N. (2003). Test review of the Young Children's Achievement Test. In B.S. Plake, J.C. Impara, & R.A. Spies (Eds.), *The fifteenth mental measurements yearbook*. Retrieved from the Buros Institute's *Test Reviews Online* web site: http://www.unl.edu/buros

Maller, S.J. (2003). Test review of the Young Children's Achievement Test. In B.S. Plake, J.C. Impara, & R.A. Spies (Eds.), *The fifteenth mental measurements yearbook*. Retrieved from the Buros Institute's *Test Reviews Online* web site: http://www.unl.edu/buros

Turner, H.C. (2006). Young Children's Achievement Test. *Journal of Psychoeducational Assessment, 24*(3), 272–277.

Information pertaining specifically to the Spanish version of the measure is in bold and italics. The remainder is equivalent information provided in the English review.

Manual

Ramos, M., Hresko, W., & Ramos, J. (2006). *Prueba de Habilidades Académicas Iniciales.* San Pedro Garza García, N. L., Mexico: PRO-ED Latinoamérica.

Publisher

PRO-ED Latinoamérica
Bosques de Canada 103-10
Col. Bosques del Valle
San Pedro Garcia Garcia, N.L. 66250
Mexico
http://www.proedinc.com

Cost

Complete kit: $124. Items sold separately.

Description of Measure

The PHAI was developed to "measure the achievement levels of preschool, kindergarten, and first-grade Spanish-speaking children with respect to those skills and abilities that ensure success in school" (Ramos, Hresko, & Ramos, 2006, p. 1).

Available Languages and Formats

The measure also is available in English.

Strengths

The English version of the measure, the Young Children's Achievement Test (YCAT), examines a wide range of preacademic domains in an interactive manner.

The PHAI was normed in Mexico. The standardization sample was nationally representative and included children from 10 Mexican states.

The Spanish translation appears to be accurate, though little information about the translation approach is provided in the manual.

The reliability statistics are strong, though temporal stability has not yet been examined among 4-year-olds.

Weaknesses

Factor analyses of the measure are not presented in the manual to support the distribution of items and subscales. Though the criterion validity data presented are generally supportive of the various subscales, the specificity of the PHAI's subtests may need further examination. According to Dr. Hresko (personal communication, July 2, 2009), these types of examinations are under way for the forthcoming PHAI–Second Edition.

The PHAI translation process took into consideration the common experiences that children have in Mexico; children from other countries may not have had the same

Type of Measure

Direct child assessment

Intended Age Range

4;0 years to 7;11 years

Key Constructs/Domains

- General Information
- Reading
- Mathematics
- Writing
- Spoken Language

experiences (or may not have the same dialect; Ramos et al., 2006). This should be considered if one is using the measure with a non-Mexican child.

As with any measure that uses different standardization samples across language versions (which is in some ways a strength), Ramos et al. warn that the "YCAT and the PHAI cannot be viewed as equivalent and cannot be compared directly, one to the other" (2006, p. 8).

ADMINISTRATION

Procedure

The five subtests can be administered in any order as well as independently. If all subtests are administered, then an Early Achievement Composite Score (EAC) can be calculated.

Time Needed

25–45 minutes for the full battery, depending upon a child's age and ability

As with many measures, the subtests begin with easier items and become more difficult as the child answers items correctly. Discontinue rules are described. The five subtests are as follows:

- *General Information.* Children are asked questions related to everyday knowledge, colors, routines, and the identification of body parts.
- *Reading.* Children are asked questions ranging from letter identification, to word recognition, to comprehension of short passages read aloud.
- *Mathematics.* Questions include counting; completing simple word problems; adding/subtracting; and working with money (for older children).
- *Writing.* This subtest begins with drawing lines and copying letters for younger children; more difficult items for older children include writing one's name, writing simple words, and writing a letter to a friend.
- *Spoken Language.* In this subtest, children point to a picture within a storybook, repeat a series of numbers, identify beginning sounds, describe how two items are alike, and detect rhymes.

Administration and Interpretation

Examiners "must be fluent Spanish speakers with knowledge of and speaking ability in the appropriate Spanish dialect" (Ramos et al., 2006, p. 5). This is important because the complete test is in Spanish, including the scoring criteria. The authors recommend that examiners have a basic understanding of statistics and test administration.

Scoring Method

The PHAI is hand-scored. It yields raw scores, percentiles, standard scores for the subtests and composite (i.e., EAC), and age equivalents (Ramos et al., 2006). Tables are provided in the manual that allow for the examination of the statistical discrepancy between subscales as well as the use of results such as stanines, normal curve equivalents, z scores, and T scores.

Children scoring less than 90 on the EAC "should be considered at risk for academic failure" (Ramos et al., 2006, p. 22). This cutoff point is based on falling below the typical range. As Carney noted in a review of the YCAT, the manual discusses that "early achievement is based on the interaction of several factors, such as physical/psychological well-being, the child's environmental experiences, informal and formal instruction, and finally, the child's intrinsic curiosity and motivation" (2003). Ramos et al. (2006) recommend that children who score below average on a given subtest be assessed further in that area.

Adaptations or Instructions for Use with Individuals with Disabilities

The manual suggests that modifications may need to be made for children with special needs.

FUNCTIONAL CONSIDERATIONS

Measure Development

Early childhood research and prekindergarten/first-grade curricula were consulted in creating the PHAI (Ramos et al., 2006). Numerous standardized measures were also reviewed. The vast majority were English measures and curricula, though a few were in Spanish. These reviews guided the construction of 186 items; 118 of these items were selected for the final version of the PHAI. (In comparison, 183 items were developed for the YCAT and 117 ultimately selected.)

As with the YCAT, details about the pilot or tryout study design are not presented in the manual. Items underwent statistical analyses, and item discrimination coefficients (corrected for part-whole effect) and item difficulties are reported in the manual. A logistic regression approach was applied to the items to detect any bias related to gender (Ramos et al., 2006). The number of identified items was in the range of that expected by chance alone. These items were reviewed and determined to not be indicative of gender bias.

Content Equivalence of Items and Measure

Both the Spanish and English versions were developed based on assessment and instruction materials, which provides a strong base for the two measures. Because the Spanish measure has generally the same items as the English one (except in varying order), it is unknown how much more the few Spanish materials were examined.

Semantic Equivalence of Translations

Little information is provided about the translation process utilized. However, it appears that many Mexican states were involved, and the manual indicates that the translation process took into consideration the common experiences that children have in Mexico. The manual's preface indicates that that the test developers "adapted YCAT items via changes in vocabulary and item content. These changes reflect the culture and the language of Spanish speaking children in Mexico" (Ramos et al., 2006, p. vii). The translation appears to be accurate.

Structural Consistency Across the English and Spanish Versions

The only difference between the two versions is in the order of the items. In other words, the two versions have the same items, but they are listed in a different order. There is no explanation in the manual regarding this difference, though it may be a result of item-level analyses, as is the case with other measures.

Standardization Sample

Normative data were collected from 2000 to 2003 for 650 children living in 10 Mexican states—Jalisco (Southwest); Queraretaro (Central); Nuevo Leon and Tamaulipas (Northeast); Baja California Sur, Chihuahua, Sinaloa, and Sonora (Northwest); and Veracruz and Yucatan (Southeast)—and the Federal District.

A site coordinator was selected for each region to supervise test administration procedures. In addition, professionals such as teachers, graduate students, speech therapists, and college professors were contracted to test children. An effort was made to assign assessors to communities whose demographic makeup was similar to their own.

The sample was representative of the Mexican population in terms of gender, residence (urban/rural), family income, and age. It generally matched 2000 Mexican census data. Approximately 49% of the sample was male and 51% female; 80% of children resided in urban areas and 30% in rural areas; and 54% of families earned 2 times the minimum wage or less, 33% earned 2–5 times the minimum wage, and 13% earned more than 5 times the minimum wage.

Norming

Norm referenced

Reliability

Test–Retest Reliability

A total of 30 children (ages 5–7 years) from private and public elementary schools were administered the PHAI twice within a 2-week interval. The (corrected) coefficient for the EAC was high at .97. The subtests were in the medium to high range (.84–.96), except for the Writing subtest (.70). The test–retest reliability has not yet been examined among 4-year-olds.

Internal Consistency

Coefficient alphas were calculated for four age groupings using the normative sample. The EAC was high (.97) across the whole sample as well as for each of the age groups. Corresponding standard errors of measurement (SEMs) for the EAC were 2–3 points. The subtests were in the medium to high range for the sample as well (.87–.93). Among preschoolers, internal consistency coefficients were in the .82–.93 range, with SEMs between 4 and 6 points.

Interrater Agreement

Two employees of the research department of PRO-ED Latinoamérica independently scored 35 completed protocols drawn at random from the normative sample. The interrater reliability across the two raters was strong (i.e., > .97).

Other Forms of Reliability (e.g., Equivalent Forms)

Not applicable

Validity

Face and Content

As described in "Measure Development," PHAI test items were developed after reviewing other early childhood assessments and curricular materials, including a few Spanish materials. In addition, item-level difficulties were examined statistically across the sample and by gender. The manual does not specify whether experts were involved in this process, though it appears that they were.

Internal Construct

Factor analyses are not reported in the manual. Intercorrelations for subtest scores from the normative sample range from .47 to .67 and are of the expected magnitudes.

External Construct

Children's performance on the PHAI subtests is correlated with their age (correlations range from .53 to .74), suggesting that the measure taps young children's changing academic abilities.

Analyses of children's performance by developmental disabilities or special needs are not presented in the manual.

In terms of convergent and discriminant validity with other measures, some support for criterion validity is present among school-age children (see "Criterion"). Similar studies need to be conducted with preschoolers.

Criterion

*Three studies conducted with 5- to 7-year-olds are described in Ramos et al. (2006). In the first study, the PHAI was correlated with the **Batería** Woodcock-Muñoz–Revisada (BWMR), **Pruebas de Aprovechamiento–Revisada.** In general, each of these correlated strongly with the EAC (.71–.96). As was noted in the YCAT review, the specificity of the PHAI's subtests may need further examination. For example, the BWMR's Reading subtest correlated .68 with Reading, .68 with Mathematics, and .39 with Writing. The BWMR's Mathematics subtest correlated .39 with Reading, .64 with Mathematics, and .68 with Writing.*

*The second study found that the **Prueba de Lenguaje Inicial** correlated as follows with the PHAI: General Information = .69, Reading = .74, Mathematics = .65, Writing = .74, Spoken Language = .79, and EAC = .85. In the third study, PHAI scores were compared with scores on the Test of Nonverbal Intelligence–Third Edition. PHAI subtest and composite score correlations ranged from .52 to .65, suggesting a moderate relationship. The PHAI's criterion validity among preschoolers remains in need of investigation.*

Comparison of Psychometric Properties Between English and Spanish Versions

Technical Equivalence in Reliability

The reliability of the Spanish and English versions is similar. However, the test–retest reliability of the PHAI has yet to be examined among 4-year-olds.

Technical Equivalence in Validity

The face and content validities of the Spanish and English versions are similar, although factor analyses have not yet been conducted for either language version. The external construct and criterion validities of the PHAI may need further examination.

RELEVANT STUDIES USING THE MEASURE

A brief literature search using PsycINFO and Google Scholar did not result in any published studies whose abstracts specified using the PHAI. However, it is possible that this measure has been utilized in studies.

ADDITIONAL REFERENCES

Carney, R.N. (2003). Test review of the Young Children's Achievement Test. In B.S. Plake, J.C. Impara, & R.A. Spies (Eds.), *The fifteenth mental measurements yearbook*. Retrieved from the Buros Institute's *Test Reviews Online* web site: http://www.unl.edu/buros

References

Administration for Children and Families. (2006). *FACES 2003 research brief: Children's outcomes and program quality in Head Start*. Washington, DC: Author.

Administration for Children and Families. (2008). *Dual language learning: What does it take? Head Start dual language report*. Washington, DC: U.S. Office of Head Start.

Administration for Children and Families. (2009, April). *Recognizing language diversity in large-scale assessments: Approaches and evidence from FACES 2006*. Presentation at the Society for Research in Child Development Biennial Meeting, Denver, CO.

Albarran-Rivero, M. (1999). *Tests for bilingual Spanish-English preschool and school-age children: Position paper from California Speech-Hearing-Language Association*. Retrieved from http://www.csha.org/documents/positionpapers/tests_for_bilingual_spanish.htm

Alberts, F.M., Davis, B.L., & Prentice, L. (1995). Validity of an observation screening instrument in a multicultural population. *Journal of Early Intervention, 19,* 168–177.

American Educational Research Association. (1999). *Laws and regulations, current practice, and research relevant to inclusion and accommodations for students with limited English proficiency in the voluntary national tests*. Washington, DC: Author.

American Educational Research Association, American Psychological Association, & National Council on Measurement in Education. (1999). *Standards for educational and psychological testing*. Washington, DC: Author.

American Educational Research Association, American Psychological Association, & National Council on Measurement in Education. (2010). *Standards for educational and psychological testing* (Rev. draft). Washington, DC: Author.

American Psychological Association. (1990). *APA guidelines for providers of psychological services to ethnic, linguistic, and culturally diverse populations*. Boston: Author.

American Psychological Association. (1999). *Standards for educational and psychological testing*. Washington, DC: Author.

American Psychological Association. (2002). *Guidelines on multicultural education, training, research, practice, and organizational change for psychologists*. Washington, DC: Author.

Atkins-Burnet, S. (2007). *Measuring children's progress from preschool through third grade*. Washington, DC: Mathematica Policy Research.

Baker, E.L., Linn, R.L., Herman, J.L., & Koretz, D. (2002). *Policy brief 5: Standards for educational accountability systems.* Los Angeles: University of California at Los Angeles; National Center for Research on Evaluation, Standards, and Student Testing.

Barnett, W.S., Epstein, D.J., Friedman, A.H., Sansanelli, R.A., & Hustedt, J.T. (2009). *The state of preschool 2009: State preschool yearbook.* Rutgers, NJ: National Institute for Early Education Research.

Barnett, W.S., & Yarosz, D.J. (2007). *Who goes to preschool and why does it matter?* Rutgers, NJ: National Institute for Early Education Research.

Barrera, I. (1995). To refer or not to refer: Untangling the web of diversity, "deficit," and disability. *New York State Association for Bilingual Education Journal, 10,* 54–66.

Barrueco, S., López, M.L., & Miles, J.C. (2007). Parenting behaviors in the first year of life: A national examination of Latinos and other cultural groups. *Latinos and Education, 6*(3), 253–265.

Basterra, M.D., Trumbull, E., & Solano-Flores, G. (2010). *Cultural validity in assessment: Addressing linguistic and cultural diversity.* New York: Routledge.

Bennett, R.E., Gottesman, R.L., Rock, D.A., & Cerullo, F. (1993). Influence of behavior perceptions and gender on teachers' judgments of students' academic skill. *Journal of Educational Psychology, 85,* 347–356.

Berry, D.J., Bridges, L.J., & Zaslow, M.J. (2004). *Early childhood measures profiles.* Washington, DC: Child Trends.

Birdsong, D. (2006). Age and second language acquisition and processing: A selective overview. *Language Learning, 56,* 9–49.

Bondurant-Utz, J.A. (1994). Cultural diversity. In J.A. Bondurant-Utz & L.B. Luciano (Eds.), *A practical guide to infant and preschool assessment in special education* (pp. 73–98). Boston: Allyn & Bacon.

Bracken, B.A. (2004). The psychoeducational assessment of preschool children (3rd ed.). Mahwah, NJ: Lawrence Erlbaum Associates.

Bravo, M. (2003). Instrument development: Cultural adaptations for ethnic minority research. In G. Bernal, J.E. Trimble, A.K. Burlew, & F.T. Leong (Eds.), *Handbook of racial and ethnic minority psychology* (pp. 220–236). Thousand Oaks, CA: Sage Publications.

Brown, C.L. (2004). Reducing the over-referral of culturally and linguistically diverse students (CLD) for language disabilities. *NABE Journal of Research and Practice, 2,* 225–243.

Brownell, R. (2001). *Expressive One-Word Picture Vocabulary Test–Spanish-Bilingual Edition.* Novato, CA: Academic Therapy Publications.

Campbell, S.B. (2002). *Behavior problems in preschool children: Clinical and developmental issues* (2nd ed.). Pittsburgh: University of Pittsburgh.

Capps, R., Fix, M., Ost, J., Reardon-Anderson, J., & Passel, J.S. (2004). *The health and well-being of young children and immigrants.* Washington, DC: Urban Institute Press.

Cizek, G.J. (2003). Test review of the *Woodcock-Johnson-III.* In B.S. Plake, J.C. Impara, & R.A. Spies (Eds.), *The fifteenth mental measurements yearbook.* Retrieved from the Buros Institute's *Test Reviews Online* web site: http://www.unl.edu/buros

Cole, K.N., & Mills, P.E. (1997). Agreement of language intervention triage profiles. *Topics in Early Childhood Special Education, 17,* 119–130.

Cote, J.A., & Buckley, R. (1987). Estimating trait, method, and error variance: Generalizing across 70 construct validation studies. *Journal of Marketing Research, 24,* 315–318.

Dana, R.H. (2005). *Multicultural assessment: Principles, applications, and examples.* New York: Taylor & Francis.

Division for Early Childhood. (2007). *Promoting positive outcomes for children with disabilities: Recommendations for curriculum, assessment, and program evaluation.* Missoula, MT: Author.

Doll, B., & LeClair, C. (2007). Test review of the Batería *III Woodcock-Muñoz.* In K.F. Geisinger, R.A. Spies, J.F. Carlson, & B.S. Plake (Eds.), *The seventeenth mental measurements yearbook.* Retrieved from the Buros Institute's *Test Reviews Online* web site: http://www.unl.edu/buros

Duarte, G., & Gutierrez, C. (2004). Best practices in bilingual early childhood classrooms. *NABE News, 27*(4), 4–7.

Duncan, S.E., & De Avila, E.A. (1998). *PreLAS 2000: Examiner's manual. English Forms C and D.* Monterey, CA: CTB/McGraw-Hill.

Educational Testing Service. (2009). *Guidelines for the assessment of English language learners.* Ewing, NJ: Author.

Eisenberg, N. (Ed.) (2011). *Child Development Perspectives*. Special Section on Dual Language Learning. Malden, MA: John Wiley & Sons.

Epstein, A.S., Schweinhart, L.J., DeBruin-Parecki, A., & Robin, K.B. (2004). *Preschool assessment: A guide to developing a balanced approach*. Rutgers, NJ: National Institute for Early Education Research.

Espinosa, L., & López, M.L. (2007). *Assessment considerations for young English language learners across different levels of accountability.* White Paper. Pew Trusts. Retrieved from http://www.pewtrusts.org/uploadedFiles/wwwpewtrustsorg/Reports/Pre-k_education/Assessment%20for%20Young%20ELLs-Pew%208-11-07-Final.pdf

Garcia, E. (2005). *Teaching and learning in two languages: Bilingualism and schooling in the United States*. New York: Teachers College Press.

Garcia, E., & Jensen, B. (2009). Early educational opportunities for children of Hispanic origins. *Society for Research in Child Development Social Policy Report, 23*(2), 3–19.

García, O., Kleifgen, J.A., & Falchi, L. (2008). From English language learners to emergent bilinguals. *Equity Matters: Research Review, 1*, 1–59.

Geisinger, K.F. (1994). Cross-cultural normative assessment: Translation and adaptation issues influencing the normative interpretation of assessment instruments. *Psychological Assessment, 6*, 304–312.

Goff, J.M. (2000). *A more comprehensive accountability model*. Washington, DC: Council for Basic Education.

Goldenberg, C. (2008). Teaching English language learners: What the research does—and does not—say. *American Educator, 32*(2), 8–43.

Goldstein, B. (2007). Phonological skills in Puerto Rican and Mexican Spanish-speaking children with phonological disorders. *Clinical Linguistic and Phonetics, 21*, 93–109.

Gunderson, L., & Siegel, L.S. (2001). The evils of the use of IQ tests to define learning disabilities in first- and second-language learners. *The Reading Teacher, 55*, 48–55.

Gutiérrez-Clellen, V.F., Restrepo, M.A., & Simon-Cereijido, G.S. (2006). Evaluating the discriminant accuracy of a grammatical measure with Spanish-speaking children. *Journal of Speech, Language and Hearing Research, 49*, 1209–1223.

Gutiérrez-Clellen, V.F., Simon-Cereijido, G., & Wagner, C. (2008). Bilingual children with language impairment: A comparison with monolinguals and second language learners. *Applied Psycholinguistics, 29*, 3–19.

Hambleton, R.K., Merenda, P.F., & Spielberger, C.D. (2005). *Adapting educational and psychological tests for cross-cultural assessment*. Mahwah, NJ: Lawrence Erlbaum Associates.

Hammer, C.S., Miccio, A M., & Rodríguez, B. (2004). Bilingual language acquisition and the child socialization process. In B. Goldstein (Ed.), *Bilingual language development and disorders in Spanish-English speakers*. Baltimore: Paul H. Brookes Publishing Co.

Hammer, C.S., Lawrence, F.R., & Miccio, A.W. (2007). Bilingual children's language abilities and early reading outcomes in Head Start and kindergarten. *Language, Speech, and Hearing Services in Schools, 38*, 237–248.

Hanson, M.J., & Lynch, E.W. (1995). *Early intervention: Implementing child and family services for infants and toddlers who are at risk or disabled*. Austin, TX: PRO-ED.

Hills, T.W. (1992). Reaching potentials through appropriate assessment. In S. Bredekamp & T. Rosegrant (Eds.), *Reaching potentials: Appropriate curriculum and assessment for young* (pp. 43–64). Washington DC: National Association for the Education of Young Children.

Hoyt, W.T. (2000). Rater bias in psychological research: When is it a problem and what can we do about it? *Psychological Methods, 5*, 64–86.

Hoyt, W.T., & Kerns, M.-D. (1999). Magnitude and moderators of bias in observer ratings: A meta-analysis. *Psychological Methods, 4*, 403–424.

Kallemeyn, L.M., & DeStefano, L. (2009). The (limited) use of local-level assessment system: A case study of the Head Start National Reporting System and on-going child assessments in a local program. *Early Childhood Research Quarterly, 24*, 157–174.

Kazdin, A.E. (2003). *Research design in clinical psychology* (4th ed.). Boston: Allyn & Bacon.

Klee, T., & Carson, D.K. (2000). Improving the positive predictive value of screening for developmental language disorder. *Disorder Journal of Speech, Language and Hearing Research, 43*, 821–833.

Kopriva, R. (2008). *Improving testing for English language learners*. New York: Routledge.

Langdon, H.W. (2002). *Interpreters and translators in communication disorders: A practitioner's handbook*. Eau Claire, WI: Thinking Publications.

Leong, F.T.L., & Austin, J.T. (2006). *The psychology research handbook* (2nd ed.). Thousand Oaks, CA: Sage Publications.

Llosa, L. (2008). Building and supporting a validity argument for a standards-based classroom assessment of English proficiency based on teacher judgments. *Educational Measurement: Issues and Practice, 27,* 32–42.

López, M.L., Barrueco, S., & Miles, J. (2006). *Latino infants and their families: A national perspective of protective and risk developmental factors.* Tempe, AZ: National Task Force on Early Childhood Education for Hispanics.

MacSwan, J., Rolstad, K., & Glass, G.V. (2002). Do some school-age children have no language? Some problems of construct validity in the Pre-Las Espanol. *Bilingual Research Journal, 26,* 213–238.

McLaughlin, B. (1984). *Second language acquisition in childhood: Preschool children.* Hillsdale, NJ: Lawrence Erlbaum Associates.

McLaughlin, B., Blanchard, A.G., & Osanai, Y. (1995). *Assessing language development in bilingual preschool children.* Washington, DC: National Clearinghouse for Bilingual Education.

McLean, M. (2004). Assessment and its importance in early intervention/early childhood special education. In M. McLean, M. Wolery, & D.B. Bailey (Eds.), *Assessing infants and preschoolers with special needs* (pp. 1–21). Upper Saddle River, NJ: Pearson.

Meisels, S.J. (1998). *Assessing readiness: How should we define readiness?*(National Center for Early Development and Learning Spotlight Series No. 3). Washington, DC: Office of Educational Research and Improvement.

Meisels, S. (2005). No easy answers: Accountability in early childhood. In R.C. Pianta, M.J. Cox, & K. Snow (Eds.), *School readiness, early learning and the transition to kindergarten.* Baltimore: Paul H. Brookes Publishing Co.

Meisels, S.J. (2007). Accountability in early childhood: No easy answers. In R.C. Pianta, M.J. Cox, & K.L. Snow (Eds.), *School readiness and the transition to kindergarten in the era of accountability* (pp. 31–47). Baltimore: Paul H. Brookes Publishing Co.

Meisels, S.J., Atkins-Burnett, S., Xue, Y., Nicholson, J., Bickel, D., & Son, S. (2002). Creating a system of accountability: The impact of instructional assessment on elementary children's achievement test scores. *American Educational Research Journal, 39,* 3–25.

Miccio, A.W., Hammer, C.S., & Rodriguez, B. (2009). Code-switching and language disorders in bilingual children. In B.E. Bullock & A.J. Toribio (Eds.), *The Cambridge handbook of linguistic code-switching* (pp. 241–252). New York: Cambridge University Press.

Midwest Equity Assistance Center. (1999). *Assessment instruments for linguistically diverse populations.* Manhattan, KS: Midwest Equity Assistance Center.

Miller, K.E., Martell, Z.L., Pazdirek, L., Caruth, M., & Lopez, D. (2005). The role of interpreters in psychotherapy with refugees: An exploratory study. *American Journal of Orthopsychiatry, 75,* 27–39.

Myford, C.M., & Wolfe, E.W. (2003). Detecting and measuring rater effects using many-facet Rasch measurement: Part I. *Journal of Applied Measurement, 4,* 386–422.

National Association for the Education of Young Children. (2005). *Screening and assessment of young English-language learners.* Washington, DC: Author.

National Association for the Education of Young Children. (2009). *Where we stand on assessing young English language learners.* Washington, DC: Author.

National Association for the Education of Young Children & National Association of Early Childhood Specialists in State Departments of Education. (2003). *Early childhood curriculum, assessment, and program evaluation: Building an effective, accountable system in programs for children birth through 8.* Washington, DC: National Association for the Education of Young Children.

National Clearinghouse for English Language Acquisition. (2006). *How has the English language learner population changed in recent years?* Washington, DC: Author.

National Clearinghouse for English Language Acquisition. (2009). *The condition of education 2009: Language minority school age children.* Retrieved from http://nces.ed.gov/programs/coe/2009/pdf/8_2009.pdf

Nicoladis, E., & Genesee, F. (1997).Language development in preschool bilingual children. *Journal of Speech-Language Pathology and Audiology, 21,* 258–270.

Olivarez, A.J., & Boroda, A. (2003). Test review of the Batería *III Woodcock-Muñoz.* In K.F. Geisinger, R.A. Spies, J.F. Carlson, & B.S. Plake (Eds.), *The seventeenth mental measurements yearbook.* Retrieved from the Buros Institute's *Test Reviews Online* web site: http://www.unl.edu/buros

Oller, K.D., & Eilers, R.E. (Eds.). (2002). *Language and literacy in bilingual children.* New York: Multilingual Matters.

Otero, M. (2006). Test review: Batería III Woodcock-Muñoz (Batería III). *The School Psychologist, 60*(2), 86–88.

Padilla, A.M., & Borsato, G.N. (2008). Issues in culturally appropriate psychoeducational assessment. In L.A Suzuki & J.G. Ponterotto (Eds.), *Handbook of multicultural assessment: Clinical, psychological, and educational applications.* Hoboken, NJ: Wiley.

Páez, M.M., & Rinaldi, C. (2006). Predicting English word reading skills for Spanish-speaking students in first grade. *Topics in Language Disorders, 26,* 338–350.

Páez, M.M., Tabors, P.O., & Lopez, L.M. (2007). Dual language and literacy development of Spanish-speaking preschool children. *Journal of Applied Developmental Psychology, 28,* 85–102.

Pan, B.A., Rowe, M.L., Singer, J.D., & Snow, C.E. (2005). Maternal correlates of growth in toddler vocabulary production in low-income families. *Child Development, 76,* 763–782.

Paradis, J., Genesee, F., & Crago, M.B. (2011). *Dual language development and disorders: A handbook on bilingualism and second language learning* (2nd ed.). Baltimore: Paul H. Brookes Publishing Co.

Pearson, B.Z., Fernandez, S.C., & Oller, D.K. (1993). Lexical development in bilingual infants and toddlers: Comparisons to monolingual norms. *Language Learning, 43,* 93–120.

Peña, E.D. (2007). Lost in translation: Methodological considerations in cross-cultural research. *Child Development, 78,* 1255–1264.

Reyes, I., & Moll, L. (2005). Latinos and bilingualism. In I. Stavans & H. Augenbraum (Eds.), *Encyclopedia Latina: History, culture, and society in the United States* (pp. 520–528). New York: Grolier Academic Reference.

Romaine, S. (1994). *Language in Society.* Oxford: Oxford University Press.

Rossi, P.H., & Freeman, H.E. (1983). *Evaluation: Asystemic approach.* Newbury Park, CA: Sage Publications.

Sandoval, J. (2003). Test review of the *Woodcock-Johnson-III.* In B.S. Plake, J.C. Impara, & R.A. Spies (Eds.), *The fifteenth mental measurements yearbook.* Retrieved from the Buros Institute's *Test Reviews Online* web site: http://www.unl.edu/buros

Santos, R.M. (2004). Ensuring culturally and linguistically appropriate assessment of young children.*Young Children, 59*(1), 48–50.

Sattler, J.M. (2008). *Assessment of children: Cognitive applications* (5th ed.). LaMesa, CA: Jerome M. Sattler Publisher.

Scriven, M. (1991). *Evaluation thesaurus* (4th ed.). Thousand Oaks, CA: Sage Publications.

Shadish, W.R., Cook, T.D., & Leviton, L.C. (1991). *Foundations of program evaluation: Theories of practice.* Newbury Park, CA: Sage Publications.

Shepard, L.,Kagan, S.L., & Wurtz, E. (1998). *Principles and recommendations for early childhood assessments.* Washington, DC: National Association for the Education of Young Children.

Snow, C.E., & Van Hemel, S.B. (Eds.). (2008). *Early childhood assessment: Why, what, and how.* Washington, DC: National Academies Press.

Stuart-Hamilton, I. (1995). *Dictionary of psychological testing, assessment, and treatment.* London: Jessica Kingsley Publishers.

Stubbe Kester, E., & Peña, E. (2002). Language ability assessment of Spanish-English bilinguals: Future directions. *Practical Assessment, Research & Evaluation, 8*(4). Retrieved from http://pareonline.net/getvn.asp?v=8 & n=4

Suzuki, L.A., & Ponterotto, J.G. (2008). *Handbook of multicultural assessment: Clinical, psychological, and educational applications.* Hoboken, NJ: Wiley.

Tabors, P.O. (1997). *One child, two languages.* Baltimore: Paul H. Brookes Publishing Co.

Tabors, P.O. (2008). *One child, two languages: A guide for early childhood educators of children learning English as a second language* (2nd ed.). Baltimore: Paul H. Brookes Publishing Co.

Tabors, P., & Snow, C. (1994). English as a second language in preschools. In F. Genesee (Ed.), *Educating second language children: The whole child, the whole curriculum, the whole community* (pp. 103–125). New York: Cambridge University Press.

Trister-Dodge, D., Herman, C., Charles, J., & Maiorca, J. (2004). Beyond outcomes: How ongoing assessment supports children's learning and leads to meaningful curriculum. *Young Children, 59,* 38–43.

Unrau, Y., Gabor, P., & Grinnell, R.M., Jr. (2001). *Evaluation in the human services.* Itasca, IL: R.E. Peacock.

Urbina, S. (2004). *Essentials of psychological testing.* Hoboken, NJ: Wiley.

U.S. Census Bureau. (2008). *Table 20: Projections of the Hispanic population (any race) by age and sex for the United States: 2010 to 2050 (NP2008-T20).* Retrieved from http://www.census.gov/population/www/projections/index.html

U.S. Census Bureau. (2009). *Table 3: Annual estimates of the resident population by sex, race, and Hispanic origin for the United States: April 1, 2000 to July 1, 2008 (NC-EST2008-03).* Retrieved from http://www.census.gov/popest/estimates.html

U.S. Department of Education. (2002). *No Child Left Behind: A desktop reference.* Jessup, MD: Education Publications Center.

U.S. Department of Education. (2000). *America's Kindergartners,* NCES 2000-070, Washington, DC: National Center for Education Statistics.

Walberg, H.J. (2002). Principles for accountability designs. In H.J. Walberg (Ed.), *School accountability* (pp. 155–183). Stanford, CA: Hoover Institution Press, Stanford University Press.

Wortham, S.E.F. (2001). *Narratives in action: A strategy for research and analysis.* New York: Teachers College Press.

Glossary

age equivalent score   The average performance on a particular measure by a certain age group based on normative data.

alternate-form reliability   The comparability of two forms of the same measure that share the same purpose but include different questions or items. Test takers complete both forms, and their scores are then correlated. Alternate-form reliability correlations are considered acceptable if greater than .80. Most measures do not have alternate forms.

basal (level)   The part of an administration at which an individual is able to master a set number of successive items. Instead of presenting even easier or similarly easy items, the assessment then progresses to more items in order to reach the *ceiling*. Many measures require administrators to identify test takers' basal and ceiling levels so as to minimize the time needed to conduct the exam.

ceiling (level)   The part of an administration at which an individual is no longer able to master a set number of successive items. Instead of presenting even harder or similarly hard items, the assessment is discontinued because the limits of the child's development or ability have been reached.

ceiling effect   The existence of a limited range of scores or variation at the upper end of a test. For example, when a test is too easy, an unexpectedly large proportion of individuals will get all or nearly all of the items correct, leaving little information to use to differentiate scores.

classification accuracy   The extent to which a measure identifies children in need of further testing and interventions from typically developing children. *See* false negative, false positive, sensitivity, specificity.

conceptual scoring   A technique that allows for scoring a child's responses regardless of the language in which he or she responds. For example, young children may answer items on a measure in English or Spanish depending upon their knowledge of the concept (i.e., they may have learned the colors in English although they speak Spanish as their first language).

concurrent validity   The degree to which an assessment correlates with performance on another measure at the same point in time. *See* criterion validity, predictive validity.

construct/domain   A theoretical concept or set of concepts covered by a particular measure. For example, a developmental assessment may cover several constructs, including physical, social-emotional, language, and cognitive development.

construct validity   A broad concept that refers to the extent to which a given assessment measures the domain of interest. *Internal construct validity* assesses the extent to which the use of separate subscales or scales is supported. For example, separate receptive language and expressive language subscale scores, rather than only a total language score, should be empirically supported. Factor analysis is an often used statistical analysis. *External construct validity* assesses the extent to which the complete measure taps a domain. For example, a test created to assess language and literacy development should be able to distinguish between younger and older children and between children with and without disabilities in this area. In addition, this test should correlate with other measures designed to assess the same domain (i.e., *convergent validity*) but not with measures designed to assess other areas of development, such as motor skills (i.e., *divergent/discriminant validity*).

content equivalence of items and measure   The extent to which the domains and items of a measure are relevant to the cultural group or population. In other words, are the domains and items appropriate for the population? For example, questions regarding children's influence in making family decisions may not be relevant in cultures that have more traditional or hierarchical family structures. Geographical differences must also be considered (e.g., asking individuals from tropical climates about winter weather may not be meaningful). Test developers may conduct interviews or focus groups or convene a panel of experts representing different cultural groups to review items for potential biases and cultural relevance.

content validity   The extent to which a measure reflects the range of content present in the domain that it is designed to measure. For example, a measure that is reported to comprehensively examine children's language development should contain both receptive and expressive questions rather than questions in only one of those areas. Generally speaking, content validity is assessed without using statistics. Activities used to assess content validity can include expert panel review and analyses of textbooks, curricula, and dictionaries.

correlation   The amount of variance in variable *a* predicted by, *although not necessarily caused by,* variable *b* (and vice versa). For example, if *a* and *b* have a correlation of .60 (and are significant), *a* predicts 36% of *b* (or r^2 : .60 × .60 = .36). This does not imply that *a* causes *b*, just that they are somewhat related. Correlation coefficients range from −1 (perfect negative correlation) to 1 (perfect positive correlation). In the social sciences, correlations are generally interpreted as follows:

r	*Interpretation*
< .50	Low correlation
.50–.80	Moderate correlation
> .80	High correlation

criterion validity   The extent to which an assessment correlates with expected outcomes, as evidenced by correlations with other measures. Two of the most common types of criterion validity are concurrent validity and predictive validity. *See* concurrent validity, predictive validity.

criterion-referenced test A type of test that assesses an individual's proficiency in certain skills or domains in relation to established standards. An individual's score does not provide information about his or her standing relative to others who have taken the same test.

differential item functioning (DIF) A statistical procedure that allows one to examine for systematic differences in the item level responses of members of different subgroups of interest. Thus, DIF analyses identify potential item bias.

domain *See* construct/domain.

equating procedure A statistical procedure that allows one to compare scores across tests. For example, one can use an equating procedure to equate scores across English and Spanish forms of the same measure.

equivalency *See* content equivalence of items and measure, semantic equivalence, structural consistency across English and Spanish versions, technical equivalence in reliability, technical equivalence in validity.

external validity The extent to which findings from a given study can be applied to the larger population.

face validity The extent to which a given assessment appears at first glance to measure the phenomenon it is designed to measure. Face validity is often examined by internal and external expert review.

false negative An erroneous test result that indicates that a condition is not present when it is. For example, children are categorized as typically developing when in fact they have special needs or delays.

false positive An erroneous test result that indicates that a condition is present when it is not. For example, children are categorized as having special needs or delays when in fact they are developing typically.

floor effect A phenomenon in which, when a test is too difficult, an unexpectedly large proportion of individuals gets no or very few items correct, leaving little information to use to differentiate their relative skills or abilities.

internal consistency The degree to which scores on items within a given scale or test correlate with one another or measure the same construct. One can assess the internal consistency of a measure using various indicators, including *split-half reliability* (i.e., correlating an individual's score on half of the items with his or her score on the other half) and *Cronbach's alpha* (i.e., using coefficient alphas to see how well items "hang together" statistically). Correlations are considered acceptable if greater than .80.

interrater or interscorer agreement The level of agreement across two or more independent scorers that demonstrates that the assessment, rather than the assessor, is measuring the ability consistently. Interrater agreement is generally reported using Pearson's *r*. Correlations of test scores $\geq$ .80 are considered acceptable.

item response theory (IRT) Statistical approach that helps to estimate the probability of individuals with specified levels of ability or skill (e.g., beginning versus advanced readers) getting an item correct or responding to an item in a particular way.

norm-referenced test A type of test in which an individual's performance is compared to that of his or her peers. In other words, the individual's score provides some sense of his or her standing relative to others who have taken the same test.

percentile or percentile rank score   An indicator that reflects the relative ranking of an individual's score in comparison to that of the normative sample. For example, if a child scores in the 60th percentile, she has scored at the same level as, or above, 60% of her peers on the measure.

predictive validity   The degree to which an assessment can be used to predict future behavior or future performance on another measure. *See* criterion validity, concurrent validity.

random error   Unsystematic error (e.g., incorrectly marking an answer or recording a response) that influences test scores.

Rasch item modeling   A technique in which a small number of items selected from a larger measure are found to have similar predictive value as the larger pool of items. This procedure allows one to estimate how well an individual would do on the entire measure if the individual completes only the smaller number of items.

raw score   A score that is often calculated as the number of items an individual answers correctly.

reliability   The extent to which a measure is free from random error. In simpler terms, *reliability* refers to how precise or trustworthy a test score is in capturing the skills, attitudes, or abilities it purports to measure. *See* alternate-form reliability, internal consistency, interrater or interscorer agreement, test–retest reliability.

scale   A subtest or set of items pertaining to a particular content area.

semantic equivalence   The degree to which versions of a measure possess the same meaning across languages or dialects. Essential questions in this area are the following: If a measure was translated, how was the translation done, and does it preserve the original meaning? If discordance was identified in particular items, how was it fixed? One way to assess the semantic equivalence of a translated measure is to translate it back into its original language and compare the result with the original measure (i.e., translation/back-translation). Dialectical variations within languages are increasingly being considered in measurement development and translation and are generally examined using a mix of qualitative and quantitative procedures.

sensitivity   A statistical approach used to examine the likelihood that a measure or approach correctly identifies the presence of an experience, such as a disability or disorder. For example, a measure with high sensitivity has a strong probability of identifying children in a classroom who have special needs or delays (i.e., they are true positives). The higher the correlation, the more precise the measure is in distinguishing children who are typically versus atypically developing.

specificity   A statistical approach used to examine the likelihood that a measure or approach correctly identifies the absence of an experience, such as a disability or disorder. For example, a measure with high specificity has a strong probability of identifying children in a classroom who are typically developing, and thus do not have special needs or delays (i.e., they are true negatives). The higher the correlation, the more precise the measure is in distinguishing children who are typically versus atypically developing.

standard score   A score that is converted to reflect the relative position of an individual's raw score to the population's mean (as measured in standardized units). Standard scores often use a mean of 100 and a standard deviation of 15.

standardization   A set of uniform procedures for treating participants in a study, interview, or experiment. Participants should be exposed to similar conditions when being assessed to ensure the appropriateness of comparing across groups.

standardization sample Sample of individuals used to *standardize* or develop set procedures for administering and scoring a measure. The standardization sample's performance on a measure will serve as a reference point for later interpretation of scores (i.e.,
norms or *normative data*). Ideally, the standardization sample will closely mirror the larger
target population. For example, the standardization sample for a measure that is intended
to be used with kindergartners across the United States should be *nationally representative,*
that is, reflect the demographics of the nation's kindergartners in terms of age, gender,
race/ethnicity, language, region, socioeconomic status, and so forth. The year a measure
was standardized is important to consider; for example, a nationally representative sample of American first graders in 1980 may not be representative of American first graders
in 2007.

Within the bilingual assessment field, particular attention is paid to the representation of
Spanish-speaking children. Was the measure standardized across various Latin American
countries? Or with bilingual children throughout the United States? Or with Spanish-
dominant children in one area of the United States? Different normative populations may
be preferred depending on the assessment's purpose and the subsequent population of
interest being assessed. Thus, there is no one correct standardization sample. However, it
is important to be knowledgeable about the standardization sample, as it assists in both
measurement selection and the accurate interpretation of results.

structural consistency across English and Spanish versions The extent to which the
structure (e.g., length, item/response format) of the original and adapted or translated
version(s) of a measure is uniform. In other words, how similar are the items and the
length and format of the measure across the languages? This *may* be important if raw
scores across both language measures are being utilized to compare children's development.

systematic error An error that occurs when a variable that is not the variable of interest influences scores systematically (e.g., students' performance on a mathematics test is
also influenced by their reading ability, suggesting that this particular math test may not
purely test mathematical ability).

technical equivalence in reliability The extent to which an adapted or translated version
of a given assessment has similar reliability psychometrics as the original assessment.
In essence, technical equivalence in reliability indicates how similar the data are across,
for example, Spanish and English versions in terms of test–retest reliability, internal consistency, and interrater agreement. Statistical coefficients are usually examined visually,
though they can be examined statistically.

technical equivalence in validity The extent to which an adapted or translated version
of a given assessment has similar validity results as the original assessment. Technical
equivalence in validity indicates how similar, for example, Spanish and English versions
are in terms of how culturally relevant the domains tested are, what their meanings are,
and how they relate to other child development measures or outcomes. This process entails a review of both qualitative and quantitative data.

test–retest reliability The stability of an individual's score on a given measure over time.
Specifically, individuals complete the same measure (or an equivalent form of the measure) on two separate occasions under as close to the same conditions as possible in a certain time interval (e.g., 2 weeks). Their scores on these two occasions are then correlated.
Test–retest reliability correlations are considered acceptable if greater than .80.

validity The degree to which all accumulated evidence supports the interpretation and
use of test scores for a particular purpose. *See* construct validity, content validity, criterion
validity, face validity.

Index

Tables, figures, and notes are indicated by *t*, *f*, and *n*, respectively.